KING COTTON

King Cotton

A tribute to Douglas A. Farnie

Edited by John F. Wilson

Crucible Books

in association with

The Chetham Society

and supported by a publications grant from

The Historic Society of Lancashire and Cheshire

King Cotton: A tribute to Douglas A. Farnie

Text © contributors, 2009

First published in 2009 by
Crucible Books
in association with the Chetham Society,
for whose third series of publications
this volume has been designated number 47

Crucible Books is an imprint of
Carnegie Publishing Ltd,
Carnegie House,
Chatsworth Road,
Lancaster LA1 4SL
www.cruciblebooks.com

British Library Cataloguing-in-Publication data
A catalogue record for this book is available from the British Library

ISBN 978-1-905472-09-3

Designed, typeset and originated by Carnegie Book Production, Lancaster
Printed and bound in the UK by Cromwell Press Group, Trowbridge

Contents

Acknowledgements

T HE EDITOR AND PUBLISHER would like to acknowledge the warm support and encouragement given by many people and organisations during the preparation of this book.

For many years Douglas was a council member of the Chetham Society, and we are particularly pleased that this august body has decided to make copies of this festschrift available to all of its subscribing members (as volume number 47 in their third series), a most suitable and appropriate tribute to Douglas' place within the pantheon of North West historians.

We are also extremely grateful to the council of the Historic Society of Lancashire and Cheshire for a grant to help with the publishing costs of this book.

Douglas Farnie: a tribute

T HIS COLLECTION OF ESSAYS has been produced to honour the life and career of a man for whom so many have the deepest respect. As both a person and historian, Douglas Farnie made an enormous contribution to a plethora of people's scholarship, from the undergraduates he taught with distinction to those with whom he worked on a wide range of projects. As one of those fortunate individuals who was both one of his undergraduates and a colleague, I can certainly testify to the kind of impact Douglas can have. I well remember the first time I sat in one of his tutorials and being confronted by questions which challenged me enormously. Apart from being called 'Mr Wilson', a salutation with which I was not accustomed, the questions provoked me into serious thought about the nature of Britain's industrialisation. When we were later colleagues in the Economic History department at the University of Manchester, Douglas confided in me that he was always keen to instil in his students the need to think, rather than offering definitive answers to his provocative questions. I tried to follow this advice throughout my career, even if in the business school world that I now occupy students always require 'the solution'.

As well as having been both an undergraduate student and colleague of Douglas, I also worked with him directly on a major research project. The fruitful result of this joint research was published as *Region and Strategy in Britain and Japan-Business in Lancashire and Kansai, 1890–1990* (edited by Douglas A. Farnie, Tetsuro Nakaoka, David J. Jeremy, John F. Wilson and Takeshi Abe; Routledge 2000). As Professor Nakaoka fondly noted to me, 'it was truly an unforgettable experience to do a collaborative work with Douglas … I was deeply indebted to him, because his method of research, which analysed Manchester as a commercial hub of regional industrial areas at Lancashire, gave a new perspective on the regional economic development of Kansai and the role of Osaka to commercially support regional industry.' How many people could make similar statements about collaborating with Douglas? How many people have received one of those file cards that Douglas always

1

used to provide detailed answers to the litany of questions he must have been asked over the last fifty years? How many people have relied on Douglas for leads and information that have been crucial to the success of a project?

Without trying to answer these questions directly, it has to be reported that I had no difficulty at all in securing the chapters which are included in this collection. Indeed, it was more a matter of keeping the collection down to a reasonable number of contributions, given the clamour to be included. Academics all over the world wanted to pay their respects to a scholar who influenced them, directly and indirectly, throughout their careers. This must be the ultimate accolade for a man whom I am proud to call a colleague, collaborator and friend. We respectfully submit this festschrift to honour Douglas Farnie, who was one of the most influential economic historians of the last half-century.

John Wilson
July 2008

The publications of Douglas A. Farnie

Books

(1969)   *East and West of Suez. The Suez Canal in History, 1854–1956*, Oxford: Clarendon Press, 860pp.

(1979)   *The English Cotton Industry and the World Market, 1815–1896*, Oxford: Clarendon Press, 416pp.

(1980)   *The Manchester Ship Canal and the Rise of the Port of Manchester, 1894–1975*, Manchester: Manchester University Press, 208pp.

(1990)   W. H. Chaloner, *Industry and Innovation. Selected Essays*, London: Frank Cass. Ed. with W. O. Henderson.

(2000)   *Region and Strategy in Britain and Japan. Business in Lancashire and Kansai, 1890–1990* London: Routledge. Ed. with Tetsuro Nakaoka, David J. Jeremy, John F. Wilson and Takeshi Abe.

(2004)   *The Fibre that Changed the World. The Cotton Industry in International Perspective, 1600–1990s*, Oxford: Oxford University Press, 614pp. Ed. with David J. Jeremy.

Papers

Major articles are marked by an asterisk

(1956)   'The Commercial Development of Manchester in the later nineteenth century', *The Manchester Review*, Spring, 326–37.

*(1956)   'The Mineral Revolution in South Africa', *South African Journal of Economics*, 24, 125–34.

*(1958)   'The Textile Industry: Woven Fabrics', in Charles Singer (ed.), *A History of Technology*, Oxford: Clarendon Press, vol. v, *The Late*

Nineteenth Century (1850–1900), 569–94. (Translated into Japanese, 1978.)

*(1962) 'The Commercial Empire of the Atlantic, 1607–1783', *Economic History Review*, second series, 15 (4), 205–18.

(1973) 'John Rylands of Manchester', *Bulletin of the John Rylands University of Manchester*, 56 (1) 93–129. Reprinted 1993.

(1978) 'Three Historians of the Cotton Industry: Thomas Ellison, Gerhart von Schulz-Gaevernitz and Sydney Chapman', *Textile History*, 9, 75–89.

*(1979) 'An Index of Commercial Activity: The Membership of the Manchester Royal Exchange, 1809–1948' *Business History*, 21 (1), 97–106.

*(1981) 'Platt Bros & Co., Ltd of Oldham, Machine-Makers to Lancashire and to the World: An Index of Production of Cotton Spinning Spindles, 1880–1914', *Business History*, 23 (1), 84–86.

*(1982) 'The Structure of the British Cotton Industry, 1846–1914', in Akio Okochi and Shin-ichi Yonekawa (eds), *The Textile Industry and its Business Climate. Proceedings of the Fuji Conference* (Tokyo: Tokyo University Press, International Conference on Business History, vol. 8), 45–91.

(1982) 'The Emergence of Victorian Oldham as the Centre of the Cotton Spinning Industry', *Bulletin of the Saddleworth Historical Society*, 12 (3), 41–53.

(1984) 'John Bunting (1839–1923)', in D. J. Jeremy (ed.), *Dictionary of Business Biography*, vol. 1, Butterworth, 506–10.

(1984) 'John Kenworthy Bythell (1840–1916), *DBB*, vol. 1, 544–47.

(1985) 'John Platt (1817–72), *DBB*, vol. 4, 725–29.

(1985) 'Samuel Radcliffe Platt (1845–1902)', *DBB*, vol. 4, 729–32.

(1985) 'John Rylands (1801–88)', *DBB*, vol. 4, 999–1004.

(1986) 'Marshall Stevens (1852–1936)', *DBB*, vol. 5, 312–25.

(1986) 'Robert Burdon Stoker (1859–1919)' *DBB*, vol. 5, 344–47.

(1984) 'The Impact of the Opening of the Manchester Ship Canal on the Greater Manchester Region', in Manchester Literary and Philosophical Society, *Report of the Seminar 'Manchester – Centre of Trade – the Future, held on July 18th, 1984*. 8–19.

*(1985) 'The Metropolis of Cotton Spinning, Machine-making and Mill Building', in Duncan Gurr and Julian Hunt (eds), *The Cotton Mills*

of Oldham, Oldham: Oldham Leisure Services. Second edition 1990, 4–11.

(1985) 'The Machine Makers', in Gurr and Hunt, *The Cotton Mills of Oldham* (1985), 12–13.

(1985) 'The Manchester Ship Canal, 1882–1984: The Transition from Salford Docks to Ellesmere Port', in Patricia M. Hodson (ed.), *The Manchester Ship Canal: A guide to Historical Sources*, Manchester: Lancashire Bibliography, part eleven, iv–viii.

*(1988) 'The Emergence of the Large Firm in the Cotton Spinning Industries of the World, 1883–1938', *Textile History*, 19 (2), 171–210. (Anglo-Japanese Conference Issue, with Shin-ichi Yonekawa.)

(1989) 'Enriqueta Augustina Rylands (1843–1908), Founder of the John Rylands Library', *Bulletin of the John Rylands University Library of Manchester*, 71 (2), 3–38. (Library Centenary Issue.)

(1990) 'John Worrall of Oldham, Directory-Publisher to Lancashire and to the World, 1868–1970', in *Manchester Region History Review*, 4 (1), 30–35.

(1990) 'The Textile Machine-Making Industry and the World Market, 1870–1960', *Business History*, 32 (4), 150–70. (Published simultaneously in book form as Mary Rose (ed.), *Competition and Strategic Response in World Textiles Since 1870*, London: Frank Cass.)

*(1992) 'The cotton towns of Greater Manchester', in Mike Williams with D. A. Farnie, *Cotton Mills in Greater Manchester*, Preston: Carnegie Publishing Ltd, for GMAU in association with the RCHME, 13–47.

*(1993) 'John Rylands of Manchester', *Bulletin of the John Rylands University Library of Manchester*, 75 (2) 3–103. Offprinted as a booklet.

*(1993) 'The Marketing Strategies of Platt Bros & Co. Ltd of Oldham, 1906–1940', *Textile History*, 24 (2), 147–61.

(1994) 'Cotton Waterway: A Hundred years of the Manchester Ship Canal, *History Today*, 44 (5) 25–29.

*(1994) 'China: a Microcosm of the World Market for Cotton Manufactures, 1868–1935', in A. J. H. Latham and Heita Kawakatsu (eds), *The Evolving Structure of the East Asian Economic System Since 1700: a Comparative Analysis*, Proceedings, Eleventh International Economic History Congress, Milan, September 1994, Milan: Universita Bocconi, B6), 9–16 (with Heita Kawakatsu).

*(1995) 'Les strategies de transport des companies petrolieres et des

armateurs et le Canal de Suez, 1929–1989', in Michele Merger, Albert Carreras, Andrea Giuntini (eds.), *Les Reseaux Europeans Transnationaux XIX–XX Siecles. Quels Enjeux?* Nantes: Ouest Editions, 384–395.

*(1997) 'Mengyo to Ajia Shijo: 1890–1997 Nen' ['The Asian Market for Cotton Manufactures, 1890–1997'], in *Nenpo Kindai Nihon Kenkyu* [*Journal of Modern Japanese Studies*] 19, 44–83 (with Takeshi Abe).

*(1998) 'The Wiener Thesis Vindicated. The Onslaught of 1994 upon the reputation of John Rylands of Manchester', in D. J. Jeremy (ed.), *Religion, Business and Wealth in Modern Britain*, London: Routledge, 86–107.

*(1998) 'The Emergence of a New Paradigm in the Museums of the North West: the Shift of Emphasis in a New Textile Gallery from Machinery to Marketing', with David J. Jeremy, in *Journal of Industrial History*, 1 (1), 107–22.

*(1999) 'The Era of the Great Inventions in the English Cotton Industry, 1764–1834', *Mitteilungen des Chemnitzer Geschichtsvereins*, 69. Jahrbuch, Neue Folge (VIII), '200 Jahre Erste Baumwollmaschinen-Spinnerei in Sachsen', 38–55.

*(2000) 'Four Revolutions in the Textile Trade of Asia, 1814–1994. The Impact of Bombay, Osaka, the Little Tigers and China', in A. J. H. Latham and Heita Kawakatsu (eds), *Asia Pacific Dynamism, 1550–2000*, London: Routledge, 49–69.

(2000) 'Money-Making and Charitable Endeavour: John and Enriqueta Rylands of Manchester', *The Journal of the United Reformed Church History Society*, 6 (6), 429–39.

(2000) 'Region and History', with Takeshi Abe, in Farnie *et al.* (2000), *Region and Strategy*, 1–8.

(2000) 'Region and Nation', with Tesaro Nakaoka in Farnie *et al.* (2000), 9–77.

*(2000) 'Japan, Lancashire and the Asian Market for Cotton Manufactures, 1890–1990, with Takeshi Abe, in Farnie *et al.* (2000), 115–57.

(2000) 'Region and Strategy', with Tetsuro Nakaoka, David J. Jeremy, John F. Wilson and Takeshia Abe, in Farnie *et al.* (2000), 300–6.

*(2000) 'The Role of India in the International Economy, 1930–1990', in Shigeru Akita (ed.), *South Asia in the 20th Century International Relations*. Research Project: Institutions, Networks & Forces of Change in Contemporary South Asia. Publications of Scientific

Research Results, no. 6. Tokyo: University of Tokyo, Institute of Oriental Culture, 1–12.

*(2001) 'A Bio-Bibliography of Economic and Social History', in Pat Hudson (ed.), *Living Economic and Social History*, Glasgow: Economic History Society, 445–80.

*(2001) 'George Unwin (1870–1925), Founder of the Manchester School of Economic History', in Hudson (ed.) (2001), 75–80.

(2001) 'The Ranking of Firms, the Counting of Employees, and the Classification of Data: a Cautionary Note', *Business History*, 43 (3), 105–118. With D. J. Jeremy.

*(2002) 'Freda Utley, 1899–1978: Crusader for Truth, Freedom, and Justice', in Hugh Cortazzi (ed.), *Britain and Japan. Biographical Portraits*, London: Japan Society, vol. 4, 361–71.

*(2003) 'Cotton, 1780–1914', in David Jenkins (ed.), *The Cambridge History of Western Textiles*, Cambridge: Cambridge University Press, 721–60, 910–15.

*(2003) 'Cotton Industry: Historical Overview', in Joel Mokyr (ed.), *The Oxford Encyclopedia of Economic History*, New York: Oxford University Press, vol. 2, 20–4.

*(2003) 'Suez Canal', in Mokyr (ed,) (2003), vol. 5, 36–7.

*(2004) John Bunting, John Kenworthy Bythell, Samuel Crompton, Sir Benjamin Alfred Dobson, Thomas Ellison, Thomas Edmund Gartside, John Kay, Evan Leigh, Hugh Mason, Haslam Mills, Platt family, Edward Potts, Enriqueta Augustina Rylands, John Rylands, Marshall Stevens, Robert Burdon Stoker, Winifred Utley, Sir Edward Leader Williams, Sir Charles Rivers Wilson. All in *The Oxford Dictionary of National Biography*, Oxford: Oxford University Press.

1

An interview with Douglas A. Farnie

A. J. H. LATHAM

Douglas, we are fellow Lancastrians and old friends from many conferences. I see you as probably the last true member of the internationally famous Manchester School of Economic History. Can you tell us a little about George Unwin and the leading lights of the School?

George Unwin was I think the first Professor of Economic History in Britain and the British Empire as it then was, although in 1892 Harvard had appointed the first Professor of Economic History in the world.

The Manchester school of economic history was a product of the Manchester school of history, created from 1890 onwards by T. F. Tout. That school supplied Oxford with three professors, in 1925, 1929 and 1948. In 1910 Tout appointed George Unwin (1870–1925) as Professor of Economic History. In return Unwin raised the department to new eminence within the world of scholarship, changing the emphasis of instruction from politics to society. His lasting achievements were fourfold. First, he established the first academic school of economic history in Britain and enlarged the horizons of the subject. He elevated it into a higher criticism of political history, locating the springs of action within the small voluntary groups of society rather than the state. Secondly, he imported into England the German tradition of research established by Schmoller and established the first British school of research into economic history. He unearthed a large clutch of business records and pioneered the study of economic history upon the basis of original sources. Thereby he set the example followed by his disciple, G. W. Daniels, who in 1931 established the first school of research in economics in the UK. Thirdly, he pioneered the publication of a series of studies of economic history by Manchester University Press, wherein ten volumes appeared during the decade 1924–34. Fourthly, he served as an inspiration to a group of notable scholars through his incandescent personality and his stimulating conversation. Those scholars included R. H. Tawney, J. L. Hammond, G. H. Tupling, H. L. Beales, Eileen Power, J. F. Rees, C. R. Fay, and Conrad Gill. T. S. Ashton in particular became the true intellectual heir of Unwin and maintained close relations with another associate, A. P. Wadsworth of the *Manchester Guardian*. In 1948 he produced the study of the Industrial Revolution which Unwin himself had always aspired to write. He also encouraged R. S. Fitton of the Manchester Polytechnic to build up an associated school of economic history and business history. His brother-in-law, Arthur Redford, had been a medievalist but was converted by Unwin and became an economic historian. In 1948 W. H. B. Court rightly ranked Unwin with R. H. Tawney and J. H. Clapham as one of the three founders of the academic study of economic history in Britain. In 2004 Unwin became the only Manchester economic historian to merit inclusion in the new *Oxford Dictionary of National Biography*.

The great days of the school have now passed, and I wonder if you can account for the decline of the School?

The school had risen in harmony with the staple trade of Lancashire and reached its apogee during the quinquennium 1920–24, when it was dominated by the trio of Unwin, Daniels and Ashton. When the cotton trade declined after the climacteric of 1926 the school also suffered a decline. In that process one may distinguish certain causative factors. First, the spread of interest in economic history throughout Britain and the emergence of new centres of excellence, especially in Cambridge and at the LSE, inevitably reduced the relative importance of the Manchester School and ultimately shifted the focus of interest away from the Industrial Revolution. Thus the golden age of economic history in the UK between 1945 and 1975 became an era of relative decline for Manchester. Secondly, the emergence during the 1930s of a new social and economic philosophy hostile to that of the Manchester School and the descent of the great wet blanket of collectivist thought upon the English intelligentsia diminished the standing of the school in the estimation of the rising generation. Thirdly, the expansion in the amount of source material available for study shattered the quasi-monopoly thitherto held by Manchester in the field of original sources. That trend was accentuated by the establishment of county record offices, by the publication of long-term series of historical statistics, by the reprint boom of the 1960s and by the advent of the photo-copier. Above all, the birth of the new economic history in the

Douglas Farnie and economic historians, 4 April 1998.
From left: 2 Dr Pamela Sharpe 3 Dr Christine Macleod 5 Prof. Douglas Farnie
6 Dr Jenny West 8 Prof. Michael [F.M.L.] Thompson 9 Prof. Roderick Floud
11 Prof. Jack Price.

USA launched a revolution in method for which Manchester was wholly unprepared.

In 1966 the annual conference of the Economic History Society was held for the first time in Manchester. On 1 April Robert W. Fogel of Chicago delivered a keynote address on 'The New Economic History' to a plenary session of the conference. The place, the speaker and the subject seem to have been chosen with some deliberation, in order to introduce the new model of the subject to Manchester. The emergence of the new economic history after 1956 undoubtedly presented a major challenge to the type of empirical economic history which had become the standard approach of Manchester scholars. Redford, as the successor to Unwin, had maintained a tradition unequalled elsewhere in its longevity (1910–1961) but one inevitably resistant to change generated from the outside. The new approach to the study of the subject matured under the influence of economics rather than of history. It deployed a formidable armoury of weapons, in economic theory, in the counterfactual hypothesis and in techniques of quantitative measurement as well as of national accounting. Phyllis Deane and W. A. Cole became the earliest English representatives of the new school and launched in 1962 a quantitative re-appraisal of British economic growth since 1688. The new economic history was extended in range to the cotton industry by the geographer E. A. Wrigley of Cambridge in 1962 and to the iron industry in 1973–77 by C. K. Hyde of Gary, Indiana.

It was of some significance that the work of both Phyllis Deane and E. A. Wrigley undermined the traditional interpretation of the Industrial Revolution and especially minimised the role played by the cotton industry in that process. It had been Manchester scholars, such as Unwin, Daniels, Wadsworth and Redford, who had first placed the study of the history of the cotton industry upon solid foundations. None of their successors took part in the process of re-interpretation or mounted an effective challenge to the revisionists. Nor did they play any role in the compilation of the great statistical compendia of 1962 and 1972, which placed the economic history of the UK and of Europe upon wholly new foundations. Only in 1974 did Manchester pay nominal homage to the new economic history by appointing Theodore Balderstone to its staff.

The relative decline in importance of the school was reflected in its loss of national status. The Economic History Society, founded in London in 1926, evolved largely independently of the influence of Manchester and held only two of its annual conferences in the city. Only one Manchester graduate, Michael Flinn, was elected to its presidency serving from 1980 to 1983. Only two local scholars, A. E. Musson and M. E. Rose, wrote pamphlets in 1972 for the society's series of studies in economic and social history. In 1971 Negley Harte published a collection of 21 inaugural lectures delivered between 1893 and 1970 but included only a single lecture delivered by a Manchester scholar, Unwin.

Manchester is also famous for the 'Manchester School' of the 1840s which forced the British Government to introduce Free Trade in 1846. To what extent did the Manchester School of Economic History reflect that open market philosophy?

The principles of free trade were accepted as axiomatic within both the Faculty of Arts and the Faculty of Commerce, even after the adoption of the principle of protection in 1932 as official government policy. Within the department of history Unwin had been 'the last of the radicals' in his deep-seated mistrust of state-power, past and present. The publications of Redford on labour, commerce, and municipal government do, however, take their due place in the great tradition of the Manchester School. The vanguard of collectivist thought in the form of Marxists from Oxford were first appointed to the section of modern history after the retirement in 1953 of Sir Lewis Namier. They then appeared among the ranks of the medievalists in 1968 but did not penetrate the economic history section until 1975–77.

Can you tell us a little about your own career? Can you tell us something of your family background, and your schooling?

My mother was Ethel Farrington (1893–1931), of an old Lancashire family. My father, Arthur Farnie (1867–1958) was born in Inverbervie on the coast of Kincardineshire. He became a tailor and migrated first to Edinburgh and then by 1886 to Eccles, which became a boom-town with the construction of the Manchester Ship Canal. There he became, in 1903, the first Labour councillor. He remained throughout his life a great reader, using the public libraries in Eccles and Salford in order to supplement his own book collection, which included the Waverley novels of Scott and Macaulay's *Lays of Ancient Rome*.

At Salford Grammar School I was introduced in 1938–39 to Egyptian history in the form of cyclostyled notes detailing the history of the country's 31 dynasties. Salford Corporation had decided, after the discovery of the tomb of Tutankhamen in 1922, that all school children in the borough should learn about the history of ancient Egypt. In my own case the method chosen proved, however, wholly unsatisfactory. I found the subject uninteresting and incomprehensible. My abiding interest in history was awakened only from 1940 by reading historical novels, especially about medieval Italy and the French Revolution. By the time I passed my School Certificate in 1942 and my Higher School Certificate in 1944 I had decided to study history at the university. In 1943 I was first introduced to the subject of economic history by R. M. Hedley, who had studied under Unwin at the University of Manchester.

Being born in 1926 you will have been a teenager during the war, just coming up to military age towards the end. I have heard you say you were in the Parachute Regiment, can you tell us something of your service days?

I served for 3½ years in the Army from November 1944 to April 1948, as a sergeant in the Intelligence Corps. I spent 15 months in India and 13 months in the Suez Canal zone of Egypt, where I read Gibbon while on leave in Moascar. I joined the Second Indian Airborne Division, originally earmarked for the invasion of Java. In February 1946 I completed a parachute training course at Chaklala, Rawalpindi, making four descents from a Dakota and four from a Halifax. Towards the end of my tour of duty in India I spent three months on detachment at Quetta on the North-West Frontier, travelling on one occasion to Chaman, on the borders of Afghanistan. Service in India and Egypt, followed by my sojourn in South Africa and my later visits to Japan and the USA widened my outlook on life. I learned much about both India and Egypt after leaving those countries but have never returned to either.

After military service, I remember you saying you were in South Africa, and at University there. Can you tell us about all this?

In 1948, at the age of 22, I became an undergraduate in the Honours School of History at Manchester. During the next two years I attended survey courses taken in the first year by Eric Stone and W. H. Chaloner and in the second year by T. S. Willan. In my final year I chose to take Arthur Redford's Special Subject, 'The Age of Economic Reform, 1830–1848'. The most truly inspiring teacher at Manchester, however, I found to be Lewis Namier in his exposition of the history of Europe 'From Vienna to Versailles' 1815–1918. In the Students' Union I was duly impressed by the personal appearances made by Charles Laughton and Greer Garson, as well as by Hewlett Johnson, 'the Red Dean' of Canterbury'.

I completed my MA thesis in two years (1951–53). On the advice of Professor Redford I undertook research upon the history of the cotton industry: I remain lastingly grateful for his recommendation of that particular subject. His intention was that I should study the business records of the firm of W. G. & J. Strutt of Belper and Milford, producing a complementary account to the work of R. S. Fitton. I found, however, the Strutt records incomprehensible: no later scholar has proved able to use them. I was able, however, to extend my range of interest from a single firm to the whole of the industry by consulting, at Somerset House in London, the original files of the 1,046 companies registered in the English cotton industry between 1845 and 1896. The subject of the cotton industry has continued to interest successive generations of students around the world, in sharp contrast to other topics that I have dallied with.

In 1953 I emigrated to South Africa, reading Toynbee while outward bound on board the *Winchester Castle*. There I spent seven happy years in the University of Natal at Durban and learned that history was not a dead subject, as in England, but a living reality, as it was also in Ulster, in Quebec and in the Deep South. There I widened the range of my interests. I lectured on the history of Western civilisation, beginning with pre-history and using as a textbook *What Happened in History* (1942) by the Australian Marxist, V. G. Childe. I also taught the economic history of South Africa from 1795. I passed under the influence of the Russian-American sociologist, P. A. Sorokin, and of the South African anthropologist, J. D. Krige. From Sorokin I learned how truly extensive the full range of social theories was. From Krige I learned of the crucial role of hierarchy in the value-system of a culture. I also compared the rise of the poor whites in South Africa and in the American South. Finally, I began research upon the history of the Suez Canal, stimulated by the outbreak of the Suez Crisis in 1956.

Then you were appointed to a post in Manchester. Who were the big names in Manchester at the time, and how did you find Manchester on your return?

In 1960 I was appointed to a lectureship in Manchester, together with Eric Robinson. Professor Redford had increased the number of economic historians within the department from four in 1945 to ten in 1958. Those ten included specialists in early modern European economic history, modern European economic history, the history of social and economic thought, local history and social history. The older generation of scholars was represented by T. S. Willan, G. H. Tupling, W. O. Henderson, W. H. Chaloner and Werner Stark. The younger generation was represented by A. E. Musson, E. R. R. Green and H. J. Perkin, together with J. M. W. Bean for medieval economic history.

The pattern of intellectual activity was essentially individualist in orientation. Each scholar pursued in isolation his own particular line of research. Redford had employed Brian W. Clapp as his research assistant and Perkin tried to persuade his colleagues to contribute a volume each to his new series of Studies in Social History. Joint activity, however, remained the exception, being limited to the publications co-authored by Henderson and Chaloner, and by Musson and Robinson. No departmental or sectional meetings were held, except for examination purposes. Even the Tout Society, established in 1922, was wound up in 1975 when members of staff lost interest in history outside their own special field. I myself replaced H. G. Koenigsberger, lecturing on the early modern economic history of both Europe and England, together with medieval economic history. My favourite course became the one devoted to the economic history of Europe, 1500–1815, wherein I came under the influence of Braudel but also deployed my knowledge of Dutch, acquired in South Africa.

During my thirty years in the department, the school increased its intake of students but suffered from a growing loss of national influence. First, Redford had himself, under pressure from the professor of ancient history, 'sold the pass' by accepting in 1958 the creation of an option for undergraduates within the department which excluded the study of economic history. He had also agreed to the down-grading of economic history to optional status within a reconstructed BA (Econ.) degree. He had sought to secure appointment to a Research Chair in Economic History, in order to cushion his retirement, but was denied that privilege by the university. Secondly, the publication in 1958 of a new edition of Engels by Henderson and Chaloner aroused widespread hostility towards them within the expanded ranks of the profession and even within the department of history at Manchester itself. The book was denied any review in the pages of the *Economic History Review*, the *English Historical Review* and the *Times Literary Supplement*. In reprisal true believers in the work of Engels as a sacred text secured the reprinting

Douglas A. Farnie.

of the out-dated translation by Florence Kelley four times (in 1969, 1988, 1991 and 1993). Thirdly, the appointment of a successor to T. S. Willan, who had been professor (1961–73) and retired at the age of 64, proved to be a long drawn-out and contested affair. The profession wanted to introduce new blood and new ideas into Manchester. Chaloner was therefore passed over. Charles Feinstein was offered the chair, but declined to accept. Finally A. E. Musson was appointed. One of his first acts was to appoint Theodore Balderstone in 1974 as a token representative of the new economic history. He then sought to secure the promotion of Chaloner to a personal chair but encountered much opposition from within the profession. Only in 1976 was Chaloner, after 22 years of service within the department, grudgingly elevated to such a chair. Musson next proposed and organised a festschrift in honour of Chaloner. Manchester University Press agreed to publish the work but then reneged upon its agreement. Sales of similar festschriften for W. O. Henderson in 1975 and for T. W. Willan in 1977 had proved disappointing. The press had made in 1973 a profit for the first time in its seventy-year history and had become enamoured of the market for textbooks and for newly fashionable themes. During the tenure of his chair Musson maintained the level of staffing within the section but proved unable to withstand the encroachment upon its traditional territory by the modern historians. Those modernists had become thoroughly bored with political history and naively aspired to embrace the 'total history' favoured by publicists of the Annales school. At least eight modern historians acquired a vested interest in the field of social and economic history without encountering any opposition from the lecturers in economic history.

Fourthly, Manchester suffered a second interregnum in 1982–88, after the first of 1925–45, when Musson, under pressure of the government cuts in university funding, took early retirement at the age of 62. The chair in economic history was thereafter allowed to lapse. The remaining members of the section pursued their own specialised research into the economic history of Germany, Russia, Spain, Africa and the Far East until in 1988 an economist, Robert Millward, was appointed to the revived chair in economic history.

Your first big book was your famous study *East and West of Suez: The Suez Canal in History, 1854–1956* (Clarendon Press, Oxford, 1969). This is a massive work of some 860 pages. How was it received, and what do you see as its major message?

This work was the subject of my doctoral thesis and set the history of the Suez Canal within a global perspective, seeking in emulation of L. J. Ragatz to avoid a blatantly Eurocentric viewpoint. It was concerned to study not the construction of the waterway (which had been undertaken innumerable times before) but the history of its commerce and shipping after the ceremonies of inauguration had come to an end. The book therefore examined the changing role of the waterway through a whole century of operation. It considered the successive emergence of the great staples of trade between east and west, from the raw cotton of Bombay in the 1870s to the crude oil of Kuwait in the 1950s, an approach which necessitated the detailed investigation of the economic history of much of Asia. I came to recognise that the canal had served as a barometer reflecting the changing relations between two worlds, and I therefore sought to examine the political, diplomatic, legal and military history of the waterway. I concluded that the canal had been less important as a trade route than as a highway of empire and that its economic function had been exaggerated at the expense of its strategic function. I nevertheless cast grave doubt upon the claim first made in 1961 that the British occupation of Egypt had been a response to 'the Suez Crisis, 1882'.

The book was very widely reviewed because it exploited the evocative appeal of the world to the 'East of Suez', it appeared in the centenary year of the opening of the canal and in the aftermath of the agonizing debates precipitated by the Suez Crisis and by the Seven Day War of 1967, which led to the decision to withdraw British forces from all their bases east of Suez. The influence of the book proved however much more limited, judging by the lack of citations made by historians. In 1895 P. H. Ditchfield published *Books Fatal To Their Authors* (244pp). The Suez book may well be ranked as one such work. For whatever reason, it seems never to have aroused the interest of scholars to the same extent that my work on the cotton industry has. There did, nevertheless, stem from it two later studies. First, an essay devoted to 'The Rise and Decline of the Oil Traffic of the Suez Canal, 1929–1991' (1994), wherein I argued that the Suez Crisis of 1956 had been the subject of innumerable political histories but that its economic significance had never received the attention it deserved. I accordingly noted the steady decline since 1961 of the share of the canal in world trade, as a direct consequence of Egypt's nationalisation of the Suez Canal Company. Secondly, a general survey published in 2003 argued that, contrary to general belief, the opening of the canal had not ushered in a new era in the economic development of Asia. It also noted the dominance of traffic first by tanker tonnage from 1948 onwards and then by container tonnage from 1987.

Then you turned your focus, not surprisingly, to Manchester and the cotton industry, resulting in *The English Cotton Industry and the World Market, 1815–1896* (Oxford, 1979). This again was a milestone in our understanding of the key industry of the Industrial Revolution. Again, what do you see as its central focus?

The 1979 book embodied a major revision and extension of my MA thesis of 1953, from which had sprung my first published articles on the commercial development of Manchester in the later nineteenth century (1956) and on textile technology (1958). The book formed a belated sequel to the work of Wadsworth and Mann and changed the emphasis apparent in my thesis from technology to trade. In particular it stressed the importance of the long waves of economic life first identified by Kondratiev in 1922, especially the long-term depression of prices during the years 1815–49 and 1873–96. In methodology it represented a distinct advance upon the Suez book because it first made effective use of growth rates, a feature which appeared in all my later work on the industry. I used the UK statistics of trade in order to study trends in the world markets and to do so with particular reference to the great markets of India and China. Within Lancashire the book focused upon the rise of the mill towns and especially upon the emergence of Oldham during the 1860s as the main centre of cotton spinning. It also included a mildly revisionist interpretation of the Cotton Famine. The work was received with respectful enthusiasm in the USA and in Japan, leading to a series of visits to both countries. The subject has supplied me with an 'iron rice-bowl', which has sustained me throughout my academic career. Most of my later work has indeed focused upon the history of the cotton industry. A rare venture into industrial archaeology took the form of a survey of the sixteen cotton spinning towns of Greater Manchester (1992), which sought to undermine the inherited stereotype of the mill town and revealed how every single town had its own distinctive pattern of development. A detailed study of Oldham, the birthplace during the boom of the 1870s of working-class investment in local industry, confirmed the value of this approach and passed through three editions (1985, 1989, 1998). A series of studies of textile technology had begun with a chapter on 'Woven Fabrics' [1850–1900] in Volume 5 of Charles Singer's *History of Technology* (1958). A statistical estimate of production by Platt Bros in 1981 was followed by five more studies of this firm, which had become in the 1850s the largest engineering firm in the world. Those studies were set in the larger context of a general essay devoted to 'The Textile Machine-Making Industry and the World Market, 1870–1960' (1990). I also surveyed the first phase of technical innovation in an article on 'The Era of the Great Inventions in the English Cotton Industry, 1764–1834' (1999).

In 1998 an essay co-authored with David Jeremy, the first of three such essays, reflected a new approach to the subject in its title, 'The Emergence of a New Perspective in the Museums of the North West: The Shift of Emphasis in a New Textile Gallery from Machinery to Marketing'. Wide-ranging syntheses of the long-term history of the industry were published in *The Cambridge History of Western Textiles* (2003) and in *The Oxford Encyclopaedia of Economic History* (2003). A biography of John Rylands, Manchester's greatest merchant, had appeared in 1973 and proved to be the first of six essays upon the same subject. Not until 1998, however, did a truly satisfactory study of John Rylands appear in 'The Wiener Thesis Vindicated. The Onslaught of 1994 upon the Reputation of John Rylands of Manchester', stressing the religious inspiration behind his entrepreneurial activity. There followed seven biographies in D. J. Jeremy (ed.), *The Dictionary of Business Biography*, and nineteen biographies in *The Oxford Dictionary of National Biography* (2004), which included entries on John Kay, Samuel Crompton and Freda Utley.

You have been very active with your Japanese contacts, including Heita Kawakatsu of The International Research Centre for Japanese Studies, Kyoto and now President of Shizuoka University of Art and Culture. This has resulted in your co-edited collection of papers *Region and Strategy in Britain and Japan: Business in Lancashire and Kansai, 1890–1990* (London: Routledge 2000). Again, what was the main line of thought in this collection?

My work on Asian economic history was fostered by my service in India, by my research for the Suez book and by my continuing interest in the history of the world market. Japan, however, proved a revelation and still remains a source of fascination. The first Japanese scholar I met, in 1978, was Heita Kawakatsu, a postgraduate student of Peter Mathias. Then in 1981, at the invitation of Shin-ichi Yonekawa, I attended the Fuji Conference on Business History and published a paper in its proceedings in 1982 on 'The Structure of the British Cotton Industry, 1846–1914'. My 1958 essay on textile technology had already been published in Japanese in 1978. Seven articles were then written jointly with different Japanese scholars, with Shin-ichi Yonekawa (1988), with Heita Kawakatsu (1994), with Takeshi Abe (1997, 2000) and with Tetsuro Nakaoka (2000). Of those the most important were 'The Emergence of the Large Firm in the Cotton Spinning Industries of the World, 1883–1938' (1988), with Shin-ichi Yonekawa, and 'The Asian Market for Cotton Manufactures, 1890–1997' (1997), with Takeshi Abe.

My interest in this field was also encouraged by you, John, by my offer of two papers at the Milan Congress of 1994 and by my organisation of a session at the Madrid Congress of 1998. Thereafter, I set the rise of 'the little tigers' (Hong Kong, Taiwan and South Korea) in the context of 'Four Revolutions in the Textile Trade of Asia, 1814–1994' (2000). Kaoru Sugihara encouraged me to consider 'The Role of India in the International Economy, 1930–1990' (2000) and strengthened my interest in the career of Freda Utley (1899–1978) as an interlocutor between east and west. Hugh Cortazzi on behalf of the Japan Society, invited me to contribute a biography of Freda to a collection of essays which was published in 2002. Such contacts were supplemented by visits paid to Manchester by Kazuhiko Kondo, Takeo Izumi, Yutaka Taniguchi and Yoshiteru Takei. On visits to Japan I enjoyed the hospitality courteously offered by Takeshi Abe and Heita Kawakatsu. My association with David Jeremy eventually produced *Region and Strategy* (2000), comprising ten chapters, each of which was written jointly by an English and a Japanese scholar. My own contributions were the four chapters devoted to 'Region and History', 'Region and Nation', 'Japan, Lancashire and the Asian Market for Cotton Manufactures, 1890–1990' and 'Region and Strategy'. The work contrasted the meteoric expansion of the region of Kansai during the century 1890–1990 with the remorseless decline of the economy of Lancashire. I concluded that the business culture of Manchester had undergone by 1990 almost total eclipse.

Are there any projects you have worked on that we have not mentioned?

There were two early articles applying the staple theory to the history of South Africa and of Anglo-American trade, 'The Mineral Revolution in South Africa' (1956) and 'The Commercial Empire of the Atlantic, 1607–1793' (1962). The latter article led me to be dubbed a 'neo-Smithian' and, later, an 'Atlanticist'. I also published a history of the Manchester Ship Canal, 1894–1975 (1980), which focused on the staple trades in cotton and oil and aroused some degree of regional interest but was then remaindered by a commercially minded

Manchester University Press. In co-operation with W. O. Henderson, I edited *Industry and Innovation. Selected Essays* (of W. H. Chaloner) in 1990.

In 2001 I was encouraged by Pat Hudson to produce not only a brief biography of George Unwin but also a Bio-bibliography of Economic and Social History, listing 700 names. That work was expanded first in 2002 to a listing of 2,200 names and then in 2004 to a listing of 3,000 names.

In 2004 I co-edited with David Jeremy *The Fibre that Changed the World. The Cotton Industry in International Perspective, 1600–1990s*. To that very large work I contributed four of the 18 chapters, on the 'The Role of Cotton as a World Power, 1780–1990', 'The Role of Merchants as Prime Movers in the Expansion of the Cotton Industry, 1760–1990', 'The Role of the Cotton Industry in the Economic Development of India, 1600–1990' and 'The Role of the Cotton Industry in Economic Development'. These essays sum up much of my life's work and suggest a new agenda for future research.

After you retired from Manchester University, you became a Research Professor at Manchester Metropolitan University, attached to the Centre for Business History. What topics are interesting you now, and what projects are you working on?

In 1992 I became associated with David Jeremy and Geoffrey Tweedale at the Manchester Metropolitan University. I found the new experience refreshingly different from the etiolated life in the Department of History at the University of Manchester. I still remain interested in the history of the cotton industry and have recently been occupied with a study of the history of the weaving towns of north-east Lancashire as a complement to my 1992 study of the spinning towns of south-east Lancashire. Because weaving had become essentially women's work, I have had to undertake a detailed study of the history of female labour within the industry, a topic which has led me once more into the sphere of comparative history, especially in relation to the USA and India.

These are difficult days for economic history, with publishers increasingly reluctant to take works on Britain and the Industrial Revolution, and more interested in issues of World Economic History. Do you see this as the direction for the future?

Economic history in Britain has been fortunate in so far as it has survived the onslaught of the cultural imperialism of the Annales School, which became manifest with the translation of Braudel's work in 1972. I would agree that world economic history may well represent the wave of the future, moderating the ineradicable parochialism and insularity of British scholars. There remain, however, certain constraints in relation to sources, languages and method, which may well limit the extent of any contribution to be made by British scholars. The left–liberal consensus within the profession may well dispose its members to favour global social history rather than global economic history. That consensus became strikingly apparent during the annual conference at Leicester in 1992, when the result of the general election resulted in a Conservative victory and so spread gloom and despondency among the delegates. Above all, British scholars may well prove as resistant to the abandonment of the study of the Industrial Revolution as they have proved to be to the sacrifice of their beloved peasantry in the wake of Alan McFarlane's *The Origins of English Individualism* (1978).

Do you have any other reflections on the state of Economic History after a lifetime in the subject?

All scholars have a threefold duty, to their subject, to their students and to the general public. Since the time of Unwin successive generations of scholars have, however, concentrated upon their subject at the expense of other commitments, writing only for one another. That trend has been accentuated by the research assessment exercises to which the British Government has subjected universities since 1990 and upon which their funding remains dependent. The result has been to widen the gap between the profession and the public to an almost unbridgeable degree. The results of research are increasingly couched in esoteric language unintelligible to the layman. Lay members of the public regularly attended annual conferences of the Economic History Society down to 1978. They do so no longer. Membership of the Economic History Society reached an all-time peak during 1976. From 1977 individual membership first sank below library membership and by 1998 total membership had declined by 40 per cent from that peak. Students have deserted the subject in droves, declining to accept the assurance made by Floud and McCloskey in 1981 that economic history is 'an exciting subject, a subject full of problems and controversy'. The prognosis for the immediate future must remain unfavourable. The subject will however return to favour when it once again associates itself with the great and permanent interests of mankind.

We will close on that optimistic note, and thank you very much Douglas for agreeing to this interview.

Interview concluded 20 October 2004.

2

Manchester's historians: archives and industry

CHRIS WRIGLEY

M ANCHESTER UNIVERSITY has played a major role in the development of economic and social history as well as of history in Britain. When the Economic History Society celebrated its 75th anniversary at Glasgow University in 2002, an interesting session of recollections by elderly eminences spoke warmly of the past contributions from Cambridge, Oxford and the LSE, but made scarce mention of Manchester, Nottingham and Birmingham or the Scottish or Welsh universities. In the case of Manchester this was an especially strange omission given its prominence.[1] The essay reassesses the contexts in which a major and innovative school of history, then economic history, emerged and developed. In the case of economic history there has been much published by Manchester historians which has investigated the massive role of Manchester and Lancashire in industrialisation in Britain and then in the international economy. Much of the economic history has also benefited from the links established between Owens College, then Manchester University, and the industrial and other enterprises of Manchester and its region.

Economic and social history fitted well into the ethos of the former Owens College. John Owens, whose legacy began the college in 1851, was a wealthy producer of cotton yarns, a Radical in politics and for long an attender at the Independent Chapel in Mosley Street. He was one of those who, in January 1839, subscribed £50 to the Anti-Corn Law League and in his will he bequeathed £100 to Richard Cobden. Owens, outraged by the exclusion of Nonconformists from Oxford and Cambridge, desired to set up a college which excluded none but, if preference were given, it was to those living within or close to the borough of Manchester.[2]

The college fostered links with the enterprises and the working people of Manchester. The links with industry ran deep, not least with engineering. Several of the college's early professors had given lectures at the Workingmen's College, and after its closure in 1861, Owens College had taken on teaching evening classes, though its enthusiasm waned. Joseph Gouge Greenwood, the first Professor of History, 1851–54 (but also of Greek and Latin) and second Principal, 1857–89, was a notable supporter of working-class education. It was later recalled of him that he 'advocated much change in the system of college teaching, in order to recommend it to Manchester businessmen'. Richard Copley Christie, the second Professor of History, 1854–66 (but also of Political Economy and Jurisprudence and Law), gave evening lectures, notably on the constitutional and legal history of the reign of James I and the earlier years of Charles I. Because of its involvement with the industrial city, in the 1870s Owens was deemed by H. E. Roscoe, Professor of Chemistry, 1857–86, to be 'the University of the Busy'.[3]

The college's links with Manchester's enterprise encouraged much reflection of a historical and even an economic history kind. In 1874, following the reconstitution and extension of the college in 1871 and the opening of new buildings by the Duke of Devonshire in October 1873, a substantial volume entitled *Essays and Addresses by Professors and Lecturers of Owens College, Manchester* was published at the request of the college's council. In his contribution James Bryce, Professor of Jurisprudence, reflected on the legal and constitutional history of Britain while discussing the Judicature Act of 1873. Towards the end of his essay he observed,

> It is surely the special function of universities ... so to train its students that they may endeavour to seize upon passing events and actual problems, apply to them an impartial analysis, and pour round them the mellowing light of history, raising them out of the dust and din of controversy, and disclosing the principles by which they must be judged, or on which their solution depends.[4]

The linking of the city's industrial concerns with the past led to consideration of economic history themes. In his contribution to the book Osborne Reynolds, Professor of Engineering, discussed 'The Use of Steam', commenting that 'at the present time steam is doing as much work as 12 millions of men could do' (an estimate whose source he gave as *Report of the Coal Commission*, 1869) while reviewing the history of the steam engine. W. Stanley Jevons, Professor of Political Economy, argued vigorously against the state control of the railways in his essay. Jevons also published elsewhere substantial work on the coal industry and on money and taxation. Henry Roscoe addressed what remains an important issue in university teaching in his essay, 'Original Research as a Means of Education'. In it Roscoe argued 'that if freedom of enquiry, independence of thought, disinterested and steadfast labour, habits of exact and truthful observation, and of clear perception, are things to be desired as tending to the higher intellectual development of mankind, then original research ought to be encouraged as one of the most valuable means of education'. Like Jevons, he roundly deplored state control, in this case of education:

> But while believing that a national system is needed in order that the potential scientific energy of the country shall become active, I for one should most strongly object to the establishment of a complete system of State education. One of our greatest safeguards and sources of national strength has been, and is, the freedom from Government control which our educational, municipal and local institutions have always enjoyed ...[5]

The importance of research to education in history became a major feature of Manchester University. An early advocate was the third Professor of History, 1866–97 (and second Professor of English and also third Principal of the college, 1889–97), Adolphus Ward. The son of a diplomat stationed in Germany, Ward was educated there and became especially interested in modern history. His contribution to Manchester's 1873 lectures was on 'The Peace of Europe', a fairly lacklustre study of the Balance of Power over the centuries. Ward, a Fellow of Peterhouse Cambridge, was an early and strong advocate of a pure history degree at Cambridge.[6] He brought his views of history and of scholarly research with him to Owens College. To the practices of scholars in writing ancient history, biblical criticism, archaeology and philosophy, Ward added emulation of German historians in his advocacy of rigorous research. Many ascribed his very efficient ways to his German upbringing. More tangibly, he drew on this background for his history, including using his father's diplomatic papers to write on the Schleswig-Holstein question and more generally for three volumes on the history of Germany, 1815–90 (1916–18). H. B. Charlton, Professor of English Literature (1921–57) and author of the college's centenary history, observed of Ward that his academic outlook could, by political analogy, be deemed that of a Whig. He went on, 'Scholarship in itself was a way of civilised life, a gentleman's contribution to the understanding of a past on which modern civilised society had perforce to build itself'. Ward encouraged undergraduate teaching of history to include 'the rudiments of research methods'. According to Charlton this 'profoundly influenced his junior colleague, Tout, who, in due course widely developed the Ward plan and brought it to fruition'.[7]

Ward was more than a St John the Baptist figure to Tout in the establishment of history at Manchester. He was a major contributor but, curiously, his own biggest contributions were made away from the department. Firstly, while at Manchester most of his prodigious output was in English. Indeed, when he went to Cambridge in 1900 he continued to publish in this area and he was the joint editor of the *Cambridge History of English Literature* (1907–16). He made his mark as a historian more at Cambridge. While at Manchester he had been assistant editor to Lord Acton on *The Cambridge Modern History*, doing much of the work. At Cambridge, with Lord Acton's resignation, Ward became a joint editor (1901–12) and, later, with G. P. Gooch, he also edited *The Cambridge History of British Foreign Policy, 1783–1919* (1922–23).[8]

Secondly, Ward's impact needs to be understood in terms of him being a major player in university and national academic affairs. Ward's standing at Manchester was mightily enhanced by him being a key figure in the successful moves of the 1870s to achieve university status, and he went on to serve as Vice Chancellor of the Victoria University, 1886–90 and 1894–96. His major role in establishing Owens as a university was recognised by Manchester conferring on him the freedom of the city in 1897. At Cambridge Ward also served as Vice Chancellor, 1901, and was knighted in 1913. His academic standing was marked by him being, among other bodies, President of the Royal Historical Society, 1899–1901, and of the British Academy, 1911–13, as well as receiving honorary degrees from Manchester and three other universities. He was a powerful friend of Manchester's history department and the university generally. When it was decided to commemorate the fallen of the First World War, Ward gave the Founder's Day oration in March 1917. Ward was a powerful and benign patron of both department and university, with a high profile in Manchester and nationally. He was the epitome of the academic statesman, though his output of publications was weightier than many of his successors a century later.

However, the major proponent of source-driven history was Thomas Frederick Tout, Manchester's fourth Professor of History, 1890–1925. He learned his trade while at Balliol from Bishop William Stubbs (1825–1901), in the year 1876–77 before he secured First Class Honours in History. Tout followed Stubbs in his emphasis on the importance of administrative history for understanding the medieval period. He carried out substantial archival research in Welsh medieval history while Professor of History at St David's College, Lampeter, 1881–90, before going to Manchester. While Tout also played a major role in Manchester University's affairs, he was also a far more substantial writer of history than Ward.

Tout was prominent in the post-Whig era of historians, one of the modernisers of Michael Bentley's Wiles lectures.[9] He built on substantial foundations laid by the generation of William Stubbs. J. R. Hale has commented of Stubbs and his contemporaries and successors: 'The study of history was becoming more exact, more preoccupied with sources, less philosophical.' For Hale, writing in 1964, Frederick William Maitland (1850–1906) was head and shoulders above his contemporaries: 'In comparison, the other institutional historians of his day, including his younger contemporary T. F. Tout, are very dull dogs indeed.'[10] John Kenyon, some twenty years later, was more positive, deeming Tout to be 'Stubbs' greatest pupil'.[11]

Tout emulated Stubbs in his impressive work in studying and editing medieval documents, and he shared his respect for such German scholars of medieval Britain as Reinhold Pauli (1823–82), Georg Waitz (1813–86) and Felix Liebermann (1851–1925) and early Scandinavian history as Conrad von Mauren (1823–1902). In an appreciation that he wrote after Liebermann's death he noted that the German's scholarship had 'a world-wide reputation by reason of its exactness, its completeness and the excellence of its methods' and he testified to his awe in seeing Liebermann analyse a thirteenth-century manuscript:

> … it gave the most vivid and impressive lesson in historical criticism and method that he has ever received. The rapt absorption, the keenness to note and compare the minutest points, the acuteness with which he based important conclusions on the faintest hints, the extraordinary rapidity and the exemplary thoroughness of the work, are never likely to escape his friend's memory.[12]

Liebermann reciprocated Tout's admiration, observing in *Deutsche Literaturzeitung* that Tout's *Chapters in the Administrative History of Medieval England*, vols 1 and 2 (1920) put him on a par with Stubbs.

Tout was more dynamic than Stubbs in respect of promoting a school of research. Tout noted of Stubbs at Oxford: 'In the end he renounced the idea, if he had ever entertained it, of organising a school of history such as had been set up by his colleagues in Germany.' He added that Stubbs, even had he been keen, 'had no fellow-workers in carrying out ideals that would have involved a radical recasting of the prevailing methods of historical teaching'.[13] In contrast, Tout had shown great energy at Lampeter in 1881–90 and, like Adolphus Ward, he was a driving force for change at Manchester.

Tout built on Adolphus Ward's foundations when developing research-based studying. He admired the special training for research provided by German scholars. In reviewing Sir Charles Firth's inaugural lecture at Oxford, Tout reflected on Manchester:

> Being Englishmen, the Manchester teachers have to pick up their own training as best they could, and they are anxious … that their pupils should enjoy more advantages than were accessible to British historians twenty years ago. They are fortunate in the traditions of research handed down from the period when Dr Ward first organised the higher teaching of history in Manchester. They are helped by the atmosphere of a society where the spirit of research is in the air, and by association with students of the physical

sciences who have long enjoyed the technical advantages denied to the medievalist.[14]

Given these views, it is not surprising that he wrote an article in a newspaper series on research in universities entitled 'An Historical "Laboratory"'. In it he argued for the ideal of research to be applied to education and that this was 'no less applicable to history than to physics and chemistry'. He argued:

> Our primary business is to find out as much as we can about the past. Our methods, then, must necessarily be the methods of the observational sciences, and we require as much training in the technique of our craft as any other skilled worker. Nay, more, the educational value of our study lies not so much in the accumulation of a mass of unrelated facts as in training in method, and evidence, and in seeing how history is made. It follows, then, that that the study of history should be largely a study of processes and method, even for those to whom history is not mainly the preparations for a career, but chiefly a means of academic education. No historical education can, therefore, be regarded as complete unless it involves training in method. The best training in method is an attempt at research.

Tout himself, like Ward and Tait, benefited greatly from writing many entries for the *Dictionary of National Biography*. He later recalled, 'Like many Oxford men of my generation, I approached historical investigation without the least training or guidance in historical method' and so Leslie Stephen's firm guidance 'constituted for many of us our first training in anything like original research'.[15] So while Stubbs provided inspiration for Tout and others it was very much learning on the job.

Tout gave primacy to the analysis of medieval history in his 'historical laboratory'. It may be that Powicke was mistaken in his British Academy Memoir of Tout in commenting of Tout's claim before the Royal Commission on Public Records that he was trying to build a school of medieval history that it only 'was referring, of course, to his own share in the work of the department'.[16] While Tout would not have excluded research in modern history, he often privileged medieval history as the area in which to develop skills. For example, in a quest for national efficiency mode in 1910, he wrote: 'With all our national cult of the amateur he is never likely to do sound work in so highly specialized a subject as medieval history.' When A. J. P. Taylor started lecturing on 1494–1914 at Manchester in 1930 he asked who had covered the period before him. He was told: 'Oh, Tout. He said that modern history was not a serious subject and anyone could lecture on it.' Taylor also observed that Tout's 'shade still dominated the department. The constitutional history of England in the middle ages came first and all other aspects of history were appendages to it.'

A. J. P. Taylor,
photographed *c*.1938/39.

In 1986, with the deaths of Goronwy Edwards and Vivian Galbraith, Taylor deemed 'an epoch had ended in English history', one marked by Stubbs and Tout and characterised by worshipping documents.[17]

Tout, like Ward before him, exemplified the assertion of professional ideals. On this Harold Perkin has written that 'the professional ideal consistently applied the tests of justification by service to society and, in one form or another, of the greatest happiness of the greatest number, to the analysis and criticisms of contemporary society'.[18] Tout readily fostered the Owens College tradition of building strong links with the city and wider society. Much of his efforts involved various forms of what now would be called outreach in education. As well as participating in his university's adult education, he was chairman of the Manchester University committee of the University Extension Movement, speaking within the city and at nearby towns for it, and also chairman of the committee setting up and supporting a Manchester University settlement. He was also a prime mover in developing good relationships between academics and the *Manchester Guardian*, which were later to be beneficial for Lewis Namier and Alan Taylor.

Tout also played a major role in developing the professional identity of historians in the Historical Association and later in the Royal Historical Society. In 1906 Tout was a founder member of the Historical Association, being with James Tait and Sir Adolphus Ward, one of its first vice presidents (fifteen in all). Tout had been on the verge of forming a Manchester based history group but readily supported the national venture. The Manchester branch was inaugurated with a lecture by the Association's first president, Professor C. H. Firth, with the other lecture of its first session being by Tout on 'Outlines versus Periods', given on 9 February 1907. Tout's paper was published as part of the Association's fourth leaflet. In the autumn of 1907 Tout spoke at the Leeds branch on 'The Historical Work of Professor Maitland and Miss Bateson', Mary Bateson of Cambridge being a historian he admired and a friend. In January 1910 he became the Historical Association's second president, standing down after the annual meeting held at Manchester in January 1912. During his presidency he helped formulate the association's policies on history teaching in schools and encouraged the expansion of its publications. His travels included speaking at the inaugural meeting of the Hertfordshire branch in Berkhamsted on 21 June 1910 and at the Historical Association of Scotland's first business meeting on 11 November 1910.[19] He was President of the Royal Historical Society in 1925–28, after his retirement from Manchester.

Tout succeeded in building up an outstanding medieval history department. Several of the early assistant lecturers were products of the Ward era. James Pounder Whitney returned after studying at Cambridge in 1882 and taught under Ward until 1887. He remained a protégé and friend of Ward's until the latter's death. Whitney was later Professor of Ecclesiastical History at King's College London, 1908–18 and at Cambridge, 1919–39, and from 1907 to 1922 a joint editor of the *Cambridge Medieval History*.[20] He was succeeded by James Tait, who had been a student of history at Owens in 1881–83 before three years at Oxford. Tait was appointed as Lecturer in Ancient History (alongside his assistant lectureship in History) in 1896. In 1902 he was made Professor of Ancient and Medieval History, at which time Tout took the title of Professor of Medieval and Modern History (instead of just History).

Tait combined with Tout and, later, Little, made Manchester an impressive centre of medieval history. Tait was a meticulous researcher who more than matched up to Tout's ideals. He was so considerable a scholar of the Domesday Book that when he wrote a review of Maitland's *Domesday Book and Beyond* (1877) for *The English Historical Review*, Maitland was so impressed that he wrote to Tait expressing his gratitude and stating, 'I have never seen a review of anything that I have written which has taught me so much or gone so straight to the points that are worth discussing'.[21] V. H. Galbraith, in summing up Tait's career, observed, 'The outstanding characteristics of Tait's work are its immense range and the exacting standards of his scholarship. He saw his medieval history as a whole, but with a temperamental caution confined himself severely to what could be demonstrated by exact proof.'[22] He and Tout set a rigorous example of best practices in research, and students were admitted to the areas of their interests and encouraged to do likewise but were not supervised in the way now expected.[23]

Tait also made a huge contribution to Manchester University as a hub of studies of Manchester and its region. Of the history professors, Christie had made his mark on local history, being chairman of the Chetham Society and writing in its publications series (notably *The Old Church and School Libraries of Lancashire*, 1885). Perhaps Tait's most eminent work was *Medieval Manchester and the Beginnings of Lancashire* (1904), the first volume in Manchester University Press's Historical Series. His work on Domesday Book led to him writing much for the *Victoria County History*, and his later work was marked by his impressive *The Medieval English Borough* (1936). He was the first President of the English Place-Names Society (1923–32). Tait was the epitome of the diligent archive-based medieval scholar. His festschrift paid tribute to his 'single-minded zeal for research' and 'the unstinted and kindly help he has given to fellow-workers within and without the universities'.[24] Such generosity was shown also by many other Manchester scholars, not least by W. H. Chaloner and Douglas Farnie.

The third key figure in the establishment of a distinguished medieval history department at Manchester was A. G. Little. Little had studied at Oxford and then in Germany before becoming a lecturer (1892–98) and then professor (1898–1901) at University College of Wales, Cardiff. His input at Manchester began in 1902. Powicke later recalled, 'A great scholar, A. G. Little, came regularly from Sevenoaks to give instructions to beginners in palaeography and kindred aids to study; he was the first man to do this as part of a training in historical method.' Little devoted much of his life to studying the Franciscans ('reverently' and 'modestly' as it was put at Oxford).[25] Little's Ford Lectures on the English Franciscans, delivered in 1916, were published by Manchester University Press in its Historical Series, while his edition of Eccleston's account of the Franciscan friars' coming to Britain was published with the assistance of the Tout Memorial Publication Fund.[26] Little was loyal to Manchester, where he was lecturer (1903–20), then reader (1920–28) in Palaeography. Like Tout and Tait he took an interest in communicating history beyond the universities. A founder member of the Historical Association, he succeeded A. F. Pollard as chair of its publications committee in 1910 and was the first editor (1910–12) of *The Annual Bulletin of Historical Literature*. He often lectured to its branches and became the Association's President, 1926–29.[27] His distinction was recognised by election as a Fellow of the British Academy in 1922.

It was in this context of a confident and innovative medieval-dominated history department, within a university with long and deep traditions of being involved with local industry that the impressive development of economic history began. Tout and Tait, when reissuing their edited collection, *Historical Essays*, in 1907 noted arrangements for palaeography (medieval lectures in alternate years, the presence of Little and also in 1908 'a course of Welsh palaeography, given by Dr J. Gwenogvryn Evans, a distinguished former student of Owens College'), oriental history with Professor H. W. Hogg (Professor of Semitic Languages and Literatures, 1903–12) and ecclesiastical history in the Theology department. In addition they noted, 'Economic history has become a separate charge and the new faculty of commerce has stimulated its study'.[28] Tout himself had been a strong supporter of the creation of a Faculty of Economics and Commerce, being one of many developments that he saw as strengthening the university's links with the city and its commerce. *Historical Essays* proclaimed what had been achieved in History at Manchester and indicated its agenda. As Powicke later observed, 'The work as a whole was a most effective manifesto'.[29]

Tout and Tait had written in the reissued volume of the need for a third chair of history 'devoted particularly to the most modern period'.[30] However, it may be that Tout, now explicitly Professor of Modern History, was enjoying lecturing in an area which he deemed less challenging than medieval. Until the First World War Tout apparently spent more time teaching modern history than medieval. Powicke had warm recollections of 'hearing Tout, in his exciting and discursive way, talk about modern history'. In the case of Mark Hovell, Tout supervised a substantial study of Chartism and finished its preparation for publication when Hovell was killed in the First World War. Whether through Tout's choice or other pressures, the chair in Modern History waited until 1914, when it was filled successively by Ramsay Muir (1914–21), H. W. C. Davis (1921–25) and J. E. Neale (1925–27).[31]

In contrast a chair of economic history did not displace Tout from his current teaching but did build on his enthusiasm for university–industry links. Before Unwin, economic history was being fostered by Sydney John Chapman holding the chair of Political Economy (1901–18), with later Henry Clay (1921–30) and G. W. Daniels (1921–37) holding this and related chairs. Chapman, educated at Manchester Grammar School and Owens College, had returned from Cambridge to be the Stanley Jevons Research Student in 1898, with the resulting essay winning in 1900 the Adam Smith Prize at the University of Cambridge. As Professor of Political Economy, with Tout's support, he secured a faculty of commerce and administration. Drawing on his prize essay and several articles as well as his contacts with businessmen and his abilities in researching economic history, Chapman wrote *The Lancashire Cotton Industry: A Study in Economic Development* (Manchester University

Press, 1904) and, later, three volumes of *Work and Wages* (London, 1908).[32] At the time the great economist Alfred Marshall (1842–1924) wrote to Chapman: 'so far as I can see your *Cotton Industry* is the best monograph of the kind that has ever been published. It is both a realistic-impressionistic study of human life, and an economic treatise.'[33] His book was the first major economic history emanating from Manchester University. It was of its times, partly in the mould of older style economics, and partly in line with the Webbs' concerns for the lot of the labour force. Douglas Farnie has commented of its economic aspect: 'His book paid homage to the influence of the German school of historical economics and was designed for the economist rather than the historian and especially for the old-fashioned economist who was concerned only marginally with marginal analysis.' Chapman's book also fitted into another notable Manchester University tradition; as Douglas Farnie has put it, *The Lancashire Cotton Industry* 'marked the forging of a new link between the university and the dominant trade of the region'.[34] From 1905 to 1908 Chapman was assisted by Hugh Owen Meredith, whose post was lecturer in Economic History and whose book *Outlines of the Economic History of England* was based on his Manchester and (earlier) LSE lectures. Negley Harte has commented that his textbook 'shows how much the outlines of the subject as it was taught at the universities owed to the work of Cunningham'. Meredith also published poetry, his *Weekday Poems* (1911) attracting Virginia Woolf's interest.[35]

George Unwin took the first chair of economic history in Britain in 1910. After Cardiff and Oxford (1890–97), he had spent six months studying economics in Berlin. Then he lived in Mansfield House, a university settlement in Canning Town, London, and through Sidney and Beatrice Webb, became secretary to Leonard Courtney, the prominent Radical MP. He combined this with not only teaching at the LSE and at Mansfield House but also carrying out substantial archival research while writing *Industrial Organization in the Sixteenth and Seventeenth Centuries* (Oxford, 1904), 'The Industries of Suffolk' for the *Victoria County History: Suffolk*, vol. 2 (1907) and *The Gilds and Companies of London* (1908). After declining a lectureship at Cardiff, he was appointed lecturer in economic history at Edinburgh in 1908, where he delivered some ninety lectures a year.[36]

Like James Tait, George Unwin was of the region, Tait being born at Broughton, Salford, and Unwin in Stockport. Unwin had a strong feeling for the past of Manchester and its region. H. B. Charlton, who arrived at Manchester University in 1912, recalled that Unwin used to invite new staff 'to walk with him anywhere in the circle of a mile around the University. Every street, every house, almost every doorway, prompted remarks on them as illustrations of different phases or aspects in the historical growth of Manchester'.[37] Charlton admired both Tout and Unwin. Of the latter he wrote memorably,

... a man in whom superb mastery of the appropriate techniques of scholarship was nothing but an instrument in the service of humanity's well-being, a man who, just out of his wealth of human kindness, opened up new lines of historical enquiry to make history serve in the search for the greater good of mankind. He himself was more of a social philosopher than an historian in the traditional sense; for him, the social aspect of history was vastly more important than the political, and even more than the economic. Indeed, even more than a social philosopher, Unwin was a social evangelist. His recurrent text was that men are linked in spiritual communion, not by legal regulation, but by the sense of belonging to this or that community (or to many communities) which have grown within society through workshop, profession, club, or church. In these the real brotherhood of man was a personal experience.[38]

Not surprisingly, given these attitudes, Unwin was also admired by, and influenced, R. H. Tawney, for whom, as Anthony Wright has observed, 'like his mentor in the discipline, George Unwin, economic history was at bottom a branch of moral philosophy'.[39] Tawney paid fulsome tribute to Unwin in his substantial introduction to Unwin's collected papers and noted with approval some of his aphorisms. For instance, 'Marx is truer than Seeley. He did not get his history right, but he was trying to get at the right kind of history. The orthodox historians ignore all the most significant facts in human development.' Perhaps, more at the core of both men's inner beliefs was: 'History is the science and art of reconstructing the spiritual past in the light of the meaning of the present. But the present is not final. There is an unknowable factor – the sphere of religion and faith'.[40] Tawney was lecturing on Unwin as late as 1955.[41]

Yet Unwin's political outlook was different from Tawney's. Unwin, a notable Nonconformist, shared the individualistic radicalism of his former employer, Leonard Courtney MP. Tawney in his Commonplace Book, recorded a conversation in 1913 with Unwin. 'Liberty means opportunity to make the world different. Everybody ought to have a chance of this. But it can only be done with much pain and anguish.' He added, in contrast to the Fabian Society's aspirations, 'To me it is incredible that committees and elected persons can ever manage the higher life of mankind.' He also aired fears of 'the levelling tendencies of democracy' and 'such things as state regulation of higher education'.[42]

Unwin turned away from state records to those generated privately and locally in order to explore economic history. As Douglas Farnie has commented in his valuable reappraisal of his predecessor: 'Unwin would have been baffled by the very idea of a Welfare State and dismayed by textbooks portraying the advent of such a state as the culmination of British history.'[43] Through the discovery of the records of the businesses run by Samuel Oldknow in a ruined cotton mill he found much he needed when he wrote his major work *Samuel Oldknow and the Arkwrights: The Industrial Revolution at Stockport and Marple* (Manchester University Press, 1924). Unwin took a deep interest in European medieval cities as well as some of the East and from them, as Tawney put it, 'he returned home to compose the glorious epic of Stockport'. His ambitions were that but more. They included what would have been a major contribution to urban history, *The Roots of the City*.[44]

Unwin was perceived to be as big a figure in Manchester University as Tout. Indeed, when A. J. P. Taylor taught at Manchester, 1930–38, he found that two of his colleagues, Arthur Redford and Ted Hughes, who were graduates of the department, 'rated [Unwin] more highly than Tout, I think rightly'.[45] Whether this was right or not, Unwin was greatly respected by both his students and his peers. Ellen Wilkinson, a student in the department in 1910–13 recalled, 'The Honours School of History under Professor Tout and Professor George Unwin was a stimulating experience', even if she later regretted it had not taught history of a more radical kind.[46] F. M. Powicke, who succeeded Tait as a Manchester professor of medieval history (1919–28) and was also a graduate of the department, wrote:

> Manchester owed an incalculable debt, during the years of Tout's greatest activity as a teacher of medieval history, to the work of George Unwin, one of the brightest spirits who ever cast his light on dark places and opened up new horizons to his pupils. Tout and Unwin were in many ways as unlike each other as two men can be, but they were alike in their belief in history, and in their capacity to inspire. The volumes of the University Press testify to Unwin's influence …[47]

Unwin also followed his Manchester colleagues in being very willing to communicate history to a wider audience. This included lecturing to branches of the Historical Association. The Manchester branch's report for 1912–13 included 'Professor Unwin … reconstructed a part of medieval economic history in an interesting lecture entitled, "A Venerable Tradition: Edward III, the Father of Commerce" in which he portrayed Edward III rather in the light of a step-father'. In 1917–18 he addressed that branch on 'some lines of continuity between Ancient and Medieval history' and to the Bury branch in 1922–23 he spoke on 'The Merchant Adventurers'.[48] In this he was not only joining Tout, Tait and Little, but in his era the first two professors of modern history, Ramsay Muir, who was also a Vice President of the Historical Association, and H. W. C. Davis.

After the age of Tout, Tait, Little and Unwin, there was a fairly rapid turn-over of professors until the arrival of Ernest Jacob, Professor of Medieval History, 1929–44, and Lewis Namier, who held the Modern chair, 1931–53.

Ramsay Muir, who had been an assistant lecturer under Tout in 1897–98, left in 1921, after seven years, for Liberal politics, being briefly MP for Rochdale (1923–24). Davis in 1925, after four years, succeeded Sir Charles Firth as Regius Professor of Modern History at Oxford (1925–28). His successor in the modern chair, John Neale, stayed only two years (1925–27), before returning to University College, London. Maurice Powicke, who earlier had been a research fellow (1902–5) and an assistant lecturer (1906–8) under Tout, remained three years after Tout's retirement (but nine in all) before succeeding Davis as Regius Professor of Modern History at Oxford (1928–47). Ernest Jacob did stay for fifteen years, from 1929 to 1944, but returned to Oxford and ended his career as Chichele Professor of Modern History (1950–61). Others also left Manchester for Oxford in the post-Tout era, including the medieval historian William A. Pantin (1902–73) and A. J. P. Taylor (1906–90) as well as others going to chairs elsewhere, such as George Unwin's former students Edward Hughes (1899–1965) to Durham and Conrad Gill (1883–1968) to Hull.

Frank Kermode, who taught English at Manchester, 1958–65, later recollected: 'It was still usual, in my youth, for English people to talk about both universities as if there were only two.' He added, 'It remains difficult for southerners to understand the distinction of, say, Manchester University in the sciences, history and biblical scholarship.' Attitudes within the university that Kermode described for his day in fact went back decades:

> The university had a kind of grim friendliness and a justified assurance of its own value, at a time when the metropolitan claims of Manchester were weakening but still pretty strong …
>
> The mood of the place was always to oppose the south, and the university had, or professed, no inferiority feelings about the ancient universities; if bright people came to Manchester, sharpened their talents, and left for Oxbridge that was their business, and they might well come to repent their foolishness in leaving a serious place for institutions that devoted themselves to feasts and gaudies.[49]

Nevertheless, there was a loss for Manchester.

While professors came and went in other areas, the chair of economic history was not filled for twenty years. Arthur Redford (1896–1961), one of Unwin's former students, after lecturing at Liverpool (1922–25) and the LSE (1925–26), returned to Manchester as Reader in Economic History. He was another local person, having been born in Droylsden of parents who both worked in the cotton industry. After publishing *Labour Migration in England, 1800–1850* (London, 1926), based on his 1922 thesis supervised by Unwin, and *The Economic History of England, 1760–1860* (1931) he turned to study Manchester merchants and then Manchester's local government. *Manchester Merchants and Foreign*

Trade, 1794–1858 (Manchester University Press, 1934) was a collaborative venture, based on six undergraduate dissertations which Redford drew on to write the book, with a second volume being published on 1850–1939 in 1956. He diverted in between to write three large volumes, *The History of Local Government in Manchester* (London, Longmans Green, 1939–40). With the first volume he was greatly helped by Tait. He acknowledged Tait had 'used his incomparable knowledge of local history to solve many problems which would have otherwise have baffled me completely' and had revised the whole volume. Redford was a Manchester person through and through and, although later embittered at being made to wait nineteen years for a chair (which he held 1945–61), he spent his career at Manchester.[50]

T. S. Ashton (1889–1968) was also one of Unwin's students and admirers. After lecturing at Sheffield and Birmingham, Unwin aided his return to Manchester as Senior Lecturer in Economics (1921–27, Reader 1927–44) where, like his brother-in-law Redford, his promotion was blocked. Ashton's first publication had been with Sydney Chapman, an article, 'The Size of Businesses, mainly in the Textile Industries' (*Journal of the Royal Statistical Society*, 1914). He wrote major studies of the industrial revolution while at Manchester as well as a centenary history of the Manchester Statistical Society. Ashton also fitted the pattern of some of his predecessors, being a nonconformist and a laissez-faire radical in outlook.[51]

Another of Unwin's intellectual legatees was A. P. Wadsworth, who worked for the *Manchester Guardian* from 1917 and became editor, 1944–56. Wadsworth, whom Alan Taylor described as 'aggressively "Lancashire"', was greatly impressed by Unwin and his approach to history. Wadsworth emulated him in painstaking research into the Lancashire cotton industry, which resulted in his book he wrote with Julia Mann (Unwin having introduced them). With the discovery of a hoard of Strutt business records at the West Mill, Belper, somewhat like the sources Unwin used in his study of Stockport and Marple, Wadsworth joined R. S. Fitton in writing on the Strutts and the Arkwrights. Redford, already busy, had encouraged Fitton to use the Strutt Papers and Ashton introduced Fitton to Wadsworth.[52]

Redford was often assisted in his work by T. S. Willan, appointed an assistant lecturer in 1934 and holding the chair of Economic History, 1963–74. Thomas Stuart Willan specialised in early modern history, especially British river transport.[53] The Redford era was also marked by major work in economic history from colleagues such as W. H. Chaloner and Otto Henderson and former students such as Douglas Farnie.

William Henry Chaloner (1914–87) was a major figure in the department during Redford's later years. He had been an undergraduate in the Manchester department being taught by Jacob, Namier, A. J. P. Taylor and Redford (1933–36) and he remained there to study his home town, Crewe, for his MA and Ph.D. (1939), resulting in *The Social and Economic Development of Crewe 1780–1923* (Manchester University Press, 1950). He taught in the department from 1945. When Redford's health deteriorated in the late 1940s he took over Ph.D. supervision of John Harris and Theo Barker, from which stemmed their classic work, *A Merseyside Town in the Industrial Revolution: St Helens 1750–1900* (Manchester University Press, 1954). His other early postgraduates included A. E. Musson (1922–2001), later Professor of Economic History (1973–87), Alan Birch and Phyllis Giles, all of whom published at least some of their work. Ted Musson's publications encompassed business history, industry and technology and labour history. Redford also encouraged Chaloner and Otto Henderson to translate Werner Schlote's *British Overseas Trade from 1700 to 1930s* (Oxford, Blackwell, 1952) and three other books including Engels' *Conditions of the Working Class in England* (Oxford University Press, 1958). This, perhaps, distracted him from writing more major monographs. Bill Chaloner, like so many other Manchester University historians, also made his mark on the history of the region. From 1955 to 1987 he was an editor of *The Transactions of the Lancashire and Cheshire Antiquarian Society* and was active in the running of the Chetham Society, 1953–87.[54]

Chaloner also followed several of his predecessors in being a Nonconformist Radical. However, by the post-Second World War era this appeared a long way from contemporary radicalism. In the Cold War era his and Henderson's edition of Engels could seem close to an anti-Marxist analysis. This image was reinforced by his 1978 piece on '1989: 1688 or 1789' in an Institute of Economic Affairs book which bewailed 'the seduction of our intellectuals, and particularly academic intellectuals, by the radical appeal of the vague French ideals of liberty, equality and fraternity, and by the spread of Marxist ideas, fostered unwittingly by a tolerant State itself through the recent expansion of higher education and subsequent infiltration'.[55]

His colleague and often close associate, William Otto Henderson (1904–93) carried out research on the cotton industry in 1859–61 under H. L. Beales at the LSE. He revised it as a book on Lancashire and the adjoining counties for his *The Lancashire Cotton Famine, 1861–1865* (Manchester University Press, 1934), with Professor G. W. Daniels providing advice.[56] While teaching at Manchester, Otto Henderson expanded his study for a second edition in 1969. Much of Henderson's major work was in German history, notably *The Zollverein* (Cambridge University Press, 1939), written while he was a tutor in adult education at the University College Hull, and *The State and the Industrial Revolution in Prussia, 1740–1870* (Liverpool University Press, 1958). However, he did combine his own German expertise with his Manchester knowledge to follow up his translation with Chaloner of Friedrich Engels, *Condition of the Working Class in England* (1951) and their edition of Engels' military articles in the *Volunteer Journal for Lancashire and Cheshire* with his two volume *The Life of Friedrich Engels* (London, Cass, 1976).

Douglas Farnie (1926–2008) had also been an undergraduate in the Manchester Department, being taught by Arthur Redford, R. M. Hedley and Lewis Namier. He was also born locally, in Salford at Ashfield, a large house then occupied by the West Salford Labour Club and Institute (his father being its steward). He began his long career as a major authority on the cotton industry with his MA thesis, 'The English Cotton Industry 1850–1896' (1953). His work studied the cotton industry internally as well as externally, the latter being marked by his classic study, *The English Cotton Industry and the World Market, 1815–1896* (Oxford University Press, 1979).[57]

Since the era of Willan, Chaloner, Musson, Henderson and Farnie, economic and social history has remained eminent at Manchester. Professor Michael Rose (1936–), Dr Iorweth Prothero (1939–), Professor Penny Summerfield and others wrote much social history of distinction. Professor Robert Milward (1939–) came from a chair of Economics at Salford and wrote major work on the public sector of the British economy. Professor Peter Gattrell (1950–) has been eminent in Russian economic history while Dr Theodore Balderston (1949–) has made a major impact on the economic history of inter-war Germany. Dr Andrew Marrison (1945–) is a major authority on British overseas trade and tariffs, while Professor John F. Wilson (1955–) is a pre-eminent British business historian. Other notable economic historians in the Manchester department have included Barrie Ratcliffe (1940–), Joseph Harrison, Colin Philips, Simon Katzenellenbogen (1939–) and A. J. Robertson (1941–). There have also been a considerable number of distinguished medieval and modern historians since Namier's time, too long a list to cite here, but including John Cooper (1947–48), Albert Goodwin, Brian Pullan, Judith Brown, Ian Kershaw, Steve Rigby and Alan Forest.

Douglas Farnie has delivered the verdict: 'The Manchester School of Economic History reached the zenith of its fame during the years 1920–1924, when the city still regarded itself as "the hub of the universe".'[58] This may be true, but 'golden ages' have a strong tendency to be back before the experience of those recollecting them. Perhaps it is best to agree, but to suggest that this zenith of economic history was in the wider context of the distinction of history, medieval and economic, in the era of Tout, Tait, Little and Unwin.

Indeed, Manchester's distinction in history has been cyclical, or a story of renewal and resurgence. There surely was another era of distinction in the 1930s, with Lewis Namier, A. J. P. Taylor and Redford at his best. Namier in his age was a scholar of massive distinction. Yet, he was not part of the pattern of Manchester scholarship before 1960, other than in his meticulous detail. Indeed, Namier rubbed up against Manchester pride, antagonising both Wadsworth and Redford in his attitudes. Alan Taylor recalled Namier's disdain for Manchester

University's ways: 'His constant references to Oxford practices, which in fact he also did not understand, did not endear him to Jimmy Redford.'[59] If not of Manchester and its concerns, nevertheless Namier could be judged to fit in with the earlier Manchester medievalists in his approach. He was very much an example of the all-pervasive modernism that Michael Bentley has identified. Hugh Trevor-Roper in 1957 complained,

> The Manchester School, in my opinion, stand condemned by their record in this respect. They have dominated English historical work for a generation and they have ended by making it mere boring antiquarianism. Now what is the use of merely switching the narrow specialist beam from the reign of Richard II to the reign of George III, from the Exchequer to the East India Company Board?

For Trevor-Roper the Namierites were worse still: 'Namierism has degenerated, in the hand of his disciples, into the cult of minutiae'.[60] This was also a danger of the Tout approach.

There was also another, and longer, distinguished era, in the last decades of the twentieth century, marked by a galaxy of stars, of which Douglas Farnie was one, and one in the tradition of upholding high scholarship on Manchester and its greatest industry.

Notes

1. The omission will be rectified with the Economic History Society's annual conference going to Manchester in the centenary year of Unwin's chair in 2010. Apart from Namier, Manchester is also near invisible in Michael Bentley (ed.), *Companion To Historiography* (Routledge: London, 1997), where, in 997 pages, none of Ward, Tout, Tait, Unwin, Ashton, Chaloner, Henderson or Farnie appears, but only one very negative reference to Powicke. The earlier major figures do appear in his excellent *Modernizing England's Past: English historiography in the Age of Modernism, 1870–1970* (Cambridge University Press, 2005).
2. James Thompson, *The Owens College: Its Foundation and Growth* (Cornish: Manchester, 1886), pp. 40–4.
3. Adolphus Ward, 'Greenwood, Joseph Gouge (1821–94)' and 'Christie, Richard Copley (1830–1901)', *Oxford Dictionary of National Biography* [hereafter *ODNB*] (2004). H. B. Charlton, *Portrait of a University, 1851–1951* (Manchester University Press: Manchester, 1951), pp. 1, 31, 64. Thompson, *Owens College*, p. 158.
4. *Essays and Addresses by the Professors and Lecturers of the Owens College, Manchester* (Macmillan: London, 1873), James Bryce (1838–1922) held the chair of Jurisprudence, 1869–75. He also held the Regius Chair of Civil Law, Oxford, 1870–93, was a Liberal MP, 1880–1906, held political office (1886, 1892–95, 1905–7) and was ambassador to US, 1907–13.
5. Osborne Reynolds (1842–1912) held the chair of Engineering, 1868–1905. Ibid.,

pp. 49, 57. William Stanley Jevons (1835–82) held the chair of Political Economy, 1866–76, then the Political Economy chair at University, London, 1876–80. Adolphus Ward wrote the entry on Jevons in the *ODNB*. Jevons' son carried on his work on coal, publishing *The British Coal Trade* (Kegan Paul: London, 1915; reprinted David & Charles: Newton Abbot, 1969).

6. A. W. Ward, *Suggestions Towards A History Tripos* (Cambridge University Press: Cambridge, 1872). Deborah Wormell, *Sir John Seeley and the Uses of History* (Cambridge University Press: Cambridge, 1980), pp. 112–13. Peter R. H. Slee, *Learning and a Liberal Education. The Study of Modern History in the Universities of Oxford, Cambridge and Manchester, 1800–1914* (Manchester University Press: Manchester, 1986), pp. 64–6.

7. Charlton, *Portrait*, pp. 69–70.

8. G. P. Gooch, 'Ward, Sir Adolphus William (1837–1924)', *ODNB*. T. F. Tout, 'Sir Adolphus Ward, 1837–1924', *Proceedings of the British Academy*, vol. 11 (1924–25), pp. 427–40. Owen Chadwick, *Acton and History* (Cambridge University Press: Cambridge, 1998), pp. 247, 259–60. Roland Hill, *Lord Acton* (Yale University Press: New Haven and London, 2000), pp. 394–5. Frank Eyck, *G. P. Gooch. A Study in History and Politics* (Macmillan: London, 1982), pp. 296, 320.

9. Bentley, *Modernizing England's Past*. See also J. W. Burrow, *A Liberal Descent* (Cambridge University Press, 1980), pp. 299–300.

10. J. R. Hale, 'Introduction' to his *The Evolution of British Historiography* (US, 1964; Macmillan: London, 1967), pp. 55–6.

11. John Kenyon, *The History Men* (Weidenfeld & Nicolson: London, 1983), p. 182.

12. T. F. Tout, 'Felix Liebermann (1851–1925)' in *History*, 10, 40 (January 1926), pp. 311–19. Liebermann had a Manchester connection in that he was of a business family and had worked for two years in a German yarn-exporting house in Manchester during a four-year stay in England in 1869–73. Conrad von Mauren was later taken up as an authority on early primitive communism by E. Belfort Bax, *Essays in Socialism* (E. Grant Richards: London, 1907).

13. T. F. Tout, 'Stubbs, William (1825–1901)', *ODNB, 1901–1910*.

14. T. F. Tout, 'The Historical Teaching of History' (from *Manchester Guardian*, 20 November 1904) in T. F. Tout, *The Collected Papers of Thomas Frederick Tout*, vol. 1 (Manchester University Press: Manchester, 1932): 76–9, p. 76.

15. T. F. Tout, 'An Historical "Laboratory"' (from the *Standard*, 3 January 1910) in ibid., pp. 79–84. Kenyon, *History Men*, p. 196.

16. F. M. Powicke, 'Memoir: T. F. Tout', *Proceedings of the British Academy*, vol. 15 (1929), pp. 491–518; reprinted in Tout, *Collected Papers of Tout*, pp. 1–24. Tout, 'Laboratory', p. 84.

17. A. J. P. Taylor, 'London Diary', *New Statesman*, 92, 2386, 10 December 1976, p. 836; quoted in C. Wrigley, *A. J. P. Taylor: A Complete Bibliography* (Harvester Press: Brighton, 1980), pp. 10, 244. A. J. P. Taylor, *A Personal History* (Hamish Hamilton: London, 1983), pp. 102–3.

18. Harold Perkin, *The Rise of Professional Society: England Since 1880* (Routledge: London, 1989), p. 123. Mary Tout, 'T. F. Tout as a Citizen' in Tout, *Papers*, pp. 27–38.

19. *First Annual Report of the Historical Association, 1906–1907*, p. 9. *Second Annual Report of the Historical Association, 1907–8*, pp. 9–10. *Fifth Annual Report of the Historical Association, 1910–11*, pp. 10–11, 14. *Sixth Annual Report of the Historical Association, 1911–12*, pp. 11–12. Donald Read, 'A Parade of Past Presidents, 1906–82', *The Historian*, 91 (autumn 2006), pp. 10–23.

20. C. W. Previté-Orton, 'Whitney, James Pounder (1857–1939)', *ODNB*.

21. F. M. Powicke, *Modern Historians and the Study of History* (Odhams: London, 1955), pp. 55–6. For Tait's review, see *English Historical Review*, 12 (1897), pp. 768–77.

22. V. H. Galbraith, 'Tait, James (1863–1944)', *ODNB*.

23. Slee, *Learning and a Liberal Education*, pp. 158–9.

24. J. G. Edwards, V. H. Galbraith and E. F. Jacob (eds), *Historical Essays in Honour of James Tait* (The Subscribers: Manchester, 1933).

25. F. M. Powicke, 'Manchester University, 1851–1951', *History Today*, 1 (May 1951), pp. 48–55, and Powicke, *Modern Historians*, pp. 73–95. A. B. Poynton's translation of his oration when presenting Little for an honorary D.Litt. at Oxford is printed in *History*, 13, 52 (January 1929), pp. 324–5.

26. A. G. Little, *Studies in English Franciscan History* (Manchester University Press, 1917) and A. G. Little, *Fratris Thomae vulgo dicti de Eccleston Tractatus De Adventu Fratrum In Angliam* (Manchester University Press, 1951).

27. A. T. Milne, 'Past Presidents', *The Historian*, 20 (autumn 1988), pp. 18–19.

28. First published in 1902, the volume was reissued as the sixth volume in Manchester University Press's Historical Series. T. F. Tout and James Tait (eds), *Historical Essays: First Published in Commemoration of the Jubilee of The Owens College, Manchester* (Manchester University Press, 1907), p. vi.

29. Powicke, *Modern Historians*, p. 33.

30. Tout and Tait, *Historical Essays*, p. vi.

31. Powicke, 'University of Manchester, 1851–1951', p. 55 and Powicke, *Modern Historians*, pp. 32–6. Charlton, *Portrait*, pp. 88–96.

32. Chapman left Manchester for a distinguished career at the Board of Trade. E. Raymond Streat, 'Chapman, Sir Sydney John (1871–1951)', *ODNB*.

33. Quoted in D. A. Farnie, 'Three Historians of the Cotton Industry', *Textile History*, 9 (1978), pp. 75–89.

34. Ibid., p. 84.

35. William Cunningham (1849–1919) taught at Cambridge and was Professor of Economic Science and Statistics at King's College, London (1891–97), publishing several editions of *The Growth of English Industry and Commerce* (1882–1910). H. O. Meredith (1878–1964) was Professor of Economics at Queen's University, Belfast from 1911 until his retirement. N. B. Harte, 'Introduction', *The Study of History* (Cass: London, 1971), p. xxv. Virginia Woolf to S. Saxon Turner, 13 April 1911 in Nigel Nicolson (ed.), *The Flight of the Mind: The Letters of Virginia Woolf*, vol. 1 (Hogarth Press: London, 1975), pp. 459–60.

36. R. H. Tawney, 'Introductory Memoir' in R. H. Tawney (ed.), *Studies in Economic History: The Collected Papers of George Unwin* (Macmillan: London, 1927), pp. ix–xlii. T. A. B. Corley, 'Unwin, George (1870–1925)', *ODNB*.

37. Charlton, *Portrait*, p. 5.

38. Ibid., pp. 89–90.
39. Anthony Wright, *R. H. Tawney* (Manchester University Press, 1987), p. 25.
40. Tawney, 'Introductory Memoir', pp. lxvi-lxvii.
41. Ross Terrill, *R. H. Tawney and His Times: Socialism and Fellowship* (Andre Deutsch: London, 1974), p. 106.
42. J. M. Winter and J. N. Joslin (eds), *R. H. Tawney's Commonplace Book* (Cambridge University Press, 1972), pp. 48–9.
43. D. A. Farnie, 'George Unwin (1870–1925): Founder of the Manchester School of Economic History' in Pat Hudson (ed.), *Living Economic and Social History* (Economic History Society: Glasgow, 2001), pp. 75–80.
44. Tawney, 'Introductory Memoir', pp. xii, liv-lvii.
45. Taylor, *A Personal History*, p. 103.
46. Ellen Wilkinson, MA, MP in The Countess of Oxford and Asquith, *Myself When Young: By Famous Women of Today* (Muller: London, 1938), pp. 399–416.
47. Powicke, *Modern Historians*, p. 32.
48. *Seventh Annual Report of the Council of the Historical Association, 1912–13* (1913), p. 22. *Twelfth Annual Report ... 1917–1918* (1918), p. 31. *Seventeenth Annual Report ... 1922–1923* (1923), p. 21.
49. Frank Kermode, *Not Entitled: A Memoir* (Harper Collins: London, 1996), pp. 65, 205.
50. W. H. Chaloner, 'Memoir of Arthur Redford' in Arthur Redford, *Labour Migration in England, 1800–1850*, 2nd edition (Manchester University Press, 1964), pp. xv–xvii. Arthur Redford, assisted by Ina Russell, *The History of Local Government in Manchester* (Longmans Green: London, 1939), p. xi. Taylor, *A Personal History*, p. 103. According to Taylor, Redford was known to his friends as 'Jimmy'.
51. D. C. Coleman, 'Ashton, Thomas Southcliffe (1889–1968)', *ODNB*. L. S. Pressnell (ed.), *Studies in the Industrial Revolution: Essays Presented to T. S. Ashton* (Athlone Press: London, 1960).
52. L. Andrews, 'Wadsworth, Alfred Powell (1891–1956)', *ODNB*. R. S. Fitton, 'Preface' in R. S. Fitton and A. P. Wadsworth, *The Strutts and the Arkwrights, 1758–1830: A Study of the Early Factory System* (Manchester University Press, 1958), p. vi. Farnie, 'George Unwin', p. 79. Taylor, *A Personal History*, p. 111.
53. On Willan (1910–94) see W. H. Chaloner and B. Ratcliffe (eds), *Trade and Transport: Essays in Economic History in Honour of T. S. Willan* (Manchester University Press, 1977).
54. He was also a President of the Agricultural History Society. D. A. Farnie, obituary in the *Times*, 2 June 1987. Memorial section of the *Transactions of the Lancashire and Cheshire Antiquarian Society*, 85, 1958, pp. 50–105. D. A. Farnie and W. O. Henderson (eds), *Industry and Innovation* (Cass: London, 1990). W. R. Ward (ed.), *Palatinate Studies* [of Chaloner] (Chetham Society: Manchester, 1992).
55. Institute of Economic Affairs, *The Coming Confrontation. Will the Open Society Survive to 1989?* (IEA: London, 1978), pp. 33–4.
56. W. O. Henderson, *The Lancashire Cotton Famine, 1861–1865*, second edition (Manchester University Press, 1969), pp. 33–4.
57. He also edited with David Jeremy the major collection, *The Fibre That Changed*

The World: The Cotton Industry in International Perspective, 1600–1900s (Oxford University Press, 2004). For a recent example of his extensive knowledge see also D. A. Farnie, 'The Cotton Towns of Greater Manchester' in Mike Williams with D. A. Farnie, *Cotton Mills in Greater Manchester* (Carnegie Publishing: Preston, 1992), pp. 13–47.

58. Farnie, 'George Unwin', p. 77.

59. Taylor, *A Personal History*, p. 11.

60. H. Trevor-Roper to W. Notestein, 2 May 1957; quoted in Bentley, *Modernizing England's Past*, pp. 230–1.

PART I

THE COTTON INDUSTRY

3

Selling English cotton into the world market: implications for the rationalisation debate, 1900–1939

ANDREW MARRISON, STEVEN BROADBERRY
AND TIM LEUNIG

I Introduction

Douglas Farnie titled his seminal work *The English Cotton Industry and the World Market, 1815–1896*.[1] The title was and is appropriate for what remains the most authoritative work on the subject, because the English cotton industry can only be understood in the context of world markets. England grows no cotton, so all of the raw material was imported. And cotton was England's largest export for 125 years, from the Napoleonic Wars until 1939, and at its 1913 peak the nation exported over 7 billion yards of cloth.[2] Even as late as 1944 John Maynard Keynes saw cotton spearheading Britain's post-war export drive, asking 'Who will export cotton goods if Britain does not – Japan, America, who?'[3]

And yet, while the dimensions of the production side of the British cotton industry are well established, surprisingly little is known about the dimensions of the merchanting section, particularly for the export trade. Farnie himself worked in this area, using subscriber numbers to the Manchester Royal Exchange as an index of commercial activity. Against this, membership was individual rather than corporate, and so the picture may not capture the merchanting sector fully.[4] Although Redford provides corporate membership figures for the Manchester Chamber of Commerce, which identifies cotton merchant firms, membership was far from complete.[5] In this paper, we use trade directories to provide a consistent series over time on the number of merchant firms in the export trade. The number continued to increase across the First World War and did not fall back below the 1913 level until the 1930s depression, despite much lower exports during the 1920s. We hope that this paper expands on a part of the cotton industry's history which, though identified as important by Farnie, has been neglected by historians.

Even less is known about the size distribution of merchant firms than of their absolute number. Kenyon's widely cited study relates to 1940,[6] some time after the sector's collapse during the 1930s, while in 1930 Ellinger and Ellinger made estimates for *circa* 1929 based largely on information about limited companies.[7] We establish the 1927 size distribution by matching firms from trade directories with data on gross estimated rental for warehouse space from the Manchester rate books. Our estimates suggest a less concentrated structure than found by Kenyon and the Ellingers, with a small number of large firms accounting for a large percentage of business, but with a long tail of very small firms.

We consider the implications for schemes of rationalisation put forward during the 1920s and subsequently. Contrary to Mass and Lazonick,[8] we see vertical specialisation as a continuing strength of the Lancashire cotton industry into the twentieth century, generating external economies of scale and delaying the loss of comparative advantage to low-wage competitors such as Japan. The heaviest market losses occurred in lower quality products, which were suitable for mass production and mass distribution. But Britain was inherently least able to compete against low-wage countries such as Japan, as well as against indigenous producers, in these goods. The fact that the merchant community remained largely intact despite the export trade's decline in the 1920s meant that: (1) producers maintained access to a wide geographic spread of markets; and (2) individual producers could continue specialising in a narrow product range while the industry continued to supply a wide product range because of the merchants' mixing function. Furthermore, there are good reasons to doubt the schemes for horizontal amalgamation in the merchant sector put forward by writers such as Ellinger and Ellinger[9] would have helped: small merchant firms could respond flexibly to detailed local knowledge, delaying the market loss in higher quality goods. Furthermore, it is far from clear that the Japan's export success owed much to its marketing organisation, when compared with the country's lower production costs.

II   The size of the cotton export merchanting sector

We pull together previous estimates of the export merchant sector between 1900 and 1939.[10] Table 1 gives data from the Royal Exchange and Slater's Directory, whose 'cotton and associated trades' classification remained unchanged in

Table 1   *Growth and decline of the cotton export merchanting sector, 1900–39*

| | Subscribers to the Manchester Royal Exchange | Merchants listed in Slater's *Directory of Manchester and Salford* | |
		Cotton shipping merchants	Grey cloth merchants and agents
1900	7,877	727	222
1911	9,921	773	226
1913	10,371		
1920	11,539		
1921	11,223	1,007	293
1927	10,215	851	303
1929	9,368	823	284
1932	7,008		
1935	5,979		
1937	5,566	534	172
1939	5,062		

Sources: Manchester Royal Exchange: Farnie, 'An Index of Commercial Activity: The Membership of the Manchester Royal Exchange, 1809–1948', *Business History*, xxi, issue 1 (1979), p. 101. Trade directories: *Slater's Directory of Manchester and Salford* (Manchester, Slater).

1900–39. For 1900–11 we have broad agreement that the number of merchants rose, but by less that the 32 per cent rise in cotton piece good exports. The most interesting developments, however, occur after the First World War. Membership of the Royal Exchange peaked in 1920, and Slater's Directory has more members in 1921 than 1911, as if in lagged response to the Edwardian boom and/or as an immediate response to the post-war boom, which suggested to contemporaries that the Edwardian boom had only been interrupted by the war. After the 1920–21 slump, Royal Exchange membership and shipping merchants declined, although grey cloth merchant and agent numbers did not fall until after 1927; even then the numbers were higher at the end of the 1920s than at the height of the Edwardian boom. It is only with the further decline during the 1930s that the dense merchant network at the heart of the specialised Lancashire system broke up: by 1935, Royal Exchange membership and the number of merchant firms had both declined to about three-quarters of their 1900 levels. These trends fit closely with information from other sources. Chapman comments that 'on the marketing side the old structure changed surprisingly little' and that 'it was only after the economic catastrophe of 1929–31 that this century-old system began to expire'.[11] Thus, in the 1920s, Lancashire still benefited from a large merchant community with the skills and experience to market its product abroad in an efficient and cost-effective manner.

III   The size distribution of merchant firms

In this section we look at the size distribution of firms. The most widely cited evidence is Kenyon's study of merchant converters operating in 1940.[12] Section II makes clear that the situation in 1940 is not a reliable guide to the merchant sector's earlier position, since the sector had declined dramatically by then. Accordingly, in this section we provide evidence on the size distribution of merchant firms in 1927, using data on gross estimated rental from the Manchester rate books. Like Kenyon, we find that a small number of firms accounted for a large share of business. However, we also find that the tail of small firms accounted for a more significant share of business than allowed for by Kenyon, reducing overall concentration.

Table 2   *The size distribution of merchant converters in 1940*

Quantity converted (yards)	Number of firms	Share of firms (%)	Share of exports (%)	Cumulative share of firms (%)	Cumulative share of exports (%)
5m +	49	4.1	50.0	4.1	50.0
0.5m – 4.99m	257	21.2	40.0	25.3	90.0
0.05m – 0.49m	468	38.7	9.5	64.0	99.5
5,000 – 49,000	306	25.3	0.47	89.3	99.97
Less than 5,000	130	10.7	0.03	100.0	100.0

Source: S. Chapman, 'The Commercial Sector', in M. B. Rose (ed.), *The Lancashire Cotton Industry: A History Since 1700* (Lancashire County Books: Preston, 1996), p. 90; derived from H. Kenyon, 'The Shape and Size of the Export Merchanting Section of the Cotton Industry', *Transactions of the Manchester Statistical Society*, Session 1944–45 (1944), pp. 1–20.

Kenyon's (1944) study is summarised in Table 2 and Figure 1. These show that the top 49 firms accounted for 50 per cent of exports, while the smallest 130 firms accounted for just 0.03 per cent of exports. In cumulative terms, just over a quarter of the firms accounted for 90 per cent of exports. This is a more concentrated structure than in cotton goods production, where average firm size remained relatively small even after the inter-war amalgamations. That

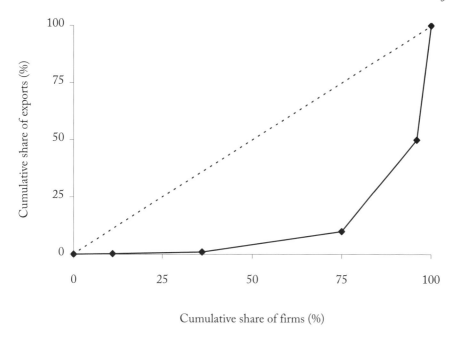

Figure 1: Lorenz curve of the size distribution of merchant converters in 1940
Source: Table 2.

concentration can be seen clearly in Figure 1, which displays the information from Table 2 graphically as a Lorenz curve. A Lorenz curve is an inequality plot, whereby firms are plotted in order, from smallest to largest. If all firms are the same size, the Lorenz curve will be a straight line, rising at 45 degrees. The further the actual line is from this 45 degree line, the greater the degree of firm size inequality. In this case the size distribution was extremely heterogeneous, with many, many small firms and a handful of larger ones.

Slater's Directory lists 1,154 merchant and exporter firms in 1927, broadly consistent with Clay's estimate that 'their number cannot be less than a thousand',[13] which is interpreted liberally by Chapman as being over 1,200.[14] Ellinger and Ellinger suggest 'some 740 merchants exporting cotton goods' in Manchester,[15] close to the 789 shipping merchants in Slater's Directory for 1930, and apparently excluding 'grey cloth merchants and agents'. For 1927, we combined the data on a sample of shipping merchants' addresses from Slater's Directory with data on gross estimated rental from the Manchester rate books for 1926–27.[16] We argue that the problems in doing so are small enough to give a valid approximation to the size distribution of firms. Of course the Directory will not have included all merchants, with smaller and more transient firms most likely to have been omitted, biasing our measure of industry concentration upwards. About one-third of merchants cannot be found in the rate books at the addresses given in the Directory. They could have failed or moved to new premises between the compilation of the Directory and the rate books; alternatively, the real occupier might have differed from the formal occupier due to sub-letting. If, as seems likely, smaller firms were more mobile between warehouses and more likely to fail, our source will overestimate industry concentration by excluding some such firms.

The second problem is that we need to assume that gross estimated rental proxies firm size. Some warehouses probably offered superior handling facilities, were more favourably located in relation to transport facilities, or were more prestigious. We rely, however, on the assumption that competitive pressures forced merchants to avoid rentals larger than necessary, so that gross estimated rental is a reasonable proxy for warehouse space and for firm size.

Our findings, based on a sample of 270 firms are presented in Table 3 and in Figure 2. Whereas in Kenyon's (1944) sample the largest 4.1 per cent of firms accounted for 50 per cent of business, in our sample the top 6.3 per cent of firms accounted for only 39.3 per cent of business. At the other end of the distribution, whereas Kenyon found the smallest 36 per cent of firms accounted for just 0.5 per cent of business, in our sample the bottom 19.3 per cent of firms accounted for 1.7 per cent of business. Overall, then, the distribution is rather less concentrated in our sample than in Kenyon's study. Hence, although there are theoretical reasons to expect a bias towards finding a concentrated structure in our study, our results show clearly that there was an extensive tail of small firms in the inter-war era.

Table 3   *The size distribution of merchant firms in 1927, based on rental*

Gross estimated rental (£)	Number of firms	Share of firms (%)	Share of rental (%)	Cumulated share of firms (%)	Cumulated share of rental (%)
2,000 +	6	2.2	22.4	2.2	22.4
1,000–1,999	11	4.1	16.9	6.3	39.3
500–999	27	10.0	20.9	16.3	60.2
300–499	35	12.9	15.8	29.2	76.0
200–299	31	11.5	8.9	40.7	84.9
100–199	53	19.6	8.8	60.3	93.7
50–99	55	20.4	4.6	80.7	98.3
Less than 50	52	19.3	1.7	100.0	100.0

Note: Results based on a sample of 270 firms.
Source: See text.

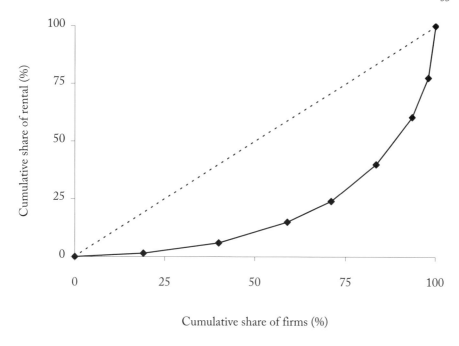

Figure 2   Lorenz curve of the size distribution of merchant firms in 1927, based on rental. *Source*: Table 3.

Our findings contrast with those of Ellinger and Ellinger,[17] who examined the size distribution of merchant firms *circa* 1929 using paid-up capital plus reserves. Their results are reported in Table 4 and Figure 3. The Ellingers divided the 742 firms in their sample into three classes, largely on the basis of personal knowledge, and defined the average size of each according to the average paid-up capital of the limited companies within it. Since only about half of the firms in Class 1 were limited companies, and this proportion fell to less than a quarter in Class 3, we might question the accuracy of this procedure. This is compounded by their supplementing paid-up capital with an allowance (also estimated) for 'declared reserves'. It is not clear that 'declared reserves' have meaning for private firms. Without the adjustment for declared reserves, the size distribution is even more concentrated, but in either case the Ellingers' estimates exhibit more concentration than in our sample. Whereas for the Ellingers the top 17.7 per cent of firms accounted for 74.1 per cent of business, in our sample the top 16.3 per cent of firms accounted for only 60.2 per cent of business. Even the top 29.2 per cent of firms in our sample accounted for only 76.0 per cent of business. The differences can be seen most obviously by comparing the shapes of Figures 2 and 3. Two points stand out. First, our data (Figure 2) show a smoother curve, reflecting their higher quality. Second, our

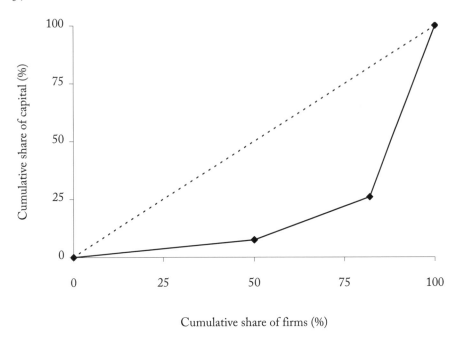

Figure 3   Lorenz curve of the size distribution of Manchester shipping merchants circa 1929, based on paid-up capital plus reserves. *Source*: Table 4.

data show less concentration, that is, the solid line in Figure 2 is closer to the 45° line than its equivalent in Figure 3.

Table 4   *The size distribution of Manchester shipping merchants circa 1929, based on paid-up capital plus reserves*

Class	Number of firms	Share of firms (%)	Share of capital (%)	Cumulative share of firms (%)	Cumulative share of capital (%)
Class 1	131	17.7	74.1	17.7	74.1
Class 2	239	32.2	18.5	49.9	92.6
Class 3	372	50.1	7.4	100.0	100.0

Source: B. Ellinger and H. Ellinger, 'Japanese Competition in the Cotton Trade', *Journal of the Royal Statistical Society*, xciii (1930), p. 215.

IV   Rationalisation revisited

Having established the key dimensions of the export merchanting section of the British cotton industry, and having noted in particular the survival of large numbers of merchants, including large numbers of small merchants, into the inter-war era, we now consider the implications for schemes of rationalisation put forward during the 1920s and subsequently. Mass and Lazonick see the combined effect of horizontal integration within merchanting and vertical integration between production and merchanting as allowing product specialisation and long production runs; they argue that this approach played a major role in the Japanese cotton industry's success during the inter-war period.[18] They cite Barnard Ellinger's comment that, 'the present organisation of the industry in Lancashire *prevents* mass production and distribution'.[19] We argue that the specialised structure of the Lancashire cotton industry and the merchanting sector delayed, rather than accelerated, the loss of comparative advantage to low wage competitors such as Japan.[20] Small producers could concentrate on particular types of cloth and gain economies of standardisation, despite the enormous variety produced by the industry as a whole.[21] Copeland sums it up thus:

> The advantage accruing from this multiplicity of middlemen is not inexpensiveness but flexibility. The tentacles of the Manchester trade reach out to all corners of the world, and whatever form of manufactured cotton is sought, whatever accommodation is desired, some one can be found in Manchester ready to accept the commission. Of all the assets which make it possible for the cotton industry to attain its largest dimensions in a country which does not produce the raw material, and which consumes only ten or twenty per cent of the yarn and cloth manufactured in its mills, none is more significant than the adaptability of the commercial organization.[22]

In the rest of this section, we show first that the areas in which Britain lost out to Japan are best explained by the product cycle model, before moving on to look in detail at the export experience. In all cases we concentrate particularly on the Indian market.

1   Quality and Britain's loss of export markets: the product cycle approach

Table 5 describes Britain's export markets losses in cotton piece goods between 1909–13 and 1937. Grey goods accounted for 40 per cent of the loss of export volumes, while India and Burma accounted for over 47 per cent of the loss, as predicted by the product cycle framework.[23] According to Vernon's model, new products are usually developed in advanced countries, because of the demands on knowledge skills.[24] However, as knowledge spreads and the technology is simplified, labour cost becomes the key factor determining location and the pioneer country loses its comparative advantage, particularly at the basic, standardised end of the market. The loss of comparative advantage will, however, be slower at the higher quality, customised end of the market, where knowledge and skills remain more important. This accurately captures the experience of British cotton exporters.

Table 5   *British exports of piece goods by type and destination (million yards)*

A. By type

	Average, 1909–13	*1937*	*Change*
Grey	2,150	317	−1,833
Bleached	1,828	572	−1,256
Printed	1,203	413	−790
Piece dyed	1,026	506	−520
Yarn dyed	268	112	−156
Total	6,476	1,921	−4,555

B. By destination

	Average, 1909–13	*1937*	*Change*
India, Burma	2,507	356	−2,151
British Empire	724	768	+44
China, Far East	973	74	−899
Near, Middle East	744	88	−656
Europe	454	269	−185
Foreign Africa	187	51	−136
Latin America	766	295	−471
Other foreign	122	22	−100
Total	6,476	1,921	−4,555

Source: J. H. Porter, 'Cotton and Wool Textiles' in N. K. Buxton and D. H. Aldcroft (eds), *British Industry between the Wars: Instability and Industrial Development, 1919–1939* (Scholar: London, 1979), p. 29.

More evidence in favour of the product cycle model comes from within the Indian market, where the British were most successful at the higher end of the market, while the Japanese were more successful at the lower end. In 1931–32 Britain still had a 74 per cent share of imports of higher value-added white goods, even though her share of low-value grey goods imports had fallen to 24 per cent, while the figures for Japan were 21 per cent and 74 per cent respectively.[25] Again, within grey goods, Britain was more successful in the higher value-added sub-sectors, such as grey dhutis, saris and scarves, as well as jaconets, madapollams, mulls and cambrics, where Britain's exports were fifteen times those of Japan even in the late 1920s, a period in which Japan's exports of simpler grey products, such as shirtings, sheetings, drills and jeans were four times those of Britain.[26] Dhutis, for example, were less standardised than plain grey goods because they were bordered, and marketed in pairs of garment pieces, often of 2–6 yards, rather than by the 30–50 yard length which was normal for piece goods. They also had to be folded and packed in specific ways. Even within the category of plain grey goods, Britain retained a strong position in the differentiated products at the higher end of the quality spectrum.

2   Assessing the role of distribution in explaining Japanese export success

We have argued elsewhere that the small merchant firms that made up the bulk of the sector served Lancashire's manufacturing base effectively.[27] Hence we reject the suggestion of Ellinger and Ellinger[28] (1930) that horizontal integration within the merchant sector would have been beneficial. Although their claim has not been supported by subsequent economic and business historians *per se*, some scholars have noted the benefits to Japanese export performance of the great trading companies. This approach has led Douglas Farnie and Takeshi Abe to pose the question of whether superior marketing could have been more important in the rapid spread of Japanese cottons into foreign markets than production-cost superiority.[29]

Like the Lancashire industry, the Japanese industry had both vertically integrated and vertically specialised manufacturing firms. Particularly under the influence of the deflation of 1927–31, the large spinning firms (some 74 in 1935) rationalised and adopted high-draft rings. These firms mostly owned wide power looms and produced 'a few standardised lines of cotton piece goods for export, especially cheap shirtings and sheetings'. But as such products encountered increasing competition in the 1930s, Japan '*had to* export a greater proportion of higher quality fancy goods which were turned out by specialist weaving sheds'. Hence the proportion of Japanese piece-goods exports supplied by the combined spinning–weaving mills fell from 60 per cent in 1928–29 to 42 per cent in 1935–36.[30] The Japanese merchant houses were instrumental in channelling orders back to these small firms.

The trading houses, which had been in existence since the early Meiji period, not only replaced local brokers and other intermediaries in overseas markets with trained Japanese staff, but also had close links with producers, links which extended to the provision of finance and the development of new technology (hence facilitating product specialisation and long production runs), purchasing raw cotton and speculating in cotton futures, and gathering market intelligence.[31] However, a descriptive cataloguing of all the activities and functions of the trading companies stands in danger of being translated into a conviction that all these activities were highly rather than marginally valuable, and that the market was incapable of providing the same services by other means. For instance, Farnie and Abe note that after 1850, Lancashire's tendency towards disintegration led to 'vertical ignorance' increasing among spinners and weavers:

> The insulation of spinners from the ultimate market for woven goods made it more difficult for them to spin the yarns best suited to specific types of cloth. Spinners could not know that a printing cloth was best made from a dense well-compacted yarn and an Indian shirting from a warp yarn more loosely spun.[32]

Yet, despite this, Lancashire prospered. In placing his order, the shipper was able to tell the weaver he wanted a print cloth for subsequent finishing, and the weaver surely knew that a dense yarn would be best for this purpose, and would order accordingly from the spinner. Britain's internal yarn market was highly developed, and the merchant's orders to the weaver and finisher very specific. Here, we argue, is a case in which Japan's visible hand was necessary to remedy the absence of the invisible one that operated in Britain, and thus offered no advantage to a country in which the invisible hand already operated so effectively.

It has been argued that an advantage of the large Japanese trading companies was their ability to penetrate the interior of foreign markets. Sugiyama argues that British failure in China stemmed from British houses' failure to branch out of their treaty port enclaves, instead relying on Chinese merchants to develop trading ties with local retailers, while Japanese firms established direct contacts.[33] Allen and Donnithorne echo this criticism, though significantly they note that during the 1930s this 'advantage' did not prevent the Japanese from being squeezed out by 'China's growing cotton industry'.[34] However, in arguing thus they neglect the fact that a considerable proportion of Chinese output now originated in foreign-owned and -operated (Japanese) mills. The truth is that, given this foreign presence, supported by successive Chinese boycotts against Britain (1926–27) and Japan (1931) and the blistering tariff of 1931, it is clearly not relevant to stress differences between Lancashire's and Japan's merchanting systems which could have only been minor in comparison. Indeed, offshore Japan's exports of yarn to China declined after 1915, and of cloth after 1925.[35]

In the Indian context Pearse, writing in 1930, stated that:

times have changed and require *more direct contact between the manufacturer and the wholesale dealer.* The three big Japanese importing houses have caused to be established in the Bombay bazaar a syndicate of 15 dealers who specialize on Japanese goods and deal in no others. Their selling brokers are in close and almost permanent touch with the syndicate, with whose chairman I had long interviews.

There is no syndicate for the sale of European goods, but there are hundreds of wholesale dealers, *each trying to compete and each depressing the price.*[36]

But Pearse supplies no detail on how the Japanese 'selling broker' at the port ensured such successful relations with the interior merchant and his claim that such syndicates prevented price falls for Japanese goods in the Indian market seems hard to reconcile with India's demand for cheapness and Japan's known emphasis on price-sensitive standardised products. Indeed, according to the Indian Tariff Board, in 1928–29 Britain supplied 38 per cent of the Indian domestic market for cotton goods, compared with 12.6 per cent for all other imports (mainly Japanese) put together. In 1932–33 the figures were 13.4 per cent and 13.9 per cent respectively, and in 1934–35 they were 12.7 per cent and 9.0 per cent. Again any marketing differences were dwarfed: nationalist influences, operating through boycott and tariffs, ensured the ascendancy of indigenous Indian production, operating first on lower qualities and ensuring that Japanese advance was only ephemeral.[37] According to such figures, between 1928 and 1935 the penetrative power of the Japanese trading company seems to have been negligible.

Nor were Japanese trading houses invariably able to deal directly with interior merchants elsewhere. In the Middle East, for example, there is plentiful evidence that Japanese trading companies dealt with local (i.e. non-Japanese) agency houses in Alexandria and other middle eastern ports.[38] Here the British often did better at penetrating the interior. Our own analysis of the day-to-day activities of middle eastern traders B. & S. H. Astardjian shows that there were excellent connections between Manchester and, through what was in effect the firm's 'main office' in Constantinople (Istanbul), the interior merchants of *several different* adjacent countries.[39] Furthermore, Shimizu's work gives strong indications from several middle eastern countries that it was Japanese exporters who had a reputation for giving credit only on the most stringent terms, and he cites the Italians as offering the most generous. Only in the early 1930s did Japan's export trade with the Middle East become concentrated mainly in the hands of Japanese firms themselves, after vigorous Japanese government effort (involving subsidies to export merchants directly and to steamship services) to assist in the late 1920s.[40]

An important part of the Japanese trading company's strength in China and India lay in proximity, and, in the case of China, in the imperial nature of Japan's relationship with Manchuria. Where markets were more distant, such as the Middle East, Japanese trading houses were much less effective. Distance seems to have been less of a bar to Manchester merchants, with 140 out of our late 1920s sample of 304 Manchester shippers stating a competence in the Chinese and Indian markets, the two areas of greatest Japanese penetration. These areas were also historically the territory of some of the largest British trading firms, firms like Ralli Brothers and Jardine Mathieson, which dealt in multiple products and had long-standing connections with shipping companies. If large Japanese-style merchanting firms were needed to export to China, then these firms would have become dominant. That they did not, and the fact that their cotton trade declined with the industry and merchanting sector as a whole, strongly suggests that it was something more fundamental, such as product cycles, that determined the ability of Lancashire to export.

There are two further reasons to be sceptical about the extent to which the rest of the world, and particularly Britain, could have gained from adopting the Japanese system of large trading houses. First, as Farnie and Abe note, the rise of the Japanese trading company began in the late nineteenth century, when Japan's penetration of world markets, especially of piece-goods, was small indeed.[41] Large trading companies were thus not sufficient for export success. Second, and perhaps most importantly, we need to realise how short was the pre-eminence of Japan in her main export markets. Japanese cloth exports became a significant presence on the world market during the First World War. While they made steady inroads thereafter, their victory in Britain's main markets, India and China, was ephemeral. For example, Japanese exports to India peaked in 1932, *three years before* Japan overtook Britain as the chief foreign supplier to the Indian market. In other words, Japanese exports were declining and only overtook British exports because the latter were declining more rapidly! As Farnie and Abe put it, 'Japan's aspirations to surpass Lancashire in the supply of the Indian market, as it had in China, were crowned with ultimate but brief success.'[42]

That there was a limited window in many of Britain's remaining export markets before even the Japanese producers would be driven from the field by (albeit tariff protected) indigenous producers supports our belief in the importance of product-cycle analysis, and makes any debate over the historical importance of differences between the marketing systems of Lancashire and Japan of trivial significance to the history of the Lancashire cotton industry. Shimizu's identification of the trend towards higher-quality goods in the Japanese export mix in the 1930s, goods turned out by specialist weaving sheds, only reinforces this conclusion.[43]

Concluding comments

As an industry employing relatively simple technology, easily exportable to countries with lower labour costs, the cotton industry was clearly subject to product-cycle analysis. The industry was never going to remain primarily located in high labour-cost countries. The interesting question is whether one form of industrial organisation was able to hasten a country's rise, or slow its decline. We argue that externalities created by Britain's many merchant firms and agents lengthened Lancashire's dominance beyond its time. We have documented how this community survived the first post-1918 onslaught on the industry and so allowed manufacturers to continue to focus on producing a narrow range of products efficiently, while offering consumers around the world the variety for which Lancashire was renowned. We end, fittingly, with a passage that, for all its international origins, is stamped indelibly with the style of Swinton's greatest scholar:

> Scholars have never tired of debating the causes of ... [Lancashire's] decline and of indulging in the pastime of 'giving lectures to the dead'. What is surely most important is not the contraction of that industry but the long duration of its primacy. The decline of the Lancashire cotton industry remains the least significant feature of its long history: its influence changed the world for ever.[44]

Notes

1. D. A. Farnie, *The English Cotton Industry and the World Market, 1815–1896* (Oxford University Press: Oxford, 1979).
2. P. Deane and W. A. Cole, *British Economic Growth, 1688–1959*, second edition (Cambridge University Press: Cambridge, 1969), pp. 186–8; L. G. Sandberg, *Lancashire in Decline: A Study in Entrepreneurship, Technology and International Trade* (Ohio State University Press, 1974), p. 4.
3. Quoted in J. Singleton, *Lancashire on the Scrapheap: The Cotton Industry, 1945–1970* (Oxford University Press: Oxford, 1991), p. 37.
4. D. A. Farnie, 'An Index of Commercial Activity: The Membership of the Manchester Royal Exchange, 1809–1948', *Business History*, xxi, issue 1 (1979), 79–106, p. 102.
5. A. Redford, *Manchester Merchants and Foreign Trade, Vol II: 1850–1939* (Manchester University Press: Manchester, 1956).
6. H. Kenyon, 'The Shape and Size of the Export Merchanting Section of the Cotton Industry', *Transactions of the Manchester Statistical Society*, Session 1944–45, pp. 1–20.
7. B. Ellinger and H. Ellinger, 'Japanese Competition in the Cotton Trade', *Journal of the Royal Statistical Society*, xciii (1930), pp. 185–231.

8. W. Mass and W. Lazonick, 'The British Cotton Industry and International Competitive Advantage: The State of the Debates', *Business History*, xxxii, issue 4 (1990), pp. 9–65.

9. See Ellinger and Ellinger, 'Japanese Competition'.

10. Merchant numbers for the nineteenth century are provided in S. N. Broadberry, *Market Services and the Productivity Race, 1850–2000: British Performance in International Perspective* (Cambridge University Press: Cambridge, 2006), p. 187.

11. S. Chapman, 'The Commercial Sector', in M. B. Rose (ed.), *The Lancashire Cotton Industry: A History Since 1700* (Lancashire County Books: Preston, 1996), 63–93, pp. 89–90.

12. Kenyon, 'The Shape and Size', pp. 1–20.

13. H. Clay, *Report on the Position of the English Cotton Industry* (Confidential Report, Securities Management Trust Ltd: London, 1931), p. 2.

14. Chapman, 'The Commercial Sector', p. 89.

15. Ellinger and Ellinger, 'Japanese Competition', pp. 214–15.

16. In addition to the 851 shipping merchants listed in Slater's Directory, we have added piece goods merchants listed in *Skinner's Directory of the Cotton Trades of the World* (1927–28 edition), when they were not listed as home trade houses in Slater's Directory. For rate data see Manchester Rate Books, Manchester Central Reference Library.

17. Ellinger and Ellinger, 'Japanese Competition'.

18. Mass and Lazonick, 'The British Cotton Industry', p. 44.

19. B. Ellinger, cited in Mass and Lazonick, 'The British Cotton Industry', p. 44.

20. S. N. Broadberry and A. J. Marrison, 'External Economies of Scale in the Lancashire Cotton Industry, 1900–1939', *Economic History Review*, lv, issue 1 (2002), pp. 51–77.

21. A. Marshall, *Industry and Trade: A Study of Industrial Technique and Business Organization; And of their Influences on the Conditions of Various Classes and Nations* (Macmillan: London, 1919) pp. 600–1.

22. M. T. Copeland, *The Cotton Manufacturing Industry of the United States* (Harvard University Press: Cambridge Mass, 1912; reprinted Augustus Kelly, 1966) p. 371.

23. Sandberg, *Lancashire in Decline*; Singleton, *Lancashire on the Scrapheap*.

24. R. Vernon, 'International Investment and International Trade in the Product Cycle', *Quarterly Journal of Economics*, lxxx (1966), pp. 190–207.

25. A. R. Burnett-Hurst, 'Lancashire and the Indian Market', *Journal of the Royal Statistical Society*, xcv (1932): 395–440, pp. 422–3.

26. F. Utley, *Lancashire and the Far East* (Allen & Unwin: London, 1931), pp. 266–7.

27. Broadberry and Marrison, 'External Economies'.

28. Ellinger and Ellinger, 'Japanese Competition'.

29. Mass and Lazonick, 'The British Cotton Industry', pp. 9–65; D. A. Farnie and T. Abe, 'Japan, Lancashire and the Asian Market for Cotton Manufactures, 1890–1990', in D. A. Farnie, T. Nokaoka, D. J. Jeremy, J. F. Wilson and T. Abe (eds), *Region and Strategy in Britain and Japan, 1890–1990*, Routledge International Studies in Business History, 7 (Routledge: London, 2000), pp. 115–57.

30. H. Shimizu, *Anglo-Japanese Trade Rivalry in the Middle East in the Inter-war Period* (Ithaca Press: London, 1986) pp. 31–2 (our emphasis).

31. Pearse notes that in January 1930 the Indian branches of the Japanese houses, which kept large stocks in Bombay, Calcutta, and Karachi, 'slaughtered' their stocks at much below replacement prices on advice from their New York and Dallas offices, where it was perceived that the raw cotton market was due for further falls following the Wall St crash. In his words: 'Such transactions are too speculative for the average-sized firm; to carry them out successfully requires a world-wide organization with a staff of first-class economists ... These hedges are not undertaken ... by [Japanese] manufacturers, but by the firms who export the cotton goods, i.e. by the shipping houses, as the term is generally used in Manchester. How many European exporters of cotton goods use hedges?' See A. S. Pearse, *The Cotton Industry of India: Being the Report of the Journey to India January–March 1930* (International Federation of Master Cotton Spinners' and Manufacturers' Associations: Manchester, 1930), p. 192.

32. Farnie and Abe, 'Japan, Lancashire and the Asian Market', p. 133.

33. S. Sugiyama, 'Textile Marketing in East Asia, 1860–1914', *Textile History*, 19 (1988), pp. 279–98; S. Sugiyama, 'The Expansion of Japan's Cotton Textile Exports into South-East Asia', in S. Sugiyama and M. C. Guerrero (eds), *International Commercial Rivalry in South-East Asia in the Inter-War Period* (Yale University Press: New Haven, 1994).

34. G. C. Allen and A. G. Donnithorne, *Western Enterprise in Far Eastern Economic Development: China and Japan* (George Allen & Unwin: London, 1954), p. 92.

35. Farnie and Abe, 'Japan, Lancashire and the Asian Market', pp. 136–9.

36. Pearse, *Cotton Industry of India*, p. 193 (our emphasis).

37. B. Chatterji, *Trade, Tariffs and Empire: Lancashire and British Policy in India, 1919–1939* (Oxford University Press: Delhi, 1992), pp. 161–7, esp. Table L, p. 167.

38. Shimizu, *Anglo-Japanese Trade Rivalry*, e.g. pp. 72, 81, 100, 192, 197.

39. Broadberry and Marrison, 'External Economies', esp. pp. 66–9.

40. Shimizu, *Anglo-Japanese Trade Rivalry*, pp. 84–6, 102, 98–123, 133.

41. Farnie and Abe, 'Japan, Lancashire and the Asian Market', pp. 127–30.

42. Farnie and Abe, 'Japan, Lancashire and the Asian Market', p. 144. It should be noted that the sequence outlined by Farnie and Abe does not correspond to that of the Indian Tariff Board figures reported in Chatterji, *Trade, Tariffs and Empire*, Table L, p. 167.

43. Shimizu, *Anglo-Japanese Trade Rivalry*.

44. Farnie and Abe, 'Japan, Lancashire and the Asian Market', p. 151.

4

The English cotton industry and the loss of the world market

STEVEN TOMS

THE JOINT STOCK COMPANY, centred on Oldham, is a central narrative in Douglas Farnie's seminal book, the *English Cotton Industry and the World Market*. Farnie was the first to highlight the idiosyncratic nature of these limited companies, including their highly democratic system of governance. Documenting the collapse of this system is a useful postscript to Farnie's analysis. The chapter will extend Farnie's contribution by examining new evidence in the pre-1896 period. It will then go on to document subsequent developments after 1896 and show that changes in governance had serious consequences for the industry. Cliques of mill owners, and the speculative stock-market capitalism they engendered, promoted over-expansion of the industry and financial instability. The over-expansion of the 1907 boom was repeated with disastrous consequences in the recapitalisation boom of 1919. It will be shown that the activities of networks of local directors, which had been established pre-1914, not financial syndicates, banks, trade unions or government, were responsible for the collapse that precipitated the industry's long decline.

Introduction

The decline of the cotton textile industry has continued until the present day and has been a dominant theme in its historiography. Following the collapse in demand for Lancashire's output in the difficult world trading conditions of the 1920s, the debate focused on attribution of blame for inaction on various groups. Keynes accused the banks of abandoning their responsibilities, referring to the bankers as 'a species of deaf mutes', and Bamberg adds that the competitive structure of bank lending to have been inimical to industry recovery.[1] Obstinate directors, with 'individualistic attitudes'[2] have also been criticised, as have the unions for lack of co-operation.[3] Subsequently, obsession with manufacturing decline in the 1970s and 1980s has coloured interpretations of pre-1914 Lancashire, and left its recent historiography dominated by the views of economists, and associated issues of efficiency and rational choice. For example it has been argued that the decline of the industry was entirely inevitable, and that attempts to preserve it represented a serious mis-allocation of resources.[4] Others have criticised the industry's leaders for their alleged conservatism, and the rationality of the choices made.[5] Lancashire's decline has also been analysed in the context of wider debates regarding the British economy; entrepreneurial failure, which has been developed and criticised from a broader sociological perspective;[6] and industry structure, particularly the impact of vertical specialisation.[7]

The town of Oldham, however, has not been a prominent feature in these stories. Indeed it has been subsumed within the larger story of cotton, the take-off industry of the industrial revolution and the dominant export sector of the British economy for a century thereafter. Yet, if the structure and ownership of this great industry are analysed in detail, it proves to be Oldham, with first its progressive brand of democratic and stock-market based capitalism, and later its domination by cliques of secretive directors, which perhaps goes furthest to explain its dramatic rise and fall.

An exception to the general neglect of Oldham is the work of Douglas Farnie, and in particular his benchmark monograph, *The English Cotton Industry and the World Market, 1815–1896*.[8] As Farnie explains, the Oldham 'limiteds' constituted the most important group of joint-stock *manufacturing* corporations in Britain and were responsible for 12 per cent of the *world*'s cotton spinning capacity in 1890 (emphasis added).[9] In the chapter on the rise of the Oldham Limiteds, Farnie describes a unique phenomenon in economic history: a system of capitalism founded on principles of democracy, where share ownership conferred the rights and obligations of participation in the management of companies by the shareholders themselves, many of whom were mill operatives.[10] Although the 'Oldham system' enjoyed a relatively short period of supremacy from its inception in around 1860, its major features were still intact at the end of the period covered by Farnie in 1896. Thereafter was a dramatic collapse, with the consequence that in almost Aristotlean fashion the virtues of the system turned into their opposites, from democratic ownership to factional block voting, from open participation and transparency to closed meetings and secrecy, from employee participation to collective bargaining, and from prosperity to collapse and prolonged decline.

The association between changes in ownership structure and fluctuation in economic performance offers a new perspective on the cause of the collapse of the industry and is intended as the first of two contributions in this chapter. It is inspired and subsumed by the second purpose, which is to extend Farnie's seminal work beyond 1896. The chapter begins with a re-examination of the democratic phase of development. A subsequent section shows how democracy was replaced quite suddenly by oligarchy in the slump of the 1890s. The new flotations of the oligarchs in 1907 and 1919 are then examined. Both flotation booms had the same characteristics and both might have had the same consequences. In comparing the two it is shown that the success of the 1907 boom led to the disaster of the 1919 boom. Subsequently, as explained in the final section, the captains of the industry who led the final advance in 1907 were incapable of managing the subsequent retreat.

The rise of democratic capitalism

'Private enterprise decays and dies, but companies may live forever'.[11] The citation that begins Farnie's chapter is from William Marcroft, the founder of Sun Mill, Oldham's first co-operative factory and high priest of industrial co-operation. The self-help based system of co-operative production advocated by William Marcroft, Samuel Smiles and others became a solution to the radicals' conflict between personal and collective improvement, and between imitating the middle class and conspiring towards its defeat.[12] Close proximity to Rochdale, the site of the earliest experiments in retail co-operation, and social conditions in Oldham created a receptive climate for co-operative ideas. Some small employers who were also labour leaders adopted 'Owenite socialism' in the 1830s, reflecting pressures from customers of their wholesale businesses and increasing working-class agitation.[13] A 'labour aristocracy' of self-acting mule minders inspired by John Bright's 'Rochdale Man' vision of co-operation, contributed to a less confrontational climate of industrial relations.[14] Karl Marx, addressing the International Working Men's Association in 1864, recommended '… the working men to embark in co-operative production rather than in co-operative stores. The latter touch but the surface of the present economical system, the former attacks its groundwork'.[15]

Indeed the practical management of the cotton spinning companies of Oldham strongly reflected the democratic ideals of the enlightenment's radical wing. As late as 1892, co-operative societies, whether retail or industrial, were still based on the 'Rochdale plan' of the original pioneers of the 1840s. Each member had one vote at the quarterly meeting, without reference to the total number of shares held and was barred proxy representation. The earliest industrial co-operative was the Rochdale Co-operative Manufacturing Society established in 1854, later known as the Mitchell Hey Spinning Company Ltd. All the promoters were members of the society; all employees were shareholders; and surpluses were paid as a bonus to labour.[16] The company was quoted on the

Oldham share market from the inception of the share list in 1875 through to 1914.[17] Links between the towns ensured that Marcroft's Sun Mill, Oldham's first co-operative mill, followed soon after. Having obtained the initial capital for the mill by 1862, shareholders were then offered employment at the company. As the original smaller operation expanded, during 1866, new capital was called at a rate of 3*d*. per week on the £1 shares. A profit-sharing scheme for operatives was introduced in 1869, although this was abolished in 1875. Similar schemes were operated elsewhere in the newer companies during the 1860s and early 1870s before being superseded by the shareholders' dividend. Sun Mill's financial success, as measured by the dividends distributed to its operatives, inspired similar projects in other districts of south-east Lancashire.[18]

These financial rewards reflected the serious approach of mill operatives to their responsibilities as investors and shareholders. Vociferous and active shareholders dominated company meetings, and their expertise often prevailed over the views of expendable and poorly rewarded boards of directors.[19] Farnie notes, 'Such shareholders proved to be the strictest of economists and were prepared to oust a whole board which failed to produce an acceptable balance sheet, displaying as much ruthlessness as the Athenian Ecclesia or the leaders of the French Revolution towards their unsuccessful generals.'[20] Such ruthlessness was well justified, and Ellison, quoting a contemporary report, explains precisely why:

> The daily discussions which take place among the shareholders as to why dividends are small or otherwise, have led almost every intelligent operative to become more economical with materials, more industrious and to see what effect his individual efforts have on the cost of the materials produced. In fact, the bulk of the working-class operatives of Oldham have more knowledge of the buying of cotton, working it up, and selling the manufactured good than most private employers had ten years ago … The competition between the managers of one company and those of another, and also between the directors of different companies and the pride which each body of shareholders take in their own mill is leading to improvements … so that *it is almost impossible for the management of any mill owned by working men to be seriously defective for any length of time* [emphasis added].[21]

Operatives' knowledge of the cotton economy and the workings of the mills helped form expectations about likely profits. Raw material prices were published in the local press and mill expenses were standard and well known. Hence operatives and other shareholders, assisted by press commentators, formed expectations about the earning power of their investments. Almost all press share market reports and many company reports discussed expected results in comparison to the actual published figures.[22]

A strike in 1875, and the flotation boom that preceded it during 1873–75, altered the course of the history of these hitherto democratic limited companies. Feelings ran high during this labour dispute and 'as the limited companies, which had been accepted as embodying the co-operative principle, were mostly ranged on the side of the capitalists ... the operatives determined to cripple these companies by withdrawing loan capital as far as possible ...'[23] Even so, many still regarded the limiteds as an extension of working-class control. At the inauguration of Industry Mill in 1875, the engine was christened the 'Oldham', as a tribute to the 3.375 million spindles 'now controlled by the working class of Oldham'.[24] Meanwhile operatives and increasingly middle-class investors were taking shareholdings in several mills. Around 70 new companies were floated on the nascent stock market in the 1873–75 boom,[25] and it became common for operatives to own shares in mills other than their own workplace. By 1875 it is clear that a hybrid system had emerged, with co-operative principle of democratic voting on the one hand and a stock-market system for buying and selling shares and collecting dividends on the other, so that Oldham earned the nickname, 'Diviborough'.[26] Some evidence of the mix of share ownership in example companies is shown in Table 1, which contrasts pre-1890 typically co-operative flotations and those that were formed later under the auspices of promotional cliques such as those led by John Bunting.[27]

Table 1   *Trends in company share ownership, 1874–1907*

Panel a) All companies	1874–76	1884–90	1894–97	1898–1907
Average number per company:				
Shareholders	384.60	338.33	255.90	195.25
Shareholder/operatives[a] (1)	78.40	42.00	26.20	14.25
Share transactions per year	78.20	71.17	10.00	31.88
Average number of shares per shareholder	27.91	37.71	73.79	157.62
Percentage of total shares per company held by:				
Operatives	22.22	11.91	9.99	5.15
Block holders (>3%)	19.41	20.27	30.62	42.25
Panel b) Companies floated before 1890[b]				
Average number per company:				
Shareholders			331.67	297.00
Shareholder/operatives			32.17	21.25
Share transactions per year			11.33	54.00
Average number of shares per shareholder			37.92	48.21

Percentage of total shares per company held by:

Operatives	9.10	5.89
Block holders (>3%)	20.81	19.40

Panel c) Companies floated after 1890[c]

Average number per company:		
Shareholders	152.80	59.67
Shareholder/operatives	18.40	2.00
Shares controlled by block shareholders (>3%)	6069.60	12513.00
share transactions per year	10.60	6.00
Average number of shares per shareholder	112.32	338.95
Percentage of total shares per company held by:		
Operatives	11.41	1.94
Block holders (>3%)	43.05	75.48

Source: Adapted from the analysis of Annual Returns (Form E) in the Public Record Office (PRO) in J. S. Toms, 'The Rise of Modern Accounting and the Fall of the Public Company: the Lancashire Cotton Mills, 1870–1914', *Accounting Organizations and Society*, xxvii, no. 1/2 (2002), p. 68.

Notes:

ᵃ Operative shareholders are defined as shareholders whose main occupation was described on the share list as related to textile factory work.

ᵇ Belgian, Henshaw Street, Livingstone, Shiloh, Thornham, and Dowry.

ᶜ Empire, Summervale and Times, floated by John Bunting post-1890 (D. Jeremy (ed.), *Dictionary of Business Biography* (Butterworths: London, 1984–86) p. 507).

Table 1 shows the changing ownership patterns for these sub-groups. Companies Act legislation of 1844, 1856 and 1862 combined with the co-operative origins of the original companies promoted companies with broad share ownership among working-class investors. Belgian, Shiloh and Thornham were typical, and many shareholders in such companies owned only one partly paid share.[28] Athough block shareholders were important in the 1870s, they too reflected the co-operative principles. Local co-operatives provided significant amounts of loan and equity capital. In the boom years of 1874–75, the Oldham Equitable Co-operative Society took up 200 shares the Equitable Spinning Company and 100 in the Glodwick and Thornham Spinning Companies, while placing £3,000, £3,000 and £1,000 respectively on deposit with the loan accounts of each company.[29] As a conduit for *local* savings, the Oldham stock market became an important institution. Another consequence of ownership structure was that some Lancashire companies' articles stated that Table A of the Companies Act did not apply and inserted clauses stating that each member shall have one vote only.[30] Such decisions closely reflected social ownership and provide historians and corporate governance regulators alike with a unique example of shareholder democracy.[31]

The crisis of democracy and the rise of the speculator

Although the benefits of one-shareholder one vote may seem desirable in the wake of Enron and other corporate scandals, it is unlikely that modern-day regulators will follow the Oldham example. Notwithstanding the implied transfer of power away from finance capital, even socially embedded democratic systems need continued regulation, lest they contain the seeds of their own demise. In the Oldham case the fault lines of the democratic governance system were embedded in the inequality of wealth distribution in late Victorian England and fractured by the vicissitudes of the economic cycle.

The downturn of 1890–91 turned into a steep and unprecedented slump lasting until 1896 and this proved the decisive event for the transformation of democratic control into corporate oligarchy. 'The darkest hour precedes the dawn', wrote an *Oldham Standard* correspondent hopefully in 1892, imagining perhaps that the recession would be of usual length and could not possibly continue much longer.[32] Lancashire's fortunes depended on export demand, but when combined with the speculative positions many firms had taken on the Liverpool market an acute scissors effect wiped out profit margins.[33] For local investors the consequence was a stock-market crash of unprecedented length and severity. By 1896 most companies had adverse balances on their reserve accounts. In some cases these balances amounted to several years' worth of average profits, so that there could have been no expectation of a dividend among the shareholders.[34] Financial adversity made operative shareholders less reliant on the 'divi' and reliant instead on effective craft-based trade union organisation.[35] Increasingly tempestuous industrial relations culminated in the 'Brooklands Lockout', the subsequent agreement of 1893 and the institutionalisation of bargaining thereafter. An important feature of the new system was its promotion of employer and operative collaboration to further collective interests, for example through political lobbying.[36] The dispute and the agreement were predicated on the vulnerability of the industry to the business cycle.[37] The long bear market finally ended in March 1896, and as new gold discoveries in Alaska and South Africa restored competitiveness in silver using export markets, there followed a general return to prosperity in the years before 1914.

In the meantime the Oldham co-operative investors had fallen victim to operators in the Liverpool market and more importantly for the longer run, to the activities of mill building syndicates within their own locality. Thus in the regular boom/recession cycle of the period 1870–90, there were mill promotion booms in 1873–75, 1883–84 and 1889–90. These mill-building booms were punctuated by temporary periods of recession. Each flotation boom created significant profit-making opportunities for cliques of mill promoters.[38] During the boom of 1888, the *Oldham Standard* published a vitriolic attack on the activities of fraudulent company promoters, describing them as 'thieves of a most destructive class'.[39] Whether fraudulent or not, 'hateful' and 'reckless' mill building was condemned both by private spinners and those committed to the existing co-operative factories. The resulting tendency to allow supply to outstrip demand posed a threat to the profits of established concerns.[40] Prior to the slump of the 1890s, promoters had attracted criticism for undermining the old limited liability system. Now, as share prices reached unprecedented low values, they had the opportunity to usurp it entirely.

A report in the *Oldham Standard* in 1898 noted the transition. 'It is said that they [promoters] are large holders of shares, many of which have been purchased within a comparatively recent period at very reasonable rates. One must hope that self-interest is not the guiding principle in their eagerness to get rid of the adverse balance, secure a dividend, and improve the selling price of the shares.'[41] The effects of systematic wealth transfers in favour of these cliques are indicated by the growth in block shareholders (Table 1). They included private spinners, for example Ralph Bagley, and Manchester-based tradesmen, such as William Kenyon. Their appearance on the share registers of John Bunting's new companies (Summervale, Empire and Times) also illustrates how promoters mobilised savings of known contacts. A further aspect of the changed structure of share ownership was the tendency for mill managers to purchase block shareholdings in their own companies and hence secure directorships and financial gain. Thomas Gartside (1857–1941), mill manager of Shiloh Spinning Company, acquired a large block of shares in the company during the period 1897–1905. Meanwhile, 'gangs of promoters' floated new mills. These comprised 'two or three mill managers who hankered after a directorship, a landowner with land to sell, a lawyer, architect, engineer and contractor in search of employment, and a yarn agent and cotton broker in quest of commission on the sale of yarn or cloth'.[42] One firm of accountants promoted 12 mills in the period 1899–1914.[43] Samuel Odgen Ward personified the transitional phase of Oldham capitalism. As an Alderman and JP, he was committed to the co-operative movement. Yet during the 1880s and 1890s he amassed directorships on the boards of several companies,[44] thereby breaking one of the movement's main rules, that committee members should hold no more than one office. Other examples in Oldham included Thomas Henthorn (1850–1913), Harry Dixon (1880–1947), William Hopwood (1862–1936), Ralph Morton (1875–1942), John S. Hammersley (1863–1933) and Sam Firth Mellor (1873–1938).[45]

In many companies during 1897 and 1898, these director-owners consolidated their control via the mechanism of extraordinary general meetings. Here they put forward and secured approval for the adoption of new articles of association. These allowed for the plutocratic one-share one-vote system, voting by proxy, minimum shareholding qualifications for directors and the removal of the obligation to forward accounts to shareholders.[46] Powerful new cliques usurped the prerogative to control company meetings and appoint directors, while disenfranchised minorities were left holding unsaleable shares. Economic and social change thereby underpinned voluntary changes in governance structures. There was a tendency for companies to move from quarterly to half yearly meetings and an increased reluctance to disclose financial information to the press, for example the resolution passed at the Glodwick Spinning Company in 1897.[47] As the new oligarchs consolidated their control, economic conditions gave them new opportunities to profit from mill flotations.

The boom of 1907

A characteristic of the slump of the 1890s was the loss of the silver-using Indian market due to the relatively high price of gold. As gold prices fell, Lancashire and in particular the coarse sector around Oldham began to recover the Indian market. Although punctuated by minor recessions, until 1914, Lancashire entrepreneurs were faced with consistent increases in demand and profits (Figure 2).[48] Accounting profit rates grew steadily from 1896 onwards and peaked in the boom of 1907.[49] In turn, this prompted an unprecedented mill-building boom in the period 1904–8, centred on the Oldham district.[50] Special features of the boom of 1907 were that promoters attracted outside investors using large amounts of loan finance, and a large proportion of the profit was distributed as repayments and bonus dividends.[51] Bunting floated the largest mill to date, the Times No. 2 in 1907, at 100,000 spindles.[52]

By the 1900s, 'empires' of individually controlled mills but otherwise un-integrated businesses, became more clearly established.[53] Profits from existing mills were channelled via the estates of these proprietary capitalists into personally administered flotations or acquisitions of other concerns.[54] The proprietors of these groups of mills possessed access to financial resources based on reputation and personal contact.[55] Strategy formulation became the exclusive preserve of these individuals while managers became nominee officials at plant level, trusted only with routine, thereby precluding the emergence of professional managerial hierarchies.[56] These changes created a highly unusual system of governance based on diversified directors and non-diversified share-holders (in the conventional model of Anglo Saxon economies it is the other way round). As a consequence capital ownership centralised and the industry increasingly fell under the control of speculative entrepreneurs.[57]

A further consequence was that speculative mill building in 1907 by these 'gangs of promoters' destroyed the profit margins of installed capacity and left the industry over-committed in subsequent slumps in demand.[58] According to a contemporary estimate in 1935, there were 13.5 million surplus spindles, of which 9.5 million were in the American section and 4 million in the Egyptian section, representing plant utilisation of just 69 per cent.[59] As early as the 1880s the industry already contained over 40 million spindles.[60] Put simply, the capacity installed by promoters in the boom period of 1896–1914 was all potentially surplus in the light of industry requirements after 1920. Over-capacity was compounded because corporate growth rates were strongest where private or family control was exercised and weakest where there was dependency on regional stock markets.[61] Yet it was in stock-market dominated Oldham, where there was the greatest expansion of capacity.

A final important consequence of oligarchic control was for the technological development of the industry. Because the commercial and technical advantages of ring spinning and the automatic loom were not yet established,[62] entrepreneurs ploughed the resources from the pre-1914 booms into specialised establishments using traditional technologies. It is for this reason that while there were few advocates of integrated production before 1914, technical issues associated with disintegration came to the fore in the 1920s and 1930s. The critique of specialisation from within the industry came from disenfranchised technical experts rather than business leaders.[63] The governance structure inherited from the nineteenth century meant the opinions of mill managers were much constrained by the actions of the directors. Before 1914 the industry ownership and its consequences dominated the issue of technical choice.

The boom of 1919

Following the gap left by the First World War, there was a further flotation boom in 1919. The overwhelming and immediate cause of the Lancashire crisis post-1922 was the collapse in demand in export markets. As Figure 1 shows, the boom of 1919–20 was dramatic even by the standards of this heavily cyclical industry. Unlike the 1907 boom that led to expansion of capacity through mill building, the 1919 boom was driven by wider margins associated with shortages and temporary dis-equilibrium in world markets. There was no physical increase in demand for Lancashire textiles. Also, a new wave of mill construction was prevented by a shortage of equipment and building supplies. Consequently, money capital was invested by financial syndicates through the recapitalisation of existing mills with bonus issues and new loan finance.[64] These aspects of the boom determined the subsequent financial characteristics of many Lancashire firms.

A crucial and previously unanswered question is who were the members of the financial syndicates? There were striking continuities between the investor groups in the Oldham section in the 1919–20 boom and the operations of similar groups, sometimes involving the same individuals, in the pre-1914 period. The syndicates investing in Oldham in 1919–20 were organised by the pre-war investor groups using the networks they had built up before 1914. Therefore important features of the booms of 1907 and 1919 were the activities of John Bunting, Firth Mellor, Hammersley and others. As a result, by 1919 promoter and share dealer Sam Firth Mellor was a director of 18 companies, and Bunting, of the same occupation, held 14.[65] Another important continuity was the involvement of successor generations. So James Henry Bunting continued his pre-war apprenticeship, while successive generations of the architects and mill designers A. H. Stott & Sons continued their practice of investing in the mills they helped to build.[66] Outside investors were attracted using pre-1914 networks, so new calls were made on the likes of Manchester-based John Kenyon and William P. Hartley (who had made money in preserves), to support the flotation of the Textile Spinning Company and the Asia Spinning Company. The Buntings, John and James Henry, were co-directors of Textile Mill. Just as in 1907, the investors of the 1919–20 recapitalisation boom were local, inter-connected, had intensive knowledge of industry finance and were continuing well-established practice from before 1914.

The oligarchs who had brought about the demise of the democratic system in the Oldham district now engineered the downfall of the whole industry. A statistical analysis of the accounts of a large sample of cotton companies taken from the period 1925 to 1931, shows that fewer recapitalised firms left the industry compared to non-recapitalised firms. However, in view of the excess capacity problem, it was imperative that some firms exited the industry. Ownership itself, in particular oligarchic control, now became an overwhelming exit barrier, preventing the reorganisation of the industry.[67] Oligrachs now pursued a rational strategy of forcing the managers of their firms to continue undercutting their competitors on marginal contracts, because the only alternative was to realise their investments at seriously deflated values, losing all the profits of their earlier speculations. In contrast to the arguments of Keynes, Bamberg and others, indebtedness to the banks seems a less important cause of weak selling, and indeed firms with greater bank debt were more likely to leave the industry. Oligarchic companies were typically larger and enjoyed stronger market position, and as a result tended to be more successful than their competitors in terms of profitability. However, most of the profit was paid out as dividend, allowing some recovery of invested capital, but starving the industry of cash for re-equipment.

The failure to re-equip had not been material in the pre-1914 expansion.

Indeed, the spinning mule and Lancashire loom system were as effective as their alternatives until that point. However, the 1920s saw major improvements in preparatory and intermediate winding processes and in high-speed drafting. With these developments ring spinning and automatic weaving organised in vertically integrated factories. International competition, most notably the US cotton industry, was well placed to exploit these advances in production methods. Lancashire, by contrast, needed to refinance before any such investment could take place, and refinancing was prevented by the ownership structure of the industry.

Epilogue: Lancashire in the 1950s

Following the end of the post-war boom in 1952, the Lancashire cotton industry once again faced problems of over-capacity and the need for reorganization. However, the ownership pattern that had developed before 1914, consolidated in the 1920s, continued to ossify along with the industry in the 1950s. Control by interlocking directorships was a crucial feature throughout the industry's decline phase. A survey using annual returns of these companies in the 1950s has revealed interlocking directorships and a rump of residual small private shareholders.[68] Table 2 shows that the typical Lancashire director sat on the boards of far more other companies in comparison to national averages. The average director of the typical large British company in 1950 held just that one board position, whereas the typical Lancashire director held three or four board positions, with a significant minority holding more than six. This governance structure reflected the nineteenth- and the early twentieth-century developments referred to above. Hence the most common type of interlock was in other cotton industry companies. The average age of each director in the Table 1 sample was 59 years, suggesting that while many had served during the crisis years of the inter-war period, a minority had also participated in the development of earlier 'Bunting-style' groups. At the same time, it is suggestive that centralisation of directors' power acted as a barrier to the development of new managerial talent.

Meanwhile share ownership was individual rather than institutional, primarily because share quotations were based on thin local stock markets, and this was also the case for the larger conglomerates and the larger number of smaller quoted firms.[69] Instead of institutional ownership there was substantial share-ownership by directors, their families and members of founding families. Oligarchic block share-ownership compounded the problem of thin markets and the general fortunes of this by now seriously under-invested and un-modernised industry meant there were few enthusiastic buyers of cotton shares.

Table 2   *The distribution of directorships in British enterprises, 1950*

	(1) Cotton textiles, 1950 %	(2) All British enterprises %
Number of directorships per person		
1	19.2%	87.4%
2	13.2%	8.5%
3–5	43.7%	3.9%
6 or more	23.9%	0.2%
	100.0%	100.0%

(1) % of directors in each category from a sample of 167 directors from 45 quoted textile companies.

(2) % of directors in each category from the top 250 British enterprises. The % is estimated from J. Scott, *Corporate Business and Capitalist Classes* (Oxford University Press: Oxford, 1997) p. 117 which provides breakdowns for the years 1938 and 1976. The figures shown here are a simple average for those two years.

Sources: Annual Returns (form E) Companies House and PRO files. Scott, *Corporate Business*, p. 117. J. S. Toms and I. Filatotchev, 'Corporate Governance, Business Strategy and the Dynamics of Networks: A Theoretical Model and Application to the British Cotton Industry, 1830–1980', *Organization Studies*, xxv (2004), pp. 629–51.

Conclusion: The English cotton industry and the loss of the world market

The English cotton industry's loss of its world market can be attributed primarily to its ownership by oligarchies of directors and their financial schemes before and after the First World War. The beginning of Lancashire's problems can be dated to 1896, which saw the end of democratic capitalism in Oldham and its replacement by the speculative oligarchs. Of course, other factors were important. The rise of overseas competition and the retreat from empire were the result of powerful forces which representatives of the cotton industry, in Oldham or elsewhere, could do little about.

With a different structure of ownership, however, the crisis of the 1920s need not necessarily have happened and cotton textiles might have retained its competitive edge for longer, in line with other textile sectors. In relation to the problem of ownership and associated financial control, the issues raised by economic historians, such as failure to restructure and failure to invest in new technology, are secondary as explanations for the poor performance and decline of the industry.

With different ownership, new investment and re-organisation would have been possible. So is this merely a restatement of the entrepreneurial failure hypothesis? In the past, this theory has been set out in terms of failure to act according to the rational requirements of the economic situation. Examples might be failure to invest, to develop marketing expertise and so on. In the case described above, however, it is clear that the problem was not that entrepreneurs failed to act. Indeed they acted decisively to exploit the short-run profit opportunities that frequently presented themselves in this cyclical industry. They acted decisively to overcome constraints that might be imposed on their actions through transparent structures of governance and accountability. They decisively seized control of the industry from other stakeholders. By 1922, they could not act decisively to reorganise the industry, because by that time they were paralysed by the consequences of their own actions.

Notes

1. J. M. Keynes, *The Return to Gold and Industrial Policy II*, Collected works (Cambridge University Press: Cambridge, 1981), p. 601. J. H. Bamberg, 'The rationalisation of the British cotton industry in the inter-war years', *Textile History*, 19 (1988), pp. 83–102.

2. G. Saxonhouse and G. Wright, 'Stubborn mules and vertical integration: the disappearing constraint', *Economic History Review*, 40 (1987), pp. 87–94.

3. W. Lazonick, 'The cotton industry', in B. Elbaum and W. Lazonick, *The Decline of the British Economy* (Oxford University Press: Oxford, 1986), pp. 18–50. Keynes, *The Return to Gold*, pp. 578–637; R. Skidelsky, *John Maynard Keynes: Economist and Saviour, 1920–1937* (Macmillian: London, 1992), pp. 261–3.

4. J. Singleton, *Lancashire on the scrapheap the cotton industry, 1945–70* (Oxford University Press: Oxford, 1991), p. 232.

5. D. H. Aldcroft, 'The Entrepreneur and the British Economy', *Economic History Review*, 2nd series, vol. 17 (August, 1964), pp. 113–34; D. Landes, *The Unbound Prometheus* (Cambridge University Press: Cambridge, 1969). D. McCloskey and L. Sandberg, 'From Damnation to Redemption: judgements on the late Victorian entrepreneur', *Explorations in Economic History*, vol. 9, no. 2 (Winter 1971–72), pp. 89–108. L. Sandberg, *Lancashire in Decline* (Ohio State University Press: Columbus, 1974).

6. Aldcroft, 'The Entrepreneur and the British Economy' pp. 113–34; M. Weiner, *English Culture and the decline of the Industrial Spirit, 1850–1980* (Penguin: London, 1981) and the contrasting analysis in W. Rubinstein, *Capitalism, Culture, and Decline: 1750–1990* (Routledge: London, 1981).

7. For the main interpretations see: Sandberg, *Lancashire in Decline*; W. Lazonick, 'Competition, Specialization and Industrial Decline', *Journal of Economic History*, vol. xli, no. 1 (1981), pp. 31–8. W. Lazonick, 'Factor Costs and the Diffusion of Ring Spinning Prior to World War One', *Quarterly Journal of Economics*, vol. xcvi, no. 1 (1981), pp. 89–109. W. Lazonick, 'Industrial Organization and Technological

Change: The Decline of the British Cotton Industry', *Business History Review*, vol. lvii (Summer 1983), pp. 195–236. G. Saxonhouse and G. Wright, 'Stubborn Mules and Vertical Integration: the disappearing constraint', *Economic History Review*, 2nd series, vol. xl(i) (1987), pp. 87–94. W. Mass and W. Lazonick, 'The British Cotton Industry and International Competitive Advantage: the state of the debates,' *Business History*, xxxii(4) (1990), pp. 9–65.

8. D. Farnie, *The English Cotton Industry and the World Market* (Clarendon Press: Oxford, 1979).

9. D. Farnie, 'The emergence of Victorian Oldham as the centre of the cotton spinning industry,' *Saddleworth Historical Society Bulletin*, 12 (1982): 41–53, p. 42. The 'Oldham District' comprised a large area of South East Lancashire (much of present-day Greater Manchester) and included Rochdale to the north, Ashton to the south and Middleton to the west.

10. Farnie, *English Cotton*, chapter 7, 'The emergence of the Oldham Limiteds, 1874–1890'.

11. Cited in Farnie, *English Cotton*, p. 244.

12. E. Hobsbawm, *The Age of Capital, 1848–1875* (Weidenfeld & Nicolson: London, 1975), p. 264.

13. J. Foster, *Class Struggle and the Industrial Revolution: Early Industrial Capitalism in Three English towns* (Weidenfeld & Nicolson: London, 1974). B. Jones, *Co-operative Production* (Clarendon Press: Oxford, 1894).

14. P. Joyce, *Work, Society and Politics: The Culture of the Factory in later Victorian England* (Gregg Revivals: Aldershot, 1991), pp. 57–8.

15. K. Marx, 'Inaugural address', International Working Men's Association, 1864, paragraph 5(c).

16. *Rochdale Observer*, 10 May 1890.

17. Jones, *Co-operative Production*, pp. 2–3.

18. For details of Sun Mill's profits, see Farnie, *English Cotton*, p. 248. Jones, *Co-operative Production*, pp. 282–90.

19. Directorships were frequently and often hotly contested. A contest at a meeting at the Higginshaw Spinning Company was likened to 'a miniature Waterloo', *Oldham Chronicle*, 30 December 1893, p. 8 (vii).

20. Farnie, *English Cotton*, p. 266.

21. T. Ellison, *The Cotton Trade of Great Britain* (Frank Cass: London, 1968, reprinted 1886), p. 138.

22. *Oldham Standard* and *Oldham Chronicle*, all Saturday issues, c. 1875–1900; for a specific example see the report on the Stock Lane Spinning company, *Oldham Chronicle*, 25 December 1897.

23. J. C. Taylor, *The Jubilee History of the Oldham Industrial Co-operative Society Limited* (Co-operative Wholesale Society: Manchester, 1900), p. 122.

24. *Textile Manufacturer*, June 1877, p. 180.

25. S. Yonekawa, 'Flotation Booms in the Cotton Spinning Industry, 1987–1890: A Comparative Study', *Business History Review*, lxi (1987): 551–81, p. 552. Ownership was diverse and, in the town of Oldham itself, may have been as large as a quarter of the adult population, Farnie, *English Cotton*, p. 261.

26. Farnie, *English Cotton*, p. 263. The term stock 'market' rather than stock 'exchange' is used deliberately. Despite attempts to establish an official exchange, promoters of the idea failed to secure permanent premises and succumbed to the tradition of *ad hoc* trading in local hotels. W. Thomas, *The Provincial Stock Exchanges* (Frank Cass and Co. Ltd: London, 1973), pp. 149–50. A possible reason was that it facilitated the trading of shares in outlying towns and industrial villages. For example the Oldham practices were copied by the 'Stalybridge Share Market', which carried on in a private house in Stalybridge (*Oldham Standard*, 13 December 1884).

27. D. Farnie, 'John Bunting', in D. Jeremy (ed.), *Dictionary of Business Biography* (Butterworths: London, 1984–86): 506–9, p. 507.

28. Respectively these companies had 639, 295 and 406 shareholders and average share-holdings of 22, 17 and 18 (PRO BT31/14469/7869, 14486/8310 and 14494/8449). See also Yonekawa, 'Flotation booms', p. 552.

29. Taylor, *The Jubilee History*, p. 75.

30. For example, Article 12 of the Thornham Cotton Spinning Company Articles of Association, 1874 (PRO BT31/14494/8449). This contrasts with the one share one vote rule adopted in the revised 1899 Articles.

31. Democratic voting systems were compatible with Table A in the 1862 Companies Act. The use of graduated voting was quite widespread in the period 1862–1900 in the USA. C. Dunlavy, 'Corporate governance in late nineteenth-century Europe and the US: the case of shareholder voting rights', in K. Hopt, H. Kanda, M. Roe, E. Wymeersch and S. Prigge (eds), *Comparative Corporate Governance: The State of the Art and Emerging Research* (Clarendon Press: Oxford, 1998), pp. 29–32. However, there are no other examples of the 'one shareholder one vote' rule, co-operative principles of member participation and stock market quotation coinciding for such a large number of manufacturing companies.

32. *Oldham Standard*, 20 February 1892.

33. The lowest prices since 1848 were recorded in Liverpool in March 1892 (*Oldham Standard*, 12 March 1892). Falling prices and their misjudgement damaged the profits of companies those companies that bought speculatively and were left holding significant stocks of 'dear cotton' (*Oldham Standard*, 7 February, 14 February, 28 February, 23 May 1891).

34. The poor condition of many companies was revealed by a survey in the *Oldham Standard*, 29 December 1894. The Belgian, Gladstone, Hope and Werneth Cotton Spinning Companies had adverse balances greater than £20,000 (the average subscribed equity capital per company in 1885 was £38,200 (calculated from the appendix data in R. Smith, 'An Oldham Limited Liability Company, 1875–1896', *Business History*, vol. 4 (2) (December, 1961): 34–53, pp. 52–3).

35. For a detailed explanation of the epistemological and technical basis of trade union power, see A. Fowler, *Lancashire Cotton Operatives and Work, 1900–1950* (Ashgate: Aldershot, 2003).

36. For example, a joint committee was established to consider 'the opening of new markets abroad, the alteration of restrictive tariffs, and other similar matters which may benefit of injure the cotton trade …', Brooklands Agreement, 1893, *Board of*

Trade Report on Wages and Hours of Labour, Part II, Standard Piece Rates, C.7567, vol. xxxi, pp. 9–11.

37. Employers were allowed to move for up to a five per cent reduction in wages; conversely up to a five per cent increase could be requested by employees, as determined by the economic cycle; K. Burgess *The Origins of British Industrial Relations* (Croom Helm: London, 1975), p. 233.

38. Farnie, *English Cotton*, pp. 250–1.

39. *Oldham Standard*, 16 June 1888.

40. *Oldham Standard*, 27 April 1889.

41. *Oldham Standard*, 24 September 1898.

42. Report of the Tariff Commission, 1905, cited in F. Jones, 'The Cotton Spinning Industry in the Oldham District from 1896 to 1914', MA thesis (University of Manchester, 1959), p. 13.

43. Jones, 'The Cotton Spinning Industry', p. 13.

44. From reports of company meetings (*Oldham Standard*, various issues, 1888/89), Ward served on the boards of Werneth, Coldhurst, Henshaw Street, Northmoor and Broadway Spinning Companies. Taylor, *The Jubilee History*, pp. 112, 125.

45. D. Gurr and J. Hunt, *The Cotton Mills of Oldham* (Oldham Leisure Services: Oldham, 1989), pp. 9–10.

46. For examples, *inter alia*, see *Oldham Standard*, 27 November 1897, 1 October, 8 October, 5 November 1898.

47. Farnie, 'John Bunting', p. 508; *Oldham Standard*, 27 November 1897.

48. Figure two refers to the coarse spinning section only.

49. S. Toms, 'Growth, Profits and Technological Choice: The Case of the Lancashire Cotton Textile Industry', *Journal of Industrial History*, vol. 1(1) (1998), pp. 35–55.

50. During the period 1897–1913 installed spindleage increased by 2 per cent per annum in Lancashire but by 2.7 per cent in Oldham (calculated from R. Robson, *The Cotton Industry in Britain* (Macmillan: London, 1957), tables 2 and 5, pp. 334 and 340 and Farnie, *English Cotton*, p. 42). The higher rate in Oldham was a function of the extraordinary boom of the middle years of the 1900s. For details of the mills constructed, see Jones, 'The Cotton Spinning Industry', pp. 221–3.

51. S. Toms, 'Windows of opportunity in the textile industry: the business strategies of Lancashire entrepreneurs, 1880–1914', *Business History*, 40(1) (1998), 1–25.

52. *Oldham Chronicle*, 28 December 1907.

53. S. Toms, 'The Supply of and Demand for Accounting Information in an Unregulated Market: Examples from the Lancashire Cotton Mills', *Accounting Organizations and Society*, vol. 23, no. 2 (1998), pp. 217–38.

54. S. Toms, 'Financial Constraints on Economic Growth: Profits, Capital Accumulation, and the Development of the Lancashire Cotton Spinning Industry, 1885–1914,' *Accounting Business and Financial History*, vol. 4 (3) (1994), pp. 364–83. S. Toms, 'The Finance and Growth of the Lancashire Textile Industry, 1870–1914', Ph.D. thesis (University of Nottingham, March, 1996). Toms, 'Windows of Opportunity'.

55. R. E. Tyson, 'Sun Mill: A Study in Democratic Investment', unpublished MA thesis (University of Manchester, 1962). W. Thomas, *The Provincial Stock Exchanges* (Frank Cass and Co. Ltd: London, 1973) p. 962; Toms, 'The Supply'.

56. Toms, 'Windows of Opportunity' pp. 1–25; Toms, 'The Finance and Growth', pp. 217–38.

57. Toms, 'The Finance and Growth', pp. 226–31.

58. Jones, 'The Cotton Spinning Industry', p. 3.

59. T. D. Barlow, 'Surplus capacity in the Lancashire Cotton Industry', *Manchester School*, 6 (1935): 32–6, p. 35; Robson, *The Cotton Industry*, Table 8, p. 344.

60. Calculated from Robson, *The Cotton Industry*, Table 5, p. 340.

61. Toms, 'Windows of opportunity', p. 3.

62. See, for example, G. Saxonhouse and G. Wright, 'New Evidence on the Stubborn English Mule and the Cotton Industry, 1878–1920,' *Economic History Review*, 2nd series, vol. xxxvii, no. 4 (1984), 507–19, p. 519. A more recent discussion of the commercial and technological factors which affected the adoption of ring spinning during the inter-war years is contained in D. M. Higgins and J. S. Toms 'Firm Structure and Financial Performance: the Lancashire textile Industry, c. 1884–1960', *Accounting Business and Financial History*, vol. 7, no. 2 (1997): 195–232, pp. 212–14.

63. Developments in intermediate processing, principally high drafting, doffing and winding that were developed and available commercially after 1914 gave a decisive advantage to the ring and automatic loom combination by the 1930s. J. S. Toms 'Growth, Profits and Technological Choice: The Case of the Lancashire Cotton Textile Industry', *Journal of Industrial History*, vol. 1(1) (1998), pp. 35–55. For examples of technicians' criticisms of industry structure, see Lazonick, 'Industrial Organization and Technological Change' and B. Robinson, 'Business Methods in the Cotton Trade', *Journal of the British Association of Managers of Textile Works (Lancashire Section)* vol. IX (1918–1919) p. 96; F. Holt, 'High Speed Winding and Warping', *Journal of the National Textile Managers' Associations*, vol. IX (1929–1930), pp. 104–5, as cited in Lazonick.

64. G. Daniels and J. Jewkes, 'The post war depression in the Lancashire cotton industry', *Journal of the Royal Statistical Society*, 91 (1928): 153–206, p. 170; W. Thomas, *The Provincial Stock Exchanges* (Frank Cass and Co. Ltd: London, 1973), p. 156.

65. Firth Mellor's interests were: Argyll, Broadway; Fernhurst, Gee Cross Mill, Gorse, Greenacres, Hartford, Marland, Mars, Mersey, Monton, Moor, Orb, Peel Mills Co, Princess, Rugby, and Stockport Ring Mill. Mellor built up a substantial shareholding in many of these companies, for example, Argyll (7.55 per cent), and Asia Mill (3.8 per cent). See D. Higgins, S. Toms and I. Filatotchev, 'Financial syndicates and the collapse of the Lancashire cotton industry, 1919–1931' (York Management School Working Paper, 2007). In total Bunting is known to have been involved in fourteen or so promotions. Farnie, 'John Bunting', p. 508.

66. For a biographical discussion of the activities of three generations of the Stott family, 1862–1937, see D. A. Farnie and D. A. Gurr, 'Design and construction of mills', in D. A. Gurr and J. Hunt, *The Cotton Mills of Oldham* (Oldham Education and Leisure: Oldham, 1998), pp. 15–18.

67. Higgins *et al.*, 'Financial syndicates'. I. Filatotchev and S. Toms, 'Financial constraints on strategic turnarounds', *Journal of Management Studies* vol. 43 (2006) pp. 407–33.

68. I. Filatotchev and J. S. Toms, 'Corporate Governance, Strategy and Survival

in a Declining Industry: A Study of Lancashire Textile Companies', *Journal of Management Studies*, vol. 40 (2003), pp. 895–920.

69. D. M. Higgins and J. S. Toms, 'Financial Distress, Corporate Borrowing and Industrial Decline: The Lancashire Cotton Textile Industry, 1918–1938', *Accounting Business and Financial History*, vol. 13 (2003), pp. 207–32.

5

Was the Lancashire cotton textile industry competitive? An alternative analysis

DAVID M. HIGGINS

Introduction

There can be little doubt that among the various explanations advanced to explain the decline of the Lancashire cotton textile industry, the role of industrial structure has been paramount. This chapter revisits this debate from a new angle: instead of assessing the relative merits of the industry's structure, the focus is on the *degree* of competitiveness which existed within the industry. In other words, did the pattern of profit rates between firms in this industry conform to the predictions of a competitive industry? Because of the large number of firms which existed in each stage of production, a key assumption made by a number of scholars is that the industry was very competitive. Using the perspective of industrial economics and a literature known as Persistence of Profits (POP), this chapter analyses the validity of this assumption and its implications for our assessment of the industry's performance.

Historiography

In 1979 Farnie summarised the structural characteristics of the industry's development as follows:

THE REPRESENTATIVE unit of enterprise in the cotton industry was the small rather than the large firm and the representative employer was a yeoman of industry rather than a captain ... The rapid expansion of the industry had in fact been achieved by a myriad of small masters, unrestrained by any barriers to entry into the trade or by any restrictions upon sales ... Throughout the nineteenth century ... the scale of operations remained small ... the industry remained readily accessible to the small capitalist because of its geographical concentration within the Lancashire area ... and the growth of a wide range of external economies offered by the auxiliary industries of the region.[1]

The key themes in this passage – small-scale operation, freedom of entry, external economies – at a time when the industry was rapidly expanding, have a much longer lineage, and can be traced back to Marshall. One particular feature of this development which has attracted considerable attention is the large number of firms which existed at each stage of production. The broad trends in the number of firms existing in the spinning and weaving sections of the industry are set out in Table 1.

Table 1   *Number of firms in the spinning, weaving, and spinning-weaving firms, in the Lancashire cotton textile industry, 1884–1965*

	Spinning firms	*Weaving firms*	*Spinning–weaving firms*
1884	683	557	446
1911	713	855	279
1955	224	675	128
1959	178	499	112
1965	115	266	77

Source: J. Jewkes and S. Jewkes, 'A Hundred Years of Change in the Structure of the Cotton Industry', *Journal of Law and Economics*, ix (1966), p. 120.

From Table 1 it is clear that the relative importance of integrated firms declined rapidly in the period 1884–1911, from just over 25 per cent to 15 per cent of total firms. The corollary of this decline was the rapid growth of specialised firms in spinning and weaving, from 75 per cent, to 85 per cent of the total. These broad trends continued until the 1960s. Effectively, therefore, the structure of the industry which existed at the turn of the twentieth century was fundamentally the same until the mid-1960s.

There is a long lineage of discussion which vividly describes the characteristics of this highly competitive industry. Ellinger and Ellinger, for example, noted of the bulk of the industry that it was, 'all without cohesion, without nucleus, loose, higgledy-piggledy, rushing hither and thither, jostling, chasing, fighting';[2] Keynes opined that, 'There is probably no hall in Manchester large enough to hold all the directors of cotton companies; they [run] into thousands';[3] Clay's Report stated that within the cotton industry there was a 'multiplicity of units in each section',[4] and the report by Political and Economic Planning commented that there was 'an excessive number of units in all sections of the industry'.[5] Without exception these commentators argued that there was an overwhelming need for amalgamation as a precursor to greater vertical integration. However, the sheer multiplicity of units precluded this. In effect, the industry was simply *too competitive* to generate, or even facilitate, the required structural change.

More recently, the views of contemporary observers have been assimilated and analysed by Lazonick, the result of which *appeared* to be a devastating critique of the industry's structure. In common with previous writers, Lazonick's attention was drawn to the high level of horizontal competition which existed within the industry. At the very least, Lazonick perceived this industry to be highly competitive. In his 1983 article, for example, Lazonick described the industry in terms of 'high degrees of horizontal competition', 'extreme competition', and 'highly competitive … structure'.[6] However, it is also the case that at various times, Lazonick has perceived the atomistic structure of this industry as being either perfectly or monopolistically competitive.[7] In the first case, Lazonick argued that, 'In Lancashire the power to implement such strategies was lacking precisely because the perfectly competitive structure of the industry made impossible the exercise of such market power and coordinated control.'[8] Similarly, in 1984, Lazonick claimed that, 'Up to the 1960s such power was lacking in Lancashire precisely because "perfect competition" … made the exercise of such coordination impossible.'[9] In the second case, Lazonick stated that, 'This horizontal specialisation (tending towards "monopolistic competition")' helped generate vertical specialisation and place further obstacles in the way of structural change.[10]

Although many of Lazonick's hypotheses have been subject to extensive empirical refutation,[11] especially the relationship between vertical specialisation and technology, no attempt has yet been made to assess whether the Lancashire industry really was as 'competitive' as claimed. By utilising the methodology employed in POP studies, I examine the degree of competitiveness which existed in this industry. If it can be demonstrated that the industry was not as competitive as claimed, then it is difficult to accept an interpretation of the industry's decline based on its structural characteristics.

Persistence of profits

On the basis of the preceding discussion it is apparent that, at least on structural grounds, the Lancashire textile industry was very competitive from the late nineteenth through to the mid-twentieth century. One way to test the degree of competitiveness in an industry is to examine the POP enjoyed by firms in an industry, and to assess the speed with which dispersion from the norm is eradicated; in other words, how quickly do the profit rates enjoyed by firms converge on the industry average?

The fundamental theme underlying much of this literature was the observation that in an efficient market economy, profits above or below the norm should quickly disappear. Such profit signals can have an important role to play in the allocation of resources, both between firms and industries. As Mueller rightly observed, much empirical work in industrial economics in the 1960s and 1970s, focused on the relationship between industry concentration and profit rates. However, once the persistence of excess profits is separated from the role of concentration in creating these profits, there is no reason why our focus should be on industry level data. In fact, the existence of firms in a given industry with profit rates continually above the industry average presents the same potential allocational inefficiencies that exist when profit rates between industries remain persistently large.[12]

Subsequent work revealed that POP could be used to throw light on a number of related issues about firm performance. For example, the distinction between a competitive industry producing homogenous products or differentiated products. In the former case, the observation that some firms were earning profits rates persistently above the industry norm would indicate that competition was inhibited because, for example, other firms were banned from using the resources or technology that enabled the more profitable firms to have lower costs, or because the more profitable firms did not exploit their competitive advantage by lowering price and expanding output at the expense of the less efficient companies. In the latter case, for example, other firms were prevented from selling a sufficiently close substitute.[13] It was also recognised that POP analyses undermined the traditional emphasis on static equilibrium in industrial structure and that they also had relevance to the treatment of welfare loss.[14]

Although some of the most recent work in this area has questioned the reliability of the standard model used to estimate POP,[15] nonetheless, perhaps the biggest advantage of POP analysis is that it surmounts the fundamental difficulty encountered when empirically examining the competitive process: the dynamic forces to which firms must adapt are difficult to observe. For example, the threat of entry, rather than entry itself, is sufficient to affect the behaviour of firms in an industry. The use of observed profit rate outcomes over time allows inferences to be drawn about the nature of the competitive process even if it is impossible to determine the particular mechanics driving the process.[16]

Methodology

The model to be estimated is defined as follows:

$$\pi^s_{i,t} = \alpha_i + \lambda_i \pi^s_{i,t-1} + \varepsilon_{i,t} \qquad\qquad \text{I}$$

Where:

$\pi^s_{i,t}$ here, is the standardised profit rate[17] for firm i in period t, defined as:

$$\pi^s_{i,t} = \pi_{i,t} - \bar{\pi}_{i,t-1} \qquad\qquad 2$$

and where $\pi_{i,t}$, is firm i's actual profit rate in year t, and $\bar{\pi}_{i,t}$, is the average (industry) profit rate in year t.

The parameters α_i and λ_i, measure long-run and short-run persistence in profitability. The sign of the parameter α_i determines whether firm i's actual long-run average profit rate is above or below the average for all firms. The parameter λ_i, measures the strength of short-run persistence in firm i's standardised profit rate. If $\lambda_i = 0$, there is no association between successive values of standardised profits for firm i. This would be the case with a perfectly competitive market structure. At the other extreme, if $\lambda_i = 1$, barriers to entry are sufficiently high that abnormal profits earned by firm i do not produce any threat of entry and therefore short-run persistence of profits is complete.[18] The intermediate case, where $0 < \lambda_i < 1$, means that short run persistence of profit is partial.[19]

Previous studies, which have focused on later and longer time periods, and which have also involved comparison between countries, have generally reported values for λ_i of 0.4–0.5.[20] In other words, the competitive process is only partial. It is also the case that firms' profit rates do not tend to converge toward the same equilibrium value in the long-run. Two interpretations follow from these findings. First, as far as the profit rates experienced by *individual* firms are concerned, there is some short-run persistence in profits. Turning to profit rates experienced by firms in an industry, the second conclusion to be drawn is that there is only limited convergence in the long-run to a norm. This latter observation might imply that firm-specific capabilities are not perfectly imitable, providing further empirical support for a resource based view perspective of intra-industry competition.

The sources used to calculate ROCE were the *Stock Exchange Official Intelligence* and Cambridge University Companies Database.[21] Limited data availability necessarily imposed severe restrictions on the sample size and the time period to be analysed. To remedy this problem, three sub-periods were selected: 1900–10, 1922–29, and 1950–59. Each of these periods correspond to different market conditions facing the Lancashire industry. In broad terms, the period 1900–10, was a general period of expansion for both capacity and exports; the second period was one of marked decline (in exports, but not capacity) and the final period witnessed a period of decline in both capacity and exports.[22]

There are a number of caveats that need to be borne in mind when comparing our results with those in the POP literature. First, data restrictions mean that the size of sample are much smaller than previous studies which have utilised sample sizes ranging between 39 and 12,986. The sample sizes used in this study for each sub-period are 15, 12, and 22, respectively. These relatively small samples obviously pose a number of econometric problems, for example, small sample bias.[23] Secondly, previous studies, focusing on the recent past, have analysed POP over longer time periods. In a summary of recent studies, Goddard and Wilson reported that the shortest time period covered was 10 years, but the average was 17 years.[24] The sub-periods covered in this study are 11, 8, and 10 years respectively. If the time period is too small there is a danger that *long-run* persistence effects might not be accurately captured. This is an especially important consideration because each of the sub-periods used were subject to powerful forces affecting profitability. For example, the second sub-period witnessed the aftermath of the collapse of the post war boom (1921), the revaluation of sterling (1925), and the formation of two major combines, Combined English Mills, and the Lancashire Cotton Corporation, both in 1929. The final sub-period encompassed the abolition of the Utility Clothing Scheme and the 'D' tax (1952), and, from the later 1950s, growing speculation about government proposals to eradicate excess capacity, which were inaugurated in the 1959 Cotton Industry Act. The final caveat to be made is that previous researchers have used much larger sample sizes and therefore they have been able to specify more sophisticated models to capture the effects of other variables which can be expected to have an influence on POP, for example, growth of sales, rate of growth of exports in relation to total sales, and ownership control.[25]

Table 2   *Regression results for persistence of profits*

	Average values of		
	alpha	*lambda*	R^2
Sub-period, 1900–10	3.3	0.54	0.35
Sub-period, 1922–29	5.6	0.6	0.65
Sub-period, 1950–59	3.2	0.62	0.38

Nonetheless, the data that are employed are the best that exist.[26] The average results for the statistically significant regressions[27] are shown in Table 2. Before discussing the observations that arise from these results, it is appropriate to state that the proportion of each sample for which statistically significant observations can be made for each sub-period, is subject to noticeable variation, being, 46.6 per cent, 92 per cent, and 27 per cent respectively.[28] Turning now to the results, a number of features are suggested. First, as far as lambda is concerned, our results seem to be slightly higher than those of previous studies,[29] ranging between 0.54 and 0.62. The reported value of lambda rests uncomfortably with the argument that the Lancashire industry was 'highly competitive'. If this was so, the value of lambda should be close to zero.

Variations in the size of lambda over our three sub-periods also deserve comment. One observation that is particularly striking is that the value of lambda increases as the industry becomes subject to increasing competition, first in export markets and then in the domestic market. *A priori*, we might have expected the opposite to hold: industries that are heavily export orientated can be expected to exhibit weaker persistence effects because fluctuations in international markets are hard to predict and control and because interna-tionally open markets may experience rapid entry driving down profits which are substantially above the norm. The second observation to be made is that lambda is much higher in second and third periods compared to 1900–10. There are a number of factors that can explain this. First, for both periods, actual or potential entry by new firms was practically zero.[30] The generally depressed condition of the industry during the 1920s, and the negative expectations about the industry's long-term future in the 1950s,[31] precluded entry and so a higher degree of persistence is to be expected.

A second factor which is relevant to the 1920s, concerns the difference in trading conditions between the American and Egyptian sections. Contemporaries were acutely aware that trading conditions were generally more prosperous in the Egyptian compared to the American section.[32] Although some attempt was made by 'American' firms to move into the 'Egyptian' section, technical reasons meant this was not always possible. The consequence was that firms in the Egyptian section – producing medium and fine combed yarns – enjoyed a higher degree of persistence in profit rates. In this context it is useful to note that two of the firms in the 1922–29 sample which had statistically significant results were renowned for their fine spinning: Crosses & Heatons, and Fine Cotton Spinners & Doublers.[33]

Turning now to the values of alpha, it is apparent that some firms did considerably better than others and this is especially pronounced for the sub-period 1922–29. One explanation has already been presented: the comparatively better trading conditions in the Egyptian compared to the American section. These average values, of course, conceal substantial differences in the experi-ences of individual firms in each sub-period. This suggests that a number of firms were able to earn persistently higher profit rates compared to their sample average in each of the three sub-periods, a finding which is also at odds with the argument that the industry was 'highly' or 'extremely' competitive.

The implication of this is that at different periods certain firms had unique characteristics (firm-specific) attributes which were not easily identifiable or transferable or imitable. In other words, although the structural characteristics of the Lancashire industry *appear* competitive, this was, in fact, a mirage: in any industry which can accurately be described as highly competitive, persistence effects should be close to zero, at least in the long-run. Even if, as I have already indicated, it is objected that the sub-periods are too short to fully capture *long-run* convergence effects, this still does not explain why some firms in each sub-period benefited from high rates of persistence.

One other observation to be made of Table 2 is that the values of R^2 indicate that the overall explanatory power of the independent variable is rather low for the sub-periods 1900–10, and 1950–59. However, the value of R^2, for the 1920s is quite high. This latter observation seems to reinforce the previous point that firms in the relatively buoyant Egyptian sector enjoyed persistently higher profit rates than those in the American section.

Discussion and conclusions

This chapter has re-assessed the competitiveness of the Lancashire cotton textile industry using persistence of profits methodology. The principal findings are that a number of firms in each sub-period benefited from persistence effects (often higher than has been reported in the previous literature), and that there is considerable evidence that firms enjoyed profit rates that were consistently above their sample averages. On the basis of these findings two conclusions are suggested.

First, reliance on the structural characteristics of an industry as a basis from which to explain performance can be misleading. While it is true that the industry had many of the features of a competitive industry such as a substantial number of firms and limited (structural) barriers to entry or exit, these characteristics did not always manifest themselves in competitive outcomes: high levels of short term persistence in profit rates have been observed for each of the sub-periods, 1900–10, 1922–29 and 1950–59. In fact, as I have already indicated, the reported values of lambda appear to have more in common with studies which have focused on the UK at a time of rapidly increasing industrial concentration, resulting in oligopolistic structures.

Following on from the above, the levels of persistence I report, which are much higher than we would expect for a highly competitive industry, suggest that the industry was composed of a number of firms which enjoyed unique advantages which were neither easily transferable or imitable: for example, the yarn market in which they operated (American or Egyptian) This suggests that a much richer and detailed analysis of firm rather than industry level behaviour is required.

Notes

1. D. A. Farnie, *The English Cotton Industry and the World Market, 1815–1896* (Clarendon: Oxford, 1979), pp. 209–10.
2. B. Ellinger and H. Ellinger, 'Japanese Competition in the Cotton Trade', *Journal of the Royal Statistical Society*, 93 (1930): 185–231, p. 211.
3. J. M. Keynes, 'Industrial Reorganisation: Cotton', in D. Moggridge (ed.), *The Collected Writings of John Maynard Keynes*, vol. 19, part II (Cambridge University Press: Cambridge, 1981), p. 631.
4. H. Clay, *Report on the Position of the English Cotton Industry* (Confidential Report for Securities Management Trust: London, 1931), p. 93.
5. Political and Economic Planning, *Report on the British Cotton Industry* (Political and Economic Planning [PEP]: London, 1934), p. 108.
6. W. Lazonick, 'Industrial Organisation and Technological Change: The Decline of the British Cotton Industry', *Business History Review*, 57 (1983), pp. 200, 204, 218. See also, W. Lazonick, 'The Cotton Industry', in B. Elbaum and W. Lazonick (eds), *The Decline of the British Economy* (Oxford University Press: Oxford, 1986), where reference is again made to 'highly competitive … industrial organisation' and 'competitive market forces', pp. 20, 45.
7. Freedom of entry is the key feature common to monopolistically and perfectly competitive industries.
8. W. Lazonick, 'Competition, Specialisation, and Industrial Decline', *Journal of Economic History*, 41 (1981), p. 36.
9. Lazonick, 'Industrial Organisation', p. 227.
10. W. Lazonick and W. Mass, 'The Performance of the British Cotton Industry, 1870–1913', *Research in Economic History*, 9 (1984), p. 15.
11. The literature is large and growing. See, in particular, D. Higgins, 'Rings, Mules and Structural Constraints in the Lancashire Textile Industry, *c.*1945–*c.*1965', *Economic History Review*, 46 (1993), pp. 342–62. D. Higgins and S. Toms, 'Firm Structure and Financial Performance: the Lancashire Textile Industry, *c.*1884–*c.*1960', *Accounting, Business & Financial History*, 7 (1997), pp. 195–232; T. Leunig, 'A British Industrial Success: Productivity in the Lancashire and New England Cotton-Spinning Industries a Century Ago', *Economic History Review*, 56 (2003), pp. 90–117.
12. D. C. Mueller, 'The Persistence of Profits Above the Norm', *Economica*, 44 (1977), pp. 369–70.
13. D. C. Mueller, *Profits in the Long Run* (Cambridge University Press: Cambridge, 1986), p. 9.
14. D. C. Mueller, *The Dynamics of Company Profits: an International Comparison* (Cambridge University Press: Cambridge, 1990) pp. 2–3, 7.
15. F. Schohl, 'Persistence of Profits in the Long Run: a Critical Extension of Some Recent Findings', *International Journal of Industrial Organisation*, 8 (1990), pp. 385–404; J. A. Goddard and J. O. S. Wilson, 'The Persistence of Profit: a New Empirical Interpretation', *International Journal of Industrial Organisation*, 17 (1999), pp. 663–87.
16. P. Gersoki and A. Jacquemin, 'The Persistence of Profits: a European Comparison',

Economic Journal, 98 (1988), pp. 375–6.

17. Profit rate is defined as the return on capital employed (ROCE). In this chapter, ROCE is defined as profit after tax and before interest and dividends divided by the total long-term capital employed. In turn, capital employed is defined as equity share capital, plus distributable reserves, plus outstanding long-term loans. These figures are expressed as percentages.

18. The possibility that $\lambda_i > 1$, means that profits above the industry norm will increase indefinitely: this can be safely ignored for the Lancashire industry!

19. If this latter case holds there is a tendency for firm i's standardised profit rate to converge towards an average or equilibrium value of: $\pi_{ip} = \alpha_i / 1 - \lambda_i$, in the long run. If $\pi_{ip} = 0$ for all firms, then all firms' profit rates converge to the same long-run average value, and there is no long-run persistence of profits. However, if π_i is greater than, or less than zero, for the sample of firms then there is long-run persistence, and no convergence to a long-run average profit rate. Because each sub-period is relatively small compared with previous studies, and because each sub-period was subject to numerous short-term shocks, calculation of a long-term equilibrium profit rate is not very informative in this context.

20. An excellent summary of these findings and the methodology employed, can be found in J. Lipczynski, J. Goddard and J. Wilson, *Industrial Organisation*, 2nd edn (Prentice Hall: London, 2005), pp. 343–7. The author is grateful to John Goddard for providing advice.

21. For a further discussion of data sources see Higgins and Toms, 'Firm Structure'.

22. These trends are covered in R. Robson, *The Cotton Industry in Britain* (Macmillan: London, 1957), table 1, pp. 332–3; table 5, p. 339.

23. This occurs when the sample size is too small to produce a reliable estimate.

24. Lipczynski, Goddard and Wilson, *Industrial Organisation*, p. 346.

25. Geroski and Jacquemin, 'The Persistence of Profits', p. 385.

26. In fact, joint work by Higgins and Toms has resulted in a comprehensive date base of ROCE for as many firms as possible in the Lancashire textile industry, c.1880–c.1960.

27. All regressions use robust standard errors. Average values for the independent variable are those which satisfy a minimum confidence level of 95 per cent.

28. These results were achieved by calculating the number of statistically significant results as a percentage of the total sample for each sub-period.

29. As reported in Lipczynski, Goddard and Wilson, *Industrial Organisation*, p. 346.

30. The increase in capacity between 1914 and 1929 is accounted for by the building of additional mills by existing firms; for example, Elk Mill was built in 1926 by Shiloh Mills. In the same year the Sir John Holden Mill was built.

31. Labour recruitment was severe during this period because other industries, such as light engineering, offered better long-term prospects. At a national level, the Lancashire industry was not thought attractive for investment purposes. The result was that even when the industry experienced buoyant conditions until 1952, this was not sufficient to attract entry.

32. Clay, *Report on the Position*, p. 9; Political and Economic Planning, *Report*, p. 52.

33. The values of lambda for these companies were 0.47 and 0.56 respectively.

6

'Working the business as one': cultural and organisational aspects of the Calico Printers' Association merger of 1899

DAVID J. JEREMY

1   Introduction

Invariably promising higher growth rates through economies of scale and market rationalisation, mergers have not always delivered their expected advantages. Research indicates that 'between 55 and 70 per cent of mergers and acquisitions failed to meet the anticipated purpose'.[1] One reason for merger failure has been a neglect of the management of culture change. This essay uses managerial insights to highlight some of the cultural and organisational problems encountered in the Calico Printers' Association (CPA) merger of 1899. For business strategists it underscores some potential problems in the corporate strategy of merger.

2   Analysing the cultural and organisational aspects of merger

Organisational culture, well established as a factor in explaining the success of organisations, has been defined by Schein as a group's basic assumptions and beliefs learnt in response to the pressures of its external environment and the problems of internal integration.[2] The dominant company culture is initially established by company founders; their successors then uphold or modify the inherited culture and defend or abandon that culture's role in the company. Schein identified a number of primary mechanisms by which leaders could establish and shape organisational culture: whatever they measured and controlled; how they reacted to organisational crises; the role model they projected; their criteria for allocating rewards and status; and their criteria for recruitment, promotion, retirement and dismissal.[3]

Culture clearly plays a part in mergers, but how and at what points could the merger be better managed by an understanding of the role of culture? In a useful survey of recent literature on the subject, Schraeder and Self reported research on elements within a prescriptive framework identified by K. Walker in 1998.[4] Some of those elements appeared prior to the merger event; some followed merger. Approximating to the Walker framework, the following pre-merger cultural elements needed to be addressed if a merger was to succeed: (1) an assessment of the cultural compatibility of the merging partners; (2) a preliminary look at strategic alternatives, followed by a due diligence examination of the chosen target; (3) the development of a flexible and comprehensive merger plan; (4) the sharing of information about the prospective merger; (5) the participation in the merger process of as many individuals as possible. During the aftermath of the merger event, culture was important in (6) enhancing commitment to the new organisation by establishing relationships and building trust; (7) constructing a new organisational culture through training, support, and socialisation; and (8) respecting individuals in the stresses they encountered in the merger process. The analysis of the CPA merger which follows addresses a number of the points made in this eight-element framework and detects within those elements some of the mechanisms noted by Schein.

The essay is in three parts: some background to the CPA merger of 1899; a cultural-organisational appraisal of arrangements prior to merger; and a cultural-organisational appraisal of post-merger leadership.

3   Trade and industry background

The CPA, incorporated on 30 November 1899, brought together 46 printing firms and 13 merchanting firms in the calico printing industry; and others soon joined. Calico printing was part of the well-known horizontal industrial structure of the UK cotton industry and formed a major component of the finishing section of the cotton textile industry (together with dyeing and bleaching). As the last step in a long processing chain, calico printing imparted colourful designs to cloth in accordance with consumers' demands for uses as diverse as ladies' dresses, curtains, furniture coverings, or children's rag books.

By the early 1890s Britain's calico printing industry printed between 1,500 million yards and 2,000 million yards per annum, of which 900 million yards to 1,000 million yards were exported, a trade worth £10 million to £11 million.[5] However, several developments put pressure on the printers' profit margins. Technologically, the adoption of roller printing machines between 1840 and 1889 increased the industry's output from about 500 million yards to nearly 2,000 million yards per annum. Roller machines drove out the hand block printers[6] and, as the industry's capacity increased from 435 to 1,100 roller printing machines, drove down production costs.[7] Prices for textile printing then moved downwards because of the competitive structure of the industry, with at least 80 printworks firms in Lancashire alone in 1898.[8] The horizontal organisation of calico printing, with the printworks relying on commission merchants for access to consumer markets, intensified competitiveness and again pushed down prices. In terms of their economic stakes in the business, printworks required much higher capital and labour costs than merchant firms: on average one roller printing machine (numbers of which became the measure of firm and industry size) and all associated fixed capital and land represented an investment of over £5,700 and a workforce of 20–30 people.[9] This allowed the merchants to exploit the printers when negotiating prices. Commission merchants allegedly controlled 80 per cent of the trade at the end of the nineteenth century.[10] While supply-side factors drove down prices, on the demand side new limits to market growth appeared with the rise of foreign rivals especially in Russia, Germany and the USA, where tariff barriers sheltered these new infant industries from British competition.[11] Thus the calico printers in the 1890s were squeezed between intensifying supply-side competitiveness and demand-side market stagnation.

Their solution, as it was for eighteen sections of the textile industries between 1890 and 1900, was a merger that would reduce competitiveness, allow price support, and cut out the commission merchant as far as possible. The 46 printing firms in the CPA reportedly commanded 830 printing machines which represented 70–80 per cent of the industry's capacity.[12] If all were running they would give employment to nearly 25,000 workers. Thus the CPA looked a formidable combine in both absolute and relative terms. (See Table 1) (Some 120 calico printers remained outside the CPA, so they would mostly have been small firms.[13]) In 1899 the CPA merger offered exciting prospects. It promised large economies of scale, reduced competition and higher prices. However, in less than three years gains from merger still lay in the future. Instead, the amalgamation was in real danger of disintegrating.

Table 1   *CPA subsidiaries, 1899 and The Management Salary Bill, 1900*

Subsidiary	Function	Date est'd	Print Works name	Location place	Location county/kingdom	Salary bill £s	Printing machines 1899
1 Black & Wingate Ltd	merchant	1816		Glasgow		2,500	
2 Shaw, James & Co. Ltd	merchant	1840		Glasgow and Manchester		1,600	
3 Allan Arthur Fletcher & Co.	merchant	1873		Glasgow and Manchester		1,500	
4 Hewit & Wingate	merchant	1858		Glasgow and Manchester		1,500	
5 Moir & Co. Ltd	merchant	1894		Glasgow		1,500	
6 Mills, James & Co.	merchant	1887		Manchester		850	
7 Bryce Smith & Co.	merchant	1860		Manchester		600	
8 Hoyle's Prints Ltd	merchant	1780		Manchester		600	
9 Waters, John & Co. Ltd	merchant	1883		Glasgow		600	
10 Gourlie, William & Sons	merchant	1831		Glasgow		550	
11 Gray, James & Sons	merchant	1888		Glasgow		500	
12 Wright & Whittaker	merchant	1895		Manchester		500	
13 Gemmell & Harter	merchant	1866		Manchester		500	
1 Potter, Edmund & Co. Ltd	printer	1825	Dinting Vale	Glossop	Derbyshire	6,000	51
2 Gartside & Co. of Manchester Ltd	printer	1865	Buckton Vale Works	Stalybridge	Lancashire	5,393	74
3 Thornliebank Printing Co. Ltd	printer	1798	Thornliebank	Glasgow	Scotland	4,100	45
4 Schwabe, Salis, & Co. Ltd	printer	1788	Rhodes Works	Middleton	Lancashire	4,090	40
5 Birkacre Printing Co. Ltd	printer	1796	Birkacre Works	Chorley	Lancashire	3,500	16

Subsidiary	Function	Date est'd	Print Works name	Location		Salary bill £s	Printing machines 1899
				place	county/kingdom		
6 Calvert, J H & Bros Ltd	printer	1835	Oakenshaw PW	Accrington	Lancashire	3,500	11
7 Rumney, William & Co. Ltd	printer	1854	Stubbins P W	Ramsbottom	Lancashire	3,400	31
8 Grafton, Frederick William, & Co. Ltd	printer	1782	Broad Oak Works	Accrington	Lancashire	3,300	34
9 Ashton, F W & Co. Ltd	printer	1816	Newton Bank P W	Hyde	Cheshire	3,100	15
10 Rossendale Printing Co. Ltd	printer	1790	Love Clough	Rawtenstall	Lancashire	2,400	24
11 Black, James, & Co. Ltd	printer	1828	Dalmonach PW	Dunbarton	Scotland	2,400	30
12 Kay, Robert & Sons Ltd	printer	1860	Adelphi P W	Salford	Manchester	2,104	8
13 Knowles, Samuel, & Co. Ltd	printer	1820	Kirklees P W	Tottington	Lancashire	2,050	19
14 Hayfield Printing Co. Ltd	printer	1858	Wood P W	Hayfield	Derbyshire	2,040	12
15 Strines Printing Co. Ltd	printer	1794	Strines P W	Disley	Cheshire	2,000	20
16 Kennedy, John Lawson & Co.	printer	1850	Hartshead P W	Stalybridge	Lancashire	2,000	16
17 Inglis & Wakefield Ltd	printer	1841	Busby P W	near Glasgow	Scotland	1,985	23
18 Gibson & Costobadie	printer	1800	Hodge P W	Broadbottom	Cheshire	1,800	16
19 Higginbotham, Samuel & Co. Ltd	printer	1800	New Springfield Works	Glasgow	Scotland	1,800	19
20 Dalglish, R, Falconer & Co. Ltd	printer	1805	Lennox Mill P W	Glasgow	Scotland	1,800	20
21 Brier, John & Sons	printer	1835	Oak Bank P W*	Bollington	Cheshire	1,800	9
22 Wood, Christopher Ltd	printer	1847	Brinscall P W	Chorley	Lancashire	1,800	13
23 Buckley, Edward & Joseph Ltd	printer	1863	Brookside P W	Leigh	Lancashire	1,800	7

| | | | | Location | | | Printing |
Subsidiary	Function	Date est'd	Print Works name	place	county/kingdom	Salary bill £s	machines 1899
24 Rumney, Edward. B., & Co. Ltd	printer	1750	Watford Bridge	New Mills	Derbyshire	1,700	18
25 Boyd, Thomas & Co.	printer	1825	Levenshulme PW	Levenshulme	Manchester	1,500	19
26 Hill, John F & Co.	printer		Bowker Bank P W	Crumpsall	Manchester	1,500	
27 Bennett, John & Sons Ltd	printer	1821	Birch Vale PW	Birch Vale	Derbyshire	1,300	20
28 Bradshaw, Hammond & Co. Ltd	printer	1838	Reddish P W	Reddish	Cheshire	1,250	13
29 Kinder Printing Co. Ltd	printer	1849	Kinder P W	Hayfield	Derbyshire	1,250	17
30 Bayley & Craven Ltd	printer	1806	Agecroft P W	Pendleton	Lancashire	1,200	12
31 Heys, Z, & Sons	printer	1842	South Arthurlie Works	Barrhead, Renfrewshire	Scotland	1,200	28
32 Bingswood Printing Co. Ltd	printer	1873	Bingswood PW	Whaley Bridge	Derbyshire	1,100	11
33 Walker, Robert & Sons	printer	1845	Quarlton Vale P W	Bolton	Lancashire	1,000	7
34 Saxby, Charles, Ltd.	printer	1794	Furness P W	Furness Vale	Derbyshire	900	9
35 Hardie, Stark & Co. Ltd	printer	1830	Locherfield P W	Bridge of Weir, Renfrewshire	Scotland	700	7
36 Macnab, A & Co.	printer	1843	Lillyburn P W	Lillyburn	Scotland	600	12
37 Whalley Abbey Printing Co. Ltd	printer	1860	Whalley Abbey P W	Blackburn	Lancashire	600	25
38 Gateside Printing Co.	printer	1881	Gateside P W	Barrhead, Renfrewshire	Scotland	600	6
39 Springfield Printing Co.	printer	1842	Springfield P W	near Glasgow	Scotland	500	7
40 Murray, Adam & Co.	printer	1860	Kincaid P W	near Glasgow	Scotland	500	6

Subsidiary	Function	Date est'd	Print Works name	Location place	Location county/kingdom	Salary bill £s	Printing machines 1899
41 Macgregor, A R & Co. Ltd	printer	1868	Mile-end Works	Mile-end, Glasgow	Scotland	500	4
42 Semple, J C & Co. Ltd	printer					500	
43 Syddall Bros Ltd.	printer		Chadkirk P W	Romiley	Cheshire	500	
44 Andrew, George & Sons	printer	1824	Compstall Works	Compstall	Cheshire	420	15
45 Laxton, F & Co. Ltd	printer	1853		near Manchester		400	8
46 Kershaw, Whittam & Taylor	printer					400	
47 Millfield Printing Co.	printer	1895	Millfield P W	Barrhead, Renfrewshire	Scotland		6
48 Low Mill Printing Co. Ltd	printer	1876		Chorley	Lancashire		8
49 Watson, William & Co. Ltd	printer	1889		near Manchester			13
50 Ferryfield Printing Co. Ltd	printer			Alexandria, Dunbartonshire	Scotland		
						97,082	824

Dalmuir Printing Co. (6 machines) had no CPA director

Sources: Manchester Central Library, Archives, CPA, Register of Directors and Managers, 1899–1905 (M75/1, Box 926); CPA Prospectus, 8 December 1899, reprinted (with slight differences in lists of participating firms) in Henry W. Macrosty, *The Trust Movement in British Industry: A Study of Business Organisation* (Longmans: London, 1907) and Geoffrey Turnbull, *A History of the Calico Printing Industry of Great Britain* (Sherratt: Altringham, 1951). Locations listed in John Worrall, *The Cotton Spinners and Manufacturers' Directory* (Worrall: Oldham, 1898), p. 233; unless indicated with * which comes from *Kelly's Directory of the Manufacturers of Textile Fabrics* (Kelly: London, 1880), pp. 144–7. Other 1890s directory information from Nerys Tunnicliffe and Jennifer Higgins of the Mitchell Library, Glasgow.

4   A cultural-organisational appraisal of CPA pre-merger arrangements

Did the framers of the merger make any attempt to assess the cultural compatibility of the merger's prospective constituents? In a formal sense the question is anachronistic: cultural compatibility was an alien concept a century ago. Nevertheless, Victorian printworks proprietors would have been well aware of the social, as opposed to the economic, characteristics of their own and of rival works.

Size had cultural implications. In the difficult trading conditions of the 1880s and 1890s, many smaller printing firms were converted into limited liability companies whose investors, many of them drysalters (dealers in dyes and chemicals), demanded low price and high throughput to achieve profits. 'Kinder' in 1892 complained that, 'they expect to get their output of 1,000 pieces a week per machine for an expenditure of a penny a piece, for designs, engraving, and sampling! The result is that "shirtings" are being done at five shillings for 140 yards, and "benzo reds and blacks" for 5s 6d for the same length. I should like to ask, Where is the scope for talent on such a base of prices?'[14] The smaller the works, the more likely it was to be producing low-quality prints at cut-throat prices, thereby attracting the less able managers, colourists and printers. In addition, a small firm had more limited market access than a large business. With under ten roller printing machines and under 2,000 copper rollers, a small firm could compete in African or Asian markets but not in the South American trade. That 'requires big assortments of designs and colourings' which only a large concern with 30 or more printing machines and 10,000 copper pattern rollers could produce.[15] Inevitably these small limited companies developed a very different ethos from that of the larger printworks whose reputations rested on quality and innovation. Merging with these small firms had only one purpose: their removal.

Age was another factor in shaping culture. Other things being equal, the older the printworks, the greater its stock of print designs and of the copper shells on which they were engraved, and the greater the accumulated knowledge and skill of the firm. Of the 45 printworks whose date of establishment is known, eight were founded in the second half of the eighteenth century. They included three of the leading printworks in the industry: Grafton's at Broad Oak, Accrington, Lancashire; Schwabe's at Rhodes, Middleton, Lancashire; and Thornliebank (the largest firm in the industry) near Glasgow. Another 11 were founded between 1800 and 1830, including Potter's, of Dinting Vale, Glossop, Derbyshire. During the seventy years prior to the CPA merger another 26 firms emerged but only one, Gartside's of Buckton Vale, Stalybridge, Cheshire, ranked with the largest and most innovative.

A works' age, with its implications for the worth of its accumulated skill and design resources, was modified by its capacity to exploit the cotton goods' value chain. Some works were dedicated, stand-alone printworks, with less potential in this direction. In contrast, Buckton Vale printworks was part of an integrated multinational empire run by J. H. Gartside. In 1890 Gartside & Co. were reported as a progressive firm which, since its foundation in 1865, had expanded from 'dyeing and finishing of figured shirtings and beetled silesias' to 'the printing of twills, angolas, sateens, and flannelettes'. In the 1880s they 'took up the general business of calico printers, aiming principally at the production of high-class cretonnes and dress prints for the home and foreign markets'. Latterly they added the 'manufacturing, dyeing, and finishing of bookbinders' cloth'. In 1890 they boasted 20 printing machines ranging from 3 to 12 colours, and 12 embossing machines, with another 12 being installed.[16]

The fundamental cultural variable which any appraisal of target firms needed to take into account was ownership. Most of the print firms started as family partnerships. As noted, the vast majority converted to limited liability companies in the difficult trading conditions of the last two decades of the nineteenth century. Even with limited liability, family control was maintained to a degree. Consequently, paternalism was a dominant culture in the constituent firms that amalgamated in the CPA in 1899. For example, at Thornliebank, five miles from the centre of Glasgow on Auldhouse Burn, where the printworks employed between 1,500 and 2,000 persons in the 1880s, the Crum family in enlightened fashion provided over 400 workers' houses, built a village hall, public baths, and school, paid the salary of a village nurse, and supplied the premises for a co-operative store. The family established a United Presbyterian church and contributed £1,500 towards the building of its rival, Thornliebank parish church. Most of these amenities were established before 1886 when the business was converted into a public limited company.[17] Thereafter, a more commercial attitude was necessarily adopted because family members no longer acted on their own behalf but on behalf of shareholders. Thus in 1887, the directors minuted, 'The Board resolved that, in its corporate capacity, it is inexpedient that the company should contribute to the funds of any religious organisation, but in consideration that the Minister of the Thornliebank United Presbyterian congregation has for many years occupied one of the company's villas free of rent, it was agreed that Mr Weilde should be allowed to continue his occupation of the manse until further notice at the nominal rent of £5 per annum.'[18] Though more distanced, paternalism persisted.

Conversion to a public company in 1886 required the psychological transfer of loyalties from the Crum family to the new public company. The former proprietors underscored and eased the transition by making key workers employee-shareholders. So while the brothers Alexander and William Graham Crum purchased 600 £100 pound shares each (and another 200 jointly held), the company's Manchester merchant bought 100 shares; the Thornliebank printworks manager 50; the Manchester salesman 30; the assistant manager 20; the secretary, printing manager, engraver, and chemist 10 each; down to two shares for two of the Manchester salesmen. In some cases the company lent employees the money to purchase shares at par.[19]

Illustrative of corporate paternalism was the generous welfare support which the Crums gave their key employees in life crises. The works' surgeon, forced by ill-health to retire, received a pension of £35 per annum.[20] The sub-manager, H. J. R. Stuart, was given leave of absence for three to four months to take a voyage to Australia for the benefit of his health, the passage money being paid for him by the company and his salary continuing.[21] Such generosity could only accumulate powerful obligations and loyalties, as well as a positive corporate reputation. Clearly small firms could not match this kind of compassion.

By the 1890s many of the larger printworks employed a scientifically trained chemist. In contrast, the smaller printworks relied on colourists with empirical rather than scientific knowledge. Thornliebank exemplified the new, progressive attitude to science and innovation. This was not surprising. The brothers' father was Walter Crum FRS, and their brother-in-law was William Thomson, later Lord Kelvin, scientist, inventor and entrepreneur. As Sir William Thomson, Professor of Natural Philosophy at the University of Glasgow, he purchased 40 £100 shares in the limited company.[22] No doubt he kept an eye on the company's chemist, William Edward Kay (1855–1938) who had been 'brilliant pupil and for years personal assistant' of Sir Henry Roscoe, Professor of Chemistry at Owens College, Manchester, 1857–85. Through Roscoe's friendship with Walter Crum, Kay was invited to Thornliebank.[23] He became one of the relatively few employee-shareholders, receiving ten shares in 1887.[24]

Another paternalist company community was developed by J. H. Gartside at Buckton Vale. However, Thornliebank and Gartside were large employers, with 1,500 to 2,000 workers. A much smaller firm like the Kinder Printing Co. at Hayfield, with 17 roller printing machines in 1892, employed 300–400 people[25] and would not have found it worthwhile to provide any more welfare facilities than two or three dozen cottages. In the Sett River valley, from Hayfield to New Mills, there were four printworks in the space of four miles.[26] With a total of 67 machines, they employed around 2,000 people and appear, from the dearth of closely located housing, to have drawn most of their workforce from New Mills. Of the four, John Bennett & Sons at Birch Vale (20 machines) owned 73 dwellings, mostly cottages, while, conversely, E. B. Rumney at Watford Bridge (18 machines) owned only one residence and four cottages.[27] The minimal employer concerns of the much smaller constituents of the CPA merger would have contrasted sharply with the enveloping paternalistic ethos associated with the largest printworks in the proposed combine.

Did the promoters of the merger examine the strategic alternatives and conduct due diligence? What was proposed was a plan of horizontal integration.

The main strategic alternative was vertical integration, of which the industry could see at least one major example. This was Gartside & Co. John Henry Gartside (1833–1906) had begun in manufacturing, at the Wellington Mills, Whitelands Road, Ashton of which he became the head. By 1888 he headed an eponymous limited company capitalised at £600,000 and owning spinning and weaving mills at Ashton, Dukinfield, Hollingworth, and Ardwick (totalling 100,000 spindles and 4,000 powerlooms in 1890), as well as a large dyeing and printing works at Buckton Vale. With 74 printing machines in 1899, Buckton Vale may have employed as many as 2,250 people, assuming each machine gave employment to 20 or 30 persons. This rare, vertically integrated business empire was completed by a merchant warehouse employing eighty people at 56 Fountain Street, Manchester.[28] In 1888 Gartside also owned a printworks in northern France: a foreign direct investment which looked particularly valuable after the Meline tariff of 1892.[29]

Gartside's example was not lost on the architects of the merger, of whom Gartside himself was one. As they announced in their prospectus of 8 December 1899,

> The strength of the Association is shown by the fact that it includes nearly every leading house of the trade, and that these supply goods not only to all branches of the home trade, but practically to every open market of the world. The businesses also deal with all sections of the trade, and include the production of every description of printed cotton, dress goods, furnitures, cretonnes, linings, flannelettes, and also of delaines and mixed fabrics. In addition, some of the businesses own large spinning and weaving plants.[30]

The primary purposes of the merger were to achieve economies of scale through horizontal integration and to stabilise prices by reducing capacity. However, the possession of a significant spinning and weaving capacity provided a valuable cushion when demand for calico printing from the commission merchants weakened. It also gave the printers some economic clout when negotiating prices with merchants. The horizontal integration appeared to have added strength in view of Gartside's foreign direct investment in French printworks.

How was the diligence exercise performed? The evidence suggests, in some haste. At Thornliebank the directors voted on 14 February 1899 to approve 'the action of two of its members who, at a preliminary meeting in Manchester of parties favourable to the project, had agreed that the heritable property, machinery etc. of the company might be valued with a view to a possible amalgamation.'[31] On 20 October 1899 the *Dyer and Calico Printer* prematurely announced the CPA merger, adding, 'it is understood that stocks and valuations were taken at the end of last month, and that all firms concerned have accepted the valuations.'[32] This suggests a minimal period of six or seven months for the due diligence exercise by the accountants and valuers. By mid-November at the latest the valuation was complete, because at that time the CPA contract was ready for the Thornliebank directors to sign – no more than 10 months for the valuation process.[33]

At 10.0 a.m. on Saturday 2 December 1899, the first meeting of the CPA board was held in the offices of their accountants and promoters of the merger, the well-established firm of Messrs Jones, Crewdson & Youatt at 7 Norfolk Street, Manchester.[34] The certificate of incorporation dated 30 November 1899 was produced and an agreement was signed by the majority of those subscribing to the company's memorandum of association, appointing them the first directors – a total of 79 men.[35] A company prospectus, inviting the public to purchase CPA shares, was issued on 8 December 1899. Thus in less than eleven months the CPA came into legal existence.

Was this enough time to perform due diligence on 59 firms (with one or two more soon joining) spread across the north-west of England and westwards of Glasgow? It depended, presumably, on the size of the teams and the time allowed for undertaking the exercise. The examination of the accounts of the firms in the prospective association was conducted by Jones, Crewdson & Youatt. The valuation of physical assets, totalling over 2,000 acres of land, a number of Manchester warehouses, plant and machinery including 830 printing machines, 277,264 cotton spindles, and 6,656 power looms, was undertaken by Edward Rushton, Son, & Kenyon, also of Norfolk Street, Manchester.[36] The accountants reported problems owing to the firms' various dates of stocktaking and therefore took an aggregate figure over a period 'mainly of five years'.[37] The valuers may not have known about some idiosyncrasies of the various printworks. For example, the water supply (on which a printworks' profitability depended as much as upon its capital equipment) differed between each of the works. Exploiting water character-istics rested on knowledge possessed by the master colourist, the chemist (where there was one), and, usually, the print works manager. Sharing that knowledge was unlikely because technical secretiveness, one aspect of corporate culture, notoriously prevailed in printworks.[38] Culture plainly had implications for due diligence, especially if diligence was conducted in haste. Neither accountants nor valuers allowed for goodwill.

Was there a flexible and comprehensive merger plan? The merger was promoted by the accountant Ernest Crewdson. His firm had already promoted two large textile mergers, English Sewing Cotton Co. (1897) and the Bradford Dyers' Association (1898) and would shortly promote the Bleachers' Association (1900).[39] So he brought some experience to the calico printers' re-organisation, for which he was paid well: 2 per cent of the £8,047,031 purchase price (i.e. £160,941), for all flotation expenses up to allotment of shares (but excluding legal expenses relating to conveyancing).[40] Evidently Crewdson negotiated with the major printing firms, one at a time, after preliminary discussions had established a willingness to combine. At the end of July 1899 four of the Thornliebank directors (William G. Crum, his son Walter G. Crum, John Jackson and Peter Moir) travelled to Manchester to discuss conditions for their entry to the CPA. They certainly had targets in mind. One was a good price for their own business (see below). Another was a target for the merger itself. They were unwilling to join unless Crewdson could bring together firms possessing in aggregate at least 600 calico printing machines.[41] Only in this way, of course, could the merged firms control pricing in the industry.

The purpose of the merger was contained in the published prospectus. It was to bring stability and revival to the trade after two years of exceptionally depressed market conditions. This would be achieved by no longer selling goods below cost price; realising economies of scale, in buying, finance and concentration of production; and preventing duplication of products between the Association's firms. The amalgamation would also be able to take the best designs and inventions from among their pooled resources; meet the competition, in quality and prices; and, with their foreign assets, break into overseas markets.[42]

Last, how extensive was corporate participation? To what extent was information communicated about the merger and its impact? How were those most affected by impending merger treated? The extent to which knowledge of the merger was relayed to the workforces of the constituent firms is unknown. However, at Thornliebank the directors took steps to cushion the transition. In November 1899 they gave five-year contracts at current salaries to three directors: John Jackson, chief salesman, Manchester; Peter Moir, company secretary; and John Riley, printworks manager (formerly a chemist at Steiners' Sunnyside Printworks in the Rossendale Valley[43]), also of Thornliebank.[44] In April 1900, just prior to the liquidation of the Thornliebank company, the directors voted to distribute £2,000, under an unspecified predetermined scheme, to their work people.[45]

How far other constituent firms made such *ex gratia* payment is unknown. Five-year contracts were certainly made with all the vendors who consented to remain as printworks managers.[46] As far as capital gains were made, several pieces of evidence suggest that the shareholders of the constituent firms (or their proprietors) were handsomely recompensed by the CPA merger. In 1892 an industry insider estimated, from national figures, that 'the value of a printworks, including land, buildings, and everything else, [was] about £5,000 per machine, overhead as a going concern.'[47] The assets of the 59 firms in the CPA merger were valued at £8,047,031.[48] If their 277,264 cotton spindles and 6,656 power looms were worth £443,264,[49] their printworks (with a total of 830 printing machines) would have been valued at £9,161 per machine. These global numbers suggest that the vendors joining the CPA made capital gains of over 80 per cent above an open market disposal (there being little inflation during the 1890s). The picture is confirmed by the shareholders' vote of thanks to the Thornliebank directors: 'we as shareholders desire to express our appreciation of the services rendered us by the Directors in making so favourable a bargain for us with the Calico Printers Association.'[50] Thornliebank printworks was valued at £522,000.[51] With 45 printing machines, that came out at £11,600 per machine: no wonder the Thornliebank shareholders were grateful.

5   A cultural-organisational appraisal of CPA post-merger developments: leadership lost, 1899–1901

Neither in the short run nor in the longer term was the CPA a great success for shareholders. The first two years' accounts to 31 December 1901 showed no ordinary dividend was paid and nothing was placed in reserves; but £202,550 was passed to the vendors. No ordinary dividend was declared in 1902 either. Meantime, F. Steiner & Co., Turkey red dyers and printers of Church near Accrington, who stayed out of the CPA, declared ordinary dividends of 8 per cent in 1899 and 1900, and 3 per cent in 1901.[52] The year 1902 was a bad one for both the CPA and Steiner. The Steiner directors blamed the state of foreign business, depreciation of stocks, and a summer drought.[53] In the long run, between 1900 and 1917 the CPA was the worst performing of nine textile conglomerates formed at the end of the nineteenth century. Its average annual dividend of 2.44 per cent was less than half those of English Sewing Cotton, Fine Cotton Spinners & Doublers, and the Bradford Dyers Association, and a tenth of the 31.5 per cent average dividend annually declared by J. & P. Coates Ltd.[54] The CPA merger became a textbook example of how not to structure a large-scale organisation – literally so because in 1907 Henry Macrosty, an academic at the London School of Economics, published a full account of the newly formed CPA (see note 9). What went wrong?

If Schein is right, the blame for failure to 'work the business as one' (the heart of the problem, according to the shareholders' Investigation Committee of 1902) rested with the original leadership. Crewdson, the merger promoter, might have given bad advice about the new corporate structure. (Similar problems occurred at English Sewing Cotton, his earlier promotion, and at the Bleachers' Association, his later one.[55]) Alternatively, his advice was ignored. In either case, the ultimate choice of the initial CPA organisational structure rested with its leaders – the first two chairmen and their closest associates, presumably the heads of the largest constituent firms in the merger. Assuming that leaders established and shaped organisational culture by how they reacted to organisational crises, the role model they projected, and their criteria for allocating rewards and status (some of the mechanisms identified by Schein), hints of what went wrong and how it was corrected lie in the profiles of the two chairmen and the rewards they permitted their vendor-managers.

The first chairman of the CPA was Francis Frederick Grafton (b. 1859), only surviving son of a better-known father. Frederick William Grafton (1825–90), a Liberal and MP for North East Lancashire, 1880–85, and for the Accrington division, 1885–86, was a merchant and calico printer and founder of F. W. Grafton & Co., who owned Broad Oak Printworks at Accrington and who left £216,000 at his death.[56] 'Kinder' (who knew the industry well), writing in 1892, spoke of 'the first houses [in the trade], such as the Potters, Graftons, or Crums'.[57]

At the inaugural meeting of the CPA on 2 December 1899 Francis Frederick Grafton was unanimously elected chairman (term, until the ordinary general meeting of 1903) by the vendor-shareholders (of whom 79 were present). Immediately, a telegram was read out from George McConnel, the highly respected and innovating head of Edmund Potter & Co., absent due to chronic ill-health, urging unanimous support for Grafton: 'his name, his character, his ability, his age, all mark him for our captain, and with such a leader we will commence the twentieth century with splendid prospects.'[58]

Grafton, with his wife, two children, and four servants, lived at Barley Grange, Bollington, near Macclesfield, on the Pennine edge of the Cheshire plain, forty miles from Broad Oak. Like his father before him, he appeared in lists of the landed gentry.[59] He evidently appealed on account of his firm's high reputation and his relative youthfulness, being just forty years of age. However, he was ranged against more than 80 co-directors, only recently many of them heads of 60 rival firms. In a matter of months, however, he proved unequal to the task of empowering his managing directors to run the newly created business efficiently.

Grafton's misjudgement and weakness appeared early on. At that first board meeting in December 1899, he conceded an imprudent precedent that spoke louder than his earlier avowals of impartiality. Samuel Knowles (of Kirklees Printworks, Tottington, Bury) rose to explain that he was unaware that the 'plan' for choosing directors allowed only one representative per constituent company on the board and that, consequently, he would resign in favour of his son Joshua Knowles. Grafton immediately proposed that an exception be made and both Knowles were appointed CPA directors.[60] The chance to check the expansion of the CPA board, indeed to shrink it massively, which was part of the organisational solution to the CPA's governance problems, was lost.

Grafton faced (and shared in forming) an impossible organisational structure. At the first meeting of the board, three vice-chairman and four managing directors were elected, all (with the chairman) forming a management board, the managing directors being full time.[61] Later a number of functional committees were formed, for buying, finance, contracts, and the like.[62] A consultative committee to advise the managing directors was formed in October 1900.[63] The printworks (branches), the larger ones with a merchant representative in Manchester, were grouped in 10 clusters, each headed by a group manager.[64]

Built into this structure were conflicts between direction and management: conflicts within the boardroom, and conflicts between legal duties and business functions. While Grafton was preoccupied with negotiating price agreements with the CPA's main rivals (F. Steiner & Co., United Turkey Red Co. and Bradford Dyers' Association), some of the bigger branches settled their own prices independently, below CPA minimum.[65] After just a few months, directors began to voice their complaints in public: some felt they were not sufficiently apprised of the decisions being taken by the management board, with respect to acquisitions – which was related to rationalisation of the CPA and the industry's capacity. Essentially, there were deep divisions between the branch managers and the head office. Assheton Clegg, manager of Grafton's, recalled, 'For the first two years we were always very hostile to the policy of the managing directors.'[66] From the centre, Lennox Lee, one of the managing directors, noted that when a specialist, such as an engineer or an experienced works manager, was sent from head office to one of the branches his advice was often ignored.[67] Nor, in mass meetings of directors, was it likely that landed magnates such as the Crums or J. H. Gartside would have regarded directors from small faltering printworks as their economic or social equals.

Under company law, the owners of the CPA were its shareholders. As the principal they delegated authority to the board of directors, their agent, to run the business on their behalf. Management below the boardroom was legally subservient to the board. Among the legal duties guiding company directors at the beginning of the century, the foremost was fiduciary duty, to act honestly and in good faith in the interest of their principal, the members of the company.[68] When the directors found themselves acting as managers their duty was to put CPA interest above the self-interest of their own printworks-merchanting branch. Too frequently this legal duty was violated.

Grafton could do nothing about the capital benefits that joining the CPA handed to its constituent firm owners. However, had he seen the problem and had he possessed enough willpower and perception, he might have struck at the salary arrangements for CPA managers. Each of the 128 vendors had an agreement giving him management of his own branch for five years.[69] As the Thornliebank boardroom minutes show, five-year salary contracts for printworks managers were part of the package negotiated before the CPA came into existence. The legality of these awards might have been challenged on the grounds that they predated the CPA. If this was not possible, a general meeting might have been convened to cut back managerial salaries: over half the ordinary shares were offered for public subscription, so in theory this might have been possible. Yet Grafton made no attempt to disturb the salary levels of the CPA's middle managers. He simply confirmed them.

Disagreements between the managing directors and the vendor managers undermined Grafton's zest for his job. Fearing for his health, he resigned on 5 September 1900, followed the day after by his managing directors. His exit was precipitous. In the 1901 Census he described himself as 'retired calico printer'.[70] From chairing the CPA, one of the largest organisations in the cotton textile industry, he descended to chairing Bollington Urban District Council.[71]

Where Grafton was relatively young, the second chairman, John Henry Gartside (noted above), was elderly. Of wide experience and formerly a CPA vice-chairman, he realised the nature of the CPA's problems when he took over on 25 October 1900 after a short interregnum. The Manchester papers in autumn 1900 reported him to be the largest CPA shareholder, which meant that he was the most powerful man in the CPA boardroom.[72] Born in Saddleworth, 'where his father owned a small property',[73] he started as a salesman for Messrs Swires, at Bank Mills, Ashton-under-Lyne in the 1850s. In the 1880s and 1890s he built a remarkable vertically integrated, multinational textile empire, already noted, and a considerable personal fortune. Gartside's seat in 1892 was Cholmondeley Castle, Cheshire.[74] Later he moved to Overstone Park, Northampton, originally built for Samuel Jones Loyd, Baron Overstone (1796–1883), one of the richest Victorian bankers.[75] At his death in 1906 Gartside left £217,000. He was unusual in other respects. As merchant-manufacturer, he travelled extensively in France, Germany and Switzerland, countries which after 1870 were overhauling Britain in the race for economic growth. His responses suggested a man of broad entrepreneurial vision and action. A multinational perspective took Gartside into mining ventures in Mexico, British Columbia, and South Africa. His sense that British businessmen must learn about their overseas competitors was so strong that he endowed the Gartside scholarships at Owens College (Manchester University) to enable a student to travel abroad and study industry and commerce on the Continent or in the USA.[76]

On the CPA board Gartside established a consultative committee of 12 directors to link the managing directors with the mass of 70 or 80 boardroom members. He too failed to run the organisation 'as one'. Printworks managers, acting as directors, could overrule anything proposed by the managing directors. Managing directors, seen as Manchester salesmen, excited the hostility of practical men in the distant works. On a weekly basis one or other of the branch printworks in the CPA was breaching Association prices.[77]

Additionally, Gartside's financial weight counted against him on the CPA board.[78] He lent the cash-strapped combine £200,000 in autumn 1900, shortly before moving to the chairmanship. The loan was repaid by April 1901, but Gartside's acquisition of power apparently alarmed the other directors. After company profits failed to improve and after he publicised the conflict between the managing directors and the vendor-managers when he addressed the share-holders' annual meeting in April 1901, he lost the confidence of his managing directors. Gartside resigned on 27 August 1901, admitting to a personal investment in a bleachworks (thereby disclosing a conflict, and a diminution, of interest in CPA affairs).[79] His managing directors followed suit. He left all his CPA directorships on 2 January 1902.[80]

For Grafton and Gartside the major problem was the economic independence of the vendor-managers. The generous valuations of their companies when sold to the CPA have been noted. Capital gains at these levels lent vendor-managers a sense of security, even invincibility. At the management level, the sale of the family printworks business to the CPA offered the best of both worlds. If the family's stream of competent managers was dwindling, now was the time to exit the trade without loss of ownership and dividend income. More sanguine prospects encouraged family members to stay in printworks management.

Evidence on CPA managerial salaries helps to explain why a CPA corporate culture eluded the first two chairmen. Initially many of these managers were vendors and directors. Within a year of its formation in 1899 the CPA had 146 managers. Two of them (Grafton, the chairman, and J. H. Gartside, the largest shareholder) had no printworks management functions. Six were based in the Manchester headquarters.[81] This left 132 in charge of the operating units, the printworks and the merchanting businesses. Of these, 22 ran 12 merchant firms and 110 the 46 printing firms.

Table 2   *Range of CPA managers' salaries, 1899–1900 (£s)*

£	number in range	Director and manager (merchant)	Manager (merchant)	Head office specialists
over 2,000	1	1 (0)		
1,500–1,999	8	5 (0)	3 (0)	
1,000–1,499	30	25 (2)	5 (0)	
750–999	22	17 (2)	5 (1)	
500–749	56	24 (7)	32 (7)	5
250–499	20	6 (1)	13 (2)	1
under 250	1	1		
Total	138 (22)	79 (12)	53 (10)	6

NB The salaries of the remaining six are unknown.
Source: Manchester Central Library, Archives, CPA, Register of Directors and Managers, 1899–1905, CPA M75/1, box 926.

As Table 2 shows, one manager (George Bolden) was paid over £2,000 (£2,013). Not only was he director-manager of Gartside's of Stalybridge, one of the largest subsidiary firms in the CPA. In addition he was in charge of the overseas selling of all the firms in the group and head of the important function of 'job settling' i.e. negotiating prices with merchants (internal or external or both, unclear) for imperfect printers' work.[82] Gartside's employed maybe 3,000 persons. Bolden's salary can be compared to the £5,000 paid in 1905 to the general manager of the London & North Western Railway, which employed 75,000 people.[83] At the other end of the scale one manager received less than £250 a year. Benjamin Pollard, manager of Gateside Printing Co. in Scotland, was on £130 for two years, but then moved up to £150 in his third year.

Other points emerge from Table 2. Nearly a quarter of the group were paid over £1,000 a year, while half were paid between £500 and £1,000. Clearly there were classes of manager, some highly valued, some little-valued (Pollard's £130 a year was little more than twice an agricultural labourer's wage), some in between. Noticeably, printworks managers were better paid than the merchant managers. Of 39 managers earning over £1,000 a year, only two were merchants; yet the ratio of printers to merchants, among the managers, was five to one. Managers' salaries grouped by firm (Table 3) reveal that while printworks managers comprised 76 per cent of the managerial workforce they received 84 per cent of the aggregate managerial salary bill. Bonuses, which are imperfectly recorded, could well have altered this picture. At any rate, while the print managers averaged £766, the merchants averaged much less, £582.

Table 3   *CPA management salary bill, 1900*

		Number of managers		Total bill £		Average salary £
1	Head office	6	4.20%	2,850	2.90%	475
12	Merchant firms	22	15.30%	12,800	12.80%	582
46	Printing firms	110	76.40%	84,282	84.30%	766
		138	95.80%	99,932	100.00%	724

(144 actual total)

Number of managers excludes F. F. Grafton and J. H. Gartside who were not paid for the management of operating units.

Source: As for Table 2.

Analysing the aggregate salary bill by subsidiary, as in Table 1, shows that among the printing firms the managerial wages, in general, positively correlated with the size of firm (as measured by the number of calico printing machines belonging to the subsidiary in 1899). The four largest firms ran up the largest management salary bills. Where size does not seem to have pushed up firm-level managerial wages, other factors presumably came into play, such as the practical skills of the individual manager, the overall value of the printworks output, and the subsidiary firm's market share.

Three broad impressions emerge from this study of the CPA's original managerial salary bill. There was a wide range between individual managers, with the highest-paid earning thirteen times the least. There was a wide range between the individual printworks, with the highest works management salary bill fifteen times greater than that of the smallest. Third, gauged by average per capita salary, the printworks managers earned 25 per cent more than merchant managers and 33 per cent more than headquarters professionals.

Rewards confirm attitudes and behaviour. The generous capital and income rewards received by the CPA's vendor-managers in the first three years of its existence sent the wrong top-down cultural message. The independent behaviour preserved by these vendor managers from their pre-merger existence prevented the CPA merger from realising its promised corporate potential. Schein's leadership theory, together with the historical evidence, suggests that this situation can be attributed to the CPA's first two chairmen.

6   Conclusion

The great amalgamations formed in the first merger wave of the 1890s and early 1900s encountered organisational and cultural challenges that only trial-and-error could satisfactorily solve and thereafter mostly avoid. This chapter has sought to explore one early example with the aid of modern management theory. The exercise illustrates the ability of family and local firm culture to resist absorption into the centralised, post-merger bureaucracy of the large-scale organisation; and the power of financial rewards in reinforcing or denying executive authority. Neither weakness nor strength in the face of the CPA's problems allowed the first two chairmen to imprint a strong and distinctive CPA culture on a congeries of firms that were bound together legally but were separated by cultural and organisational independencies.

Acknowledgements

I am grateful to the Leverhulme Trust and Manchester Metropolitan University Business School for supporting my research on North West business leaders and boardroom cultures. Staff and resources in the Manchester Central Library (Archives and the Main Reading Room) have facilitated my work. My understanding of the CPA has been advanced by the late Stuart Scofield, also Rex Collins, Derek Moorhouse and Maurice Cribb. Finally, I must thank Professor Douglas Farnie and Dr Geoffrey Tweedale for commenting helpfully on an earlier version of this paper.

Notes

1. Mike Schraeder and Dennis R. Self, 'Enhancing the Success of Mergers and Acquisitions: An Organisational Culture Perspective', *Management Decision*, 41 (2003), pp. 511–22 quoting R. J. Carleton, 'Cultural Due Diligence', *Training*, 34 (1997). My thanks to Geoff Tweedale for this reference.

2. Edgar H. Schein, *Organisational Culture and Leadership* (Jossey-Bass Inc.: San Francisco, 1985), p. 6.

3. Schein, *Organisational Culture*, pp. 223–43.

4. Schraeder and Self, 'Enhancing the Success of Mergers' citing K. Walker, 'Meshing Cultures in a Consolidation' *Training and Development* 52, no. 5 (1998), pp. 83–8.

5. P. Lesley Cook and Ruth Cohen, *Effects of Mergers; Six Studies* (George Allen & Unwin: London, 1958), p. 136.

6. Capacity in hand block printing was estimated by the number of printing tables. These fell in England from a maximum of 8,129 in 1840 to 700 in 1889. Geoffrey Turnbull, *A History of the Calico Printing Industry of Great Britain* (Sherratt: Altrincham, 1951), p. 114, 423–6.

7. Turnbull, *History*, p. 114.

8. *Cotton Spinners and Manufacturers Directory … for Lancashire* (John Worrall: Oldham, 1898).

9. Henry W. Macrosty, *The Trust Movement in British Industry: A Study of Business Organization* (Longmans: London, 1907), p. 371; R. Robson, *The Cotton Industry in Britain* (Macmillan, 1957), p. 143.

10. Cook and Cohen, *Effects of Mergers*, p. 137.

11. Turnbull, *History*, p. 114; Cook and Cohen, *Effects of Mergers*, p. 136.

12. CPA Prospectus, 8 December 1899, reprinted in Macrosty, *Trust Movement*, p. 365.

13. Douglas A. Farnie, 'The Calico Printing Industry and the World Market, 1890–1940: The Survival of Independent Printing Firms in Co-existence with the Calico Printers' Association' (unpublished paper given at Manchester Polytechnic (now MMU), September 1991), Table 5 gives 182 calico printers in the Manchester trade in 1898.

14. 'Kinder', *Kinder Printing Company: Its Strange History* (Manchester, July 1892), p. 31. My thanks to Douglas Farnie for bringing this to my attention.

15. *Manchester City News*, 22 September 1900.

16. *Dyer and Calico Printer* 10 (1890), 104–5, issue for 15 July.

17. Nicholas J. Morgan, 'Alexander Crum' in Anthony Slaven and Sydney Checkland (eds), *Dictionary of Scottish Business Biography, 1860–1960*, vol. I (Aberdeen University Press, 1986); Eastwood District Libraries Local History Project, *Crum's Land: A History of Thornliebank* (Eastwood District Libraries: Glasgow, 1988).

18. Thornliebank Co. Ltd, Directors' Minute Book (27 December 1886 to 1 June 1900), 8 March 1887, Glasgow City Archives, TD585/1, Mitchell Library, Glasgow.

19. Thornliebank, Directors' Minutes, 29 December 1886, 29 August 1887.

20. Thornliebank, Directors' Minutes, 5 September 1893.

21. Thornliebank, Directors' Minutes, 10 January 1895.

22. Thornliebank, Directors' Minutes, 29 December 1886.
23. Calico Printers' Association Archive, Manchester Central Library. [hereafter CPA], M75/1, Box 926, Register of Directors and Managers, 1899–1905, sv Kay. *Journal of the Chemical Society* 1939 Part 1: my thanks to Dr Gerrylyn Roberts of the Open University for this reference. See also *Society of Dyers and Colorists Journal* 55 (April 1939), pp. 212–13.
24. In the 1890s these shares could be sold back to the company at around £130 each. Thornliebank. Directors' Minutes, 29 August 1887.
25. 'Kinder', *Kinder Printing Company*, pp. 3, 30.
26. John V. Symonds, *The Mills of New Mills* (New Mills Local History Society, 1991).
27. CPA, M75, Inventory and Valuation volumes for Bennett, 1909 and Rumney, 1904.
28. *Manchester of Today* (1888) p. 92 (my thanks to Douglas Farnie for this reference); *Dyer and Calico Printer* 10 (July 1890).
29. France's 1892 tariff raised import duties on cotton and linen fabics 'considerably': J. H. Clapham, *The Economic Development of France and Germany, 1815–1914* (Cambridge University Press, 1928) p. 264. Gartside's printworks were at Malaunay, near Rouen.
30. Macrosty, *Trust Movement*, p. 365.
31. Thornliebank, Directors' Minutes, 14 February 1899.
32. *Dyer and Calico Printer* 19 (1899), p. 45.
33. Thornliebank, Directors' Minutes, 15 November 1899.
34. Derek Matthews, Malcolm Anderson, and John Richard Edwards, *The Priesthood of Industry: The Rise of the Professional Accountant in British Management* (Oxford University Press, 1998) p. 309.
35. CPA, DM I, Directors' Minutes, vol. 1 (2 December 1899 to 15 March 1905), pp. 1–4.
36. They were replaced in 1914.
37. Macrosty, *Trust Movement*, 367.
38. One example: in 1890 *The Dyer and Calico Printer* began publishing monthly profiles of notable print- and bleachworks. Half-a-dozen appeared and then the series was stopped. Since no explanation was given, it is assumed that they met no more cooperation with the feature.
39. *Dyer and Calico Printer* 20 (1900) p. 49, issue for 20 April.
40. Macrosty, *Trust Movement*, p. 369.
41. Thornliebank, Directors' Minutes, 27 July 1899.
42. Reprinted in Macrosty, *Trust Movement*, pp. 360–9.
43. Thornliebank, Directors' Minutes, 19 January 1892.
44. Thornliebank, Directors' Minutes, 15 November 1899.
45. Thornliebank, Directors' Minutes, 30 April 1900.
46. Macrosty, *Trust Movement*, p. 149.
47. 'Kinder', *Kinder Printing Company*, p. 38.
48. Macrosty, *Trust Movement*, p. 368.
49. Douglas Farnie estimates that looms could be valued at £25 each and spindles at

£1 each at this time.

50. Thornliebank, Directors' Minutes, 1 June 1900.

51. Thornliebank, Directors' Minutes, 22 March 1900.

52. Macrosty, *Trust Movement*, pp. 153–4.

53. *Dyer and Calico Printer* 22 (1900) 130, issue for 20 September.

54. Douglas A. Farnie, 'The Structure of the British Cotton Industry, 1846–1914' in Akio Okokchi and Shin-ich Yonekawa (eds), *The Textile Industry And Its Business Climate: Proceedings of the Fuji Conference* (University of Tokyo Press, 1982), p. 78.

55. Macrosty, *Trust Movement*, pp. 133–4; David J. Jeremy, 'Survival Strategies in Lancashire Textiles: Bleachers' Association Ltd to Whitecroft PLC, 1900–1980s' *Textile History* 23, 2 (1993) pp. 174–8.

56. Michael Stenton and Stephen Lees, *Who's Who of British Members of Parliament: A Biographical Dictionary of the House of Commons*, 4 vols (Harvester Press: Hassocks, Sussex, 1976–81).

57. 'Kinder', *Kinder Printing Company*, p. 12.

58. CPA, Directors' Minutes, 2 December 1899,

59. Edward Walford, *The County Families of the United Kingdom; Or Royal Manual of the Titled and Untitled Aristocracy of England, Wales, Scotland, and Ireland* (Chatto & Windus, 1881, 1891); *Kelly's Directory of Cheshire* (Kelly's Directories Ltd), 1896. Simon Pitt, 'The Political Economy of Strategic and Structural Change in the Calico Printers' Association, 1899–1973' (London Business School Ph.D., 1990), pp. 44–5 confused Francis Frederick Grafton with his father Frederick William Grafton. His source, Turnbull, *History*, p. 78 did not. However, Turnbull's a source, R. S. Crossley, *Accrington Captains of Industry* (Wardleworth: Accrington, 1930), p. 59, was mistaken in reporting Frederick William Grafton as a Rugby School pupil. There is no evidence of either him or his son in the Rugby School registers. My thanks to the Rugby School archivist for this information.

60. CPA, DM I, Directors' Minutes, 2 December 1899.

61. CPA, DM I, Directors' Minutes, 2 December 1899.

62. CPA, DM I, Directors' Minutes, 26 July 1900.

63. CPA, DM I, Directors' Minutes, 25 October 1900

64. CPA, MDMB 1 & 2, Managing Directors' Minutes, 4 January 1900, 5 November 1901.

65. Pitt, 'Political Economy', pp. 47–51.

66. Quoted by Pitt, 'Political Economy', p. 57.

67. Pitt, 'Political Economy', p. 57.

68. In the oft-cited dictum of Cairns LC, in *Parker v Mckenna* (1874): 'No man can in this Court, acting as agent, be allowed to put himself in a position in which his interest and his duty will conflict'. Francis Beaufort Palmer, *Company Law* (Stevens: London, 1901), pp. 130–3, 140.

69. Macrosty, *Trust Movement*, p. 149.

70. CPA, Register of Directors and Managers, 1899–1905, CPA, M75/1, Box 926. My thanks to Alison Gill of the Greater Manchester County Record Office for help in searching genealogical databases.

71. *Kelly's Directory of Cheshire*, 1906–11.

72. *Manchester City News*, 22 September 1900.

73. *Manchester Courier* 14 November 1906.

74. *Kelly's Directory of Cheshire*, 1892.

75. *Directory of Directors* 1901; Ranald C. Michie, 'Samuel Jones Loyd' in David J. Jeremy and Christine Shaw (eds), *Dictionary of Business Biography* (6 vols, Butterworths: London, 1984–86); Mark Girouard, *The Victorian Country House* (Yale University Press: New Haven CT, 1979), p. 415; William D. Rubinstein, *Men of Property: The Very Wealthy in Britain since the Industrial Revolution* (Croom Helm: London, 1981); CPA, M75/1, Box 926, Register of Directors and Managers, 1899–1905.

76. W. T. Pike and W. B. Tracy, *Manchester and Salford at the Close of the Nineteenth Century* (W. T. Pike: Brighton, 1899), p. 111; *The Ashton-under-Lyne Reporter* 17 November 1906; *Manchester Guardian*, 13 November 1906; *The Times* 20 November 1906. My thanks to Douglas Farnie for Gartside's death date.

77. Pitt, 'Political Economy', pp. 57–8.

78. Pitt, 'Political Economy', pp. 55, 60.

79. CPA, Directors' Minutes, 27 August 1901.

80. CPA, MDMB 1, Managing Directors' Minutes, 2 January 1902.

81. They were: Registrar (company secretary); Controller of Home Trade and Colonial Prices; Cloth Buyer; Selling Office Manager; Chief Engineer; Head Chemist.

82. My thanks to Rex Collins, former senior CPA executive, for an account of this lively haggling process in which the merchant tried to beat down the printer and the printer did all he could to defend his quoted prices.

83. National Archives, LNWR Directors' Minutes, RAIL 410/39, 19 January 1906.

7

High-performance Lancashire: knowledge, skills and mountaineering clothing before 1953

MIKE C. PARSONS AND MARY B. ROSE

Introduction

The evolution of the Lancashire cotton industry, from the eighteenth to the twentieth century, drew on a rich combination of knowledge and skill. These were influenced and shaped by machinery, machine making, yarns and fabrics. Driven by buoyant and diverse overseas markets, the spatial and organisational specialisation of cotton Lancashire, from the 1830s onwards, led the county to be described by Alfred Marshall as the first industrial district. The extreme level of specialisation included a commercial sector centred on Manchester's numerous shipping houses, production and machinery specialised by town and the separation of spinning and weaving from finishing. Cotton spinners and weavers, and indeed finishers, were normally metaphorically and physically separated from their end users by the complex network of middlemen, based in Manchester. These intermediaries negotiated and co-ordinated all elements of activity. This chapter focuses on the end-products and users of Lancashire cotton goods, rather than on yarn and cloth production or trade. High-performance fabrics have been described as the neglected legacy of the Lancashire cotton industry.[1]

This chapter explores the challenges of producing fabrics for extreme activities and the complex relationships between fabric, garment and equipment design and their use in mountaineering and exploration. The chapter will be divided into three substantive sections. The first section traces the development of high-performance clothing and equipment for exploration and mountaineering, examining the interplay along the supply chain between manufacturers and users. It will show how competition, especially at the top end of the market, combined with military demand, led to the development of high-performance functional fabrics and clothing. It will show how these influenced and were influenced by both polar exploration and the development of outdoor sports from the second half of the nineteenth century onwards. A combination of economic and social changes has meant that during the twentieth century and into the twenty-first century there has been considerable loss of textile knowledge. Clearly the collapse of the Lancashire cotton industry has led to loss of technical capability, while among mountaineers there has also been a loss of understanding of how their clothing functions. The final section of this chapter explores how we should judge the performance of these fabrics in comparison with the present way as a way of placing the sophistication of Lancashire cotton in context. By comparing with modern fabrics and designs, it demonstrates the level of fabric and clothing system sophistication which had been achieved by the 1920s.

Lancashire cotton and high-performance clothing for extreme climates

Animals, birds and insects have evolved to stay warm and dry. Man also originally had a deep instinctive understanding of survival and of staying warm and dry, by using combinations of insulating furs, plant materials and even animal intestines. Yet one of the greatest technical challenges for textile manufacturers has been the development of weatherproof fabrics, which are comfortable to wear during vigorous activity. When we exercise we become warm, and sweat. If fabrics do not allow the water vapour to permeate out, or in other words do not breathe, this leads to chilling. The quest to develop waterproof, windproof, breathable textile fabrics began long before the development of Gore-Tex® in the 1970s; it started with natural textiles, including silk and wool, in ancient civilisations and continued with cotton and linen in the nineteenth and twentieth centuries. Oiled silk is strong, waterproof, windproof and extremely light and was one of the first high-performance fabrics. It was first used in umbrellas by the Chinese over 1,000 years ago. This section traces the development of waterproof and windproof cotton fabrics in Lancashire from the early nineteenth century onwards. It explores the problems associated with developing functional fabrics and garments.

Despite problems of breathability, the commercialisation of rubberised fabrics revolutionised rainwear and made an enormous and lasting contribution to the Lancashire economy. It also influenced and was influenced by the history of clothing and equipment for both exploration and mountaineering. Rubber is a natural polymer which came to Europe with Christopher Columbus in the fifteenth century and was used to proof fabric in Mexico from the seventeenth century. In Britain, the patent records from the second quarter of the seventeenth century bear witness to numerous attempts to waterproof fabrics, including experiments with rubber.[2] However, in 1823 Charles Macintosh, a Glasgow chemist, patented a double textured fabric which bore his name. Rubber, softened with naphtha, was sandwiched between two layers of cloth to form a waterproof material. His 1823 patent claimed:

> A manufacture of 2 or more pieces of linen, woollen, cotton, silk, leather or paper or other the like substances ... cemented together by means of a flexible cement, the nature of which said manufacture is that it is impervious to water and air.[3]

Macintosh used virtually any fabric, but his rubber coating became especially associated with cotton, when he sought and gained financial backing from two Manchester cotton manufacturers, the Birley Brothers and R. W. Barton. Charles Macintosh & Co., of Cambridge Mills, Chorlton-on-Medlock and began trading in 1824.[4] Even the earliest Macintosh products were used in the Arctic, and Franklin's 1824 expedition was equipped with inflatable Macintosh bags, the first airbeds. Three years later Parry's North Pole expedition was supplied with waterproof bags and covers.[5] However, they were problematic, because the original Macintosh not only smelt terrible, but went rigid in the cold, a problem only alleviated with the patenting of vulcanisation by Thomas Hancock in 1843 (in parallel with the better known and virtually identical innovation by Charles Goodyear in the United States).

Without this development, which made the rubber less sensitive to changes in temperature, Macintosh's rubber coating would have made just a fleeting appearance. But vulcanisation brought versatility to rubber products, made elastic a viable proposition and meant that single-coated fabrics became an alternative to the old double fabrics. Since Macintosh had formed a partnership with Hancock in 1830, his company was in a position to benefit from Hancock's advance and the new and improved Macintosh received awards at the Great Exhibition of 1851. But he did not enjoy a monopoly, and the success of his rubber goods promoted competition. This helped to make Manchester the home of the UK rainwear industry which, before the First World War, supplied 90 per cent of the world market.[6]

Improved Macintosh was extremely versatile and was developed for fashionable wear and sporting activity. Indeed, an exceptionally lightweight garment was designed to fit in a cigar case:

> Hellewells's waterproof 5 oz, weight reversible paletot [loose cloak] surpasses all others for fine and wet weather. Can be carried in a coat sleeve of a packet and folded up in the space of a cigar case. The lightest, the best and the most portable protection from rain and dust, adapted for fishing, rowing, yachting, riding, driving, hunting, shooting, coursing and deerstalking.[7]

As a cloak this garment also had the advantage of easy ventilation, because, along with the unpleasant smell, the major disadvantage of Macintosh was that it was not breathable. This made it downright uncomfortable, and the chilling effect potentially dangerous for high-exertion sports such as mountaineering. Early mountaineers, like the Reverend Girdlestone, suggested tweed was a better waterproof, since it was 'impossible to walk long in a Macintosh without oppressive heat'.[8] In any event Macintosh had a fatal flaw – it was damaged by salt and hence by sweat.[9] Woollen fabrics, such as box cloth, had no such problems. They breathed and could be made almost impervious to wind and water through felting and so did not need to be coated. They were, however, excessively heavy and were designed, not for activity, but for sitting on exposed stage coach boxes.

Linen was a highly versatile natural fibre and its ability to swell and become impervious to moisture meant that it was used for fire buckets and hoses right up to the Second World War. It was also widely used in agricultural work wear. Agricultural labourers wore loose linen smocks which

> were cool in summer and warm in winter; they could easily be washed and, finally, although self ventilating, they to a great extent kept their wearer's dry. Curious observation suggested that the ability of smock frocks to exclude wet depended somewhat on their being voluminous, so as to fit loosely, and on their being made of closely woven texture, which water could contract, and therefore render as it became saturated with moisture more impervious to rain.[10]

These provided the model for garments and fabrics which were, ironically, to revolutionise weatherproofing at the top end of the market from the 1880s onwards, and have significant implications for polar explorers and mountaineers for the next 50 years.

It was allegedly his observation of these highly functional garments which encouraged Thomas Burberry, the Hampshire sports outfitter, to experiment and develop his breathable gabardine rainwear. These appeared in the 1860s and were at first made of linen; like many innovations these were ridiculed at first, but

> they reduced the tendency to overheat the body and excite perspiration, and,

at the same time, they kept out wet more effectually than garments of cloth woven from wool, even when the later was dipped in solutions of sugar of lead or other deleterious chemicals.[11]

The trade mark for Burberrys' self-ventilating weatherproof combination patent was registered in 1879 and, as its name suggests, was a direct response to the problems of breathability associated with Macintosh.

The competitive success of Burberrys' at the top end of the market can be traced to three causes. It stemmed partly from the versatility of the Lancashire cotton industry. Burberrys' were not cloth manufacturers and it was only in 1920, when they went public, that they acquired their cloth suppliers Pandora Mills of Farnworth near Bolton and became a fully integrated company. However, they engaged with the industry on fabric development and finishing. Following experiments Burberry was supplied with proofed cotton substitute for linen – gabardine which was effectively triple proofed – once in the raw material, once in the yarn and once after weaving. The fabric required long stapled, high-quality Egyptian cotton and high-quality weaving. Burberry was anything but cheap, however, and it was the impervious nature of Macintosh which was the other source of Burberrys' success with wealthy and increasingly health-conscious customers. The patent records show how much energy was devoted to making rubber-coated fabric less unpleasant to wear, with the insertion of eyelet holes and even tubes to move away moisture. But this was the period of Dress Reform and calls for hygienic clothing systems, and the 1884 International Health Exhibition highlighted the deleterious effects on health of rubberised fabrics. Burberrys, on the other hand, pointed out the health benefits of their clothing coming from its natural properties:

> Like the plumage of birds and the scales of fish, Burberry prevents penetration by wet without sacrifice of the ventilating principles essential for health and comfort. Water is excluded by fine transversal threads which fill up the minute interstices formed by warp and weft, though air being more plastic, still finds an easy passage through the invisible spaces remaining.[12]

Burberrys milked this for all they were worth and just four years later took out a patent for 'Improved materials specially adapted for Garments of Sportsmen', which made Burberry garments so distinctive and so effective:

> A compound fabric specially adapted for making sportsmen's garments consists of two layers, the outer twill or plain linen of the like and the inner of waterproofed or semi waterproofed cloth … and the former may or may not cover the whole of the latter …[13]

For the next 40 years Burberry's marketing campaign hinged upon the ways in which Macintosh damaged health, culminating in a volume of over 200 pages entitled *Open Spaces*. From the 1880s no opportunity was lost to point to the dangers of Macintosh both as a process and for clothing and the health card was relentlessly played. In 1910 we are reminded that:

> Modern enlightenment in the principles of hygiene realises that to obtain protection by a material impervious to air is to run risks to health far greater than those of getting wet. Burberrys, by associating the most advanced chemical knowledge, the most modern methods of therapeutics and the most skilled weaving and dyeing manufacture for outdoor pursuits weatherproof cloths that are at once healthful, reliable and beautiful. Their inventions provide weatherproof garments which, owing to their conformity with hygienic principles – supersede those proofed by the dangerous system of rendering fabrics even more impermeable to air than they are to water by solutions of rubber which, as in the case of Macintosh block up the interstices of the web and necessitate artificial ventilation to make it endurable. Burberrys' having first discovered an agent that makes any woven fabric non-absorbent, invented machinery to force proof first into the strands of the raw material before it is twisted into yarn, secondly into the yarn as prepared for the loom and thirdly into the finished cloth.[14]

Ten years later *Burberrys' Protection* implied that only bad parents would expose their children to Macintosh:

> The lightest rubber or cemented coat keeps in the natural heat [and] bakes the body. If adults choose to take risks it is their own look out; but they don't put children in airtight coats. It is better to get wet from precipitation than to get wet from perspiration.[15]

Burberrys' success was a combination of fabric and innovative clothing designs. They were after all, first and foremost outfitters. Their designs depended upon impeccable tailoring which brought an understanding of functionality. However, their tailoring was also innovative for one of their hallmarks was the development of features, such as the pivot sleeve, patented in 1901, which drastically improved freedom of arm movement.[16]

In the 1890s and early 1900s Burberrys secured their market through identifying a niche in high-quality clothing for sporting activity at the very top of the market. By the 1920s their list of patrons ran to six pages, and included just about every aristocratic family in the UK and Europe, although whether a limerick submitted to the *Morning Post* quite fits this image is doubtful:

Said the Queen to Sir Walter, I vow
If the road's wet I'll kick up a row
Said Raleigh. 'Well Liz'
I don't mind if it is
I carry a Burberry now.[17]

They recognised that survival depended upon developing a range of niches, rather than relying on just one; therefore, by 1914, they combined the sale of high-class sporting clothing, including by this stage, ski-wear with fashion wear. Alongside this, and a source of considerable pride and advertising, was their supply of explorers and mountaineers from the 1890s until the 1930s. Their largest market was, like so many suppliers of high-performance clothing, military. In 1901, almost certainly through their aristocratic network, they received War Office instructions to design a new uniform for British officers. Interestingly the conservative image of the British armed forces initially squeezed out many of the most innovative features of Burberry designs. But it secured a crucial bulk market for them which in no way undermined their exclusive image. In addition, the re-designed First World War Trench coat saw functionality later translated into fashion in the Burberry Trench Coat. This bulk market was to be further reinforced by an Air Ministry contract in 1923.[18]

Burberry created their exclusive niche through the use of a combination of high-quality fabrics, innovative designs and their relentless attack on rubberised fabrics. In doing so they changed the market but did not undermine the production of rubberised clothing. This continued to expand so that by the 1890s there were 70 Macintosh companies in Manchester. Instead the exclusivity of Burberry helped to drive rubberised rainwear into the mass market, a move which was also facilitated by the growing number of Jewish émigré rainwear manufacturers in the Salford and Cheetham Hill areas of Manchester. Several of these, including Mandleburgs and Frankensteins, were also exceptionally innovative and were responsible for a number of registered designs, including Mandleburgs' patented odourless Macintosh.[19] In their different ways and for different reasons, Burberrys, Mandleburgs and Frankensteins also had a lasting impact on the supply of polar explorers and mountaineers.

The principal function of the original Burberry gabardine was as a waterproof, but the twill fabric was very versatile and could be produced in a startling array of weights using either cotton or wool. These included Tropical, Airylight, Summer, Autumn and Winter and according to their advertising was:

ideal for sport, games and other outdoor use involving exposure to rain, mist sleet or snow, to fluctuating temperatures; to cold winds or burning sun, to thorns, fish hooks and general rough usage.[20]

The origins of modern layering systems lay in the much maligned nineteenth-century British naval expeditions to the Arctic. On the Nares expedition of 1875 hand-sewn canvas windproofs were added, in preference to the unwieldy and unsuitable box cloth, and these garments were hooded in the style of the Eskimo anorak. In the 1880s Nansen also incorporated a hood and, in the 1890s used the new Burberry gabardine which was lighter, a prime concern for this pioneer lightweight explorer. The combination of tight weave, finish, lightness, durability and its snow-repellent qualities made Burberry an ideal windproof for polar exploration. From the 1890s it was used for both tents and as an integral part of a layering system of clothing, which frequently also included Jaeger underclothing. The fabric was further improved for Shackleton's 1902 Antarctica expedition, and the design of the windproof smocks themselves adapted, though they were not hooded. Burberry was also used by Robert Falcon Scott both for tents and windproofs on his ill-fated expedition of 1910–12. Amundsen was also an enthusiastic user of lightweight Burberry hooded anoraks and overalls, which he used in conjunction with a number of air trapping layers. He recalled:

> Our clothing in moderate temperatures consisted of thick woollen underclothing and Burberry windproof overalls. This underclothing was specially designed for the purpose; I had myself watched the preparation of the material, and knew that it contained nothing but pure wool. We had overalls of two different materials: Burberry gabardine and the ordinary green kind that is used in Norway in the winter. For sledge journeys where one has to save weight, and to work in loose easy garments, I must unhesitatingly recommend Burberry. It is extraordinarily light and keeps the wind out completely. For hard work I prefer the green kind. It keeps the wind out equally well, but is heavier and more bulky, and less comfortable to wear on a long march. Our Burberry wind clothes were made in the form of anorak [blouse] and trousers, both very roomy. The others consisted of trousers and jacket with hood.[21]

Burberrys' experience as polar suppliers before the First World War gave them a depth of knowledge which was readily transferable into mountain sports. By 1910 they had developed an exclusive range of sportswear which included the Burberry climbing suit, the ladies' climbing gown and ranges of skiing and skating wear. The performance of this clothing depended upon a combination of the choice of fabric and the quality of tailoring.

During the inter-war period Everest replaced the North and South Poles in the public's imagination, taking centre stage on the Royal Geographic Society (RGS) and Alpine Club's agendas after the First World War. By 1939 there had been seven British expeditions to Everest, which contributed to a pyramid of knowledge of clothing for high altitudes. George Bernard Shaw described the 1922 Everest expedition as looking like a 'Connemara picnic surprised by a snowstorm'. Knowledge certainly grew with each successive expedition and, by 1924, practical experience of the conditions, combined with improvements and adaptations to polar kit, demonstrated progress and understanding of the requirements for Himalayan climbing. The sketchy kit-list for 1921 is replaced in 1924 by a detailed, well-researched set of guidance notes, which drew heavily on the experience and research by climber and scientist, George Finch, from the 1922 expedition. Edward Norton's 1924 Everest list described a layered clothing system for active climbers at high altitudes and was adapted from the combination of polar windproofs, insulation and air-trapping layers. In both 1922 and 1924 Burberry windproofs were used. The 1924 climbing team were instructed, when they went to Messrs Burberry in Haymarket, to ask for Mr Pink for a careful fitting, crucial if the outer-garment was to fit over multiple layers.[22] There were also notable innovations since Sandy Irvine used custom-made zip fasteners.[23] Their clothing was clearly state of the art, and breathable cotton windproofs had been found very effective and versatile at the poles and especially during high-exertion activities. Indeed the most uncomfortable part of the 1920s Everest trips will have been the walk in through tropical rain, since no really effective waterproofs had been developed.

Burberry then was almost inseparable from the 1920s Everest expeditions, and their garments were the first truly breathable weatherproofs. But, after 40 years of dominating exploration as well as fashion rainwear, they were outraged when they found they faced competition. Indeed, in 1932, when Hugh Ruttledge began to investigate what to take to Everest, Burberrys got wind of a potential change in suppliers and wrote:

> By this post we are forwarding you a publication entitled *Open Spaces*, in which we should like to draw your attention especially to pp. 53 to 71 and pp. 165 to 167, as they deal with Polar and Mountaineering equipment.
>
> During the last 40 years we have accumulated evidence in the records of famous explorers, which proves that Burberry Gabardine is a material unrivalled for ensuring protection against cold, wind, snow and rain. Though extremely light in weight, it is at the same time the most durable cloth woven for rough usage – two qualities of utmost importance to expeditions such as the one you are about to lead.[24]

Competition did not come from their principal rivals in the rainwear sector, Aquascutum, but from within Lancashire: from Burnley cloth manufacturers Haythornthwaites. Invented for the Arctic missionary Sir Wilfred Grenfell in 1923, Grenfell cloth was a tightly woven, high-quality, cotton gabardine that was used for flying suits, high-quality leisure wear and, in the 1930s, for mountaineering for both tents and clothing. Just why Grenfell did not go to Burberry in the first place is unknown, but he wanted to make his own clothing, rather than having ready-made clothing and it is possible that Burberrys refused to supply the fabric separately.[25] It was an extremely specialist and technical fabric, which needed skilled weavers to produce it without a flaw and was exceptionally difficult to finish. It is a measure of the high relative skill of Lancashire textile workers that, when the Americans, with their more standardised textile traditions, tried to copy it to make 'Byrd' cloth, they could not produce it in any volume.[26] Tested by the Manchester Chamber of Commerce against Cupra – another windproof considered by the Mount Everest Committee – Grenfell was both lighter (at less than 6 oz per square yard) and stronger, and in this outperformed Burberry.

As well as being chosen by the Labrador Missionary, Grenfell began to be used for other high-performance purposes. It went to the South Pole with Byrd in 1931 and a Grenfell suit was used in the flight over Everest in 1933. During the 1930s Haythornthwaites marketed the cloth through the Manchester company of Baxter, Taylor & Woodhouse, and it was within this association that the key to its popularity for mountaineering lies. The secret of the success of Grenfell in this period lay in the combination of a light windproof fabric, with Eric Taylor's specially designed climbing suit, which became a classic for a decade. It was far more sophisticated than the Shackleton's overalls and more modern than the Burberry climbing suits. A climber himself, Taylor recognised that however good a cloth was, it was useless if the design of the suit was inappropriate. He developed a 'standardised' climbing suit, with variations for winter and summer, including a detachable hood, a jacket with zipped front and windproof wrists which could then be made up by a tailor. But like all good outdoor designers he wanted to improve it, and invited readers to contact him.[27] The response he got from climber Marco Pallis, published in the next edition of the *Mountaineering Journal*, could not have been more helpful. It incorporated suggestions from Howard Flint, whom Pallis believed was the only man in the country who really knew how to make a climbing suit. It is the first article to address one of the most crucial issues faced by any expedition climber – the subject of passing water – though interestingly he stopped short of discussing defecation. Flint's main suggestion was for the front fastening:

This is a Zip with an inner lining of cloth to prevent the metal searing the flesh. It may be due to reasons of false modesty, but the question of passing water is generally ignored in discussions of this type, and more damage has been caused to climbers through this than any single thing. There are scores of young men today suffering from internal troubles caused by inattention to this important problem. In the past, suits designed for low temperature wear have not had front fastenings. Obviously the fly front would not do as it admitted the wind and the snow. The practice was, therefore, to have a completely enclosed front, and when relief was desired partially to remove the garment. Now as the diet of most expeditions consists largely of hot liquid food, the necessity of relief is comparatively more frequent than in normal life, and this meant that often during the day, there was an exposure of the body to the cold. But worse than this followed. After the function had occurred, the climber found it quite impossible in the open to tuck in his shirt etc., into their positions, leaving that part of the body semi-unprotected. The result is now apparent in the frequency of stomach trouble among members of recent expeditions. The Zip fastener on the trousers designed by Mr Flint obviates this as far as the male is concerned.[28]

Taylor's Everest suit was an adaptation of the general-purpose suit, and appears to have taken on board many of Flint's suggestions, while adding some of his own. The crucial innovations included an integrated quilted hood with a windproof gusset, a draw string and fur linings, wind traps on the cuff, and zip fasteners on both pockets and flies. It was also made double thickness to increase wind resistance. He recognised that high-altitude clothing needed to be comfortable, windproof and sun-proof as well as being easy to manipulate. Crucially he grasped that kit should be 'invisible' saying:

> I had to take into consideration the men working at such high altitudes could be subject to nervous tension so that the slightest irritation in the lie of their kit would become an intolerable burden.[29]

Grenfell cloth was used for clothing and for some tents for Everest right the way through the 1930s and, like Burns, Taylor was always trying to improve what he made. The choice of Taylor's Grenfell Everest suit for the 1933 expedition marked the end of Burberrys' position as premier expedition supplier.

War often stimulates innovation, and changes in the competitive position of manufacturers and the Second World War was no exception. During the first 18 months Haythornthwaites produced 5 million yards of Grenfell cloth for the three services, but then faced a bombshell. The grave cotton shortage, brought on by the need to conserve scarce shipping space for food and armaments, led to an acceleration of the policy of concentration of production in far fewer mills. This meant that around half of spindleage and loomage across Lancashire was made compulsorily idle.[30] Only those mills concentrating on government orders or for export could remain open. Walter Haythornthwaite was incandescent when he found that although 84 per cent of their machinery ran on government orders, they were to be closed down. He complained to his MP that:

> If a closing down order by the Cotton Control is their interpretation of

JUSTICE and RIGHT we can only presume that they have been educated upon different lines to ourselves or is there a faint suspicion of 'Fifth Column Activity' impeding the War Effort.[31]

He had a point, for Grenfell cloth was a highly specialist cloth, ideally suited for military purposes. But family rumour has it that the problem lay, not with the cloth or the efficiency of the factory, but with relations between the Ministry of Supply and Haythornthwaite himself. He could be short-tempered, but impatience with the bureaucracy of the Ministry of Supply often had one result – shifting contracts – and he certainly was not the only manufacturer to be deprived of a contract by sometimes vindictive officials.[32] Whatever the cause, Grenfell cloth went out of production in 1941 and did not reappear until 1945, by which time it had lost its position at the top of the market for high-performance goods.

But crucial wartime fabric and clothing development was to have a lasting impact on what was available for peacetime mountaineering and exploration. Fine cotton/nylon fabrics were developed for parachutes, while Ventile – poplin rather than gabardine – was developed by Dr F. T. Pierce, when he was head of the Shirley Institute. The first impetus for this breathable fabric came from a shortage of flax used for canvas fire hoses and water storage tanks during the Second World War. As Thomas Burberry had found, linen fibres swelled as they absorbed water, closing the pores between the yarn, obviating the need for a rubber lining. Like Burberry, Pierce used long stapled Egyptian cotton and used an Oxford weave, where the warp threads run in pairs. If the origin of Ventile was fire hoses, wartime demands altered the direction of the research somewhat. The high level of casualties for airmen on convoy duty, ditching into icy waters of the Atlantic, created a new requirement. This became a problem because home based RAF fighter convoy escort was impossible – they just did not have the range, and so Churchill had promoted the idea of catapulting Hurricane aircraft from the decks of merchant ships to provide local cover. Of course they then had nowhere to land and the pilot could either ditch or bail out. Although the airmen were relatively easy to find as they had lights, within only minutes most died of exposure. Ventile was adapted for this and many military purposes and dramatically improved airmen's survival chances from a few minutes to 20 minutes, making rescue a real possibility. As a result 80 per cent of anti-submarine pilots who fell into the sea survived, as compared with a mere handful previously.[33]

As a potential peacetime outdoor fabric Ventile was not impermeable – like rubber or plastic coated cloths – and so was also breathable, making it ideal for a wide range of active pursuits. While there were some doubts about the durability of the lighter versions, the tests on British Ventile clothing in the Arctic in late 1940s 'proved superior to any other type of arctic clothing similarly tested'.[34] Almost as soon as the war ended, its benefits were trumpeted in the press by a cotton industry anxious to recover:

> Lancashire has found a new world beating use for cotton. It has produced a cotton cloth which is rainproof, storm proof, windproof and warm.[35]

It proved to be an effective competitor for Grenfell, which never regained its pre-war status as an expedition fabric. In comparing the characteristics and construction of Ventile and Grenfell, David Haythornthwaite reluctantly gave Ventile the edge in performance terms.[36] Neither Ventile nor Grenfell went to Everest in 1953, as a nylon-cotton mix was used. But it was used by Chris Bonington on Everest in both 1972 and 1975. In 1985 it compared very favourably with modern fabrics such as Gore-Tex®, and for Polar work it still remains the preferred option of some explorers.[37]

Conventionally discussion of Lancashire cotton, from the late nineteenth century to the end of the Second World War, has emphasised its competitive decline. This chapter, with its discussion of high-performance fabrics, offers an alternative perspective. Yet the question remains of how these fabrics compare with their modern equivalents. As part of a Heritage Lottery Fund Project, carried out on behalf of Mountain Heritage Trust, we replicated the clothing used by British climber, George Leigh Mallory, on the 1924 Everest expedition. These were subsequently field-tested on Everest at 21,000 feet. It took nearly three years of intensive scientific analysis and detective work to transform the fragments brought back from Everest into testable replicas. This work involved teams from the four universities of Southampton, Derby, Leeds and Lancaster.

The project was not just about a set of textile fragments, nor even a set of replicated clothes, but about understanding their position in the history of mountaineering and the wider innovation process. This unusual and collaborative project involved historians of innovation, textile conservators and replica makers, working alongside performance clothing specialists, textile and clothing manufacturers and mountaineers. The replicated fabrics and garments all had to meet precise specifications, and the collapse of textile skills in Lancashire made this particularly challenging. Our primary worry was whether there would be machinery available capable making the fabrics. A full set of clothing was made and several fabrics, such as the Burberry windproof, the wool flannel and the silk woollen vest, the cotton long-johns and the puttees, were custom-made and many garments hand-knitted. Modern silks had to be specially treated or de-gummed, to match 1920s processes.

All contributors to the project were committed to conserving the textile fragments. So testing was non-intrusive and did no damage. The aim was to produce a testable replica that would perform just like the original clothing on Everest rather than simply garments for museum display. Before full replication began, the experts were curious to understand how windproof the fabrics were and what kind of insulation they gave. So the first destination was the Performance Clothing Research Centre at the University of Leeds where Dave Brook, an expert in analysing modern textile performance, tested the materials thoroughly, exactly as he would modern fabric samples. First he measured the TOG value (the same measure used for assessing the warmth of a duvet) and found that together the layers were equivalent to 3.5 TOG, which was the insulation worn by Ranulph Fiennes and Mike Stroud when they were working hard at −40°C in Antarctica in 1996. Brook also tested the jacket fragments and found they were very close to modern Pertex fabric in terms of windproof quality. He concluded that George Mallory was sufficiently well insulated to survive on Everest, provided he was moving, though not for a bivouac. These first signs indicated that the fabrics were high performance and that the layering of the clothing was effective. The primary fabric and fibre analysis was carried out by a team of researchers led by Amber Rowe at the Textile Conservation Centre (University of Southampton). Analysis confirmed that Mallory was indeed wearing a Burberry windproof climbing suit for the outer layer of a sophisticated, layered, lightweight clothing system.

Eighty-two years after the ill-fated 1924 expedition, Graham Hoyland, himself an Everest veteran, tested the clothing first at 3,658 metres at Everest Base Camp and again at 4,877 metres on the Rongbuk Glacier. His reports, received by e-mail on 27 April and 6 May 2006 from Everest Base Camp, were clear and revealing. On dressing in layers prior to testing, he was especially struck by the contrast between these natural fibre garments and modern polypropylene. 'Warm to slip into rather than cold and clammy,' he wrote. His report confirmed that this was, indeed, an advanced clothing system:

> When exposed to a cutting wind blowing off the main Rongbuk glacier, I found the true value of the Burberry outer layer. This resisted the wind and allowed the eight layers beneath to trap warmed air between them and my skin. The patented pivot sleeve of the jacket enabled me to lift my arm right above my head (as when, say, striking a blow with an ice axe) without displacing any layers.[38]

Conclusions

This chapter has shifted the emphasis away from the production of cotton textiles, to the design and functionality of high-performance sportswear from the late nineteenth century to 1945. It explores the forces behind the shifting competition at the top end of the cotton fabric and clothing market. While the history of the Lancashire cotton industry has been characterised by the separation of user and manufacturer, this chapter shows that where, at the specialist top end of the market lead user innovation and collaboration added significantly to the functionality of the end product. The interplay between garment design and fabric is noticeable both for Burberry and Grenfell where in both cases a symbiotic relationship existed between garment design and fabric performance. Whereas Burberry would not have secured its market strength without a close relationship with their Lancashire suppliers, Haythornthwaites needed the expertise and climbing knowledge of their Manchester distributors and associated designers. The chapter comes forward to 2006 when comparisons are made between modern and inter-war fabrics, demonstrating the considerable fabric and garment sophistication, at the top end of the market.

Notes

1. Mike Parsons and Mary B. Rose, 'The Neglected Legacy of Lancashire Cotton: Industrial Clusters and the UK Outdoor Trade, 1960–1990, *Enterprise and Society*, 6 (4) (2005), pp. 682–709.

2. Patent abridgements for India Rubber and Guita Percha: air, fire and waterproofing, 1627–1855.

3. British Patents: BP4804/1823.

4. S. Levitt, 'Manchester Macintoshes: A history of the rubberised garment trade in Manchester', *Textile History*, 17 (1) (1986) pp. 51–2.

5. D. W. F. Hardie, 'The Macintoshes and the Origins of the Chemical Industry', *Chemistry and Industry*, June 1952, reprinted in A. E. Musson, *Science, Technology and Economic Growth in the Eighteenth Century* (Longman: London, 1972), 188.

6. Levitt, 'Manchester Macintoshes', p. 52; Alison Adburgham, *Shops and Shopping, 1800–1914* (George Allen & Unwin: London, 1964), p. 82.

7. Levitt, 'Manchester Macintoshes', p. 53.

8. A. G. Girdlestone, *The High Alps without Guides* (Longmans: London, 1870), p. 170.

9. Anon., *How to dress on £15 a day as a lady by a lady* (Frederick Warne and Co.: London, no date).

10. Corocias Garrulus (ed.), *Open Spaces* (Burberry: London, c.1927), pp. 22–3.

11. Garrulus, *Open Spaces*, p. 23.

12. *Burberry for Ladies*, XIX edition (Burberry: London, c.1910), p. 10.

13. British patents: BP 17928/1888.

14. *Burberry for Ladies*, p. 6.

15. *Burberry Protection: Children's' Burberry* (Burberry: London, c.1927).

16. British Patents: BP 25,506/190.

17. Garrulus, *Open Spaces*, p. 239.

18. Extract from Victoria and Albert Museum Burberry Exhibition notes, 1989.

19. Levitt, 'Manchester Macintoshes', pp. 56–8.

20. *Burberry for Ladies*, p. 6.

21. Roald Amundsen, *The South Pole: An Account of the Norwegian Antarctic Expedition in the Fram, 1910–1912*, translated by A. G. Chater (C.Hurst & Co.: London, 2002), pp. 39–40.

22. Royal Geographical Society (RGS), Everest Files, Equipment List, 1924.

23. Clothing list for Irvine, 1924. We are grateful to Julie Summers, Sandy Irvine's great niece and biographer for supplying a copy of this list.

24. RGS Everest Files, Box 45 16 September 1932, Burberrys' Ltd to Hugh Ruttledge.

25. Suggestion from David Haythornthwaite to Mary Rose, e-mail 21 August 2003.

26. Erna Risch and Thomas Pitkin, *Clothing the Soldier of World War II* (QMC Historical Studies, 1946), p. 92.

27. Eric H. Taylor, 'Climbing Suits', *Mountaineering Journal*, 1 (1932–33), pp. 168–71.

28. Carl K. Brunning, 'Further remarks on Climbing Suits', *Mountaineering Journal*, 1 (1932–33), p. 251.

29. Interview with Eric Taylor in *Daily Mail*, 20 January 1933.

30. John Singleton, 'The Cotton Industry and the British War Effort', *Economic History Review*, 47 (1994), pp. 601–18.

31. Haythornthwaite Archive, in possession of David Haythornthwaite, Statement to Wilfred Andrew Burke MP by Walter Haythornthwaite.

32. Interview with David Haythornthwaite by Mary Rose, July 2000.

33. Public Record Office (PRO) WO/32/13587 'The Development and Use of "Ventile" Cloths' Directorate of Equipment and Stores, Ministry of Supply 1949; Ventile Cloth Website: www.ventile.co.uk; H. M. Taylor., 'Ventile Fabrics: How and Why they were developed', *Textile Institute and Industry*, 27 (1975), pp. 359–60. We are grateful to Derryck Draper and Dave Brook for alerting us to this research.

34. PRO WO 32/12960 Arctic Mountain Warfare trials, 1947–49.

35. *Daily Express*, January 1946.

36. E-mail from David Haythornthwaite to Mary Rose, 21 August 2003.

37. 'Trading Post', *Great Outdoors*, July 1985. Taylor, 'Ventile Fabrics', p. 259; C. Bonington, *Everest: South West Face* (Hodder & Stoughton: London, 1973), p. 293.

38. Mike Parsons and Mary Rose, *Mallory Myths and Mysteries, The Mallory Clothing Replica Project* (Mountain Heritage Trust, 2006).

8

Enterprise, opportunity and bankruptcy in the early Derbyshire cotton industry

JOHN MASON

The rise of the Derbyshire cotton industry in the late eighteenth century has been extensively studied. Fitton and Wadsworth's account of the early spinners, Arkwright and the Strutts, and others exploring the differing fortunes of the firms that swarmed in their wake, have identified the principal themes.[1] By Arkwright's death in 1792 the best sites for water spinning had been taken; indeed the firms that occupied them were soon to face war-induced crises and competition from urban, steam-powered, mule-spinners. Yet, on both sides of the Pennines, there were still many looking for new sites and ready to invest in the technologies that had brought the leaders their success.[2] This study will examine attempts to establish a cotton industry in Derbyshire's Amber valley and in particular near Toad Hole Furnace in Shirland parish. Successive sections will consider the establishment and running of the firms, the 'structural' factors that were to limit their success, the commercial context, and the experience of failure.

I

Early descriptions of the Amber valley record an area engaged in agriculture and extractive and manufacturing industry.[3] Sandwiched between the Derwent cotton firms and the Nottinghamshire hosiery and lace districts, its inhabitants, at Alfreton and some twenty or more villages and hamlets, were to be touched by both. By 1789 framework knitting had taken root in many communities;

there is evidence too of a limited amount of wool working and calico weaving. In the early 1790s, perhaps inspired by the nearby Strutts, tradesmen, dealers and landowners from the middling ranks, initially from Alfreton and Fritchley, but subsequently from outside the region, were to build and run textile mills at South Wingfield, Fritchley (Crich parish), Shirland and Kelstedge (Ashover). Though confirming much held opinion of entrepreneurial origins,[4] in particular their having access to capital, their experiences display a considerable degree of variation and complexity.

The first cotton mill was erected in 1792 in Wingfield Park, South Wingfield. Four storeys high, powered by the Cowbourne stream and equipped for spinning, it was built by or for William White, maltster, of Alfreton and a landowner there and at South Wingfield and Shirland. Upon his death in 1795 his sons George and William disposed of much Alfreton property including a brewhouse, 'a small Weavers shop' and a 'very large new erected building, three storeys high, calculated to hold a quantity of Machinery for Spinning or Weaving', but retained the Wingfield mill. In 1800, possibly protecting George's interests, the South Wingfield properties were divided and William, 'a cotton manufacturer', took the mill. Within a year, 'by reason of divers losses and other misfortunes', his property was made over to creditors. The transactions reveal a network of possible relatives – a Sheffield grocer and an Alfreton butcher – and a number of Alfreton's middling sort. Among the latter were Thomas Green, a grocer, draper and mercer – and the purchaser and unsuccessful operator of White's Alfreton mill – and William Brookshaw, a cutler and hardwareman. In March 1801 these two purchased the Wingfield mill. The venture may not have been plain sailing, for in 1807 Brookshaw left the partnership and in 1813 Green was gazetted. Green, whose assignees were to consider taking Counsel's advice concerning 'the title and circumstances attending part of his freehold estates', had many interests: the mill and land at South Wingfield, houses, shops, warehouses, building land and land in Alfreton, and at Selston, Nottinghamshire, a house and windmill and 45 acres with the prospect of enclosure rights and underlying beds of coal and ironstone. Green may have sought to maintain his interest in the mill – occupied from 1814 to 1816 by Thomas Green Junior (in 1806 a gazetted calico-weaver) – but from 1816 William Wilson, of Morley, Wilson & Morley of Nottingham, hosiers, and tied too through marriage and religion, was to take it. Conducted initially by his sons as W. & S. Wilson it was to be worked by the family until 1856.[5]

The mill at nearby Fritchley, in Crich parish, was erected on land leased in 1793 for £43 per annum by James Turton, a local freeholder and enclosure awardee, whose interests came to include quarrying, lime-burning, and a specu-lative sough. Previously taxed on the ownership of 'a shop', Turton may already have worked textiles. The mill, four storeys high, was built in The Dimple, a valley to the east of the village. Turton subsequently passed the business

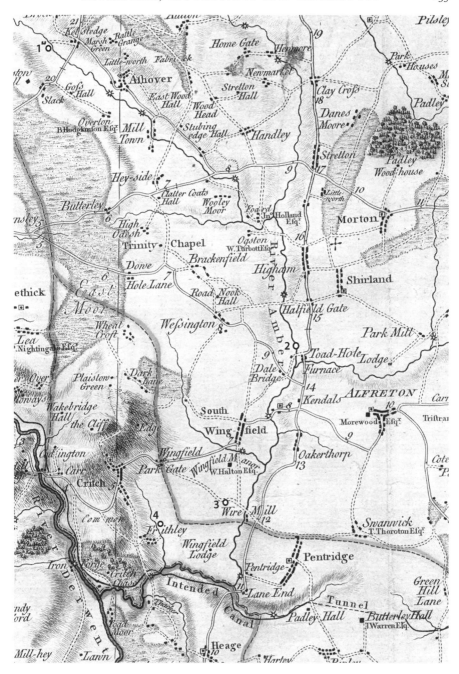

Location of mills in the Amber valley, Derbyshire mentioned in the text. Set in Burdett's *Map of Derbyshire*, revised edn, 1791. By permission of Derbyshire Record Office.

1. The Amber Mill, Kelstedge   2. The Amber Mill, Shirland
3. Park Mill, South Wingfield   4. Fritchley Mill.

to two sons, John and Thomas, who ran it as a spinning and manufacturing enterprise. In May 1802, possibly seeking to expand, the family purchased a newly built three-storey mill, originally erected for the manufacture of straw bonnets. Perhaps this brought dissension, for in 1803 the partnership was dissolved; Thomas was to conduct it alone, albeit later alongside his father. In 1805, presumably seeking to withdraw from the trade, the mill and associated buildings and land were put to auction. Adverts suggest that the mill had become the centre of a complex at once part factory and workshop: preparatory machinery and water-frame and mule spindles complemented a warp room, two loom-shops, a 'Boil, Size and Dye House' and a warehouse. The works went unsold and the Turtons, apparently concentrating on yarn and thread, continued the enterprise. Perhaps they had built a business incapable of sustained profitability: in 1813 father and son were gazetted and the complex again went to auction. The machinery was still being offered in 1814. Cotton working ceased, and the mill eventually became a bobbin-making factory.[6]

The largest enterprise was that at Toadhole Furnace, Shirland, another area then attracting interest from Alfreton. In 1792 eleven acres of meadow were advertised for auction:

The River Amber runs down the Estate seven hundred Yards in Length, hath 14 FOOT fall, well adapted for COTTON or other Mill, plenty of Water, good Stone for building very near, not more than 200 Yards from the Chesterfield or Matlock Turnpike Roads, and great Numbers of Hands all round who are in great Wants of Employment

and purchased by George and Charles Lowe. Of unknown origins – but probably springing from nearby Derbyshire or Nottinghamshire landed or trades families – they evidently had access to capital. Additional purchases of property, particularly around 1794–95 – and, land taxes suggest, sales to raise fresh capital – in Shirland and adjacent Wessington, Crich parish, created an estate of 21 acres and enabled them to construct a dam, a four-storey mill, 'The Amber Mill', and a substantial house and farm buildings. Spinning cotton and silk, their aim, seems to have been to supply the Manchester (cloth-making) and Nottinghamshire (hosiery) trades. In 1806 they went bankrupt. Though land purchases and building must have absorbed resources, a persistent failure to settle a small account with McConnel & Kennedy in 1804 and the presence of the Manchester cotton merchant Jeremiah Whittenbury as an assignee indicate trading difficulties.[7]

The estate and mill were purchased by the Manchester cotton merchant Robert Spear, a sometime partner of, among others, Whittenbury and the younger Arkwright. Shortly to retire, he was to part lease and sell the property to John Gould and Thomas Williamson, two partners in the calico manufacturing firm of Gould, Williamson & Bythesea of Derby and London. Williamson took up residence at Shirland and may have acted as managing partner at the site that was to be expanded to include a large loom-house and an apprentice house. Plans for expansion possibly caused discord between the partners for in October 1807 they split, Gould taking the whole business. He soon purchased adjacent land in South Wingfield and particularly in Wessington, where he erected cottages. By February 1809 cloths were being manufactured and sent for finishing at the Stockport works of William Sykes. To supervise the works Gould employed as manager Joseph Hulse (1781–1825), resident, at least since April 1807, at the Amber Mill and probably introduced to Gould by Spear – Spear's second wife was Anne Hulse. Despite his exertions Gould gained little, dying in January 1810 at Exeter where he had gone 'for the sake of his health'. His executors, including William Sykes, were to dispose of his property, with the proceeds, after minor bequests, going to his widow. She took up residence at Oxford, dying there in 1811. An exception concerned two parcels of land at Wessington and South Wingfield which Gould instructed be given to 'my good friend, Abel Walford Bellairs, banker'.[8]

Bellairs, in partnership with two sons and others, operated banks at Derby, Leicester and Stamford. The Derby bank was based at his residence in Full Street, once the home of Dr Darwin. Gould's 'Amber Cotton Works Company' probably had an account at the Derby bank – Hulse certainly had – and a knowledge of that and the bequest presumably whetted Bellairs' appetite, for he quickly took control of the Amber works and, with Hulse as manager, traded as the 'Amber Mill Company'. Under Bellairs and, spanning the latter years of the wars, the firm more than survived: in 1813 Hulse brought apprentices from Bristol and Derby to work there; then, in July 1814, a run on the Bellairs' Stamford bank, followed by runs at Leicester and Derby, saw the throwing into liquidation of Bellairs' entire interests. The Stamford bank's liabilities of £216,514 12s. 4d. exceeded assets of £169,469 12s. 2d.: among the latter were 'stock at Amber £13,000' and a mortgage of £300 on the mill. As the Amber Mill Company, 'a separate trade carried on by a separate fund and solvent in itself' had borrowed £16,000 from the Derby bank, itself indebted to the Stamford bank, the trail led to Shirland. The Chancellor in bankruptcy allocated the sum to the Derby creditors with any surplus [of the mill company's assets] being divided between creditors at Stamford and Leicester. For the first three required meetings at Derby the solicitors booked the County Hall; the assignees were to be busy for two decades.[9]

The Shirland works, perhaps because the acreage and the mill rendered each a poor buy, failed to sell at auction or privately. With fears of a banking crisis[10] compounding trading difficulties and marginal sites becoming less attractive, the assignees must have been anxious for an income. Hulse, presumably by lease, took over operations on his own. Cyclical swings and the increasing

Park Mill, South Wingfield, by J.B. Smith, late nineteenth century, from R. Jewell, *Memory Lane*. Built 1792. Note the design, the later chimney, the outbuildings and mill cottages and the rural surroundings. By permission of R. Jewell.

mechanisation of lower counts weaving must have made his task difficult, though Midlands, Manchester and London connections must have helped. Though his marriage to Martha, the daughter of William Sykes, perhaps brought social advantages, he was to slip from survival into crisis. On 10 August 1822 he was gazetted. Bellairs' assignees repeatedly put the mill estate for auction at different places, but without success. In October 1824, and possibly indicating the expected price, prospective purchasers were offered an incentive, £6,000 upon security at £4 per cent. Hulse, the person to contact by those wishing to view the site, died at Amber Mill on 25 February 1825. After repeated failures to sell, the mill and the greater part of the land was eventually purchased by William Eaton Mousley, the Derby solicitor for Bellairs' assignees. The house and land became a farm; the mill ground corn.[11]

That small enterprises could prosper is evidenced by 'The Amber Mill' at Kelstedge, where William Milnes, agent to Sir Joseph Banks, sometime President of the Royal Society, facilitated the construction of a four-storey mill on the site of a redundant lead cupola besides the Amber. Milnes kept Banks closely informed. The scheme was initiated in 1794 by a Mr Bromby of

Retford, Nottinghamshire, seeking to spin coarse yarn for use in his sailcloth business. By 1795 he was planning to advance his partner, Harvey, '£800 for ye purpose of erecting the Mill & Machinery & allow him a certain price per stone for Spinning the raw material'. The lease – in 1796 Milnes, who initially offered 21 years, finally agreed 28 years at £27 p.a. after accepting 'they are disposed to lay out a good deal of money' – was only settled in 1798. The partners had a short tenancy: in 1800 the mill 'with a good dam of water, and lately in the occupation of Mr Richard Hervey, as a mill to spin hurds' was offered to let. The lease was taken by George Caywood (later Cawood), from a Matlock copyholder family, and his associates, William Lowe and John Seddon. The partnership, Caywood & Co., was dissolved in 1812 from when Cawood operated alone. He spun flax and later cotton, and turned out thread and bleached, until his retirement in the 1830s. Having purchased the freehold in 1829 – and becoming indebted – he let the mill. Taken by William Cartledge, possibly of Nottingham, a thread manufacturer, and later by others, it was to operate until the late nineteenth century.[12]

II

The Amber Valley mills (see table 1), though not comparable with Derbyshire's largest, were typical of the many built by those seeking to emulate the industry's founders. All slip into the category defined by Chapman as B1: 'four-storeyed … designed for about 1,000 spindles, and 70 to 80 ft long by 25 to 30 ft wide'. In 1839 the then working mills at Kestledge and South Wingfield ranked 30th and 31st out of 36 Derbyshire cotton mills. The redundant mill at Fritchley would have ranked similarly; Shirland, with around 100 hands in 1802 but 128 in 1818, would have ranked 20th. Erected when rural water-spinning was about to give way to urban mule-spinning, they nevertheless exhibit that combination of power, machinery and labour that to Ure defined the factory.[13]

With ancillary buildings and workers' cottages, the mills were among the largest structures and complexes in their neighbourhoods. Destruction by fire of the Fritchley mill, and the conversion of Kelstedge into a castellated ballroom limits description, but the earliest, South Wingfield, with three storeys, each side lit by nine sixteen-paned windows, and a worked gable and roof-lit attic, was a classic Arkwright type. Fritchley, similar in scale to South Wingfield, nestled in The Dimple, the valley in which it sat, with the hat works and corn mills to north and south. The Kelstedge complex, built around a courtyard, its dam and reservoir, and the proprietor's adjacent Amber House, dominated the Amber's headwaters. At Shirland the mill was larger, albeit less regular than at South Wingfield; light and ventilation for the three principal storeys came predominantly from multi-paned iron-framed windows, with central vents, on the south-facing side – and the site's acreage, the waterworks and

Table 1   *The mills of the Amber Valley*

Mill Date built	Size in feet all 4-storey	Power W=water S=steam	Spindles WF/T/M[a]	Looms	Owner's/manager's house	Number of cottages	Acreage (ARP)	Farm: farm bldgs	Number of employees
S. Wingfield 1792	75' x 22' (external)	W: 7HP (est) S: 7HP (1839)	'Spinning & Roving[c] Frames' (1801)	No	Yes	0 (1813) 7 (1839)	7A 2R 0P (1813)	Yes	32 (1839)
Fritchley 1794–95	Unknown	W: 6HP (est) S: 6HP (1813)	444 WF 336 M	2 shops =16+ quantity of looms (1805) None (1813)	Yes	2 (1805) 4 (1813)	5A (1805) 15A 1R 9P (1813)	Yes	Unknown
Shirland c. 1794	100' x 24' (external)	W: 14HP S: 14HP							c. 100 (1802)
1806			1500 WF 700 M	No	Yes		21A (1806)	Yes	
1810			unknown	92	Yes	26 (1810)	109A (1814)	Yes	
1822		17 HP (est)[b]	1246 T 2160 M (+12 Mules in pieces)	92	Yes	26 (1822)	83A (1822)		128 (1818)
Kelstedge 1798	100' x 21' (internal?)[e] (1839)	W: 30HP (1839)	unknown	No but Bleaching	Yes	5 (1858)	24A 0R 23P (1858)	No (20 Acres let)	34 (1839)

Sources: See relevant paragraphs.

Notes:

a WF=Water-frame, T=Throstle, M=Mule (their usage), estimate: (est).

b Estimate based on Spindle/HP ratios (See G. N. Von Tunzelmann, *Steam Power and British Industrialization to 1860* (Oxford University Press: Oxford, 1978), p. 177.)

c S. Wingfield: Spindle/HP ratios would suggest similar spindleage as Fritchley.

d 1822 *DM* adverts detail all Shirland machinery.

e survey 1955 internal size?

Gould's additions, made it more complex. Among Gould's new buildings were a loom-house, 132 ft by 33 ft, an apprentice house – described as a 'hospital' or 'schoolhouse', capable of sleeping 200–300 children – smith's and joiner's shops, a turning room and a casting shop. At Amber Row, a short walk from the mill, he built cottages each with 545 square yard gardens for his employees and at nearby Toadhole Furnace six more.[14]

The mills' machinery reflected the buildings, the processes pursued, and their source. Fritchley, the first to fail, combined preparatory, spinning, weaving and finishing equipment on a scale almost Lilliputian. In contrast at the most long lived – South Wingfield and Kelstedge – processes were limited: at the former the spinning and later doubling of cotton; at Kelstedge the spinning of flax and later cotton for thread. Though Shirland was initially equipped for the 'spinning of cotton or silk, or both', Gould's business, 'calculated for carrying on a spinning and weaving concern in an extensive manner' extended the product range. Descriptions of mill rooms, ancillary buildings and machinery indicate the range of equipment that even smaller firms required, and indicate Gould's transformation of a primarily water-frame mill into a throstle- and mule-spinning and manufacturing enterprise. Adverts regularly described the machinery as 'quite new', 'newly fitted up' and 'in complete repair'. While the standard size of the mules suggests their being made and bought to order, varying individual throstle-spindleages indicate possible second-hand purchase. The first mill, at Wingfield Park, was apparently equipped with second-hand machinery brought from Manchester, and Hulse certainly purchased parts and second-hand machinery there – including from Peel & Williams – and at Stockport. The winding-up of the Shirland works hints at further possibilities. While references to a 'forcing and other pumps, fire engine, 1300 brass and iron wheels, lamps, bobbins, baskets, scales, beams and weights, spouting … iron, nails' indicate the everyday calls of mill life, the specification of a 'wheel cutting clock engine, joiner's bench, vices and tools; turner's benches, lathes and tools, blacksmiths benches, vices, bellows, anvils, drill bench, and tools; models, castings' suggests an ability to repair if not manufacture equipment on site, and the part of mills in training engineers in machinery and machine-tool making.[15]

All the mills occupied sites disproportionately large and therefore expensive because of the need to store water. Though the Amber and its tributaries powered many corn mills, only two converted to textiles: Higham, which John Radford, a candlewick maker, operated as a Bunk mill and Pentrich which became a silk mill. Maps and surviving plans demonstrate how water needs governed the form of sites.[16] At Wingfield Park the builders dammed the stream to create two reservoirs and constructed a mill-race that powered an 18 ft overshot wheel housed in the end of the mill. At Fritchley, in 1805 an 'overshot water-wheel, 20 feet high, with eight feet head from reservoir which is large', captured the stream's flow, albeit insufficiently in 'very dry seasons', when steam was used. At Kelstedge the dammed river created a reservoir sufficient for a 35 ft wheel. At Shirland the shallow valley required a different solution: the builders excavated land to the west of the river and constructed a dyke, some 660 yards in length, to its east, so channelling the flow south to a double sluice that provided the river outlet, and a third sluice that directed the flow to a 12 ft head sufficient to power the wheel (which was built with iron buckets). Small in output compared with the great Derwent mills – Belper and Milford combined produced 200–300 HP – the works were well inside the competence of local millwrights.[17] Yet even Shirland's water proved insufficient. In 1819 Hulse, by having 'wrongfully raised the height of a certain Dam or Weir', was to face action for causing silting and flooding upstream. Ironically, John Farey commented favourably upon dam and sluice systems such as Shirland's, as distinct from the weir and leat systems of water extraction, which he blamed for causing floods downstream.[18]

With water supply a constraint for all except Kelstedge, supplementary power was essential. Fritchley 'in the midst of plentiful coal country' boasted in 1805 'a Steam Engine 7 horse power, made under the direction of Mr Woodhouse, upon a wood frame' and 'so constructed, that with a small expence it may be removed to a coal or other mine'. In 1813 the South Wingfield Mill was advertised with 'a good steam engine'. In 1839 the mill was described, probably mistakenly, as being totally dependent upon steam: coal came from the nearby Oakerthorpe colliery.[19] At Shirland, notwithstanding its builders' efforts, the Lowes had, by 1806, acquired a steam engine 'nearly new, of 14 horses power complete, so as to work the machinery with or without the water wheel'.[20] Sherratts of Manchester were to repair its boiler 'as good as new' in August 1817. That these firms, close to supplies of coal and the Butterley iron working and engineering firm, did not develop a larger steam-based textile industry begs the question why.[21] Estimates that each steam generated HP required around 12½–15 lbs of coal per hour suggests that the answer might lie in the roads. Farey described one near Kelstedge as 'tremendous sudden and steep' and some of Shirland's as 'very deep miry and bad', while Blore, in 1793, wrote of South Wingfield 'the publick roads, not turnpike, are all in summer bad, and in winter nearly impassable'. Transport deficiencies arguably limited or lay behind the decline of firms too small to demand changes to infrastructure.[22]

The operation of factories, even the smaller ones, demanded a diverse labour force. Absentee owners required managers and in a 'non-cotton' area clerks, overseers and skilled workers were sometimes difficult to obtain and retain. The original advert for the Shirland site suggests that the rural surplus, presumably unemployed hands in framework knitters' and labourers' cottages, could be drawn on for semi-skilled work. While the operation of the valley's mills indicates that demands were met, local labour might have been unwilling.

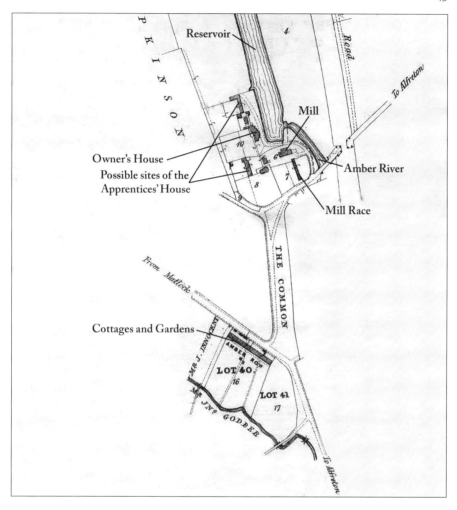

Amber Mill, Shirland. Plan of 1854. By permission: Derbyshire Record Office

Blore, describing South Wingfield in 1793, distinguished framework knitters and those of maturer years in agriculture from 'the younger part, and of the lowest order, in the cotton mill'. Indeed local poor law overseers seem to have been reluctant to place children in mills. Gould's construction of cottages and an apprentice house presumably reflected deficiencies in supply as much as a preference for tied and indentured labour. The employment of apprentices, even for calico weaving, suggests, despite the poverty of the area, recruitment problems unknown to most North West firms. An 1818 employee list for Shirland, possibly partial but including some apprentices, has 128 names; of these 45 per cent fall into possible family or sibling groupings. The female to

Amber Mill, Shirland, and ancillary building, photographed in 2007.

male ratio of 2:1 compares with those for South Wingfield and Kelstedge in 1839 (81 per cent and 79 per cent respectively). In the latter two mills, 53 per cent and 71 per cent respectively of the employees were under 18 years of age.[23]

In 1818 Hulse's employees, presumably at his behest, petitioned the House of Lords against proposals to limit the hours for children in cotton manufactories. The first record of hours at Shirland – ignored by visiting magistrates in 1802 as the mill (they noted the rooms 'were lofty, clean and airy') did not employ apprentices – is for 1821 when three ex-overseers apparently gave evidence concerning Hulse's apprentices. Then, and without any indication of shorter Saturday or winter working, Shirland worked from 6.00 a.m. to 7.30 p.m. with stoppages of thirty minutes and one hour respectively for breakfast and dinner. On one evening each week apprentices were instructed in reading and writing, on four 'in the following branches – the little ones Knitting when they were perfect in the art, they were placed with those making new or Mending – about from 14 to 20 of the oldest were employed in washing and mangling ...' Every Sunday brought school from 9.30 to 11.30 a.m. and then, 'when fine they run', and preaching every other Sunday and a sermon and prayers every Sunday evening. The mill farm doubtless contributed to the breakfast and supper of boiled milk and bread (gruel when milk was unavailable in the winter) and meat and potatoes every day for dinner. Similar to the diet of other Derbyshire apprentices, it bettered the local Ashover workhouse, which provided meat on two days. The intensity of work at Shirland is unknown. One of the Wilsons' Radford overseers who had worked at their South Wingfield mill from around

Amber Mill, Shirland – owner's house and farm ancillary buildings, 2007.

1813 to 1829 reported hours left unchanged by the 1819 legislation, and at Radford, where a short breaks regime operated, fines and physical punishment for the youngest that possibly applied at South Wingfield too. While the Shirland apprentices' experience was perhaps more regular, certainly than that of the surrounding framework knitters and labourers who joined the Pentrich rising, fixed and maintenance costs may have made their employment more expensive than at 'free labour' mills such as South Wingfield: that factory survived when Shirland was to fail.[24]

III

The business of the valley's firms, be it the sale of goods, raw materials and equipment acquisition, or financial services, drew them into extensive networks: to Alfreton – certainly for professional services at times of bankruptcy; to regional centres at Derby or Nottingham; and to Manchester and London. While the setting of Hulse's signature alongside those of other Nottinghamshire and Derbyshire cotton masters petitioning the Lords against the 1818 Bill suggests a tight business community, the Amber Valley's firms were to develop differently.[25]

Though not venturing overseas, unlike Derbyshire firms such as the Strutts and indeed the smaller Longsdon enterprise, there was little uniformity about the trades they pursued. Perhaps anticipating Habakkuk's successful small producers,[26] the two longest lived undertakings were to specialise: South Wingfield though twice failing as a yarn producer – under White and Green – was to survive into the late nineteenth century as a cotton doubler;

Amber Mill, Shirland. Cast-iron window frames, photographed in 2007.

Kelstedge, originally a flax mill, was similarly to have a long trade as a lace thread manufacturer. Fritchley, though abandoning the loom shops that had produced printers and sheetings, continued to spin, bleach and dye a range of low count 'Twist Cotton Sewings Indias and working Cottons' that, given the firm's size and competitive markets, must have rendered the Turtons' bankruptcy inevitable. The Lowes were unusual in producing both cotton and silk yarn, presumably for sale to cloth manufacturers and hosiers; however their purchase, presumably for a customer, of 100 lbs of 100s Georgia mule twist from McConnel & Kennedy in 1804, perhaps indicates an inability to meet orders. While Gould's business was more typical of the Manchester area than of the east midlands, he evidently found markets at Derby and London. This was the business continued by Bellairs and then by Hulse. Though finishing was central to the sale of cloths, few Derbyshire firms engaged in that trade. Charles Callow of Derby and John Gould and the successor firms at Shirland sent their cloths to Stockport's William Sykes.[27]

During 1809 Gould's bill for finishing at Sykes's came to £1601 8s. od. Given finishing's share of costs, this would suggest cloths to the value of about £16,000. In the nine months to September 1810 (including eight under his executors), finishing to the value of £2,013 was apparently done.[28] The Sykeses' letter books detail this trade when Hulse was operating Shirland on his own account. Entries indicate, after the 10 per cent discount offered to regular customers, some £200–300 of business each quarter.[29] The cloths included low count, 3s, 4s and 9s, ginghams, shirtings, twills, etc. of varying lengths – but chiefly c. 38–42 yds – and widths. A great deal of effort went into determining the appropriate finish – soft or fine, calendered or glazed, and 'as per Irish' – and indeed the widths cloths were to be pressed to. Some cloths, 'what we call fragile – i.e. the weft has separated in places owing to the cloth being manufactured almost without Twist', demanded filling and finishing at the limits of the bleacher's craft. Others including 'menders' and older cloths, many apparently from the bankrupt Bellairs' stock, caused continuing problems.

Finished goods were returned to Hulse or, at his request, sent by Sykes to London customers. The bulk of Hulse's London business went to three dealers in Manchester wares: Thomas Martin Son & Hughes, Rowlandson Burra & Co. and Deacon Son & Ellis. The cloths were finished to the specification of the customer, and the bleacher bore the risk associated with defects in the finished article. To Sykes' consternation, during 1816–17 all three London firms complained of the cloth's condition and in particular mildew. Sykes rejected blame, attributing the defects to transport, storage by others – including at Shirland – and old cloth. However, in order to preserve his firm's name, he had little choice but to accede to the London houses' demands for a considerable abatement. Hulse made visits to London – offering to help Sykes – and was perhaps inspired: in December 1817 he requested his cloths be stamped with the Prince of Wales feathers and in March 1819, evidently aware of a changing fashion, expressed a preference for shirtings to be finished soft (as normally done for the higher counts) rather than hard.

Transport of Hulse's finished, London bound, cloths – to Manchester, where Sykes had a warehouse, and then by canal with Pickford's or Aspull's – was less fraught than the carriage of goods on the trans-Pennine route from Stockport to Shirland. Correspondence continually returned to themes such as the merits of wagons and carts (though of lower capacity the latter, perhaps because of conditions on the roads, were generally used); the number of and demands upon horses; Hulse's readiness to load more than beast and machine could safely pull; the desire to avoid excess weight charges and conversely the need to send full loads in order to ensure maximum use of resources; and the sometimes sloppy counting on and off at Shirland. Sykes and Hulse eventually arranged a route via Tideswell, but their exchange of carts and horses at the mid-way point (Hulse's carrying grey cloths, Sykes' finished cloths and the many items that Hulse ordered) became subject to pillage by robbers. Though the carters were questioned by the fearsome John Lloyd,[30] Sykes had no doubts of his own man 'who would not [otherwise] suit us as a Collector in Manchester & Stockport where carts are continually beset with thieves'.[31] For Hulse transport was evidently a time-consuming issue and a probably significant addition to merchanting and manufacturing costs. Besides finished cloths and bales of raw cotton, machinery, and even his iron boiler, came from Manchester or Stockport by road: conveyance of the latter took a month of planning and three teams of three horses, one each from Hulse and Sykes and another from Sherratt's, the repairer. Sykes evidently came to feel that Hulse was taking advantage and by 1818–19 Potter and Hibberson of Manchester, professional carriers to the east midlands, were also being used.

Transport difficulties emphasise the marginality of the Amber Valley mills, and in particular Hulses' dependence on the goodwill of others. Though the valley's firms seem to have bought raw cotton directly from merchants – Jeremiah Whittenbury's Manchester firm was involved with the failed White and Lowe enterprises – Hulse sometimes used Sykes as an intermediary. Sykes sold Hulse's cotton waste and unwanted and defective warps and negotiated for the purchase of second-hand machinery. Sykes' accommodation of his customer was to extend from matters as small as the provision of domestic salt and flour and seed potatoes – reciprocated by Hulse's supply of grain seed – to issues more substantial. While Hulse's settlement of his quarterly account was seemingly regular and without complaint he could stretch Sykes' tolerance: on 7 June 1816 Sykes curtly wrote, 'advising of Bill being refused acceptance for want of advice', and again 10 February 1817, '[your] enclosure £386 13s. 2d. came duly to hand this morning: I was disappointed to find it so long dated – as we wanted it to meet some acceptances and our Bank do not take to a/c any beyond 3 mos – I hope we shall be able to get it discounted and that you will bear in mind our poverty.' Though Hulse had other connections than Sykes, it is possible that he, given their family relationship and, not least, his readiness to oblige, became the most significant.

Hulse's career, though sparsely documented, would not have been atypical. With good early connections and well paid as a manager to Gould and the Bellairs – his salary rose from £400 p.a. in 1810 to £600 p.a. in 1814 – he was even able to accumulate monies in the three per cents and to lend sums, not always wisely, to others.[32] Despite the harsh experience of Bellairs' bankruptcy in 1814, its threat to his position and his initial loss of £616 5s. 9d. at Bellairs' Derby Bank, Hulse was able, when operating on his own account, to weather the turmoil of the post-war years. However there were pointers: while Sykes in April 1817 could boast of 'such a stir in goods which makes us very busy', the number of cloths sent to Sykes by Hulse in 1820 was no greater than that despatched by Gould in 1810. Structural factors – the firm's isolation and a probable growing inability to compete with power-looms in low-count weaving – must have been at work. So too were personal factors which suggest a growing loss of control: the prevarications and sloppiness that attracted Sykes' rebukes; the legal action over the Amber dam; a rates dispute with the Wessington churchwardens; the apprentices' case; the presumably disaffected ex-overseers; and the financial juggling.[33] After his gazetting in 1822 his father-in-law, William Sykes, doubtless from concern for his daughter and grandchildren, became involved in Hulse's affairs: among his discoveries was a debt of £200 to the Manchester merchant J. H. Heron – Hulse had used £70 of this to pay wages.[34] His firm had simply run out of the wherewithal to continue.

IV

The experience of the Amber Valley's mills is an example of the potential for reverse in even the most dynamic economic process. While the mills' development coincided with the high tide of water-spinning and war, more substantial determinants were at work. In short the failure of the valley's firms to build on the advances of the 1790s was largely due to an absence of those advantages natural and acquired that underwrote the development of Lancashire's cotton industry.[35]

What the valley did not lack was a supply of businessmen willing to try their hand. Between 1792 and 1840 the four mills were controlled by 23 men operating 19 differently named firms. Though their principals came from the middling ranks, they differed from those in the north-west in that only four – Spear, Gould and Hulse at Shirland and Wilson at South Wingfield – can definitely be described as being rooted in textiles. Excluding Cawood and Cartledge at Kelstedge and the Wilsons, the life expectancy of these firms was about five years: a turnover that matches the experience of small firms at Manchester.[36] It is notable that the 'survivor' firms at South Wingfield and Kelstedge produced commodities, yarn or thread for hosiery and/or lace, that brought forward linkages to Nottinghamshire industries; Fritchley and Shirland manufactured for intensely competitive markets that their location and mode of production merely exacerbated.

The history of failure in the cotton industry is unwritten. Of the Amber valley's businessmen, seven were gazetted, one passed his assets to creditors, and eleven dissolved their partnerships. The Lowes apart, the failures do not correlate with the wider industry figures; however, all the partnerships dissolved when cotton bankruptcies peaked.[37] While Green was to rebuild a business, albeit not in cotton, and survive a second bankruptcy,[38] White, the Turtons, the Lowes and Bellairs were to slip from the record. Hulse was to die within three years of his bankruptcy, followed within a year by his wife. Her father, William Sykes, sold her household effects and found foster care at Alfreton for his three granddaughters, two soon to die. He also provided for the keep and education of his two grandsons, William Wilson Hulse and Joseph Sykes Hulse, and remembered them in his will.[39] The fate of the Shirland mill's labour force and the apprentices is unknown – they may have found work in other Derbyshire mills or drifted to the east midlands towns and villages.

There is a footnote to the Shirland mill's history. Among those signing the employees' petition to the House of Lords in 1818 was the fifteen-year-old son of Hulse's sister Sarah. He had been fostered and put to learn the trade at Shirland following his mother's death in 1814 and his father's decision to abandon his family and train as a minister. In 1821 the nephew, Joseph Whitworth, was to embark on a career in Manchester and London that was to take him to the heights of the engineering profession and the armaments industry. It is not unreasonable, as his obituary part asserts, to suggest that the speed with which he found employment in Manchester, and his later success, was down to early years spent amid the machine tools, the machinery, the steam engine, and his uncle's guns, at Shirland. His memories of the Amber Mill cannot have been entirely negative: his cousins William Wilson Hulse and Joseph Sykes Hulse found employment with him and became part of the design team that brought his machine tools to fruition; Whitworth himself was to build his house, Stancliffe Hall, at Darley Dale, not too distant from Shirland.[41] From there, albeit attenuated, a thread can be drawn, through Hulse and Sir Joseph Whitworth's educational legacies, to the historians of 'the Manchester tradition'[42] and their contribution to the understanding of cotton's history.

Notes

1. R. S. Fitton and A. P. Wadsworth, *The Strutts and the Arkwrights, 1758–1830* (Manchester University Press: Manchester, 1958); S. D. Chapman, *The Early Factory Masters* (David & Charles: Newton Abbot, 1967); K. Honeyman, *Origins of Enterprise* (Manchester University Press: Manchester, 1982), pp. 192–6.

2. C. Aspin, *The Water-Spinners* (Helmshore Local History Society: Helmshore, 2003); G. Ingle, *Yorkshire Cotton: The Yorkshire Cotton Industry, 1780–1835* (Carnegie: Preston, 1997).

3. J. Pilkington, *A View of the Present State of Derbyshire Vol. II* (Drewry: Derby, 1789), pp. 237–41, 313–28. And see B. Cooper, *Transformation of a Valley: the Derbyshire Derwent* (Heinemann: London, 1983).

4. Honeyman, *Origins of Enterprise*, ch. 5.

5. T. Blore, *A History of … South Winfield in Derbyshire* (Brewman: London, 1793), p. 84. Derbyshire County Record Office [DCRO]: D6579/1/1–2 Deed etc. South Wingfield Mill. R. Johnson, *A History of Alfreton* (R. Johnson: Alfreton, 1970), p. 108. *Derby Mercury [DM]* 11 June 1795; 19 March 1801; 18 March, 4 November 1813. *London Gazette [LG]* 1806, p. 839; 1813, p. 491. Nottinghamshire CRO [NCRO]: DR.WW William Wilson MSS. William Wilson (1769–1833) the purchaser. William Wilson (1800–66) became sole proprietor 1833, his principal business a large cotton spinning and Merino thread mill at Radford, Nottingham. DCRO: QR/E Land Tax, 1790–1830 (all sites). Commercial directories, 1792–1846.

6. *DM* 13 May, 2 August 1802; 8 December 1803; 4 July 1805; 14 January, 15 April, 30 December 1813; 28 April 1814. *LG* 1813, pp. 98, 147. DCRO: Crich Parish Registers, burials; Q/R1 2/351 Crich Enclosure Award 1788. J. G. Dawes, *A History of Crich* (Landmark: Ashbourne, 2003).

7. *DM* 27 September 1792, 24 July 1806. *LG* 10 June 1806; John Rylands University Library: McConnel & Kennedy MSS [M&K] MCK/2/1/10 & MCK/2/2/2 (all indexed).

8. R. S. Fitton, *The Arkwrights: Spinners of Fortune* (Manchester University Press: Manchester, 1989), p. 214. *Manchester Mercury* 25 October 1801. *DM* 2, 9, 16 October 1806; 8, 15 February 1810. *LG* 1807, p. 1443. *Gentleman's Magazine* 1810, p. 285; 1811 p. 678. PRO: PROB 11/1507 WILL John Gould. DCRO: 430z/T23 Deed: Joseph Hulse to William Hopkinson. Quarry Bank Mill Styal: BAA [BAA] 132 A+B William Sykes Nominal Ledger.

9. Stockport Local Studies Library [LSL]: Sykes MSS [Sykes MSS] 178/17/9 Miscellaneous Accounts Book. Derby LSL [DLSL]: Derbyshire Deeds 1813(04111), 1814(000989&000990). *LG* 1814, pp. 1448–9, 1570. L. S. Pressnell, *Country Banking in the Industrial Revolution* (Clarendon Press: Oxford, 1956), p. 471, misses Bellairs though noting falling grain prices helped reduce bank liquidity. National Westminster Bank Archives: typescript note Bellairs Son & Co. University of Nottingham Library: Dr. E 89–102 Papers Bankruptcy Bellairs & Co. Bank Derby.

10. M&K MCK/2/2/5 M&K to John Bennett 14 July 1814.

11. *DM* 18 August 1814, 19 January 1815, 11 December 1822, 13 October, 1 December 1822, 5 October 1825, 19 March 1828. Manchester Central Library: Mf Cheadle Parish Registers, Marriages, 25 May 1818. *LG* 1822 p. 1329. Lichfield Diocesan Record Office: Will, Admin, Joseph Hulse. DCRO: D295M/T6 Estate W. E. Mousley.

12. *Ooford Dictionary of National Biography* [*ODNB*] (Oxford University Press: Oxford, 2004). Derbyshire County Library: Mf26352 Sir Joseph Banks Correspondence (Lyon Playfair Library, Imperial College) Milnes to Banks ff. 119, 175, 207, 233, 234, 299, 309. *DM* 20 February 1800, 5 November 1812. Cawood's partners were William Lowe (see *LG* 1807, p. 1134 for Lumsdale Mill: 'William Lowe' & 'Thomas Green' were partners there). DCRO: 475z/z/1/3/4/5 Valuation of Property 18 July 1853 and Will of George Cawood (d. 1846).

13. S. D. Chapman, 'Fixed Capital Formation in the British Cotton Industry, 1770–1815' *Economic History Review*, 2nd series XXIII.2 (1970), p. 239. PP 1839 (41) *Persons employed in Cotton, Woollen, Worsted, Flax and Silk Factories etc.*, pp. 210–21 (ranking based on counting and averaged estimates). For Shirland see n. 24 below. A. Ure, *The Philosophy of Manufactures* (Knight: London, 1835), p. 13.

14. Unless stated mill references can be found under the earlier relevant paragraphs. For Kelstedge see also DCRO: z/z4 D2404/3 Sale Particulars Amber House. See illustration of South Wingfield mill complex in R. Jewell, *Memory Lane* (Breedon Books: Derby, 1998), p. 191. N.E. Derbyshire District Council Planning Office: plans, elevations etc. for the Amber Mill complex (Listed building(s) now flats). DCRO: D595 R/1/1/3 4685–4705 Amber Row.

15. W. H. Brighouse, *Derbyshire Life and Countryside*, vol. 32 no. 10 (October 1967), p. 47.

16. For plans of mills, watercourses, dams etc. see the OS 1879 1:2500 series for Fritchley (Crich), Kelstedge (Ashover), South Wingfield. D295M/T6 Plan of Amber Mill, Shirland. DCRO: D 161/Box 17/61 Plan no. 2 for South Wingfield.

17. Fitton and Wadsworth, *Strutts and Arkwrights*, p. 207 n. 1.

18. G. Turbutt, *A History of Shirland and Higham* (Ogston Estates: Derbyshire, 1978), pp. 253–4. John Farey, *General View of the Agriculture of Derbyshire Vol. II* (B. Millan: London, 1815), pp. 489–90.

19. PP 1839 (41) *Persons employed*, p. 216.

20. But *DM* 18 August 1814: 'The mill is worked by Water and Steam'.

21. Cooper, *Transformation of a Valley*, pp. 113–15.

22. G. N. Von Tunzelmann, *Steam Power and British Industrialization to 1860* (Oxford University Press: Oxford, 1978), pp. 67–70. Blore, *South Winfield*, p. 83. Farey, *Agriculture of Derbyshire*, vol. III, pp. 224–5, 263.

23. Blore, *South Winfield*, p. 84. For the destinations of Shirland parish's apprentices see Turbutt, *Shirland and Higham*, pp. 275–8. House of Lords Record Office [HLRO] Main Papers 243k 1 May 1818 Petition of the Workpeople employed in the Cotton Mill of Mr. Joseph Hulse at Shirland in Derbyshire [HLRO: Workpeople]. PP 1839 (412) *Persons employed*, pp. 210–21.

24. HLRO: Workpeople. PP House of Lords 1819 (66) III, *An Account of the Cotton and Woollen Mills and Factories in the United Kingdom etc.* pp. 46, 50. DLSL: RF

331 MSS/24287 Statement of food and clothing of the apprentices with hours of working and meals. Farey, *Agriculture of Derbyshire*, p. 557. PP 1833 (450) XX *Employment of Children in Cotton factories, 1st Report*, C1, pp. 42–7, 53–4, 58–9. Though meeting in a quarry near the Wingfield mill, the Pentrich men did not attack it: see Cooper, *Transformation of a Valley*, pp. 278–83.

25. HLRO Main Papers 243d 13 May 1818 Petition of the Cotton Spinners of Mansfield, Nottinghamshire & the Neighbourhood.

26. H. J. Habakkuk, *Industrial Organisation since the Industrial Revolution* (University of Southampton: Southampton, 1968), p. 13.

27. Fitton and Wadsworth, *Strutts and Arkwrights*, ch. IX. S. D. Chapman, 'James Longsdon, 1745–1821, Farmer and Fustian manufacturer: the small firm in the early English cotton industry', *Textile History*, I (1968). R. Lowe, *General View of the Agriculture of the County of Nottinghamshire etc.* (Macrae: London, 1794), p. 54. See n.7 above for M&K.

28. BAA 132 A+B Nominal Ledger for William Sykes: a/c John Gould.

29. Unless noted Sykes MSS 173/17/4 Letter Book (73 to Hulse) and BAA 139 Sykes Letter Book (5 to Hulse) for Hulse's commercial dealings.

30. For whom see R. Glen, *Urban Workers in the Early Industrial Revolution* (Croom Helm: London, 1984), pp. 58–9.

31. Sykes MSS 173/17/4, 8 February 1817.

32. Sykes MSS 178/17/9 Misc. Accounts Book for Hulse's finances.

33. DCRO: Q/SO 1822/3 Hulse Joseph and Wessington Churchwardens and Overseers.

34. *LG* 10 August 1822, p. 1325; BAA 133 William Sykes Cash Book, attachment f. 122.

35. D. A. Farnie, *The English Cotton Industry and the World Market, 1815–1896* (Clarendon Press: Oxford, 1979), p. 46.

36. R. Lloyd-Jones and A. A. Le Roux, 'Marshall and the Birth and Death of Firms: The Growth and Size distribution of Firms in the early Nineteenth-Century Cotton Industry', *Business History*, XXIV.2 (1982), p. 144.

37. R. Burn, *Statistics of the Cotton Trade* (Simpkin Marshall: London, 1847), p. 25.

38. *LG* 1821 p. 2043.

39. DCRO: Shirland Parish Registers, burials. BAA 133 William Sykes Cash Book, 1812–1837; BAA 134 William Sykes Cash Book, 1825–38.

40. Norman Atkinson, *Sir Joseph Whitworth* (Sutton: Gloucester, 1996) is incorrect in rejecting (the *ODNB* (2004) in avoiding) Victorian accounts (*The Times*, 24 January 1887) of Whitworth's youth, albeit useful on the Hulse brothers, later the machine-tool makers, J. S. Hulse & Co. of Salford. See *DM* 25 January 1826 for the Hulses' household and personal possessions.

41. Prof. P. Mathias in Fitton, *The Arkwrights*, p. xii.

PART 2

TEXTILES OVERSEAS

9

Catalan cotton goods and colonial markets, 1880–1914*

JOSEPH HARRISON

THROUGHOUT the nineteenth century Catalonia, in the north-eastern corner of the Iberian peninsula, constituted Spain's first industrial region.[1] While most other Spanish regions, apart from the Basque Country, are generally portrayed by scholars as prime examples of economic backwardness, a leading economic historian famously dubbed the principality 'Spain's factory'.[2] Even so, the Catalan economy was notoriously lopsided, heavily dependent on its leading sector, cotton textiles. At the beginning of the twentieth century, Catalonia's cotton mills employed around 80,000 men, women and children,[3] while the cotton industry accounted for 49.2 per cent of Catalan industrial output.[4]

With a few notable exceptions, the Catalan cotton textile industry was characterized by its lack of specialization, uncompetitiveness, and atomised production in a myriad tiny enterprises, the majority of them family firms.[5] Àngel Calvo calculates that, in 1900, 68.4 per cent of companies possessed fewer than 1,000 spindles; 12.2 per cent had between 1,000 and 5,000; 15.2 per cent 5–10,000; 3.0 per cent 10–20,000; while only 1.0 per cent boasted more than 20,000 spindles.[6] On top of this, Catalan cotton manufacturers had to organize their own sales structure. In contrast to Lancashire, where mill owners performed few commercial functions and were spared the expense of having to

---

* I wish to thank the staff of the Biblioteca de Catalunya for their help and encouragement, as well as Carlos García Pons, librarian of the Foment del Treball Nacional, for granting me access to his unrivalled collection despite the presence of the builders.

provide credit to their customers, Catalan manufacturers were forced to act as 'manufacturers, merchants and bankers at one and the same time'.[7]

The Catalan cotton industry, whose origins date from a ban on imports of Asian textiles in the 1720s,[8] consolidated its position between 1830 and 1860.[9] During these three decades, the consumption of cotton fibre rose more than eightfold.[10] That said, any progress that was achieved by the industry was hard-won since, by common consent, the odds were stacked against manufacturers.[11] On the supply side expansion was constrained by Catalonia's poor endowment of natural resources, not least coal, the cotton industry's main energy source.[12] Most of the coal used in the region's steam-powered mills had to be imported, at considerable cost, mainly from the United Kingdom. The principal alternative was to use low-grade domestic coal, which itself had to be transported long distances from Asturias, initially by coastal shipping and later by rail.[13] From the early 1840s, when geological surveys suggested the existence of significant reserves of coal near the town of Sant Joan de les Abadesses, in a remote valley of the Pyrenees, the Catalan middle classes unwisely sank their savings into building a railway from Sant Joan to Granollers, linking the embryonic mining zone with Barcelona and other manufacturing centres along the Mediterranean littoral.[14] Sadly, neither the coal mines nor the railway were a commercial success. Indeed, the period 1844–66 witnessed the collapse of two companies set up to construct the 88-kilometre stretch of railway track.[15] As a result, Catalan manufacturers abandoned what Nadal terms 'the British model of industrialization', which required plentiful supplies of cheap coal.[16]

In their search for a new solution, from the 1870s Catalan cotton manufacturers began to relocate their production to the lower Pyrenees, an area known as the *Muntanya*. Two main factors lay behind this decision. First, decentralization, away from Barcelona and the coastal region, allowed manufacturers to take advantage of cheaper water power from the fast-flowing rivers of the pre-Pyrenees, among them the Llobregat, Ter, Freser, Cardener, and Fluvià. Second, by constructing new mills in the countryside, away from the revolutionary atmosphere of the old industrial towns, the mill owners could substitute female and child labour for more expensive male operatives.[17] By 1910, two thirds of the region's 1.8 million cotton spindles were situated on or near river banks.[18]

On the demand side, Catalan manufacturers were the perennial victims of the chronically low purchasing power of Spain's overwhelmingly rural population.[19] Worse still, from the mid-1880s, when the country was suddenly inundated with imports of cheap wheat, the cotton textile industry began to show signs of overproduction, due above all to a dramatic fall in demand from the cereal growers of Old Castile.[20] An editorial in *El Trabajo Nacional*, mouthpiece of the Catalan employers' federation, lamented that: 'Agriculture is ruined, that is the cry of pain which is heard from one corner of the Peninsula to another.

The ruin began with falling wheat prices. American competition first, then India and Chile, but above all Russia and the Danubian states.'[21]

In a desperate attempt to remain competitive, mill owners sought to raise productivity by incorporating the latest technology.[22] During the final decades of the nineteenth century, the main technological improvements took place in spinning, where – along American lines – self-acting mules were gradually replaced by ring-frames.[23] Apart from taking on an increasing proportion of women and girls, the hard-nosed mill owners also endeavoured to keep down costs through production speed-ups, pay cuts, longer working hours, and by dismissing trade unionists.[24]

Latter-day critics of the Catalan mill owners condemn them for their conservatism and lack of entrepreneurial spirit. Why, they ask, didn't the cotton manufacturers of the principality imitate their Swiss or Italian counterparts, who compensated for the limitations of their domestic markets by specializing in the production of high value-added goods, directed towards foreign sales?[25] However, Catalan cotton mill owners insisted that the option of specialized production was not open to them, due to low levels of aggregate demand in the impoverished home market. For instance, in his submission to a government inquiry of 1913 on working conditions in the Spanish textile industry, Sr Gorris, a cotton manufacturer from the *Muntanya*, maintained that:

> For multiple reasons, the output obtained by the textile industry in Catalonia, is well below the output that is obtained in England … The internal market, being so restricted, does not permit the specialization that takes place in the big English mills, where a factory which has 2,000 to 3,000 spindles, works on two, three, or four different types, whereas in our factories, since we produce for a relatively small market, we have to produce nearly all numbers and almost all types … This cannot be attributed to one factor or another, it is the product of the conditions in which our industry has developed; if the latter were larger and our market stronger we could have built factories with greater capacity and we could have specialized, but, for the moment, this is not possible.[26]

Other commentators, however, contended that the mistaken choice of manufacturers to produce a range of items in a single factory, often on the same machine – a process known as *enciclopedisme* – led to over-manning and the production of cheap, low-grade fabrics.[27] All the same, it is widely held by economic historians that the Catalan cotton industry adapted remarkably well to the well-known deficiencies of the Spanish market.[28] However, denied the advantages of economies of scale, the price that the mill owners paid for their refusal to specialize was an almost complete failure to compete in world markets.[29] In this respect, of course, Catalonia was not alone.

Douglas Farnie recounts how, during the nineteenth century, nine regions of continental Europe developed a cotton industry. Yet none of them evolved into a 'mini-Lancashire'. In his opinion, the European cotton textile industry was incapable of building up a low-cost structure comparable to that of north-west England.[30]

Following the loss of Spain's empire in the New World after 1808, with the exceptions of Cuba, Puerto Rico, and the Philippines, the Catalan cotton industry – which imported large quantities of raw cotton, coal, and machinery – came to depend for its very survival on selling practically the whole of its production in the protected home market.[31] To paraphrase Douglas Farnie, unlike their English counterparts, Catalan mill owners were never in a position to break free from their overwhelming reliance on the domestic market.[32]

Despite this unpromising situation, Catalan economists, prominent among them José Ferrer i Vidal and Andrés de Sard, were adamant that tariff protection was a precondition for the advancement of the Spanish cotton industry, due to insurmountable cost differentials *vis-à-vis* its principal competitors, namely England, Switzerland and Alsace.[33] Elsewhere in the peninsula, however, apart from Castilian wheat growers and Basque ironmasters – their livelihoods threatened by cheap imports – the doctrine of protectionism attracted few advocates. In his 1908 study of the Catalan economy, the French economist Édouard Escarra observed that 'the Catalans are naturally proud of their industries', adding that, 'for their part, the Spanish consider the Catalans as "egotists", who have got rich at their expense, by exploiting Spain, thanks to excessive tariff protection'.[34] In a similar vein, modern Spanish economists generally dismiss Catalonia's mill owners as rent seekers.[35]

The role of colonial markets

While open competition in international markets was a chimera – Catalan producers looked longingly towards the Caribbean island of Cuba, with its wealthy planter class.[36] Writing in 1853, Joan Güell i Ferrer, who had previously amassed a large fortune in Havana, argued that:

> It is clearly demonstrated that Catalonia's principal market is the other Spanish provinces, just as *their* principal market is Catalonia ... These reciprocal markets are the only certain ones, since the rest are exposed to a thousand eventualities. That of our Antilles is, without doubt, after [Spain] of great importance because of the system of protection'.[37]

Two decades later, in the throes of Cuba's first separatist rebellion (the Ten Years' War of 1868–78), Güell i Ferrer declared that 'the rich and Spanish island of Cuba is the first external market for our agricultural products, and perhaps our industrial ones', further asserting that 'the irreparable loss of [Cuba] would reduce the political and economic importance of Spain by more than half'.[38]

Well before the so-called Agricultural Depression made its appearance south of the Pyrenees, a number of Spain's businessmen, including the Catalan mill owners and the flour millers of Santander, were convinced that 'the Pearl of the Indies' offered producers the possibility of a 'reserved market' for goods they could dispose of in the home market.[39] Following concerted pressure, in June 1882 Sagasta's Liberal government introduced an Act of Commercial Relations with the Overseas Provinces.[40] For customs purposes, the Act defined Spain's overseas provinces (Cuba, Puerto Rico and the Philippines) as part of the peninsula, decreeing that all trade between the metropolis and these islands should be treated as cabotage (coastal shipping). As Table 1 shows, helped by a phased reduction in customs duties over the period 1882–91,[41] sales of cotton goods to Cuba, Puerto Rico and the Philippines nearly doubled between 1880 and 1885, and more than quadrupled over the following five years.[42]

Table 1   *Exports of cotton goods from Catalonia, 1875–90, in tonnes*

Year	colonies	total	percentage of total output
1875	378.7	402.2	1.5
1880	548.5	642.4	2.1
1885	1,002.2	1,148.7	3.0
1890	4,205.7	4,498.2	10.8

Source: Jordi Maluquer, 'La gran transformació. Industrialització i modernització a la Catalunya del segle XIX', in Jordi Nadal *et al.*, *Història econòmica de la Catalunya contemporània*, 1, *La formació d'una societat industrial* (Barcelona, Enciclopèdia Catalana, 1994), 228.

While Catalan mill owners accepted that colonial trade did not offer a lasting answer to the problem of overproduction, the new legislation was greeted with enthusiasm within the principality. In their evidence to a government commission of 1889, representatives of the region's employers maintained that consumption of cotton goods in Spain had fallen by 14 per cent between 1882 and 1888.[43] It was their considered opinion that '[without] the advantages obtained in the markets of Cuba and Puerto Rico, thanks to the Law of Commercial Relations of 20 July 1882, which opened a safety valve for our products, the Spanish cotton industry might not have been able to save itself from a catastrophe'.[44]

Catalan demands for a bigger share of the colonial market are best seen against the background of the principality's lengthy campaign for greater tariff protection.[45] To this end, in March 1889 the region's two main employers' organizations, the Institut Industrial and the Foment de la Producció Nacional, merged to form what was to become Spain's most influential business lobby, the Foment del Treball Nacional.[46] Two years later, pressure from the Foment was rewarded with the ultra-protectionist Cánovas tariff of December 1891. Moreover, either side of this legislation, the Philippine tariff of April 1891 and the Cuban tariff of July 1892 raised customs duties on goods entering the overseas provinces from outside the metropolis.[47]

With these advantages, Catalonia's struggling cotton industry embarked on a new phase of prosperity. In his report of 1895 to the Overseas Ministry, the president of the Foment, Juan Puig y Saladrigas, stated that:

[Trade] with the Antilles has given a decisive impulse to the manufacturing industries of the peninsula. More than thirty million pesetas of cotton goods were exported to the Antilles through the port Barcelona in 1894. It is no exaggeration to calculate that 1.5 million pieces of cotton were exported to the overseas provinces; an enormous quantity which was enough to keep going 8,000 looms and 850,000 spindles. If to this considerable sum for cotton goods, we add all the other textiles, the number of workers thrown out of work by the closure of the Antilles market would be disastrous. Every branch of the country's production … lives and breathes from the trade with our provinces in America and Oceania.[48]

When separatist rebellions broke out in Cuba (1895) and the Philippines (1896), the Catalan cotton textile industry received an added boost, owing to 'significant shipments of clothing to the numerous battalions sent out to combat the insurrection'.[49] According to the British consul in Barcelona, twenty-five firms produced a type of cotton cloth known as *rayadillo*, which was worn by Spanish troops serving in the tropics.[50] Not surprisingly, the Catalan business community vociferously opposed any concession to the insurgents.[51]

On the eve of Spain's ignominious naval defeats at Cavite and Santiago de Cuba in the Spanish–American War of 1898, Cuba, the Philippines, and Puerto Rico accounted for nearly one-fifth of the entire output of Catalan cotton mills.[52] Thanks to a clause in the Paris peace treaty of December 1898, Spain was granted equal treatment with the victorious United States in its trading relations with Cuba over the next decade. More ominously, the lucrative markets of the Antilles and the Philippine archipelago were now open to all comers.[53]

The impact of Spain's 1898 disaster

By the end of 1898, an atmosphere of deep pessimism had engulfed the Catalan business community, not least the cotton industry.[54] Most observers bemoaned the fact that the peninsular market was unable to absorb a similar volume of goods to that previously sent to the former colonies. Without new markets, it was asserted, the sector surely faced a spate of bankruptcies, factory closures and job losses.[55]

Before long, however, the mood changed to one of optimism as a number of factors came to the rescue of the mill owners.[56] First, a sharp depreciation in the value of the peseta, caused by the extraordinary cost of the three-year military campaign, stimulated foreign sales while making imports more expensive.[57] Conversely, manufacturers had to pay more for their basic inputs: raw cotton, artificial dyestuffs, coal, and machinery.[58] Second, as the British consul in Barcelona informed the Foreign Office in 1899:

> About 200,000 soldiers, returned to Spain from Cuba and Manila during the year, these men on arrival here were clothed in the usual drill suits while campaigning in the tropics, but as they all received on returning home the arrears of pay due to them, considerable sums were spent on new outfits to the manifest advantage of the Barcelona shopkeepers.[59]

Third, bumper harvests in 1898 and an above-average crop in 1899 resulted in a pronounced increase in the purchasing power of rural consumers.[60] Fourth, relations between Catalan producers, the export houses, and their customers in the former colonies were sufficiently well established as to avert an overnight breakdown in trade.[61]

To everyone's relief, 1899 was a year of excellent fortunes for the Catalan cotton textile industry. In a message to the Silvela government, representatives of the Foment stated that 'the immediate consequences of the war have not been as terrible as was feared nor have they given rise to the sharp crisis that everyone predicted'.[62] Indeed, throughout the summer of 1900, work in the region's cotton mills proceeded at a feverish pace. Amid fears that domestic orders would not be fulfilled, manufacturers built new factories and accumulated huge stockpiles of raw cotton at fancy prices.[63]

Sadly for the mill owners, the post-colonial boom turned out to be ephemeral. By 1900, the nation's conscript army had spent its back pay; the sequence of good harvests came to an end; and textile production in the *Muntanya* was badly disrupted by strike activity.[64] Throughout the autumn of that year, the economic press reverberated with stories of industrial recession.[65] Factories shut their doors, and thousands of operatives had to be laid off.[66] A committee set up by the Foment recommended the intro-duction of short-time working (*el short times inglés*) as the most effective way of spreading the misery among the labouring classes.[67] Thereafter, over the next few years, the cotton industry fell victim to a variety of setbacks. In 1902 a violent and disruptive general strike, in support of striking metal-workers, triggered economic meltdown throughout the principality.[68] Later, a debilitating drought, which lasted from 1904 to 1906, bringing famine and starvation to large parts of central and southern Spain, further depressed already weak rural demand.[69]

The search for new markets

The 'mortal blow' of the loss of empire in 1898 presaged a sharp fall in sales of Catalan cotton goods to the former colonies.[70] In addition to facing competition from France, Germany and Italy, Catalan manufacturers had to meet a strong challenge from the cotton mills of New England, with their vertically integrated, high-throughput technology.[71] Moreover, in Latin American markets, US manufacturers enjoyed lower transport costs and more regular shipping services.[72]

According to Carles Sudrià's calculations, based on Spanish trade statistics, sales of cotton goods to Cuba declined from 4,500 tonnes a year in the peak years of 1893–97 to 1,800 tonnes in 1898–1902. Over the same period, exports to the Philippines, which was at war with the United States from 1899 to 1902, fell by an even greater extent, from 2,500 tonnes to 800 tonnes per annum. As for Puerto Rico, itself annexed by the Americans in 1900, exports of Catalan cottons had by 1902 dwindled to almost nothing. Overall, Sudrià estimates, sales of cotton goods to these islands collapsed by as much as 70 per cent between 1898 and 1902 (see Table 2).

In the specific example of Spanish cotton exports to Cuba, Sudrià's findings have been questioned by new data from Jordi Maluquer. Basing his calculations on Cuban trade statistics, Maluquer suggests that Catalan mill owners were reluctant to surrender the valuable Antilles market to outsiders.[73] As Table 3 shows, while the contribution of Catalan cotton goods to total Cuban imports fell by roughly fifty per cent between 1899 and 1907, there is evidence of a modest recovery in sales to the island after 1901.

Maluquer's more optimistic interpretation is supported by statistics from the ill-fated Mutua de Fabricantes de Tejidos de Algodón (see below). As Table 4 demonstrates, a dramatic fall in exports of white goods to Cuba after 1897 was partly offset by a steady, albeit irregular, rise in sales of dyed and printed goods over the next decade.[74] In marked contrast, exports to the Philippines dried up almost completely in the aftermath of the colonial débâcle.

How can we explain the survival in sales of Catalan cotton goods to Cuba after 1898, without the benefit of protective tariffs? Two main factors probably contributed to this development. First, despite losing possession of the island in the Paris treaty, emigration from the peninsula did not come to a halt. Indeed, the Cuban census of 1907 shows the presence of 228,000 inhabitants of Spanish origin, 11.1 per cent of the population, compared with only 129,000 in 1899.[75]

Table 2   *Exports of cotton goods from Spain, 1897–1910, in tonnes*

Year	Cuba	Argentina	Europe	Philippines	Total
1897	4,246	?	?	3,960	10,298
1898	2,140	77	706	1,769	5,871
1899	2,679	52	627	995	5,959
1900	1,551	30	572	1,882	5,017
1901	1,485	53	824	732	4,247
1902	1,292	55	664	943	4,073
1903	1,632	149	509	531	4,366
1904	1,725	378	643	734	5,337
1905	2,225	580	772	961	7,111
1906	1,652	730	737	766	6,125
1907	1,920	490	1,050	961	6,925
1908	1,473	1,015	1,086	416	7,065
1909	1,923	1,484	1,615	548	8,291
1910	1,512	1,447	634	365	6,292

Source: Carles Sudrià, 'La exportación en el desarrollo de la industria algodonera española, 1875–1920', *Revista de Historia Económica*, 1 (ii) (1983), 383–5.

Table 3   *Cuban imports of Spanish cotton goods, 1899–1907*

Year	value (millions of dollars)	percentage of total imports of cotton goods
1899	2.13	34.2
1900	1.61	26.4
1901	1.37	22.4
1902	1.48	27.0
1903	1.44	22.5
1904	1.51	18.3
1905	1.86	20.6
1906	1.57	18.0
1907	1.66	18.0

Source: Jordi Maluquer, 'La gran transformació', 324.

Second, unlike their new competitors, Catalan manufacturers mainly supplied the bottom end of the Cuban market in terms of quality and price.[76]

Table 4   *Export of cotton goods to Cuba and the Philippines, 1897–1906, in millions of pesetas*

Year	white goods		dyed and printed goods	
	Cuba	*Philippines*	*Cuba*	*Philippines*
1897	15.40	9.71	7.71	10.73
1898	4.51	2.62	7.75	7.08
1899	4.42	1.22	11.49	3.08
1900	2.63	1.68	6.40	7.32
1901	2.99	0.52	5.90	2.97
1903	2.14	0.12	8.00	1.18
1904	1.51	0.09	9.55	1.45
1905	0.95	0.08	23.13	2.13
1906	0.78	0.07	9.63	1.71

Source: *El Trabajo Nacional*, xvi, no. 411 (16 January 1908), 309–10.

One branch of the industry which fared remarkably well at this stage was hosiery and cotton knit. This enterprising sector, which employed approximately 10,000 operatives, was located on the Mediterranean coast, north of Barcelona, around the town of Mataró. In 1908, as much as one-third of its entire output of undergarments, socks, caps, etc. was exported, mostly to Latin America, including Spain's former colonies.[77] Recent estimates by Montserrat Llonch indicate that sales to Cuba and the Philippines almost doubled from 460,572 kilogrammes in 1899 to 797,904 in 1907, despite growing competition from France and Japan respectively.[78] A report of 1903 from the US consul in Havana, cited by Llonch, warned Washington that Catalan merchants showed a better understanding of the Cuban market and offered more favourable terms than their American counterparts.[79]

The main obstacle to the sector's further expansion in the New World appears to have been the absence of well-organized commercial networks. Writing in 1911, the Catalan deputy Frederic Rahola revealed that: 'on many occasions [manufacturers] find themselves obliged, due to the lack of Spanish export houses, to abandon their article to a European intermediary, who removes the label of origin, and sells that product made in Catalonia with a German or French brand.'[80]

In an orchestrated assault on the 'crisis of overproduction',[81] Catalan cotton manufacturers engaged in a vigorous campaign to discover new markets, above all in South America, whose tastes were considered similar to those of the peninsula.[82] Argentina and Uruguay, in particular, with their large Spanish populations, were singled out for special treatment.[83] In 1903 Rahola and his fellow parliamentarian José Zulueta led a delegation of Spanish industrialists to the River Plate to study the markets of the Southern Cone. Their aim was to inform Spanish manufacturers which products were in greatest demand.[84] As Ralph Odell informed the US Commerce Department:

Samples of the kinds of goods sold in these markets were sent home, publicly exhibited, and copied by the manufacturers. It is realized that Spain must look to South America in expanding its export trade, and everything possible is being done to enable the home industry to compete successfully with the United States, Germany, England, and France.[85]

Odell went on to spell out the notable progress in exports of Catalan cotton textiles to the River Plate republic in recent years, noting that:

Goods shipped to [Argentina] are not confined to any one line, although dyed and printed fabrics predominate. In these fabrics Spain ranks fourth as a supplier of Argentina's needs, following England, Italy, and Germany. These goods are mostly drils[86] and trouserings. The exports of corduroy and velvets to Argentina alone are more than the amount shipped to all other countries. Hosiery, handkerchiefs, and yarn for matches make up the remainder of the exports.[87]

Indeed, the success of Rahola's mission to the Southern Cone spurred on the beleaguered mill owners to more ambitious schemes. Perhaps the most daring attempt to discover new markets for the large stockpiles of cotton goods that had been accumulating in Catalan warehouses since 1898 was the short-lived Mutua de Fabricantes de Tejidos de Algodón (Mutual Association of Cotton Weavers). This cartel was formed in June 1907, and involved most of the region's largest companies. In addition to facilitating the export of white goods, printed and dyed goods, and coarse cloth which manufacturers were unable to dispose of in the peninsula, the association promised to indemnify participating companies for losses incurred in sending their products to new and untested markets.[88] In all, 83 per cent of mill owners joined the scheme, which began operations in July. The association was managed by five directors, assisted by a council of fifteen members, all manufacturers. Each member paid an entrance fee of around $100 and assumed a liability to pay all calls made upon him by the directors, in proportion to the number of looms in his factory. By the end of August 1909, it was calculated, 920,425 pieces of one hundred metres, had been dispatched to 176 destinations, with a total value of $7.5 million.[89] The most favoured destinations were Argentina and Turkey.[90]

Unfortunately for the Mutua, the cotton manufacturers' best-laid plans were soon in disarray. As the well-informed Odell observed:

> To reimburse the manufacturers for the losses sustained by the sale of these goods in foreign markets, heavy calls had constantly been made on all members of La Mutua, and, as usually happens in such cases, great discontent began to be shown by the subscribers. It was contended that the sacrifice was out of proportion to the results obtained. The policy of the directors in sanctioning the exportation of 25,000 pieces of Spanish cretonne to Manchester (which seemed very like sending coal to Newcastle) was severely criticized, and several members refused to contribute to the very heavy losses entailed by this experiment, protests were made, legal proceedings followed, and the relations between directors and shareholders became very unsatisfactory.[91]

Amid bitter recriminations, the association was finally wound up in April 1910, having done little to tackle the worrying problem of overproduction. Nor did the Catalan cotton textile industry manage to increase its share of world production. According to Jordi Nadal, on the eve of the First World War, Spain accounted 0.8 per cent of world exports of cotton goods, compared with 58 per cent for the United Kingdom, 12 per cent for Germany, and 8 per cent for neighbouring France.[92]

The Catalan cotton industry's failure to consolidate new export markets for its uncompetitive products made manufacturers ever more reliant on securing ever larger doses of tariff protection from the Madrid authorities. The Salvador tariff, introduced in June 1906 following a heated national debate, including strong representations from the Foment del Treball Nacional,[93] had among its aims encouraging the production of fine-quality cottons and yarns. Such products, it was hoped, would find a market in Latin America.[94] Within the principality, however, the 1906 tariff was seen as belated compensation for the 'collapse' of colonial trade after the 1898 disaster.[95] In the long term, cut-throat competition from low-cost producers, coupled with the appearance of artificial fibres, ensured that the relative demise of the cotton industry was merely a matter of time. Indeed, long before the disappearance of the overseas provinces, the Catalan economy was in urgent need of diversification. Yet the widening of the region's industrial base proved to be a difficult task, not least before the advent of cheap electricity liberated manufacturers from their dependency on expensive coal and water power.

Notes

1. In 1900, Catalonia, with less than 10 per cent of Spain's population, accounted for 40 per cent of industrial added value; Daniel A. Tirado, Elisenda Paluzie, and Jordi Pons, 'Economic integration and industrial location: the case of Spain before World War I', *Journal of Economic Geography*, 2 (2002): 343–63, p. 343. For a recent survey of Catalan industrialization, see Jordi Maluquer, 'La industrialización de Cataluña: un balance historiográfico', in Antonio Di Vittorio, Carlos Barciela, and Giovanni Luigi Fontana (eds), *Storiografia d'industria e impresa in Italia e Spagna in età moderna e contemporanea* (CLEUP: Padua, 2004), pp. 63–102.

2. Jordi Nadal, 'Cataluña: la fábrica de España: la formación de la industria moderna en Cataluña', in *Moler, tejer y fundir: estudios de historia industrial* (Ariel: Barcelona, 1992), pp. 84–154.

3. Federico Rahola, 'Del comerç i de la indùstria de Catalunya', in Francesc Carreras i Candi (ed.), *Geografia general de Catalunya* (Establiment Editorial de Albert Martin: Barcelona, 1913), p. 461.

4. Jordi Maluquer, 'El índice de la producción industrial de Cataluña: una nueva estimación, 1817–1935', *Revista de Historia Industrial*, 5 (1994): 45–70, p. 59. According to one comparative account, Spain ranked eighth in the world in 1907–8 measured by the number of cotton spindles in place; Gary Saxonhouse and Gavin Wright, 'Technological evolution in cotton spinning, 1878–1933', in Douglas A. Farnie and David Jeremy (eds), *The Fibre that Changed the World: the Cotton Industry in International Perspective, 1600–1990s* (Oxford University Press, 2004), p. 130. Another study puts Spain in eighth position in 1912–13, in terms of the quantity of raw cotton consumed, and tenth by the number of spindles; Àngel Calvo, 'La indústria cotonera a començaments del segle XX', *Recerques. Història, Economia, Cultura*, 44 (2002): 91–100, pp. 95–6.

5. Calvo, 'La indústria cotonera', p. 93. A report from the US commercial agent in Spain pointed out that: 'Practically all the mills are owned by private companies, usually composed of one or two families. One frequently finds them operating under the name of "The Widow of —", "The Brother of —," "The Nephew of —", etc.'; Ralph M. Odell, *Cotton Goods in Spain and Portugal*, US Department of Commerce and Labor, Bureau of Manufactures, Special Agents Series, no. 46 (Government Printing Office: Washington, 1911), p. 18.

6. Odell, *Cotton Goods*, p. 101.

7. Nadal, 'Cataluña: la fábrica de España', p. 118. According to a more recent interpretation, the triple role of manufacturer, merchant, and banker had the advantage of providing the mill owners with important feed-backs, not least it allowed them to detect changing tastes in the domestic market; Marc Prat and Raimon Soler 'La formación de redes comerciales y el fracaso de la penetración internacional de los tejidos catalanes', *Revista de Historia Industrial*, 21 (2002): 201–24, p. 205.

8. See J. K. J. Thomson, 'Explaining the "take-off" of the Catalan cotton industry', *Economic History Review*, 58 (2005), pp. 701–35.

9. A new textbook refers to an 'authentic revolution' in cotton manufacturing south of the Pyrenees in the period 1830–60; Albert Carreras and Xavier Tafunell, *Historia económica de la España contemporánea* (Crítica: Barcelona, 2004), pp. 172–3. Cf. Jordi Maluquer, 'La gran transformació: industrialització i modernització a la Catalunya del segle XIX', in Jordi Nadal *et al.*, *Història econòmica de la Catalunya contemporània*, 1, *La formació d'una societat industrial* (Enciclopèdia Catalana: Barcelona, 1994), pp. 125–86.

10. Carreras and Tafunell, *Historia económica*, pp. 169–70; Jordi Nadal, *El fracaso de la Revolución industrial en España, 1814–1913* (Ariel: Barcelona, 1975), app. 7.

11. Catalonia's high level of industrialization has been attributed to a combination of the relative scarcity of land, the professions, and agricultural labour, and an abundance of artisans and capital; Joan Ramon Rosés, 'Why isn't the whole of Spain industrialized? The new economic geography and early industrialization, 1797–1910', *Journal of Economic History*, 63 (2003): 995–1022, p. 1013.

12. For a case study of 'industrialization without natural resources', see Jordi Maluquer, 'The industrial revolution in Catalonia', in Nicolás Sánchez Albornoz (ed.), *The Economic Modernization of Spain, 1830–1930* (New York University Press: New York, 1987), pp. 172–3.

13. In 1910, Asturian coal used in Catalan cotton mills sold at 31 pesetas ($5.55) per tonne, while imported coal from Cardiff and Newcastle cost $7.20 and $5.65 respectively at the quayside in Barcelona; Odell, *Cotton Goods*, p. 20.

14. Pere Pascual, 'Ferrocarrils i industrialització a Catalunya', *Recerques. Història, Economia, Cultura*, 17 (1985), pp. 43–72.

15. Pere Pascual, 'El ferrocarril carbonífero de Sant Joan de les Abadesses (1867–1900): la frustración de una empresa estratégica', *Revista de Historia Industrial*, 14 (1998): 11–41, p. 12; Albert Carreras, 'Cataluña: primera región industrial de España', in Jordi Nadal and Albert Carreras (eds), *Pautas regionales en la industrialización española (siglos XIX y XX)* (Ariel: Barcelona, 1990), p. 280.

16. Jordi Nadal, 'La indústria cotonera', in Jordi Nadal *et al.*, *Història econòmica de la Catalunya contemporània*, 3, *Segle XIX: indústria, transports i finances* (Enciclopèdia Catalana: Barcelona, 1991), p. 50.

17. On the reasons for the relocation of the cotton industry, see 'A orillas del Fluviá', *El Trabajo Nacional*, i, no. 13 (20 August 1892), p. 101 and 'La industria catalana en las márgenes del Fraiser (*sic.*)', *El Trabajo Nacional*, i, no. 16 (10 September 1892), p. 125. Cf. Gracia Dorel-Ferré, 'L'eau ou le charbon? L'alternative énergétique de l'industrie catalane au XIXe siècle', in Albert Carreras, *et al.* (eds), *Doctor Jordi Nadal. La industrialització i el desenvolupament econòmic d'Espanya* (Universitat de Barcelona: Barcelona, 1999), pp. 2, 1057–67.

18. Odell, *Cotton Goods*, p. 20.

19. In 1900, Spain's per-capita GDP was 65.2% of the western European average; Carreras and Tafunell, *Historia económica*, app.

20. Before the spread of phylloxera across the Pyrenees in the early 1890s, Spain's agricultural crisis mainly affected the cereal growers of the central meseta, while the wine-growing regions of La Rioja, Catalonia, and the País Valenciano prospered thanks to foreign sales; Ramon Garrabou and Jesús Sanz, 'La agricultura española

durante el siglo XIX: ¿inmovilismo o cambio?', in Ramon Garrabou and Jesús Sanz (eds), *Historia agraria de la España contemporánea*, 2, *Expansión y crisis (1850–1900)* (Crítica: Barcelona, 1985), pp. 164–87.

21. 'Certamen agrícola', *El Trabajo Nacional*, ii, no. 6 (20 July 1893), p. 41.

22. Joan Ramon Rosés, 'The choice of technology: Spanish, Italian, British and US cotton mills compared, 1830–60', in Şevket Pamuk and Jeffrey G. Williamson (eds), *The Mediterranean Response to Globalization before 1950* (Routledge: London, 2000), p. 144.

23. In 1908, three-fifths of spindles were ring-frame, one of the highest ratios in Europe; Saxonhouse and Wright, 'Technological evolution', p. 131. Mules were preferred for higher quality yarns; Maluquer, 'La gran transformació', p. 331. One of Spain's leading economist opined: 'the machinery is extremely varied; in general, spinning has modern machines and occasionally the best type'; Francisco Bernis, *Fomento de las exportaciones* (Minerva: Barcelona, 1917), p. 136.

24. Angel Smith, 'Social conflict and trade-union organisation in the Catalan cotton textile industry, 1890–1914', *International Review of Social History*, 36 (1991): 331–76, pp. 336–8.

25. Gabriel Tortella, *The Economic Development of Modern Spain. An Economic History of the Nineteenth and Twentieth Centuries* (Harvard University Press: Cambridge Mass., 2000), p. 76; Joan Ramon Rosés, 'La competitividad internacional de la industria algodonera española (1830–1860)', *Revista de Historia Económica*, 19, special issue (2001): 85–109, p. 88.

26. Instituto de Reformas Sociales, *La jornada de trabajo en la industria textil: trabajos preparatorios del reglamento para la aplicación del Real decreto de 24 de agosto de 1913* (Imprenta de la Sucesora de M. Minuesa de los Ríos: Madrid, 1914), p. 48. Ralph Odell noted that: 'the average number of yarn is 30, although yarn up to number 100 is spun in a few mills for the manufacture of fine goods from Egyptian cotton'; Odell, *Cotton Goods*, p. 18.

27. Alfredo Ramoneda, *Introducción al estudio del precio de coste en hilatura de algodón* (Sociedad General de Publicaciones: Barcelona, 1915), p. 190.

28. For a defence of *enciclopedisme*, see Maluquer, 'La gran transformació', pp. 326–7.

29. Rosés, 'La competitividad internacional', pp. 106–7.

30. Douglas Farnie, 'The role of the cotton industry in economic development', in Farnie and Jeremy (eds), *The Fibre that Changed the World*, pp. 566–70.

31. On the social division of labour between Catalonia and the rest of the country, with Spain supplying Catalan industry with foodstuffs and raw materials while acting as the principal market for the region's textiles, see Josep Maria Fradera, *Industria i mercat: les bases comercials de la industria catalana moderna (1814–45)* (Crítica: Barcelona, 1987), p. 277.

32. Cf. Douglas Farnie, *The English Cotton Industry and the World Market, 1815–1896* (Clarendon Press: Oxford, 1979), pp. 81–134.

33. José Ferrer y Vidal, *Conferencias sobre el arte de hilar y tejer en general y especialmente sobre el hilar y tejer el algodón hechas en el Ateneo Barcelonés* (Establecimiento de Jaime Jepús Roviralta: Barcelona, 1875), p. 46 and Andrés de Sard, *Comparación entre el actual estado de desarrollo de la industria algodonera en Inglaterra y el de la propia*

industria en España (Imprenta de Jaime Jepús: Barcelona, 1884), p. 36. Ferrer y Vidal, p. 106, calculated that in 1870 a kilo of coarse cloth cost 20.30 francs to produce in Spain, compared with 17.50 francs in France, 16.40 francs in Switzerland, and 15.20 francs in England.

34. Édouard Escarra, *Le Développement industriel de la Catalogne* (Arthur Rousseau: Paris, 1908), p. 205–6.

35. Pedro Fraile, *Industrializacion y grupos de presión: la economía política de la protección en España, 1900–1950* (Alianza: Madrid, 1991), pp. 59–63. For a rejection of such arguments, see Jordi Nadal and Carles Sudrià, 'La controversia en torno al atraso económico español en la segunda mitad del siglo XIX (1860–1913)', *Revista de Historia Industrial*, 3 (1993): 199–227, pp. 221–4.

36. In the late 1870s, exports of cotton goods accounted for less than two per cent of imports of cotton fibre; Carles Sudrià, 'La exportación en el desarrollo de la industria algodonera española, 1875–1920', *Revista de Historia Económica*, 1 (ii) (1983): 369–86, p. 386.

37. Juan Güell y Ferrer, *Comercio de Cataluña con las demás provincias de España y observaciones sobre el mismo asunto y otras cuestiones económicas* (Imprenta de Narciso Ramírez: Barcelona, 1853), p. 23.

38. Juan Güell y Ferrer, *Rebelión cubana* (Impreso de Narciso Ramírez y Compañía: Barcelona, 1871), p. 36.

39. For a discussion of Cuba as a 'captive market' for uncompetitive Spanish manufactures, see José A. Piqueras Arenas, 'Mercados protegidos y consumo desigual: Cuba y el capitalismo español entre 1878 y 1898', *Revista de Historia Económica*, 16 (1998), pp. 747–81.

40. The 1882 Act has been described as a second line of defence for Catalan manufacturing, after protectionism; Maluquer, 'La gran transformació', p. 191.

41. Customs duties between Spain and the overseas provinces were reduced by 5 per cent annually between 1882 and 1884, 10 per cent in each of the next four years, and 15 per cent between 1889 and 1891; Pablo de Alzola y Minondo, *Relaciones comerciales entre la Península y la Antillas* (Imprenta de la Viuda de M. Minuesa de los Ríos: Madrid, 1895), p. 36.

42. Maluquer, 'La gran transformació', p. 228.

43. Submission of the Fomento del Trabajo Nacional, in *La Reforma arancelaria y los tratados de comercio. Información escrita de la comisión creada por el real decreto de 10 de octubre de 1889*, vol. 2 (Sucesores de Rivadeneyra: Madrid, 1890), p. 8.

44. Fomento del Trabajo Nacional, *La Reforma*, p. 8. By contrast, the Act provoked loud protests in the colonies, especially from planters and merchants who were naturally free traders; Carlos Serrano, *Final del imperio: España, 1895–1898* (Siglo XXI: Madrid, 1984), p. 14.

45. For a history of the protectionist movement in nineteenth-century Spain, see Manuel Pugés, *Cómo triunfó el proteccionismo en España: la formación de la política arancelaria española* (Juventud: Barcelona, 1931).

46. Guillermo Graell, *Historia del Fomento del Trabajo Nacional* (Imprenta de la Viuda de Luis Tasso: Barcelona, 1910), pp. 355–7. The defence of Catalan business interests in Madrid is summarised in Soledad Bengoechea, 'Els empresaris catalans en els

segles XIX i XX: actituds i aspects organitzatius', *Revista de Catalunya*, 214 (2006): 25–49, pp. 26–30.

47. Even so, economic historians argue that the Cánovas tariff of 1891 strengthened the 'agrarian bias' of Spanish protectionism; Daniel Tirado, 'Protección arancelaria y evolución de la economía española durante la Restauración: un ensayo interpretativo, *Revista de Historia Industrial*, 9 (1996): 53–81, pp. 59–60.

48. Fomento del Trabajo Nacional *Informe sobre los aranceles antillanos* (Tipografía Española: Barcelona, 1895), p. 15. Another study claimed that: 'Many factories are working day and night, their main halls lit by powerful electric lights'; Manuel Escudé Bartolí, *La producción española en el siglo XIX. Estadística razonada y comparada. Territorio. Población. Propiedad. Agricultura. Industria y Comercio* (Librería de Antonio Bastinos: Barcelona, 1895), p. 211.

49. Pablo de Alzola y Minondo, *La política económica mundial y nuestra reforma arancelaria* (Imprenta y Encuadernación de la Casa de Misericordia: Bilbao, 1906), p. 239.

50. Parliamentary Papers, *Diplomatic and Consular Reports on Trade and Finance* (Barcelona), xciii (1897), p. 442, henceforward PP.

51. 'El problema cubano', *El Trabajo Nacional*, v, no. 141 (15 January 1897), p. 191; 'Memoria leída en la junta general ordinaria celebrada por el Fomento del Trabajo Nacional el día 30 de enero de 1898', *El Trabajo Nacional*, vi, no. 179 (3 February 1898), p. 183. Cf. Serrano, *Final del imperio*, pp. 122–5.

52. Sudrià, 'La exportación', p. 375.

53. José Prats Aymerich, 'La crisis de la industria manufactura catalana', *Revista de Economia y Hacienda*, iv, no. 3 (20 January 1901), pp. 60–2.

54. Juan Sallarés y Plá, 'Mirando al porvenir', *El Trabajo Nacional*, vi, no. 179 (5 August 1898), p. 57.

55. 'Memoria leída en la junta general ordinaria celebrada por el Fomento del Trabajo Nacional el día 29 de enero de 1899', *El Trabajo Nacional*, vi, no. 189 (29 January 1899), p. 188; 'Carta de Barcelona', *La Estafeta: Revista Económica y Financiera*, vii, no. 294 (9 January 1899), pp. 20–1.

56. 'Desde Barcelona', *El Economista*, xiv, no. 660 (14 January 1899), pp. 22–3.

57. 'La cuestión de los cambios', *El Trabajo Nacional*, ix, no. 245 (30 July 1901), pp. 51–61.

58. 'La crisis catalana', *El Economista*, xv, no. 749 (29 September 1900), p. 745. The escalating cost of coal is discussed in Enrique Mercader, 'Los carbones nacionales en Barcelona', *Revista de Economia y Hacienda*, iv, no. 33 (18 August 1901), pp. 774–6, and *Revista de Economia y Hacienda*, iv, no. 35 (1 September 1901), pp. 823–4. On the 'ruinous price of cotton', which many attributed to American speculators, see Eduardo Calvet, *et al.*, *Memoria del congreso celebrado en Bremen los días 25 al 29 de junio de 1906* (J. Sabater: Barcelona, 1906), p. 47.

59. PP (Barcelona), xcvi (1900), p. 265.

60. PP (Barcelona), xcvi (1900), p. 265; Diputación Provincial de Barcelona, *Exposición elevada al Excmo. Sr. Presidente del Consejo de Ministros al objeto de remediar la actual crisis industrial que se siente en Cataluña según acuerdo del Cuerpo provincial de 11 de Diciembre de 1900* (Sucesor de F. Sánchez: Barcelona, 1901), p. 11.

61. Eusebio Bertrand y Serra, 'Un estudio sobre la industria textil algodonera', *Boletín del Comité Regulador de la Industria Algodonera*, iv, no. 33 (1931): 81–98, p. 84.

62. 'A los representantes de la nación', *El Trabajo Nacional*, vii, no. 196 (15 May 1899), pp. 3–5. Cf. 'Carta de Barcelona', *La Estafeta: Revista Económica y Financiera*, vii, no. 314 (22 May 1899), p. 324.

63. 'El precio del algodón y los tejidos', *La Estafeta: Revista Económica y Financiera*, viii, no. 389 (15 October 1900) p. 652; Pedro Corominas, 'Actividad económica de Cataluña', in Pedro Estasen, *Cataluña. Estudio acerca las condiciones de su engrandecimiento y riqueza* (F. Seix: Barcelona, 1900), pp. 868–72.

64. PP (Barcelona), lxxxiv (1901), p. 723; Smith, 'Social conflict', pp. 355–7.

65. See for instance 'La crisis', *El Trabajo Nacional*, viii, no. 224 (20 September 1900), pp. 85–6; 'La crisis catalana', *El Economista*, xv, no. 747 (15 September 1900), pp. 699–700.

66. According to one estimate, between 1896 and 1901, the number of spindles and power looms in active use fell by 42% and 25% respectively; Jordi Nadal and Carles Sudrià, *Història de la Caixa de Pensions* (Edicions 62: Barcelona, 1981), p. 19.

67. 'La crisis industrial', *El Trabajo Nacional*, viii, no. 225 (30 September 1900), p. 93.

68. On the impact of the 1902 general strike on the Catalan business community, see Gemma Ramos and Soledad Bengoechea, 'La patronal catalana y la huelga general de 1902', *Historia Social*, 5 (1989), p. 77–95. Cf. Angel Smith, 'Anarchism, the general strike and the Barcelona labour movement, 1899–1914', *European History Quarterly*, 27 (1989): 5–40, pp. 20–3.

69. Joaquín Aguilera, 'Los enemigos de la industria', *El Trabajo Nacional*, xvi, no. 349 (16 January 1906), p. 33; PP (Barcelona), cxxvi (1906), p. 591.

70. 'La industria algodonera', *El Trabajo Nacional*, ix, no. 254 (30 December 1901), p. 196. On sales to the former colonies, see Aurelio Ras, 'Nuestro comercio con Filipinas', *Revista de Economía y Hacienda*, iv, no. 20 (19 May 1901), p. 469, and Aurelio Ras, 'El comercio exterior de Barcelona', *Revista de Economía y Hacienda*, iv, no. 50 (15 December 1901), p. 1188–9.

71. That said, high throughput technologies may well have constrained American manufacturers to a narrow range of product lines, making them 'ineffective competitors outside the US'; Gary Saxonhouse and Gavin Wright, 'Stubborn mules and vertical integration: the disappearing constraint?', *Economic History Review*, 55 (1987): 87–94, p. 93.

72. 'El tratado de comercio con Cuba', *Revista de Economía y Hacienda*, v, no. 34 (24 August 1902), p. 805. Odell (*Cotton Goods*, p. 39) calculated that the cost of transporting cotton goods from New York to Havana was 10 cents per cubic foot, compared with $7.17 per cubic metre (plus 10 per cent primage) from Barcelona to Havana. By my reckoning, Catalan mill owners faced shipping charges twice those of their American competitors.

73. Maluquer, 'La gran transformació', p. 324. The same author plays down the impact of 1898 'disaster' on the Spanish economy as a whole; Jordi Maluquer, *España en la crisis de 1898: de la Gran Depresión a la modernización económica del siglo XX* (Península: Barcelona, 1999), passim.

74. *El Trabajo Nacional*, xvi, no. 411 (16 January 1908), pp. 305–11. On the survival of

Spain's export trade with Cuba in the aftermath of the 1898 disaster, see Yolanda Blasco and Anna Carreras, 'Las exportaciones de España a Cuba (1891–1913): pervivencias históricas en la demanda cubana de productos españoles', *Secuencia: Revista de Historia y Ciencias Sociales*, 59 (Mexico, 2004), pp. 131–58.

75. Jordi Maluquer, *Nación e inmigración: los españoles en Cuba (ss. XIX y XX)* (Jucar: Gijón, 1992), p. 127.

76. Piqueras Arenas, 'Mercados protegidos', p. 758.

77. This figure is considerably higher than that for the United Kingdom, which exported around one-fifth of its total output of hosiery goods at this stage; Montserrat Llonch, 'La capacitat exportadora de la indústria catalana de gènere de punt (1876–1935)', *Recerques. Història, Economia, Cultura*, 37 (1998): 165–92, pp. 166–7.

78. Montserrat Llonch, 'La competetividad de la industria española de géneros de punto en el siglo XX: factores y obstáculos de su proyección exterior', pp. 6–7, <http://www.usc.es/estaticos/congresos/histec05/b4_llonch.pdf>.

79. 'American versus European manufactures in Cuba', *US Consular Reports*, lxxii, no. 274 (July 1903), pp. 353–6, cited in Llonch, 'La competetividad', p. 4.

80. Federico Rahola, 'La industria de Mataró', *Mercurio. Revista Comercial Hispano-Americana*, xi, no. 131 (24 August 1911), p. 283.

81. Overproduction was defined as the inability of manufacturers to sell their products in the domestic market at remunerative prices; 'Producción y comercio de algodón', *El Trabajo Nacional*, xii, no. 304 (1 April 1904), p. 26.

82. José Puigdollers, 'Las relaciones entre España y América: manera de fomentarlas', *Mercurio. Revista Comercial Hispano-Americana*, ii, no. 4 (4 February 1902), p. 57; Odell, *Cotton Goods*, p. 32.

83. Escarra, *Le Développement industriel*, pp. 168–71.

84. Federico Rahola, *Sangre nueva: impresiones de un viaje a la América del Sud* (Tipografía 'La Académica' de Serra hermanos y Russell: Barcelona, 1904), passim.

85. Odell, *Cotton Goods*.

86. The term 'drils', not to be confused with 'drills', was applied to twilled fabrics, either dyed in the piece or woven from coloured fabrics.

87. Odell, *Cotton Goods*, p. 37. A similar concentration on dyed goods occurred among British exports to Latin America before 1914. This has been ascribed to rising per-capita incomes and changing tastes; Andrew Marrison, 'Great Britain and her rivals in the Latin American piece goods market, 1880–1914', in Barrie M. Ratcliffe (ed.), *Great Britain and her World, 1750–1914. Essays in Honour of W. O. Henderson* (Manchester University Press: Manchester, 1975), pp. 309–48.

88. *Antecedentes acerca la constitución de la Mutua de Fabricantes de Tejidos Reguladora del Mercado y Exportación* (Casamajó: Barcelona, 1907), pp. 10–12.

89. Odell, *Cotton Goods*, pp. 33–4.

90. The association sent 1,000 tonnes of cotton goods to Argentina in 1908, and over 1,400 tonnes in 1909 (a figure only exceeded by exports to Cuba). Sales to Turkey expanded from 287 tonnes in 1907, to 880 tonnes in 1908, tailing off to 694 tonnes in 1909; Sudrià, 'La exportación', p. 379.

91. Odell, *Cotton Goods*, p. 34.

92. Nadal, 'La indústria cotonera', p. 85. Nadal's figures are calculated from

Andor Kertész, *Die Textilindustrie sämtlicher Staten. Entwicklung, Erzeugung. Absatzverhältnisse* (Viewig & Sohn: Braunschweig, 1917), pp. 28–9. The industry's poor performance owed a great deal to its inability to develop commercial and financial networks outside the peninsula; Prat and Soler 'La formación de redes comerciales', p. 203.

93. Among the committee which drafted the 1906 tariff was the Conde de Sert, a local textile magnate; Marcela Sabaté Sort, *El proteccionismo legitimado: política arancelaria española a comienzos de siglo* (Civitas: Madrid, 1996), p. 163.

94. Alzola y Minondo, *La política económica mundial*, p. 240. The adoption of ring spinning after 1870, although bringing important gains in productivity, also increased a general trend in the cotton industry towards the manufacture of low-quality fabrics. This tendency was reinforced by the 1891 tariff; Sabaté Sort, *El proteccionismo legitimado*, p. 147.

95. Sabaté Sort, *El proteccionismo legitimado*, p. 147.

10

The diversification of a Japanese cotton spinning company: the case of Kanebo

TAKESHI ABE

Introduction

The purpose of this paper is to trace how Kanegafuchi Spinning Company (Kanebo[1]) of Japan developed its range of products from the early days to the first half of the 1960s.[2] Kanebo has been not only one of the most important companies in Japan, but also one of the well-known Japanese large-scale cotton spinning companies in the world. In December 1913, Kanebo was the fifth largest textile firm in the world by the number of spindles.[3] Kanebo ranks in the top one hundred industrial and mining companies of Japan by total assets in several years: 1st in 1896, 2nd in 1914, 4th in 1919 and in 1929, 3rd in 1936, 7th in 1940, 11th in 1955, 26th in 1965, 47th in 1972 and 88th in 1990. These figures show that Kanebo was a conspicuous giant by the inter-war period. In and after World War II it gradually declined, but had kept itself in the top one hundred by the end of the twentieth century.[4]

1 The outline of development of Kanebo

First, the outline of the development of Kanebo should be explained. In 1886, some of the ginned cotton merchants in Tokyo established Tokyo Men Shosha [Tokyo Raw Cotton Trading Co.] with the capital of 100,000 yen, in order to trade in Chinese ginned cotton. In the following year, the company increased the capital stock to 1,000,000 yen and secured the land for a mill at Kanegafuchi, Sumida-mura, Minami-Katsushika-gun in Tokyo-fu (now Sumida-ku in Tokyo Prefecture). In August 1888 Tokyo Men Shosha changed its name to Kanegafuchi Boseki Kaisha [Kanegafuchi Spinning Co.], the main purpose of which was to spin cotton yarn. Kanebo began to operate its equipment in April 1889, and to sell its products in August. At the end of the year, it finished installing ring spinning machines with 28,920 spindles, which were imported from the UK, making it the largest Japanese cotton spinning companies at that time. Though the panic of 1890 seriously hit Kanebo, the company was able to survive, supported by the finance of Mitsui Bank. Thereafter, Kanebo had been an affiliated company of Mitsui *zaibatsu* both in terms of capital and management at least until 1905, when Mistui Bank began to sell many stocks of Kanebo in the market.[5]

In 1893 Kanebo established the second mill with 10,400 spindles, tried to export cotton yarn to China, and changed its name to Kanegafuchi Boseki Kabushiki Kaisha [Kanegafuchi Spinning Co. Ltd]. In 1894 Sanji Muto became the manager of the Hyogo branch near Kobe, the mill of which with 39,900 spindles was under construction. Muto (1867–1934), the son of a rich farmer, graduated from Keio Gijuku in Tokyo, which was established in 1858 by Yukichi Fukuzawa, further studying at the Pacific University in San Jose in California State of the USA during the period 1885–87. He entered Mitsui Bank in 1893, and was ordered by Hikojiro Nakamigawa, the leader of Mitsui *zaibatsu*, to move to Kanebo in the following year. Later, Muto became managing director of the company in 1908, and was the president for the years from 1921 to 1930.[6]

Under the leadership of Muto, who insisted that many Japanese cotton spinning companies should be merged into bigger ones, Kanebo merged or purchased seven firms after the Sino-Japanese war (1894–95), merged three firms after the Russo-Japanese war (1904–05), and had reached the total number of 298,303 spindles by 1910. Kanebo also reinforced its equipment in silk spinning and cotton weaving (see Table 1). After the Sino-Japanese war, Kanebo secured high-quality raw cotton, which was indispensable to the improvement of cotton goods, through a special contract with Mitsui Bussan Kaisha, one of Mitsui *zaibatsu*'s subsidiaries and a famous general trading company.[7] Around the beginning of the twentieth century, especially after the Russo-Japanese war, Muto made efforts to establish the personnel management system and developed welfare facilities.[8]

Kanebo gained enormous profits in the boom of World War I. In and after the war, Kanebo further propelled the diversification within the textile industry as follows: silk-reeling, finishing textiles at the newly established Yodogawa mill, and cotton spinning in China (*zaikabo*. See table 1). In 1930 Shingo Tsuda became the company president. Tsuda (1881–1948) entered Kanebo soon after he graduated from Keio Gijuku in 1907, was ordered by Muto to complete the Yodogawa mill, and settled its labour disputes. With his initiative, Kanebo subsequently promoted diversification in the new field of wool and rayon manufacture. Tsuda also diversified into the marketing of products.[9]

After the outbreak of the second Sino-Japanese war in July 1937, Kanebo apparently advanced in the fields of heavy and chemical industry. Later in 1938 such departments or affiliated firms were concentrated into the newly founded Kanegafuchi Jitsugyo Kabushiki Kaisha [Kanegafuchi Business Co. Ltd], while Kanebo itself survived. In 1943, when Japan was fighting with the allied powers, cotton spinning companies in Japan were compelled to be merged into ten big firms, each of which had to have over one million spindles. As Kanebo had reached 1,312,096 spindles in 1942, it was allowed to remain independent, but in February 1944 Kanebo and Kanegafuchi Jitsugyo, both of which promoted diversification, were finally dissolved, and the newly created company, Kanegafuchi Kogyo Kabushiki Kaisha [Kanegafuchi Industry Co. Ltd], merged with them. The above-mentioned organizational changes seem to have been aimed at facilitating fund-raising under the severe limitations of a government-controlled economy.[10]

As Kanegafuchi Kogyo had a lot of equipment not only in mainland Japan but in colonial Korea and some parts of China, where Japan occupied territory during the conflict, and remarkably diversified into the munitions industry, the company was much more seriously hit by the defeat of Japan than the other Japanese cotton spinning companies. Kanegafuchi Kogyo changed its name to the original Kanegafuci Boseki Kabushiki Kaisha in 1946. Kanebo abolished some departments of its business, and separated chemical departments as Kanegafuchi Kagaku Kogyo Kabushiki Kaisha [Kanegafuchi Chemical Industry Co. Ltd. Now Kaneka] in 1949.

Although Japanese cotton spinning companies could reconstruct their capital equipment and reopen to produce textile goods, it was very difficult for them to recover quickly from the damage in and after the war. The Korean War (1950–53) did bring about a remarkable boom for the cotton spinning companies, but from 1952 they came to suffer from the structural depression. Kanebo was not exceptional. President Itoji Muto hammered out the 'Greater Kanebo Scheme' in 1961 as one of the counter-measures against the slump. Muto (1903–70), the son of Sanji Muto, studied at a school at Maidenhead in Berkshire in the UK from 1924 until 1929, and entered Kanebo in 1930. He became a director of the new Kanebo in 1946, was inaugurated as the president in the following year,[11] and stayed in the position until 1968, when Junji Ito assumed the chair.

The purpose of the Greater Kanebo Scheme was to propel the diversification of domestic consumer goods, and Kanebo soon realized it through entry into the fields of synthetic fibres, toiletries, foodstuffs, drugs, real estate and so on. The company kept propelling the diversification, which seems to have been

Table 1 Foundations and acquisitions of mills and Branches in the prewar period by Kanebo

Year	Month	Name of Kanebo's mill or branch	Product	Scale		Merged or purchased company
1889	5	The 1st Mill of Tokyo Main Office	Cotton Yarn	30,440	s	
			Twist Cotton Yarn	6,660	s	
1894	3	The 2nd Mill of Tokyo Main Office	Cotton Yarn	14,800	s	
1896	5	The 1st Mill of Hyogo Branch	Cotton Yarn	42,288	s	
1899	9	The 2nd Mill of Hyogo Branch	Cotton Yarn	19,840	s	Shanghai Boseki
	10	Suminodo Branch	Cotton Yarn	10,368	s	Kashu Boseki
	11	Nakajima Branch	Cotton Yarn	10,368	s	Kunijima Boseki
1900	1	Sumoto Branch	Cotton Yarn	10,368	s	Awaji Boseki
1902	10	Miike Branch	Cotton Yarn	31,104	s	Kyushu Boseki
	10	Kurume Branch	Cotton Yarn	14,760	s	Kyushu Boseki
	10	Kumamoto Branch	Cotton Yarn	10,368	s	Kyushu Boseki
	10	Nakatsu Branch	Cotton Yarn	10,368	s	Nakatsu Boseki
	12	Hakata Branch	Cotton Yarn	11,136	s	Hakata Kenmen Boseki
1905	10	Weaving Experimental Mill of Hyogo Branch	Cotton Cloth	176	1	
1907	10	The 2nd Mill of Kyoto Branch	Silk Yarn	5,000	s	Nihon Kenmen Boshoku
	10	Sumoto Branch	Cotton Yarn	20,708	s	Nihon Kenmen Boshoku
	10	Nakatsu Branch	Cotton Cloth	300	1	Nihon Kenmen Boshoku
1908	3	The 1st Mill of Kyoto Branch	Silk Yarn	12,300	s	
			Twist Silk Yarn	4,896	s	

Year	Month	Name of Kanebo's mill or branch	Product	Scale		Merged or purchased company
			Handspun Silk Yarn	4,626	s	
			Twist Silk Yarn	660	s	
	5	The 3rd Mill of Tokyo Main Office	Cotton Gas Yarn	34,640	s	
			Twist Cotton Yarn	13,200	s	
1909	3	The 2nd Mill of Sumoto Branch	Cotton Yarn	27,856	s	
			Twist Cotton Yarn	4,740	s	
			Cotton Cloth	1,205	l	
	9	Weaving Mill of Nakatsu Branch	Cotton Cloth	352	l	
	10	Takasago Branch	Cotton Yarn	37,440	s	
1910	4	The 3rd Mill of Hyogo Branch	Cotton Cloth	1,010	l	
	8	Weaving Mill of Hakata Branch	Cotton Cloth	411	l	
1911	3	Okayama Mill	Cotton Yarn	13,376	s	Kenshi Boseki
			Cotton Cloth	1,028	l	Kenshi Boseki
	3	Wakayama Mill	Cotton Yarn	11,136	s	Kenshi Boseki
	3	Kamikyo Mill	Silk Yarn	9,000	s	Kenshi Boseki
	3	Shimokyo Mill	Silk Yarn	7,800	s	Kenshi Boseki
	3	Shinmachi Mill	Handspun Silk Yarn	4,890	s	Kenshi Boseki
	3	Maebashi Mill	Handspun Silk Yarn	1,214	s	Kenshi Boseki
	3	Okayama Silk Spinning Mill	Silk Yarn	12,600	s	Kenshi Boseki
	3	Bizen Mill	Cotton Yarn	36,668	s	Kenshi Boseki

Year	Month	Name of Kanebo's mill or branch	Product	Scale		Merged or purchased company
	3	Saidaiji Mill	Cotton Yarn	7,936	s	Kenshi Boseki
			Cotton Cloth	518	1	Kenshi Boseki
	3	Shanghai Silk Spinning Mill	Silk Yarn	5,000	s	Kenshi Boseki
1912	4	Weaving Experimental Mill of Tokyo Main Office	Cotton Cloth	100	1	
1913	5	The 4th Mill of Hyogo Branch	Cotton Gas Yarn	33,808	s	
			Twist Cotton Yarn	13,640	s	
	7	Weaving Experimental Mill of Kyoto Branch	Silk Cloth	539	1	
	9	The 5th Mill of Hyogo Branch	Cotton Cloth	422	1	
	12	Osaka Branch	Cotton Yarn	28,456	s	Asahi Boshoku
1914	6	The 4th Mill of Tokyo Main Office	Cotton Cloth	302	1	
1918	5	Yodogawa Branch	Finishing (Dyeing, Printing)			
	6	The 5th Mill of Tokyo Main Office	Cotton Yarn	22,000	s	
			Twist Cotton Yarn	6,160	s	
1919	5	The 2nd Mill of Yodogawa Branch	Finishing (Bleaching)			
1920	10	The 3rd Mill of Sumoto Branch	Cotton Yarn	31,200	s	
			Twist Cotton Yarn	18,040	s	
1921	5	Silk Reeling Dept. of Shinmachi Branch	Raw Silk	330	c	
	5	Hikone Silk Reeling Mill	Raw Silk	288	c	Kokka Seishi
	5	Kofu Silk Reeling Mill	Raw Silk	708	c	Wakao Seishi

Year	Month	Name of Kanebo's mill or branch	Product	Scale	Merged or purchased company
	5	Kumamoto Cocoon Drying Mill	Cocoon Drying		
	6	Kameyama Cocoon Drying Mill	Cocoon Drying		
			Raw Silk	23 K	
	6	Fukuchiyama Cocoon Drying Mill	Cocoon Drying		
			Raw Silk	28 K	
	7	Silk Reeling Experimental Mill of Sales Dept.	Raw Silk		
1922	4	Gong Da Sha Chang(Shanghai)	Cotton Yarn	48,528 s	
			Twist Cotton Yarn	11,880 s	
			Cotton Yarn	1,280 s	
	6	Yamashina Silk Weaving Mill	Twist Silk Yarn	15,000 s	Nihon Kenpu
			Silk Cloth	300 l	
1923	3	Oyodo Cocoon Drying Mill	Cocoon Drying		
			Raw Silk	40 K	
	4	Zhong Yuan Sha Chang(Tsiungtao)	Cotton Yarn	133,496 s	
			Cotton Cloth	4,412 l	
	4	Fukushima Cocoon Drying Mill	Cocoon Drying		
			Raw Silk	40 K	
1923	6	Hiratsuka Cocoon Drying Mill	Cocoon Drying		
	6	Matsuzaka Branch	Cotton Yarn	8,240 s	Nansei Boseki
	10	Gifu Silk Reeling Experimental Mill	Raw Silk	158 c	

Year	Month	Name of Kanebo's mill or branch	Product	Scale	Merged or purchased company
1924	3	Yamashina Silk Reeling Experimental Mill	Raw Silk	56 c	
	6	Nagahama Cocoon Drying Mill	Cocoon Drying		
1925	5	Ohi Cocoon Drying Mill	Cocoon Drying		
	5	The 2nd Mill of Gong Da Sha Chang	Cotton Yarn	45,000 s	Laou Kung Mow Cotton
			Cotton Cloth	515 l	Spinning and Weaving
	12	Seoul Silk Reeling Mill	Raw Silk	60 K	
	12	Hikawa Silk Reelng Mill	Raw Silk	40 K	
1926	5	Ohta Cocoon Drying Mill	Cocoon Drying		
	9	Tsingtao Silk Reeling Mill	Raw Silk	26 K	
	12	Sakamoto Silk Reeling Mill	Raw Silk	60 K	

Key: s-spindles.
l-looms.
c-caldrans.
K-Kanebo-type machines.
The facts which occurred after 1927 are not written.
Source: Kanebo Co. Ltd (ed.), *Kanebo Hyaku Nen Shi* (Kanebo Co.: Osaka, 1988), pp. 92–4, 158–61.

a representative strategy of a cotton spinning company in Japan under the structural textile depression from the latter half of the 1960s. Kanebo further changed its name from Kanegafuci Boseki to Kanebo in 1971. The following sections will scrutinize the diversification of Kanebo, to which I often referred in this section.

2 The development of the vertical integration in the textile industry (1887–1929)

Under the leadership of President Sanji Muto, Kanebo propelled diversification within the textile industry as energetically as such larger cotton spinning companies as Toyobo, established by the merger with Osakabo and Miebo in 1914, and Dai Nihonbo, established by the merger of Amagasakibo and Settsubo in 1918. The company originally produced only cotton yarn. Table 1 shows that Kanebo increased its equipment for yarn in 1899–1902, 1907, 1911, 1913 and 1921–23, usually during depressions through mergers and acquisitions. For Japanese cotton spinning companies, mergers and acquisitions enabled them not only to acquire the fixed capital very cheaply but also to inherit workers and markets.[12] Naosuke Takamura classified the strategies of Japanese cotton spinning companies in the depression at the beginning of the twentieth century into three groups: (1) mergers and acquisitions, and improvement of cotton yarn for export (Kanebo, Osaka Godobo and Settsubo); (2) enlargement of integrated weaving sector (Osakabo and Miebo); and (3) production of finer yarn (Amagasakibo and Tokyo Gasubo).[13] The most important strategy of the early Kanebo was mergers and acquisitions of other textile mills.

Kanebo adopted this strategy for a number of reasons, including the serious depression caused by the adoption of gold standard system in 1897 and the Boxer Rebellion in China in 1900.[14] In those days modern enterprises were very few in Japan, and most were companies in such limited fields as cotton spinning, shipping and railways, besides several large firms owned by *zaibatsu*. Many owners of the above-mentioned companies were apt to desert the firms whenever they could not gain dividends from them. Such an attitude of the owners also accelerated the merger movement.

In addition, Sanji Muto insisted that most of the Japanese weak cotton spinning companies should be merged, and in 1901 he published a book entitled *Boseki Dai Godo Ron* [On the Significance of the Great Merger Movement of Japanese Cotton Spinning Companies]. Muto seems to have had such an idea through his superior, Hikojiro Nakamigawa.[15] Nakamigawa (1854–1901) was the son of *samurai*, and a graduate of Keio Gijuku, the founder of which was his uncle, Y. Fukuzawa. When Nakamigawa stayed in the UK for the period from 1874 to 1877, he met governmental officers, the president of Sanyo Railway Company and so on. Nakamigawa entered Mitsui Bank in 1891, came to preside over all of the Mitsui's businesses, and strongly propelled industrialization of Mistui *zaibatsu*. Kanebo was an important part of the industrialization as well as Shibaura Seisakujo (now Toshiba) and Oji Seishi (Oji Paper Company, which is still alive) and so on.[16] Muto's intention must have influenced Kanebo's mergers. Kanebo grew up to be one of the big businesses in prewar Japan through mergers.

As we can see from Table 1, it is interesting that Kanebo reinforced the facilities in silk spinning. This strategy was also based on Nakamigawa's idea that the silk industry should be foremost among Japan's industries because Japan could supply enough silk cocoons and raw silk, and the industry could earn much foreign currency.[17] Fuji Boseki Kaisha [Fuji Spinning Company, Fujibo], another of the biggest cotton spinning companies, promoted the development of silk spinning and weaving. The leader of Fujibo was Toyoji Wada, who had also been a subordinate of Nakamigawa. Fujibo developed Fujiginu, a famous silk fabric, for export.[18] The cotton spinning companies which advanced the silk industry were rather rare, but we can know that there existed Nakamigawa's unique idea through these cases.

After the Russo-Japanese war Kanebo reinforced the weaving sector in the same way as the other large cotton spinning companies of Osakabo and Miebo. Adding to that, Kanebo advanced towards textile finishing, including bleaching, printing and dyeing, in the boom of World War I. In 1916 the company began to construct Yodogawa mill at Johoku-mura, Higashinari-gun (now Miyakojima-ku in the city of Osaka) in Osaka Prefecture, not so far from the centre of Osaka, completing it in 1924. Shingo Tsuda, the future president, took full responsibility for the construction. In those days most of the cotton textile finishing mills were located in and around the cities of Osaka and Nagoya. In 1929 the number of the bleaching mills in Osaka Prefecture was 126, while the total number in Japan was 676. In the same year, the number of the dyeing mills in Osaka was 383, of the total of 12,361 in Japan.[19] In Osaka Prefecture, though large firms such as Inabata Senkojo and Yamatogawa Senkosho were highly developed, most of the mills were small- and medium-sized firms.[20] In such a situation, Muto decided the construction of an unprecedentedly huge mill in order to compete with the cotton industry in Manchester of the UK. Though it took a long time till Yodogawa mill earned profits, it began to develop impressively from around 1927. Indeed, it came to be called 'the largest finishing mill in the Orient', and became a source of enormous profits[21] for Kanebo.

It is noteworthy that Kanebo began to construct spinning mills in China during the boom of World War I. After the war, the larger cotton spinning companies of Japan were keen to have *zaikabo*. Japanese scholars pointed out the following facts as the reasons why *zaikabo* were established after the war: the rise of wages in Japan; the delay of delivery of imported spinning machinery; the international prohibition against the night work by female spinning workers; and the raising of the rates of maritime customs by Chinese Kuomintang government, and so on. However, it is more likely that the rising Chinese domestic cotton spinners came to encroach upon the Japanese market was the most important reason.[22]

Though Kanebo already had a strong interest in the export of cotton goods to China and even in the construction of *zaikabo* in the days of Nakamigawa,[23] the company became rather more prudent in the foundation of *zaikabo* after the First World War. In short, Kanebo propelled the diversification both of cotton and silk, and the vertical integration within the textile industry, led by Sanji Muto.

3   The development of full-line production of textile goods and the inclination to munitions (1930–1945)

New president Shingo Tsuda was more aggressive than Muto in pressing forward with diversification. The products of Kanebo in the 1930s and the former half of the 1940s were not only textiles but also miscellaneous goods, especially munitions. As Japan was militarised, especially after the 1930s, Tsuda cooperated closely with the army, and Kanebo quickly turned into a huge munitions company. As for the diversification of textile goods, it is noteworthy that the vertical integration in both sectors of cotton and silk was continuously propelled until the 1930s. Though in the former half of the 1930s enlargement of both sectors was generally remarkable, Yodogawa mill for finishing particularly developed, supported by the rapid increase of the export of cotton cloth. In 1932 the mill could produce 300,000 *tan* of bleached cloth, 250,000 *tan* of dyed cloth and 150,000 *tan* of printed cloth per month. Tsuda aimed to double its bleaching capacity by 1933.

Tsuda further eagerly made efforts to sell Kanebo's textile goods. He raised the slogan: 'Kanebo goods to all over the world except the South Pole and the North Pole', and executed marketing activities. First, from 1933 Tsuda established bases for sales in Lyon, Berlin, London, Stockholm, Paris and so on, where the specialist products of Kanebo were sent. In sales Kanebo's brands were usually used. Second, Kanebo endeavoured to grasp the information on fashion and to purchase new designs in cooperation with two excellent designers, Katsujiro Kinoshita and Chiyo Tanaka. President Muto well recognized the significance of fashion and design, and opened the Kanebo showroom at Shinsaibashi in Osaka in 1924. Tsuda developed this room into Kanebo Seihin Senden Kabushiki Kaisha [Kanebo Goods Publicity Co. Ltd] as a directly affiliated concern. The same year this company changed its name into Kanebo Service Co. Ltd. Another showroom was established at Ginza in Tokyo in 1935. Cotton spinning companies in prewar Japan were strongly interested in the purchase of cheap raw cotton, but most of them were indifferent to the sale of products, which was usually deemed to be the work of trading companies. In such a situation the case of Kanebo was exceptional.

While Kanebo developed the above-mentioned sectors, it also entered the unknown fields of textiles in the 1930s. One of them was the wool manufacturing. It was not easy for the wool industry to develop in Japan because of the difficulty in rearing sheep. However, the industry began at the end of the Russo-Japanese War, using imported raw wool, and in 1933–34 its golden age arrived. Each of the cotton spinning companies entered into the wool industry. Kanebo also constructed an experimental corner in Yodogawa Mill in 1934, and started spinning and weaving wool at the corner of Takatsuki Mill in Osaka Prefecture of Takatsuki Kenshi Co. Ltd, which had been consigned to Kanebo in 1935. In April 1936 the wool weaving section was newly set up at the sales department of Kanebo. In October of the same year Keori Kogyo Kabushiki Kaisha [Wool Weaving Co. Ltd] consigned six mills (Oi, Minami-senju, Ogaki, Imazu, Tonouchi and Nakatsu of Osaka) to Kanebo. In 1941 these mills were formally merged into Kanebo. In the same year Kanebo acquired three mills (Nagoya, Saya and Naka-izumi) through the purchase of Ogiwara & Co., and three mills (Yokkaichi, Kameido and Nerima) through the amalgamation of Toyo Boshoku Kabushiki Kaisha [Orient Spinning and Weaving Co. Ltd]. In this year Kanebo erected Shizuoka Felt Mill and actually entered into felt producing. Besides, Kanebo came to have some wool spinning and/or weaving mills in China, five of which had been started by July 1944. While the conflicts over trade between Japan and the British Empire, including Australasia, which was a main supplier of raw wool, grew more serious in the 1930s, Kanebo began to breed Angora rabbits in 1933, and wool sheep in 1935.

Another new field of textile was rayon manufacturing. After Toyobo founded the subsidiary, Showa Rayon Co. Ltd at Katada in Shiga Prefecture in 1927, especially after 1932, when the yen was drastically depreciated, many cotton spinning companies entered the rayon industry.[24] Tsuda dispatched three members of Kanebo to Europe and the USA in 1932, let them investigate the industry, and finally decided to introduce the Italian technology. In 1934 Kanebo began to construct Hofu Mill in Yamaguchi Prefecture and Takasago Mill in Hyogo Prefecture for rayon manufacturing. The former started operations in 1935, the latter in 1936.

Tsuda had a special interest in making full use of resources or in recycling. Such a viewpoint is found particularly in the silk sector. During 1931–39 Kanebo produced recycled silk yarn that was made from the waste of spun silk, a process that had been invented in 1923. At that time, as a chrysalis occupied 80 per cent of the total weight of a cocoon, and cocoons were dealt in weight, Tsuda proposed the utilisation of chrysalises. Concretely, Kanebo started the sales of 'Savon de Soie', the high-quality soap for export through Kanebo Service

Company, which was made from the grease of a chrysalis. Further, oilcake was utilised as the material for amino acid soy sauce.

In 1934 Tsuda made a business trip to Korea, one of the colonies of Japan, invited by General Kazushige Ugaki, the Viceroy of Korea. Kanebo already had two silk reeling mills, in Seoul and Kwangju in Korea. Tsuda, who accepted Ugaki's request, decided to construct cotton spinning mills in Korea. In 1935–36 two mills began to operate in Seoul and Kwangju. In 1939 a rayon mill in Pyongyan also started to work. Pyongyan mill produced fibre acetate, briquette and so on, as well as rayon made from the pulp of a reed. As the Japanese wartime economy was promoted, Kanebo came to undertake coal mining, iron manufacturing and so forth in Korea.

After Tsuda visited Tientsin, Tsingtao and Manchukuo in autumn 1935, he became more enterprising in the activities in the Chinese continent. In 1936 Kanebo purchased two cotton spinning mills, which the Chinese persons had in Tientsin and suffered from loss. Kanebo became a pioneer of *zaikabo* in north China. In those days Tsuda reached the idea that Kanebo should share its profits among the Japanese government, the Asian natives and Kanebo, and should advance into heavy and chemical industries.

It is, however, impossible to elucidate the entire picture of the diversification of Kanebo in wartime. A few cases will be shown. First, in 1937 an agriculture section (later, the agriculture and forest department) was established in the sales department. The outline of the agriculture and forest department in the first half of the 1940s is shown on Table 2. Second, in 1937 Kanebo founded Karafuto Saitan Kaisha [Sakhalin Coal Company], which stemmed from a coal mine of Fujita *zaibatsu* in the southern Sakhalin, one of the colonies of Japan. The establishment of this company was Kanebo's first step to the mining industry. The coals of Karafuto Saitan were sold to Amagasaki Seitetsu Kaisha [Amagasaki Iron Manufacturing Company], in which Kanebo invested capital in 1938.

In November 1938 Kanegafuchi Jitsugyo [Business] Kabushiki Kaisha was set up and Tsuda took up the post of its president. Since 1937 the control of Japan's economy had advanced, and the Japanese government obliged many cotton spinning mills to merge. In the end, by 1943 ten big companies were established, but Kanebo kept independent in this restructuring process. In those days the textile industry was generally treated coldly by government, except for the munitions activities. Most of the mills of Kanebo converted to the production of weaponry. Some of their spinning and weaving machines were delivered to the government as scrap iron, and others were transferred to East Asia. Consequently, the number of cotton spindles of Kanebo decreased from 1,312,096 in 1942 to only 157,808 in August 1945, when Japan surrendered to the Allied Powers.

Kanegafuchi Jitsugyo (KJ), however, had vigorously diversified its product

Table 2 *The outline of the Agriculture and Forest Department of Kanebo in the prewar period and wartime*

Area	Name of a Farm or a Mill	Established		Activity	Areas (Unit: chobu)
		Year	Month		
Japan	Fukuchiyama Farm of Stud Rabbits	1935	1	farming of stud Angora rabbits	2
	Beppu Farm of Stud Livestock	1935	7	farming of sheep	265
	Kanoya Farm of Stud Livestock	1936	11	farming of sheep	30
	Tokachi Farm of Laccoon Dogs	1937	7	farming of Ezo Laccoon Dogs	43
	Nemuro Farm	1939	1	farming of a stallion	1,836
	Shizuoka Forestry	1940	3	forestry and lumbering	1,100
Korea	Sinuiju Farm	1938	4	cultivation of reeds for the pulp for rayon	3,437
	Jueul Mills	1938	4	cultivation of flax and production of its textile	1,600
Manchukuo	Wang Fu Farm of Stud Livestock	1936	11	breed improvement of sheep, cultivation of soybeans and so on	6,308
	Ying Kou Farm	1938	4	cultivation of reeds for the pulp for rayon	19,600
	Xing An Farm	1938	10	breed improvement of military horses	120,000
	Kai Shan Tun Hemp Mill	1939	2	cultivation of flax and hemp, and production of their goods	2,500
	Yi Da Flour Mill	1940	6	production of flour	7
China	Qi Ming Farm	1938	1	construction of the model of a farm village and paddy fields	7,183

Area	Name of a Farm or a Mill	Established		Activity	Areas (Unit: *chobu*)
		Year	*Month*		
	Ji Ning Sheep Laboratory	1938	7	breed improvement of sheep	70
	Tai Yuan Fram of Stud Livestock	1938	8	improvement and breeding of sheep	114
	Meng Jiang Farm	1938	10	improvement and breeding of sheep	9,086
	The Department of Agriculture of Jiang Bei Gong Si	1939	6	breed improvement of cotton and instruction of stockbreeding	41

Key: One *chobu* approximately equals to one hectare.
Source: Kanebo Co. Ltd (ed.), *Kanebo Hyaku Nen Shi*, pp. 315–16.

Table 3   *The outline of Kanegafuchi Kogyo in July 1944*

Organization	Japan	Taiwan	Korea	Sakhalin	Manchkuo	China	Mongolia	Southern Foreign Country
Head Office	4							
Branch	2		1					
Small Branch	3				3	5	1	
Laboratory	2							
Mining	2		4	1	(7)	(3)		
Heavy Industries	11 (30)	1	4 (2)			(1)		1
Parts of Aircraft	8 (25)		1					
Chemicals	9 (22)	(1)	1 (2)		1			
Pulp & Paper	2		1 (2)		(3)	(7)		
Cotton & Rayon	9 (1)		3		(2)	1 (7)		1 (1)
Silk	12 (4)		3					
Wool & Hemp	11 (1)		2 (3)		(2)			
Agriculture & Forestry	5	1	2		8	1	2	1
Miscellaneous	5 (2)		2		1	17	1	

Key: Unit: number of establishments.

Figures with asterisks show the number of subsidiaries.

Source: Kanebo Co. Ltd (ed.), *Kanebo Hyaku Nen Shi*, pp. 399–409.

range in wartime. Its main new enterprises are listed here. In 1938 KJ purchased a gold mine in Tientsin in China, founded Kanegafuchi Hokushi Kogyo [North China Mining] Co. Ltd and began the gold mining. In the following year, 1939, KJ invented *Kaneviyarn*, the first synthesized fibre in Japan, invented by Professor Ichiro Sakurada and his colleagues at Kyoto Imperial University, which was industrialized after 1940 and was renamed *Vinylon* in 1950 by Kurashiki Rayon Co. KJ entered also aircraft manufacturing through the foundation of Kokusai Kogyo [International Industry] Kaisha, a subsidiary. KJ began to produce magnesium for aircraft, and brom, an additive of the aircraft fuel. In 1940 KJ industrialized the synthesized rubber manufacturing by the vinyl acetylene method. About that time KJ started to produce oils and fats, vitamin drugs and hormone drugs made from a whale. MK began to manage Nippon Diizeru Kogyo [Japan Diesel Industry] Kaisha which manufactured diesel engines. Kanebo was entrusted with this company by Riken Arumaito Kogyo [Riken Anodized Aluminum] Kaisha. In 1942 Nihon Diizeru Kogyo changed its name to Kanegafuchi Diizeru Kogyo. In the same year KJ began iron manufacturing. Its main materials were powder of iron ore and iron sand, and it utilized electric power. KJ entered into timber manufacturing relating to manufacturing parts of an aircraft. In 1943 KJ amalgamated Umeda Seikosho [Umeda Steel Manufacturing] and Umeda Kikai Seisakusho [Umeda Machine Manufacturing], and newly erected Kanegafuchi Kikai Kogyo Kabushiki Kaisha [Kanegafuchi Machine Industry Co. Ltd]. Umeda Seikosho and Umeda Kikai Seisakusho had produced a full-fashioned socks knitting machine, supported by Kanebo. Kanegafuchi Kikai Kogyo started to produce parts of an aircraft.

In February 1944 Kanebo and KJ merged, and Kanegafuchi Kogyo [Industry] Kabushiki Kaisha was set up, with Tsuda as the president of this company. The outline of Kanegafuchi Kogyo in July 1944 is shown on Table 3. Here we can confirm the fact that the company diversified its product range extensively. At the end of the war Kanegafuchi Kogyo was a huge arsenal.

4   The return to production of textile goods and the reopening of the diversification in the non-textile field (1945–64)[25]

Of the ten big cotton spinning companies, the Kanebo that remarkably inclined to the production of the munitions was most seriously hit by the defeat of Japan.[26] In the middle of 1949 Kanebo estimated the loss by the repeal of the governmental wartime indemnity, the forfeiture of the overseas assets, and so on, at 1,246 million yen, while the losses of Toyobo and of Dai Nihonbo were, respectively, 616 million yen and 489 million yen. Though Kanegafuchi Kogyo Co. Ltd changed its name to the original Kanegafuchi Spinning Co. Ltd in May 1946, Tsuda was detained in Sugamo Prison on suspicion of being an A-class war criminal, and the top managers of Kanebo were purged. In June

Table 4   Kanebo's sales in postwar period (1)

Year	Cotton Goods (%) A		Wool Goods (%) B		Silk Cloth (%) C		Rayon Goods (%) D		A+B+C+D (%)		Total (%)	
1950	14,621	(55.6%)	4,839	(18.4%)	2,621	(10.0%)	1,440	(5.5%)	23,521	(89.5%)	26,295	(100.0%)
1951	30,380	(59.9%)	7,879	(15.5%)	2,629	(5.2%)	4,852	(9.6%)	45,740	(90.2%)	50,725	(100.0%)
1952	17,930	(48.7%)	8,511	(23.1%)	1,488	(4.0%)	4,203	(11.4%)	32,132	(87.3%)	36,811	(100.0%)
1953	19,209	(47.4%)	9,393	(23.2%)	1,674	(4.1%)	5,472	(13.5%)	35,748	(88.1%)	40,561	(100.0%)
1954	18,122	(47.6%)	8,963	(23.6%)	1,723	(4.5%)	5,239	(13.8%)	34,047	(89.5%)	38,044	(100.0%)
1955	19,485	(48.0%)	9,365	(23.1%)	1,386	(3.4%)	6,301	(15.5%)	36,537	(89.9%)	40,628	(100.0%)
1956	21,732	(44.0%)	12,552	(25.4%)	1,662	(3.4%)	9,181	(18.6%)	45,127	(91.4%)	49,353	(100.0%)
1957	20,636	(44.4%)	12,297	(26.5%)	1,506	(3.2%)	8,018	(17.3%)	42,457	(91.4%)	46,450	(100.0%)
1958	17,688	(46.0%)	10,030	(26.1%)	1,722	(4.5%)	6,070	(15.8%)	35,510	(92.4%)	38,449	(100.0%)
1959	21,363	(45.9%)	12,077	(25.9%)	1,919	(4.1%)	7,897	(17.0%)	43,256	(92.9%)	46,586	(100.0%)
1960	26,711	(49.5%)	13,303	(24.6%)	2,105	(3.9%)	7,690	(14.2%)	49,809	(92.3%)	53,976	(100.0%)
1961	27,599	(46.5%)	16,260	(27.4%)	2,732	(4.6%)	7,358	(12.4%)	53,949	(90.9%)	59,358	(100.0%)
1962	34,602	(39.4%)	18,624	(21.2%)	4,515	(5.1%)	7,652	(8.7%)	65,393	(74.5%)	87,824	(100.0%)
1963	39,806	(32.3%)	25,670	(20.9%)	4,716	(3.8%)	8,929	(7.3%)	79,121	(64.3%)	123,100	(100.0%)
1964	35,642	(24.9%)	31,266	(21.8%)	2,760	(1.9%)	9,757	(6.8%)	79,425	(55.4%)	143,314	(100.0%)
1965	27,954	(20.9%)	30,027	(22.5%)	1,549	(1.2%)	8,504	(6.4%)	68,034	(50.9%)	133,728	(100.0%)

Key: Unit: million yen. Data of handspun silk yarn and synthetic fibre are not available, which are included in total.
Source: Kanebo Co. Ltd (ed.), *Kanebo Hyaku Nen Shi*, pp. 598, 626, 629, 632 and 633.

1947 Itoji Muto took up the post of president, remaining in this position until June 1968.

In the postwar restructuring, Kanebo closed the lumbering, machine manufacturing and mining departments, and in September 1949 Kanegafuchi Kagaku Kogyo [Chemical Industry] Kabushiki Kaisha was established to concentrate the manufacturing departments of chemicals, paper, pharmaceuticals, toiletry and wire. Kanebo came to devote itself to the production of textile goods. It was not easy for Kanebo which suffered from the deficiency of funds to restore itself. In the boom of the Korean War that broke out in June 1950, Kanebo, however, enjoyed prosperity, and in July 1950 it hit the target of 415,426 cotton spindles which had been set in February 1947.

On Table 4 in 1950 we can see that cotton goods and other textile goods occupied the greater part of sales. While Kanebo had been a general textile maker until 1961, we can find some interesting changes for this period when we scrutinize the data.

First, the percentages of cotton goods tended to decrease. Though after the defeat Japan had only ten cotton spinning firms left, twenty-five firms were newly approved to enter the cotton spinning industry in order to promote competition among the firms, when General Headquarters-Supreme Commander of the Allied Powers (GHQ) deemed four million spindles the provisional target of the reconstruction of this industry in 1947. Just after the outbreak of the Korean War, the limit of four million spindles was removed, and many newcomers appeared.[27]

In the boom of the Korean War, when the cotton industry was extremely prosperous, many cotton spinning firms including the ten biggest companies competitively invested in plant and equipment. After the mid-1950s when the boom passed away, the Japanese cotton spinning industry came to be concerned about the chronic surplus of equipment. Nevertheless, cotton cloth was the most important Japanese export in Japan during the 1950s and early 1960s, and the competitive advantage of the Japanese cotton industry was not easily weakened. The sign of its collapse was, however, found after the boom of the Korean War.[28] Though Kanebo endeavoured to introduce new and powerful technologies, and made efforts to export cotton goods by sending representatives overseas, sales of cotton goods did not increase much under such stagnant situations.

The second to be drawn from Table 4, is that the percentage of silk cloth fell remarkably. Though Kanebo was greatly committed to the silk industry, the Japanese silk industry had already lost its competitive advantage just after the Second World War because of the development of the rayon industry since the 1920s, the stagnant prices of silk goods during the Great Depression, the coercive conversion of planting from mulberry tree to rice in the wartime period, and the emergence of nylon after 1937.[29] Though data on silk spinning are not available, the slump in sales of Kanebo's silk cloth reflected such a situation. In 1958, Kanebo separated the silk reeling department, which became a newly erected Kanegafuchi Sanshi Kabushiki Kaisha [Kanegafuchi Silk Reeling Co. Ltd].

On the other hand, the percentage of woollen goods tended to rise. The wool department is said to have been 'the Ever Victorious Army' in Kanebo. This success was the fruit of the newly developed products such as wool yarn for hand-knitting, the entry into the field of worsted in 1950, and the sale of *College Flano* [flannel suiting] in 1952. Particularly the sales of *College Flano* are said to have reached about 25,000,000 pieces per year in terms of slacks for twenty-five years after 1952. Kanebo also regarded marketing of wool goods as important. For example, the brand of wool yarn for hand-knitting was named *Kanebo Keito*, which became popular among many Japanese people through the radio and TV commercials of the 1950s. By 1953 *Kanebo Keito* was proud to occupy first place in sales of the firms of wool yarns for hand-knitting.

In April 1945 Kanebo disposed of Hofu mill in Yamaguchi Prefecture, the main mill in this field, withdrawing from the rayon industry. Merging Nihon Serurosu Kogyo Kabushiki Kaisha [Japan Cellulose Industry Co. Ltd], the former Hofu mill, in 1950, Kanebo recommenced production of spun rayon yarn at the new Hofu mill and some other mills. Through the 1950s spun rayon yarn was a very important product of Kanebo.

After the boom of the Korean War, first of all the cotton industry suffered from the chronic surplus capacity in the Japanese textile industry. For fifteen months after March 1952, every cotton spinning company reduced operations according to the administrative guidance (*Kankoku Sotan*) of the Ministry of International Trade and Industry. For fourteen months after May 1955 when the Japanese economy began to enjoy the High Speed Growth Era, the second *Kankoku Sotan* was put into practice. In addition, in 1956 the Provisional Law on the Equipments of the Textile Industry was promulgated and enforced. It regulated the enlargement of textile equipment. For about one year after the middle of 1957, the Japanese economy was in recession. At this time not only the cotton industry but also the entire textile industry (except synthetic fibre manufacturing) came to be affected by the slump. *Kankoku Sotan* in 1957–58 aimed at the fields of cotton, rayon and wool.[30] Kanebo also took such measures as the closing of some mills, wage reductions and lay-offs in order to overcome the depression.

Under these circumstances, President Muto launched 'the Greater Kanebo Construction Scheme' (GK Scheme), from November 1961 to October 1964.[31] The main points behind this scheme were as follows: (1) Kanebo propelled forward integration in every textile sector, especially integrating sewing, knitting, selling and so on, and sought to increase the added value in these products; (2) Kanebo advanced further towards synthetic fibres; (3) Kanebo advanced

Table 5   Kanebo's sales in postwar period (2)

Period	Cotton goods	Wool goods	Silk goods	Chemicals	Nylon	Service shop	Toiletry & medicine	Food	Total
October 1960–April 1961	13.3	6.8	1.9	4.6	–	–	–	–	26.6
	50.1%	25.5%	7.2%	17.2%	–	–	–	–	100.0%
October 1966–April 1967	14	16.4	5.1	7.4	15.6	1.3	6.7	2.5	69
	20.3%	23.7%	7.4%	10.8%	22.6%	1.9%	9.7%	3.6%	100.0%

Unit: billion yen
Source: Kanebo Co. Ltd (ed.), Kanebo Hyaku Nen Shi, p. 696.

towards such non-textile products as toiletry, foodstuffs, drugs and real estate. Though Kanebo failed to accomplish the first target, as for the second target in 1962 the introduction of the nylon manufacturing technology of Snia Viscosa Co. in Italy was authorized by the government, and in June 1963 production was started at Hofu mill. Kanebo continued producing *Kaneviyarn*, a sort of synthetic fibre invented in 1939, until 1955, the sales of which did not increase. The entry into nylon manufacturing was the real advance towards the field of synthetic fibres.

Kanebo achieved good results on the third target. One of these areas was toiletry manufacturing. After the sales of the above-mentioned 'Savon de Soie', Kanebo continued developing toiletry. In 1939 Kanebo set up a laboratory for toiletries in Ohi mill, where foundation cream, toilet water, brilliantine, powder, perfume, shampoo, special hair lotion and so forth were developed. In the 1940s, output of toiletries was inevitably obliged to decrease. After World War II, toiletry manufacturing was moved into Kanegafuchi Kagaku Kogyo. As a part of the GK Scheme, Kanebo repurchased the toiletry manufacturing facilities from the company, created the new Kanebo Keshohin Kabushiki Kaisha [Kanebo Toiletry Co. Ltd] as a subsidiary in January 1961, and merged it in April 1962. For the period from 1961 to 1964, Kanebo Keshohin Hanbai Kabushiki Kaisha [Kanebo Toiletry Sales Co. Ltd] worked, and chain stores for the sales were founded in each prefecture. Kanebo endeavoured to reinforce its sales network.

It is also noteworthy that Kanebo entered the food industry. During the war Kanebo produced foods as part of the processing of farm products and stock farm products. In the early years just after the Second World War, Kanebo made some foods, but it actually came to be interested in food processing after the GK Scheme was launched. Since 1948 Kanebo had been producing a chewing gum base, founded on the technology of producing *Kaneviyarn*, and had supplied Harris Co. Ltd with it. In 1963 Kanebo dispatched some top managers to Harris, separated department of sales from Harris, and erected Kanebo Harris Co. Ltd. In April of the same year Kanebo merged with Harris.

After the GK Scheme was launched, Kanebo increased the sales of synthetic fibres and of non-textile products (see Table 5), while the percentage of the established textile departments decreased significantly (see Table 4). In the 1960s, while cotton and silk industries were declining, Kanebo did recommence its vigorous diversification strategy, as well as in the days of President Tsuda.

Concluding remarks

Though Kanebo had been a remarkably large cotton spinning firm from its start, in and after World War I it became one of three largest cotton spinning companies in Japan, including Toyobo established in 1914 and Dai Nihonbo established in 1918. Shin'ichi Yonekawa considered the differences between these 'big three', arguing that Kanebo's principal feature was its market-oriented or consumer-oriented strategy, while the other two companies pursued technology-oriented strategy. He further suggested that the personnel who graduated from Keio Gijuku, founded by Yukichi Fukuzawa, were promoted to the top management in Kanebo, while both in Toyobo and Dai Nihonbo the engineers such as Takeo Yamanobe, Tsunezo Saito and Kyozo Kikuchi played important roles in the top management.[32] At the earlier stage of Japan's industrialization, managerial ability was generally scarce, but the above-mentioned spinning companies succeeded in securing excellent managers.

In Kanebo, among the key personnel Sanji Muto had occupied the crucial position, owing to his supreme ability, and made the important decisions almost solely by himself. The market-or consumer-oriented strategy in Kanebo was very advanced compared to most of the Japanese cotton spinners, who were not interested in marketing in the pre-war days. The diversification within textiles in Kanebo up to the 1920s was the result of such a strategy promoted mainly by Muto. This feature was also imitated in the post-war Kanebo, and actually gave it a competitive advantage among Japanese firms.

In the 1930s Shingo Tsuda added another aspect to the diversification of Kanebo, which was related to non-textiles, especially heavy and chemical industries. Tsuda strongly encouraged such industries to cooperate with Japanese governmental policy. His strategy was seemingly very unique, but it is true that he greatly contributed to Kanebo's diversification in non-textiles, which Kanebo and Kanegafuchi Kagaku imitated in the post-war period, providing a clear insight into why Kanebo enjoyed such long life until the late twentieth century.

Notes

1. *Bo* in Japanese means 'spinning'.
2. The sentences, the source of which are not shown, are written on Kanebo Co. Ltd (ed.), *Kanebo Hyaku Nen Shi* [A Centennial History of Kanebo] (Kanebo Co.: Osaka, 1988).
3. Douglas A. Farnie and Shi'ichi Yonekawa, 'The Emergence of the Large Firm in the Cotton Spinning Industries of the World, 1883–1938', *Textile History*, 19(2) (1988), p. 174.
4. Data compiled by Seishi Nakamura in the appendices in Keieishi Gakkai [Business History Society of Japan] (ed.), *Nihon Keieishi no Kiso Chishiki* [Japanese Business History: Basic Facts and Concepts] (Yuhikaku: Tokyo, 2004). Kanebo rapidly declined at the end of the twentieth century, and account rigging became apparent. In February 2006 only the toiletry department was sold to Kao Company, and in June 2007 Kanebo was dissolved. The causes of Kanebo's collapse must be

considered someday.

5. Mitsuru Kawai, 'Jugyoin no Rieki to Kabunushi Rieki ha ryoritsu shiuruka?: Kanebo ni okeru Muto Sanji no Kigyo Tochi' [The Corporate Governance of Sanji Muto: Satisfying both the Shareholders and the Employees], *Keieishigaku* [Japan Business History Review], 40(2) (2005).

6. Yoshinaga Irimajiri, *Muto Sanji* (Yoshikawa-kobun-kan: Tokyo, 1964).

7. Naosuke Takamura, *Nihon Boseki Gyo Shi Josetsu* [The History of Cotton Spinning Industry in Modern Japan], 2 vols (Hanawa Shobo: Tokyo, 1971); Hatsu Nishimura, 'Kanegafuchi Boseki Kaisha' in Kazuo Yamaguchi (ed.), *Nihon Sangyo Kinyu-shi Kenkyu: Boseki Kinyu Hen* (Tokyo Daigaku Shuppankai: Tokyo, 1970).

8. Tetsuya Kuwahara, 'The Development of Factory Management in Japan during the Early Stages of Industrialization: The Kanegafuchi Cotton-Spinning Company before the First World War' in Douglas A. Farnie and David J. Jeremy (eds), *The Fibre that Changed the World: The Cotton Industry in International Perspective, 1600–1990s* (Oxford University Press: Oxford, 2004).

9. Eiichi Ishiguro, *Taiga: Tsuda Shingo Den* [A Big River: the Biography of Shingo Tsuda] (Daiyamondosha: Tokyo, 1960); Takeshi Abe, 'Organizational Changes in the Japanese Cotton Industry during the Inter-War Period: From Inter-Firm-Based Organization to Cross-Sector-Based Organization' in Farnie and Jeremy (eds), *The Fibre that Chaged the World*, pp. 480–2.

10. AuKi Joung, 'Senji-ki "Kanebo Guruupu" no Henyo to Kanegafuchi Kogyo no Seturitsu' [Transformation of 'Kanebo Group' in the Wartime and Foundation of Kanegafuchi Kogyo], *Keiei Shigaku*, 32(3) (1997); A. Joung, 'Senji-ki "Kanebo Guruupu" to Kanegafuchi Jitsugyo no Setsuritsu' ['Kanebo Group' in the Wartime and Foundation of Kanegafuchi Jitsugyo], *Keizai Ronso* 159(1/2) (Kyoto University, 1997).

11. Yoshitaro Tsutsui, *Muto Sanji Den, Muto Itoji Den* [Biographies of Sanji Muto and Itoji Muto] (Toyo Shokan: Tokyo, 1957).

12. The talk by the late Mr Kiichi Yamada, vice-president of Kanebo.

13. Takamura, *Nihon Boseki*. Osaka Godobo was merged into Toyobo in 1931, and Tokyo Gasubo was bought by Fujibo in 1906, which changed the name Fuji Gasubo.

14. Takamura, *Nihon Boseki*.

15. Hatsu Nishimura, 'Muto Sanji no Boseki Keiei Ron' [Muto Sanji's Opinion on the Management of Japanese Cotton Spinning Industry], *Bijinesu Revyu* [Business Review], 24(3) (1976); Tetsuya Kuwahara, *Kigyo Kokusaika no Shiteki Bunseki* [Historical Analysis on the Internationalisation of Japanese Firms] (Moriyama Shoten: Tokyo, 1990).

16. Shuko Sirayanagi, *Nakamigawa Hikojiro Den* [Biography of Hikojiro Nakamigawa] (Iwanami Shoten: Tokyo, 1940). The reason why Mistui Bank began to sell many stocks of Kanebo in the market in 1905 was that Nakamigawa's strategy of the industrialization was criticized by such managers as Takashi Matsuda of Mistui Bussan after the death in 1901.

17. Nishimura, 'Muto Sanji'; Satoshi Matsumura and Takeshi Abe, 'Wada Toyoji to Fuji Gasu Boseki Kaisha: *Wada Toyoji Nikki* Kanko ni Yosete' [Toyoji Wada and

Fuji Gas Spinning Company], Keio Gijuku Fukuzawa Kenkyu Sentaa, *Kindai Nihon Kenkyu* [Modern Japanese Studies], vol. 10 (1994).

18. Teikichi Kita (ed.), *Wada Toyoji Den* [The Biography of Toyoji Wada] (Wada Toyoji Den Hensanjo: Tokyo, 1926); Matsumura and Abe, 'Wada Toyoji to Fuji Gasu Boseki Kaisha'.

19. Noshomu Sho [Japanese Ministry of Agriculture and Commerce] (ed.), *Noshomu Tokei Hyo* [The Statistical Tables of Ministry of Agriculture and Commerce] (Governmental Periodical Publication: Tokyo).

20. Noshomu Sho (ed.), *Kojo Tsuran* [Data Book on Japanese Mills] (Governmental Periodical Publication: Tokyo).

21. Ishiguro, *Taiga*.

22. See Takeshi Abe, 'The Chinese Market for Japanese Cotton Textile Goods, 1914–30', in Kaoru Sugihara (ed.), *Japan, China, and the Growth of the Asian International Economy, 1850–1949* (Oxford University Press: Oxford, 2005).

23. Shanghai Spinning Company of Mitsui *zaibatsu* in Kobe, which was later merged into Kanebo, had originally aimed at *zaikabo*.

24. Hiroaki Yamazaki, *Nihon Kasen Sangyo Hattatsu Shi Ron* [The History of the Rayon Industry in Prewar Japan] (Tokyo Daigaku Shuppankai: Tokyo, 1975).

25. See Shin'ichi Yonekawa, 'Men Boseki' [Cotton Spinning] in Shin'ichi Yonekawa, Koichi Shimokawa and Hiroaki Yamazaki (eds), *Sengo Nihon Keiei Shi* [Business History of Postwar Japan], vol. 3 (Toyo Keizai Shinposha: Tokyo, 1991).

26. See Masayasu Miyazaki, Norio Tominaga, Osamu Ito, Isao Arai and Hideaki Miyajima, 'Senryo Ki no Kigyo Saihensei' [The Reorganisation of Big Companies in the Occupied Japan], *Kindai Nihon Kenkyu* [Journal of Modern Japanese Studies], vol. 4 (Yamakawa Shuppansha: Tokyo, 1982).

27. Takeshi Abe, 'Kei Kogyo no Saiken' [Reconstruction of Japanese Light Industry] in Tsusho Sangyo Seisaku Shi Hensan Iinkai (ed.), *Tsusho Sangyo Seisaku Shi* [History of the Policy on International Trade and Industry], vol. 3 (Tsusho Sangyo Chosakai: Tokyo, 1992).

28. Takeshi Abe, 'Kei Kogyo no Saiken'.

29. Nihon Sen'i Kyogikai (ed.), *Nihon Sen'i Sangyo Shi Kakuron Hen* [History of Japanese Textile History] (Sen'i Nenkan Kanko-kai: Tokyo, 1958), Ch. 3.

30. Nihon Boseki Kyokai [Japan Spinners Association] (ed.), *Sengo Boseki Shi* [History of the Cotton Spinning Industry in Postwar Japan] (Nihon Boseki Kyokai: Osaka, 1962).

31. This is accurately the first scheme. The second GK Scheme covered the period from November 1964 to October, 1967.

32. Shin'ichi Yonekawa, 'University Graduates in Japanese Enterprises before the Second World War', *Business History Review*, 24(2) (1984).

11

Broader-width cotton cloth mechanical weaving in a Japanese rural area: a case study of the Giseidô factory in Syûtô around 1916

1. Introduction

The object of this paper is to explore the Japanese women working in a small rural weaving factory floor through a case study of the Giseidô factory, which produced broader-width cotton cloth for the national market in Syûtô region covering Kuga, Kumage and Ohshima-gun in Yamaguchi Prefecture (see Map 1) around 1916.

Syûtô had developed as a weaving district producing narrow-width white cotton cloth (*kohaba-shiromomen*), narrow-width white cotton crepe (*kohaba-shirochidimi*) and narrow-width striped cotton cloth (*kohaba-shimamomen*) for the national market since the Edo period (1603–1868). Giseidô was one of the enterprises established in Yamaguchi Prefecture of early Meiji Japan through the government's programme called '*shizoku jusan*', the samurai rehabilitation policy. In 1878 the Giseidô handloom weaving factory was established at Iwakuni town in Kuga-gun.[1] At the end of the nineteenth century, Kokura-fabrics (*Kokura-fukuji*) and broader-width cotton crepe (*hirohaba-menchidimi*) for the national market were woven by handlooms in the workshop.[2] We can

202

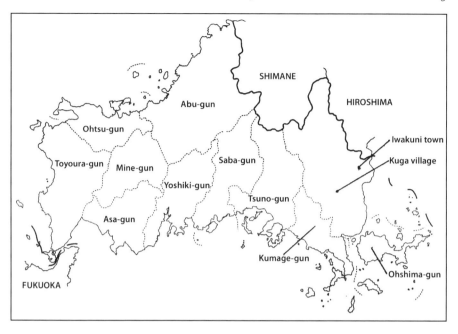

Map 1. Yamaguchi Prefecture
Source: Jun Sasaki, *Ajia no Kôgyô-ka to Nihon*, pp.142–3

say that Giseidô had an exceptional handloom factory among rural weavers who produced narrow-width cotton cloth in Syûtô.

While demand for Kokura-fabrics (*Kokura-fukuji*) for military uniforms had increased, in 1905 Giseidô imported thirty-six broad-width power looms from Britain and started to operate its own power loom weaving factory.[3] In the production of broader-width cotton cloth for the national market, the nation-wide number of power loom weaving factories to the total number of weaving factories ratio increased from 7.3 per cent in 1909 to 63.9 per cent in 1920 (see Table 1). We can assume that Giseidô introduced power looms at a comparatively early stage among producers of broader-width cotton cloth for the national market.

During the first and second decade of the twentieth century, Giseidô continued to import broad-width power looms from Britain: six shuttle-changing looms in 1907, and twenty-two looms with dobbies in 1910 and 1914.[4] Of the sixty-four power looms that were imported from Britain, we can confirm the fact that six shuttle-changing looms, which were called 'Platt Loom' in Giseido MSS; *Hataorikôchin-chô*, were ordered from Platt Bros & Co. Ltd of Oldham by Giseidô on 25 June 1907 and were bought through the sole agency of Platt Bros, Mitsui Bussan Kaisha (MBK).[5]

Table 1 Weaving factories classified by production area for the national broader-width cotton cloth market in 1909, 1917 and 1920

Prefecture	City or gun or ku	‡@ the end of 1909			‡A the end of 1917			‡B the end of January 1920		
		Powered factories	Non-powered factories	Total factories	Powered factories	Non-powered factories	Total factories	Powered factories	Non-powered factories	Total factories
Saitama	Kita'adachi-gun	0	23	23	7	2	9	11	3	14
	Iruma-gun	0	0	0	1	0	1	0	0	0
	Minamisaitama-gun	0	0	0	0	0	0	0	1	1
Osaka	Kitakawachi-gun	0	0	0	1	0	1	5	0	5
	Higashinari-gun	1	1	2	1	0	1	1	0	1
	Osaka City	0	2	2	0	0	0	0	0	0
	Nakakawachi-gun	0	0	0	1	0	1	1	0	1
	Nishinari-gun	0	1	1	0	0	0	0	0	0
Aichi	Nagoya City	0	3	3	1	1	2	2	2	4
	Kaifu-gun	0	0	0	0	4	4	0	4	4
	Nakajima-gun	0	1	1	0	0	0	2	4	6
	Aichi-gun	0	0	0	0	0	0	1	0	1
	Haguri-gun	0	0	0	0	0	0	1	0	1
	Nishikasugai-gun	0	0	0	0	0	0	1	0	1
	Higashikasugai-gun	0	0	0	0	0	0	0	1	1

Production area		‡@ the end of 1909			‡A the end of 1917			‡B the end of January 1920		
Prefecture	City or gun or ku	Powered factories	Non-powered factories	Total factories	Powered factories	Non-powered factories	Total factories	Powered factories	Non-powered factories	Total factories
Tokushima	Tokushima City	0	3	3	1	1	2	2	2	4
Okayama	Kojima-gun	0	0	0	2	7	9	5	6	11
	Shitsuki-gun	0	0	0	0	0	0	7	11	18
	Oda-gun	0	0	0	1	1	2	2	4	6
	Asaguchi-gun	0	1	1	1	0	1	0	1	1
	Tsukubo-gun	1	0	1	1	0	1	0	0	0
Yamaguchi	Kuga-gun	1	0	1	1	0	1	2	0	2
	Asa-gun	0	0	0	0	0	0	1	0	1
Hiroshima	Fukayasu-gun	0	2	2	0	0	0	5	0	5
	Ajina-gun	0	0	0	0	0	0	4	0	4
	Fukuyama City	0	0	0	0	0	0	1	0	1
	Kure City	0	0	0	0	0	0	1	0	1
Hyôgo	Kawabe-gun	0	1	1	0	0	0	0	0	0
	Katô-gun	0	0	0	0	0	0	1	0	1
Tochigi	Aso-gun	0	0	0	1	2	3	4	0	4
	Ashikaga-gun	0	0	0	0	0	0	2	0	2

| Production area | | #@ the end of 1909 | | | #A the end of 1917 | | | #B the end of January 1920 | | |
Prefecture	City or gun or ku	Powered factories	Non-powered factories	Total factories	Powered factories	Non-powered factories	Total factories	Powered factories	Non-powered factories	Total factories
Shiga	Siga-gun	0	0	0	1	0	1	0	0	0
	Takashima-gun	0	0	0	0	1	1	0	0	0
Toyama	Toyama City	0	0	0	0	1	1	0	0	0
Fukui	Ōno-gun	0	0	0	0	1	1	0	0	0
Shizuoka	Hamana-gun	0	0	0	0	0	0	5	2	7
	Hamamatsu City	0	0	0	0	0	0	4	1	5
Ni'igata	Kitakanbara-gun	0	0	0	0	0	0	0	1	1
	Nakakanbara-gun	0	0	0	0	0	0	1	0	1
Mie	Tsu City	0	0	0	0	0	0	2	0	2
Tokyo	Honjyo-ku	0	0	0	0	0	0	1	0	1
Fukuoka	Kokura City	0	0	0	0	0	0	1	0	1
	No. of total	3	38	41	21	21	42	76	43	119

Source: Nōshōmushō [Ministry of Agriculture and Commerce], *Kōjyō Tsūran* [Directory of Japanese Factories] (Tokyo, 1909, 1917 and 1920)

In 1916 sixty-eight power looms, including the Toyoda broad-width power looms, were operating in the Giseidô factory. The looms were all attached to the power source, an 85-horsepower steam engine, by a system of shaft-and-belt transmissions. The operation of individual power looms could be halted by detaching the power transmission belt, which was hooked up to the power loom's crankshaft.

2   Residence, employment age and employment terms

It was possible to collect personal information on 122 women weavers who were engaged in the weaving process in the Giseidô power loom weaving factory between 1905 and 1916 from Giseido MSS; *Hataorikôchin-chô* (Book of wages statistics calculated per weaver) and *Kôdanjyo-meibo* (Worker List of Names). In this section I would like to examine the residence, employment age and employment terms of these 122 women.

Table 2 shows women weavers classified by their place of residence. The data include the place of residence for 122 women weavers, of whom 119 lived in Yamaguchi Prefecture. Of these 119 women weavers, 99 lived in Kuga-gun. Of the remaining 20 women weavers, 12 were dwellers of Ohshima or Tsuno or Kumage-gun, in neighboring Kuga-gun. A breakdown of the data by Iwakuni town and the nineteen villages in Kuga-gun shows that Iwakuni town, where the Giseidô power loom weaving factory was located, headed the list (see Map 1). This information shows that most of the workers went back and forth to the factory from their own farm households which were in villages as near as possible to Iwakuni town.

The distribution of 109 women weavers whose ages at first employment were known by age are as follows: age of 15–19: fifty-four; age of 20–24: twenty-six; age of 10–14: eleven; age of 25–29: ten; and age of 30–40: eight. The majority of them were young female weavers who were 15–25 years old and were engaged in the weaving process (through a piecework system) which took place after learning by doing of about two weeks (a daily wage calculation system). For example, Rinu Fujino, after learning by doing of fifteen days (22–29 May and 2–8 June 1916, wages ¥1.800 [¥ 0.12 a day]), wove 12 tan 20 shaku[6] of Kokura-fabrics (*Kokura-fukuji*) during six days (9–14 June 1916, wages ¥9.880 [¥ 0.78 a tan, ¥0.026 a shaku]), so that she received earnings of ¥11.680 which were equal to her total wages.[7] The remaining examples in this type included eight occasions from 15 November until 14 December 1916. Not only in the weaving process but also in the drawing-in process, we can see this skill acquisition through learning by doing for the first few weeks. Hunter points out that the learning of shopfloor workers in Japanese textile factories by watching others, by imitation and by a process of trial and error, remained a major method of skill acquisition throughout the prewar period.[8]

Of the number of 109 women weavers whose ages at first employment were known, the dates at first and last employment of 22 women weavers were known. Twenty of these retired within one year. A breakdown of the data by the age is as follows: age of 15–19: seven; age of 20–24: five; age of 25–29: two; and age of 30–40: six. The employment terms of the remaining two women weavers were, respectively, one year and eleven months, and two years and three months, and the ages at first employment were respectively twelve and sixteen. Of the number of twenty women weavers who retired within one year, thirteen women weavers were compelled to retire because of absence without permission and misbehaviour, four left the factory to marry or as a result of death from diseases,[9] one left the factory to nurse her father, one was transferred to another factory, and finally one was compelled to retire because she was regarded as an incompetent. Two women weavers whose employment terms exceeded one year, respectively, retired because of family commitments (the twelve-year-old girl) and left the factory to nurse her mother (the sixteen-year-old girl).

Table 2   *Women weavers classified by their place of residence, 1905–1916*

Place of residence	Number
Iwakuni town in Kuga-gun in Yamaguchi Prefecture	34
Kitakouchi village located in Kuga-gun	6
Fujikawa village located in Kuga-gun	4
Marifu village located in Kuga-gun	4
Shigino village located in Kuga-gun	3
Kwashimo village located in Kuga-gun	1
Oze village located in Kuga-gun	1
Takamori village located in Kuga-gun	8
Kawagoe village located in Kuga-gun	4
Yonegawa village located in Kuga-gun	1
So'o village located in Kuga-gun	1
Kuga village located in Kuga-gun	13
Sakaue village located in Kuga-gun	5
Kamibata village located in Kuga-gun	3
Kuwane village located in Kuga-gun	5
Yanai town in Kuga-gun	2
Hidumi village located in Kuga-gun	1
Yota village located in Kuga-gun	1

Place of residence	Number
Takane village located in Kuga-gun	1
Fukasu village located in Kuga-gun	1
Total	99
Okiura village located in Ohshima-gun in Yamaguchi Prefecture	3
Gamano village located in Ohshima-gun	3
Hirai village located in Ohshima-gun	1
Suetakekita village located in Tsuno-gun in Yamaguchi Prefecture	1
Nakazu village located in Tsuno-gun	1
Fukugawa village located in Tsuno-gun	1
Asae village located in Kumage-gun in Yamaguchi Prefecture	1
Yashiro village located in Kumage-gun	1
Kushi village located in Saba-gun in Yamaguchi Prefecture	1
Hôfu town in Saba-gun	1
Kôsei village located in Asa-gun in Yamaguchi Prefecture	1
Kotô village located in Asa-gun	1
Hagi town in Abu-gun in Yamaguchi Prefecture	1
Kayoi village located in Ohtsu-gun in Yamaguchi Prefecture	1
Mine-gun in Yamaguchi Prefecture	1
Narazaki village located in Toyoura-gun in Yamaguchi Prefecture	1
Total	20
Ohno village located in Saeki-gun in Hiroshima Prefecture	1
Asayama village located in Ano-gun in Shimane Prefecture	1
Uncertainty	1
Grand Total	122

Source: Giseido MSS; *Hataorikôchin-chô* (Book of wages statistics calculated per weaver), *Kôdanjyo-meibo* (Worker List of Names)

Of the 78 women weavers who seemed to be employed as of January 1911, in which the last women weaver entered the Giseidô weaving factory, 63 women weavers entered the factory at the age of 15–24. A breakdown of the data by the passing employment term is as follows: within one year: one; within two years: ten; within three years: twenty-eight; within four years: sixteen; within five years: six; and within six years: two. In addition, two women weavers of these, whose passing employment term were, respectively, within one year and within two years, were respectively employed as of the period of 15 May–14 June 1916 and as of the period of 15 August–14 September 1914, therefore both their extended employment term was less than six years. However, the latter woman weaver was likely to leave the factory at the latest by the period of 15 November–14 December 1916 because no evidence of her working was recorded during the year of 1916. As we can see from the above-mentioned, women weavers entered the Giseidô weaving factory from the latter half of their teens to the former half of their twenties.

The employment records of the remaining nine women weavers show that they were dismissed, but that they were able to rejoin the Giseidô weaving factory. For example, Nao Sunahara whose place of residence was Iwakuni town in Kuga-gun, was taken into employment at the age of eighteen on November 1902 and was dismissed on October 1905, but rejoined the factory at the age of twenty-three on October 1907 and passed the employment term on three years and three months as of November 1911. We can consequently see that the case of Nao Sunahara suggests a pattern of work participation among women weavers.

3   Production of Kokura-fabrics (*Kokura-fukuji*) and broader-width cotton crepe (*hirohaba-menchidimi*)

I would now like to consider the production of Kokura-fabrics and broader-width cotton crepe by the women weavers working in the Giseidô power loom weaving factory during the former half of the First World War period. The women weavers were classified into three types of female workers: those engaged in the weaving process; those engaged not in the weaving process but also in the drawing-in process; and those engaged in the weaving process as temporary workers. Table 3 shows the number of women weavers, classified by type, additionally with payment of wages. The number of temporary workers was very small.[10] Most of the women weavers received wages according to the quantity of piece-work they had done. In this section, given a breakdown of the data shown in Table 3, we can focus on the women weavers who received piecework wages and examine attendance patterns, payment of wages and weaving patterns in the Giseidô weaving factory.

3.1.   Attendance patterns

The rate of going to work, namely, the rate of the number of weaving days to the number of days except holiday at each period, can be calculated per woman weaver who received piecework wages. Table 4 shows their frequency distribution. The average rate of going to work was, respectively, 76.7 per cent (15 August–14 September 1914), 75.3 per cent (15 April–14 May 1916), 72.1 per cent (15 May–14 June 1916), and 71.8 per cent (15 November–14 December

Table 3 *The number of women weavers, 1914 and 1916*

Women weavers	Payment of wages	1914	1916		
		15 August– 14 September	15 April– 14 May	15 May– 14 June	15 November– 14 December
The female workers who were engaged in weaving process	A piece-wage payment	33	54	50	36
The female workers who were engaged not only in the weaving process also in the drawing-in process	A piece-wage payment (weaving process), a daily wage calculation system (drawing-in process)	20	8	15	35
The female workers who were engaged in weaving process as temporary workers	A daily wage calculation system	5	1	1	1
Total		58	63	66	72

Source: Giseido MSS; *Hataorikōchin-chō* (Book of wages statistics calculated per weaver)

1916). It had decreased a little from 1914 to 1916. The women weavers who received piecework wages produced 3,268 tan 3 shaku during the period of 15 August–14 September 1914, 5,088 tan 11 shaku during the period of 15 April–14 May 1916, 4,820 tan 2 shaku during the period of 15 May–14 June 1916 and 4,452 tan 13 shaku during the period of 15 November–14 December 1916. The output had increased by about 50 per cent from 1914 to 1916. The demand for Kokura-fabrics and broader-width cotton crepe seemed to rise towards the boom years of the First World War. To sum up, in order to meet the rising demand, Giseidô increased output, but the average of the rate of going to work tended to decrease. The reason for this was because Giseidô tried to assure supplies by increasing the total number of the women weavers, while the number of them of rate of going to work 60 or more per cent was kept.

Table 4   *The distribution of the rate of going to work of women wavers (a piece-wage payment), 1914 and 1916*

the rate of going to work (%)	1914	1916		
	15 August–14 September	15 April–14 May	15 May–14 June	15 November–14 December
100	7	12	0	4
90–99	8	4	14	7
80–89	14	14	17	14
70–79	15	15	9	21
60–69	1	5	7	6
50–59	1	6	10	13
40–49	1	2	2	1
30–39	2	0	1	3
20–29	1	2	4	1
10–19	1	0	1	0
0–9	2	2	0	1
total	53	62	65	71

Source: Same as Table 3

Why could Giseidô not try to assure supplies by increasing the number of weaving days of each woman weaver? We can identify 284 female workers' reasons for leaving the Giseidô weaving factory earlier than usual, which were recorded from 8 June 1914 until 29 July 1915. The list of reasons in the records are as follows: leaving because of bad health (diseases – 209; headache – 10; stomachache – 8; toothache – 2), 229;

leaving because of family commitments, 17; leaving because of family's and relative's sicknesses, 14; leaving off without permission earlier than usual, 12; leaving because of accident, 8; leaving because of the relative's death, 3; uncertain, 1. It is important to stress that there were 35 cases of women who left the factory earlier than usual because of domestic circumstances (including family commitments, family's and relative's sicknesses, a relative's death). As we saw in the previous section, some women weavers were dismissed, but that they were able to rejoin the Giseidô weaving factory. It consequently seems safe to assume that the responsibilities for not only agricultural chores but also housework were the main reason why female workers were not able to work more regularly. Therefore, Giseidô could not try to assure supplies by increasing the number of weaving days of each woman weaver.

Then, why could not Giseidô try to assure supplies by compelling each woman weaver to operate two or more power looms? Each woman weaver worked on only two power looms at most. The number of women weavers who operated two power looms at each period were respectively six (15 August–14 September 1914), seven (15 April–14 May 1916), one (15 May–14 June 1916) and three (15 November–14 December 1916). Most women weavers respectively worked on only one power loom. Therefore, Giseidô tried to assure supplies by compelling each woman weaver to operate two or more power looms. Even if the number of women weavers increased, the number of operating power looms did not increase rapidly. In fact, the number of operating power looms at each period were respectively 51 (15 August–14 September 1914), 62 (15 April–14 May 1916), 60 (15 May–14 June 1916) and 70 (15 November–14 December 1916), which kept pace with the number of women weavers. The integrated cotton spinning and weaving mills in 1903 1.17 power looms per weaver, in 1912 1.12 looms per weaver and in 1926 1.36 looms per weaver, until the automatic loom spread.[11]

As we have seen, Giseidô could not assure supplies by increasing the number of weaving days of each woman weaver because the responsibilities for not only agricultural chores but also housework were the main reason why female workers were not able to work more regularly. They assured supplies by compelling each woman weaver to operate two or more power looms while most women weavers respectively worked on only one power loom. As a result, the average rate of going to work decreased a little from 1914 to 1916.

3.2 Payment of wages

As we have seen in the Introduction, Giseidô imported from Britain 36 broad-width power looms, 6 shuttle-changing looms in 1907, and 22 looms with dobbies in 1910 and 1914. These three types of power looms were operated during the first half of the First World War period. In the Giseidô weaving factory, the woven cotton cloth was distinguished through combining the sign of cotton cloth (i-gô, sin-ichi-gô) with the type of power loom. The piece-wage rates of each distinguished cotton cloth were set according to the factory's own standards.

Table 5   *Piece-wage rates, 1914 and 1916*

The type of power loom	1914	1916		
The sign of cotton cloth	15 August–14 September	15 April–14 May	15 May–14 June	15 November–14 December
Broad-width power looms				
i-gô		10.2	10.2	10.2
ki-gô		9.0	9.0	
kuro-i-gô		10.2	10.2	
gen-gô	9.3			9.3
ko-gô		9.9	9.9	
sa-gô		8.1	8.1	8.1
jin-gô	9.0		9.0	10.2
dai-roku-gô	10.2	10.2		10.2
nu-gô		9.0	9.0	
no-gô		9.0		9.0
haru-ichi-gô		10.2	10.2	10.2
ma-gô		9.0	9.0	
mi-gô		8.4	8.4	
ri-gô		7.8	7.8	
ye-gô	9.0	9.0	9.0	
hi-gô		9.9		9.9
shin-go-gô		10.2	10.2	
haru-san-gô		10.2	10.2	
Shuttle-changing looms ('Platt Loom')				
i-gô	13.8			13.8
ki-gô		11.7	11.0	
sa-gô			13.8	12.0
shin-ichi-gô		13.5	13.5	13.5
shin-san-gô		16.5	16.5	
no-gô		11.7	10.8	
ra-gô	15.6	15.6		15.6

The type of power loom	1914	1916		
The sign of cotton cloth	15 August– 14 September	15 April– 14 May	15 May– 14 June	15 November– 14 December
ri-gô		10.14	9.3	
Looms with dobbies				
shin-ichi-gô		13.5	13.5	
shin-san-gô		16.5	16.5	
su-gô		13.2	13.2	13.2
se-gô		13.2		13.2
dai-nana-gô	14.4	14.4		14.4
dai-hachi-gô	13.8	13.8	13.8	13.8
tsu-gô	14.4	14.4	14.4	14.4
toku-chû-yon-gô		13.2	13.2	13.2
toku-chû-go-gô		13.2	13.2	13.2
toku-chû-roku-gô		13.2	13.2	13.2
ni-gô	13.2			13.2
yo-gojyûni-gô		15.6	14.7	
ra-gô		15.6	15.6	15.6
ran-gô	13.2			13.2
dai-roku-gô		13.2	12.8	

Source: Same as Table 3.

Table 5 shows the piece-wage rates for two or more periods, classified by the type of power loom. Let us examine the trend of piece-wage rates for the same cotton cloth. Of the 41 kinds of cotton cloth woven for two or more periods, we can identify the piece-wage rates of 1 kinds during the period between 15 August and 14 September 1914. Of this number of eleven kinds, only one piece-wage rate of cotton cloth (jin-gô) woven by broad-width power looms rose by about 13 per cent from 1914 to 1916. The piece-wage rates of ten other kinds of cotton cloths did not change at all. The piece-wage rates of six kinds of cotton cloths other than jin-gô fell by about 3–13 per cent during 1916. Thus, the piece-wage rates of only seven of the forty-one kinds of cotton cloths changed during 1916. We can see that few piece-wage rates changed during the first half years of the First World War.

Women weavers were paid according to the amount of cloth they had finished weaving during one month, but 20 per cent or 30 per cent of the piece-wage rates were subtracted when they wove some defective cotton cloths. The numbers of women weavers who wove defective cotton cloths were respectively ten (15 August–14 September 1914), nine (15 April–14 May 1916), nine (15 May–14 June 1916) and six (15 November–14 December 1916). A few women weavers were paid some amount in advance per month and the numbers were respectively six (15 August–14 September 1914), ten (15 April–14 May 1916), five (15 May–14 June 1916) and three (15 November–14 December 1916). To the female workers who were engaged not only in the weaving process but also in the drawing-in process received fourteen kinds of daily wages: ¥0.132; ¥0.150; ¥0.180; ¥0.210; ¥0.230; ¥0.240; ¥0.250; ¥0.270; ¥0.280; ¥0.290; ¥0.300; ¥0.320; ¥0.330; and ¥0.350.

3.3   Weaving patterns

In order to focus on the weaving patterns of the specific cotton cloth, we need to consider the data on not only the type but also the number of power looms each woman weaver operated. During the period under consideration (15 November–14 December 1916), three types of cloth (broader-width cotton crepe, black Kokura-fabrics and white Kokura-fabrics) were woven by numbered broad-width power looms. Table 6 shows the production of these three types of cloth by the women weavers who received piecework wages. As we can see from this data, all of the women weavers, except for two weavers (Fude Muraoka and Shimo Shimizu), did not spend all weaving days producing a particular type of cotton cloth. In general, one weaver seemed to produce two types of cloth, at least per one power loom during the period.

Let us focus on each weaver's date of weaving. The period of weaving of concerned type of cloth divided into three sections (the first, middle and the latter). Thus, first, for broader-width cotton crepe, Nami Nakai, Kimi Yoshinaka, Suma Hayashi, Nobuko Kugimoto and Toyo Morikane produced cloth in the first section, Nobuko Kugimoto and Toyo Morikane in the middle and Kiriyo Hayashi, Yuki Tominaga and Fude Muraoka in the latter section; secondly, for black Kokura-fabrics, Kuni Yoshiyama in the first section and in the middle and Riu Ninomiya/Kimi Yamasaki, Shimo Shimizu, Tame Kurashige, Suma Hayashi and Michi Chô in the latter section. Finally, for white Kokura-fabrics, Kimi Yoshinaka, Yuki Yonemoto, Yuki Tominaga, Uta Yoshiyama and Aya Ishida in the first section, Yuki Tominaga, Uta Yoshiyama and Aya Ishida in the middle and Aya Ishida in the latter section. That is to say, the weaving of different types of cloth was assigned to each weaver as time passed. We can imagine that by using these methods the Giseidô weaving factory was able to meet demand for each type of cloth under conditions in which young female workers were not able to work more regularly because of their responsibilities for not only agricultural chores but also housework.

Table 6 *Weaving patterns (15 November–14 December 1916)*

Weaver	Number of power looms	Date of weaving	No. of days	Output	No. of weaving days	No. of drawing-in days	No. of working days	Rate of going to work
Weaving of broader-width cotton crepe								
Nami Nakai	12	16–17, 19–20 November	4	16 tan	16	0	16	57.1
Kimi Yoshinaka	*31*	*16, 18–21 November*	*5*	*20*	*27*	*0*	*27*	*96.4*
Suma Hayashi	*28*	*17–18 November*	*2*	*7*	*20.5*	*0.5*	*21*	*75.0*
Nobuko Kugimoto	21	17–19, 21–23 November	6	22	25	0	25	89.3
Toyo Morikane	11	17–18, 20–21, 23–24, 26 November	7	28	17.5	0.5	18	64.3
Kiriyo Hayashi	18	24, 26, 28–29 November, 2, 4–5, 7–8 December	9	36	18	0.5	18.5	66.1
Yuki Tominaga	*34*	*25, 27–30 November, 2, 4–6, 8–12 December*	*14*	*52*	*22*	*0*	*22*	*78.6*
Fude Muraoka	32	2–3, 5, 7, 9, 11–12, 14 December	8	26	8	9	23	82.1

Weaver	Number of power looms	Date of weaving	No. of days	Output	No. of weaving days	No. of drawing-in days	No. of working days	Rate of going to work
Weaving of black kokura-fabrics								
Kuni Yoshiyama	9	16–18, 20–22, 24–26 November	9	36 tan	22	0	22	78.6
Riu Ninomiya/ Kimi Yamasaki	uncertainty	3–5, 7 December	4	4	26	0	26	92.9
Shimo Shimizu	13	5, 7–9, 11–14 December	8	32	8	2	10	35.7
Tame Kurashige	23	6–8, 10–12, 14 December	7	24 tan 3 shaku	19.5	0.5	20	71.4
Suma Hayashi	28	*9–10, 12–14 December*	5	*20 tan 8 shaku*	*20.5*	*0.5*	*21*	*75.0*
Michi Chô	29	10–11, 13 December	3	10 tan 4 shaku	22	0	22	78.6
Weaving of white kokura-fabrics								
Kimi Yoshinaka	25	*16–17 November*	2	*8 tan*	*27*	*0*	*27*	*96.4*
Yuki Yonemoto	36	16–18 November	3	12	28	0	28	100.0
Yuki Tominaga	34	*17–18, 20–21, 23–24 November*	6	*24*	22	0	22	78.6
Uta Yoshiyama	32	17–19, 21–23, 25 November	7	30	20	5	25	89.3
Aya Ishida	14	17–18, 20–22, 24–25, 27–29 November, 2–4 December	13	50	23	0	23	82.1

Source: Same as Table 3.

Note: (1) The data on women weavers produced cotton cloth over two types is expressed by Oblique characters.
(2) Fude Muraoka learnt her skill by watching others on the job and received daily wages for six days between 16 and 21 November (¥0.120 per day) before she began to engage in the drawing-in process. Her working days includes these six days. Afterwards she engaged in the drawing-in process between 22 and 30 November and started on the weaving of broader-width cotton crepe on 2 December.
(3) Riu Ninomiya and Kimi Yamasaki were always registered in joint names and were paid as one person. The case like this was extremely rare.

4 Concluding remarks

Giseidô had produced broader-width cotton cloth such as Kokura-fabrics and broader-width cotton crepe for the national market since 1878, when its handloom weaving factory was established in Syûtô. While the demand for Kokura-fabrics for military uniforms had increased, in 1905 Giseidô imported broad-width power looms from Britain and started to operate its own power loom weaving factory. During the first half of the 1910s the Giseidô weaving factory was able to meet demand for each type of cloth under conditions in which young female workers were not able to work more regularly because of their responsibilities for not only agricultural chores but also housework. This fact means that using the labour of young women in a rural setting did not prevent a rural factory from being equipped with about seventy British broader-width power looms in the early twentieth century. Thus, the evidence from Syûtô shows the patterns of work participation among rural female workers in a village weaving factory in this period.[12]

Notes

1. Giseidô (ed.), *Giseidô Hyakunenshi* [A 100-Year History of Giseidô] (Osaka University Press: Yamaguchi, 1974), p. 63.

2. Giseidô, *Giseidô Hyakunenshi*, p. 142; Giseidô MSS: *Keireki-sho* [Career book], *Jigyôgaikyô-sho* [Business report].

3. Giseidô, *Giseidô Hyakunenshi*, p. 144.

4. Giseidô MSS: *Hataorikôchin-chô* [Book of wages statistics calculated per weaver], Giseidô, *Giseidô Hyakunenshi*, pp. 144, 146, 152.

5. Platt Bros, Loom Order Books, No. 21, April 1906–October 1909, listed at DDPSL 1/70/21, in the Lancashire Record Office at Preston, p. 97.

6. The tan is a unit of measure. One tan of cloth is 30 shaku long. The shaku used in this case is the measure known as the Kujira-shaku. One Kujira-shaku is 37.5 cm.

7. Giseido MSS: *Hataorikôchin-chô*.

8. Hunter, J., *Women and the Labour Market in Japan's Industrialising Economy: The textile industry before the Pacific War* (Routledge: London, 2003), pp. 130–1.

9. The names of the diseases responsible for their deaths are not recorded.

10. The ratio of the output by temporary workers to the total number of production of cotton cloth was less than 10 per cent at each period: 9.5 per cent (15 August–14 September 1914), 1.2 per cent (15 April–14 May 1916), 1.6 per cent (15 May–14 June 1916) and 3.8 per cent (15 November–14 December 1916).

11. Tadashi Ishii, 'Sen'i Kikai Gijutsu no Hatten Katei' [The Develpoment Process of the Textile Mechanical Technology], in T. Nakaoka *et al.* (eds), *Kindai Nihon no Gijutsu to Gijutsu Seisaku* (United Nations University Press: Tokyo, 1986), p. 127.

12. For the contemporary and similar evidence on women working on rural small weaving factory floor from Banshû, a weaving district specializing in the production

of yarn-dyed, narrow-width striped cotton cloth, see Jun Sasaki, 'Factory Girls in an Agrarian Setting *circa* 1910', in Masayuki Tanimoto (ed.), *The Role of Tradition in Japan's Industrialization* (Oxford University Press: Oxford, 2006); Jun Sasaki, *Ajia no Kôgyô-ka to Nihon* [Asian Industrialization and Japan] (Koyo Shobo: Kyoto, 2006).

PART 3

THE REGIONAL ECONOMY

12

Lancashire and the Great War: the organisation and supply of munitions to the Western Front

ROGER LLOYD-JONES AND M.J.LEWIS

S PEAKING at Manchester in June 1915 the newly appointed Minister of Munitions, David Lloyd George, asserted that Britain was 'fighting against the best organised community in the world'. What concerned him was whether the nation had sufficiently recognised the protracted and dangerous nature of the struggle. For too long, the British had employed 'haphazard, leisurely, go-as-you-please methods', which were placing the nation in great peril.[1] The creation of the Ministry of Munitions represented a break with 'business as usual' and an acceptance that in attempting to satisfy the insatiable demands of the Western Front the British engineering industry would be called upon to deliver unprecedented supplies of munitions, especially shell.[2] Logically this directed attention towards the organisation of domestic production, and consequently for politicians such as Lloyd George and certain business leaders, there would inevitably have to be a radical re-think of business–state relations, which would in all probability have to be restructured. This chapter examines the organisation of war production in one of the country's most important industrial regions, Lancashire, with particular reference to the development of contractual relations between the Ministry, local boards of management, and private engineering contractors.

The first section outlines the structure of Lancashire's engineering sector, describing its size, composition and growth during the Great War. Section two then considers the circumstances leading to the establishment of local boards of management under the Ministry. Employing principal agent theory as a method of analysis, we focus on the board of management of the Manchester and District Armaments Output Committee (MDAOC). This was the local institution to coordinate, manage, monitor, review and evaluate contracts between the Ministry and local engineering firms, establishing a set of relations that often resulted in considerable tension. Section three examines the pressures associated with the enormous demand for shells and the drive to increase output. How successful were Lancashire firms in meeting their targets?; did the MDAOC enable local firms to make a smooth transition from general engineering to munitions production?; what constraints did local contractors face?; and to what extent were they given adequate support by the MDAOC and the Ministry? From the summer of 1915 to the great Somme offensive that began on 1 July 1916, the priority of the munitions authorities at both national and local levels was to increase output.[3] Thereafter, as section four explores, the continued drive to increase output led to increasing tensions in contractual relations, complicated by a prioritisation on quality, government control over wages and prices, and by general constraints on raising output. In this context, the role of the MDAOC in repositioning and managing its relationship with contractors becomes essential in any assessment of the effectiveness of the contractual relationship between the Ministry and Lancashire's engineering firms. The jurisdiction of the MDAOC did not cover the whole of Lancashire, but its remit did stretch out to towns such as Ashton, Bolton, Bury, Oldham, Rochdale, Stalybridge, Stockport and Warrington, and while these towns had their own local committees, representatives from the MDAOC sat on them, and munitions contracts were sanctioned and distributed by the Manchester Board. The study, therefore, allows for a representative coverage of Lancashire's engineering sector and an understanding of the complexity of the organisation of munitions supply at the local level.[4]

Lancashire engineering during the Great War

Engineering was an important sector of Lancashire's industrial economy, and in 1914, the North West, consisting predominantly of Lancashire, employed a larger share of Britain's engineering labour force than any other region (Table 1). Textile machine making, which owed its origins to the cotton industry, formed an important sector, shaping the pattern of engineering in Lancashire. Table 2 lists a few of the leading textile machine makers in 1921, which produced munitions during the war. In total, around 80 to 100 textile machine makers in Lancashire produced munitions, the largest being Platt Bros Ltd of Oldham, the world's leading maker, and a company that had diversified into collieries and general engineering.[5] Another large producer was Dobson & Barlow, Bolton, a firm where family control remained important,[6] as it did in the large firm of Howard & Bullough, Accrington. Other major producers included Mather and Platt of Newton Heath and Asa Lees of Oldham, but Manchester itself boasted few textile machine makers, with the exception of J. Hetherington & Sons.[7]

Table 1 *Percentage of engineering labour force employed in the five largest regions, 1914–1919*

December	1914	1915	1916	1917	1918	1919
North Western	20.4	19.1	18.7	18.5	17.3	17.3
East and West Midlands	17.5	19.0	19.3	20.2	18.2	18.6
Yorkshire	12.4	12.8	12.5	12.5	11.6	11.6
London	9.7	10.5	11.2	13.0	13.4	12.3
Scotland	15.2	14.8	14.4	14.3	13.5	14.3
% total engineering labour force	75.3	76.2	76.1	78.5	74.0	74.1

Source: *Board of Trade Labour Gazette*, xxiv, no. 1 (1916), p. 16; xxv, no. 1 (1917), p. 14; xxvi, no. 1 (1918), p. 2; xxvii, no. 1 (1919), p. 81; xxviii, no. 1 (1920), p. 19.

Table 2 *Leading Lancashire textile machine makers and munitions producers*

	Employment	Paid-up share capital (£)	Outstanding debentures (£)
Platt Bros & Co.	7,000	3,710,160	1,030,000
Dobson & Barlow	5,500	400,000	230,722
Howard & Bullough	5,000	15,000	250,000
Mather & Platt	4,000	1,763,660	–
Asa Lees & Co.	2,300	360,000	–
J. Hetherington & Sons	2,000	–	–
Brooks & Doxey	900	551,031	–
J. Stubbs	500	–	–
Taylor & Lang	300	–	–
W. Ayrton	100	–	–
Hacking & Co.	–	–	–

Source: H. Clay and K. R. Brady (eds), *Manchester at Work: A Survey* (Manchester Civic Committee, 1927), p. 111.

Lancashire engineering was not restricted to textile machine making. Other branches in the region included locomotive making, machine tools, electrical engineering, boiler and steam engine manufacture, motor vehicles, cranes, hydraulic plant, printing machinery, and wire and wire netting.[8] Firms themselves tended not to pursue a strategy of narrow specialisation, growth often premised upon 'widening ... the class of articles manufactured'.[9] Naysmith, Wilson & Co., for example, locomotive builders of Patricroft, also manufactured steam hammers, hydraulic presses and general engineering products.[10] In 1913 there were 231 mechanical engineering firms in Lancashire, of which 81 were limited companies, and between 1914 and 1918 there were probably over 200 'general' engineering firms.[11] In Manchester and its outskirts alone were clustered a number of large firms. These included locomotive makers such as Beyer, Peacock & Co., The Vulcan Foundry, and Naysmith, Wilson & Co.; boilermakers and general engineering concerns such as Galloways Ltd, Lancaster & Tonge, The National Gas Engine Co.; printing machine makers, including Linotype Ltd; chain makers: Hans Renold; motor vehicle makers: Ford Ltd, Crossley Bros and Belsize Motors; electrical engineering: British Westinghouse and Metro-Vic Electrical; and in armaments Armstrong Whitworth. All these firms engaged in armament and munitions production during the war, as did the Bolton general engineering firms of John Musgrave & Son, Hicks & Hargreaves, and J. & E. Wood.[12] Beneath this layer of large enterprises there was a thick undergrowth of small-scale firms, and while a clear trend towards company incorporation had begun before the war, the typical Lancashire engineering firm remained a sole proprietorship, or a partnership, 'the scale at which they operated requiring comparatively little fixed capital expenditure'.[13]

Table 3   *Insured workers employed in engineering in the five largest regions, 1916–1919*

December	1916	1917	1918	1919	% increase, 1916–18
North West	195,942	227,226	239,988	220,780	22.5
East and West Midlands	201,375	247,848	251,829	237,127	25.1
Yorkshire	130,432	153,930	161,104	147,333	23.5
London	116,972	159,172	186,346	157,002	59.3
Scotland	151,027	176,017	187,305	181,770	24.0
Total engineering labour force	1,045,982	1,226,731	1,386,833	1,274,336	32.5

Source: *Board of Trade Labour Gazette*, xxv, no. 1 (1917), p. 14; xxvii, no. 1 (1919), p. 81; xxviii, no. 1 (1920), p. 19.

While the North West was the largest engineering region by employment in 1914, the trend over the war period saw its relative position decline (Table 1).

Although employment in absolute terms grew (Table 3), by the end of the war, the East and West Midlands had overtaken Lancashire, and the growth of employment, a proxy for engineering activity, was significantly higher in London. Compared to the other important regions the North West experienced the slowest rate of growth from 1916 to 1918, which suggests that Lancashire itself was the least dynamic of the major centres of engineering production. The region's engineering firms faced a number of daunting challenges during the war, as its local management boards strove to satisfy the Western Front's enormous appetite for munitions.

Munitions supply: The Manchester Board of Management and the contract system

Visiting Lancashire in June 1915, Lloyd George attempted to encourage a greater organisation of engineering resources, and his theme for Manchester manufacturers concentrated on the vital role of 'the workshop'. Victory depended 'more upon the master and men who are occupied in running the workshops of this country, than upon almost any section of the community'.[14] Thus Lloyd George articulated his view of an 'Engineers' War'.[15] Lancashire responded by establishing the MDAOC, one of a number of local committees that sprang up in the early months of 1915 as disquiet grew over the effectiveness of the War Office (WO) procurement system. Before the start of the war there had been a general optimism that the WO, through officially listed armament producers, would provide munitions in sufficient quantities,[16] the consensus predicting reserves sufficient for six months.[17] By April 1915, however, George Macaulay Booth, the Liverpool and London merchant and ship-owner[18] appointed by Kitchener to chair the Armaments Output Committee, acknowledged that the methods adopted by the WO for the procurement of munitions, 'by concentrating on a rather limited number of people', had proved a failure. The 'curve of delivery is behindhand', and while Booth accepted that the output of shell had increased, deliveries were 'already 60 to 90 days late'.[19] At the end of December 1914, cumulative orders for shell stood at 10,389,073, but the number delivered at the end of May 1915 was only 1,972,558, or 19 per cent of the total ordered.[20] Booth believed that if targets were to be met, then the 'engineering facilities' of the country would have to be employed more efficiently. Consequently there was a need for changes in the procurement system, allowing for a much wider range of firms to contract for government business.[21] Booth challenged the preferred system adopted by the WO of contracting out orders to a 'circle of listed suppliers', a policy that excluded local engineering firms from direct orders and left them dependent on sub-contracts from the elite armament firms.[22]

In June 1915, with the creation of the Ministry of Munitions by the new coalition government, the policy focus under Lloyd George shifted to the organisation of supply, aimed at procuring the necessary resources in materials, machine tools and labour, from a much wider range of producers. An important element in the Ministry's strategy was the establishment of National Shell Factories under the local management boards, as well as 'co-operative schemes' for sub-contracting for munitions components. These initiatives concentrated upon small calibre shell, while the major armaments firms managed heavy shell production in newly created National Projectile Factories, together with National Filling Factories.[23] The National Factories became 'a vast network of munitions workshops',[24] but were often ad hoc affairs administered by local firms, and central to the system of organisation was the wide spectrum of private firms who contracted with local boards of management to supply shells and a range of other munitions components, such as fuses, to the Ministry. The MDAOC demonstrates the complexity of the local system for contractual organisation, and the problems of 'moral hazard' in its relationship to the Ministry.

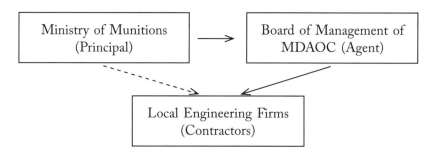

Figure 1: Principal agent: contractual relations in munitions production
Note: dotted line denotes that in certain circumstances a department of the Ministry might contract directly with local firms.

Figure 1 illustrates the contractual relations between local engineering firms, the MDAOC, and the Ministry of Munitions, informed by principal agent theory.[25] The Ministry was not a direct producer, but acted as a principal, hiring as agents local boards of management to distribute contracts, organise the supply of physical and human resources and the production of munitions in their local district.[26] Thus, as the Manchester Board accepted, 'the law of agent and principal' determined its relationship to the Ministry.[27] In their capacity as agents, the boards placed contracts with local engineering firms, monitoring the ability of the latter to meet production targets and delivery dates. To ensure the carrying out of Ministry policy, and to provide production specifications, labour and material supply and quality inspection, boards were subordinate to Area Offices established by the Ministry.[28] Given that boards were managed by small groups of local businessmen, the potential for a conflict of interest with the principal ('moral hazard')[29] was high, since the board consisted of members of contracting firms. Agency 'problems are easily solved if it is feasible to write a complete contract', defining 'each party's responsibilities and rights for each and every contingency that could conceivably arise during the transaction'.[30] In the case of the MDAOC, however, complete contracts were not feasible because disputes arose over the technical specifications of products contracted for, and, as will be shown later, over the constraints placed upon engineering firms in an environment of scarcity. Such were the contractual problems that the MDAOC employed H. O. Simpson, a leading Manchester contract lawyer, to 'personally give legal advice'.[31]

Table 4   *Board of management of the MDAOC, 1915*

W. Collingwood (Chair)	MD, Vulcan Foundry (locomotive manufacturers)
Hans Renold	Chair and MD, Hans Renold Ltd (chain manufacturers)
H. Mensforth	Director of British Westinghouse Electrical & Manufacturing Co. Ltd.
A. P. Wood	MD, Lancashire Dynamo & Motor Co.
J. Taylor	Vice-Chair and MD, Mather & Platt (textile machinery)
E. G. Goodbehere	Director, Brooks & Doxey (textile machinery)

Source: MA, MS F 623.4 M1 no. 1, 27 July 1915.

In 1915 the Board of Management of the MDAOC consisted of W. Collingwood, together with five local business leaders (Table 4). Prominent local representation, however, did not guarantee a smooth relationship with its principal. For example, from the outset, the Board complained that the Ministry was delaying the production of munitions by issuing enquiries for shell that lacked clear technical specifications, and not ensuring 'sufficient' supplies of materials.[32] Fearing a loss of trust and credibility with local contractors, the Board insisted that they should be kept fully informed of the Ministry's intentions, so that they could effectively 'guide' firms on 'their future manufacturing programmes, enable them to train the necessary labour', and meet their contractual obligations.[33] Such was the Board's concern that they sought a meeting with Lloyd George, where it was agreed that while the Ministry and WO would continue to deal directly with armament firms and railway companies, it 'would as a rule deal only through the Board of Management', making optimum use of the organisational capabilities of the Board to organise local contractors.[34] Both parties considered this a 'very satisfactory' compromise, but contractual problems persisted. In September, for example, disputes arose over anomalies in contract prices, the Ministry reprimanding the Board for setting prices for the partial machining of 3.3-inch shell significantly above those which other firms were offering to the armaments firms, the latter directly contracting to the Ministry. The price differential was 65 per cent above what the Ministry considered 'an ample figure', the Board prejudicing 'deliveries to the armament firms'.[35] The Ministry inferred that the Board was exploiting its agency role by colluding with local engineering firms, a classic example of 'moral hazard', where agent and contractor attempt to maximise remuneration.[36] Despite strong representation from J. Bowden, the Ministry's Superintendent Engineer at Area Office, the Board denied any collusion, confirming its responsibility as an agent to its principal.[37]

Nevertheless, this episode raised the question of the autonomy of the Board to supervise local contracts, and the authority of the Ministry to dictate terms and bypass the local agency. Such an organisational dilemma could manifest itself in contractual duplication, as for example in the actions of the Ministry's Trench Warfare Department, which, according to Goodbehere, had contracted directly in the Lancashire district for shell for Stoke Trench Guns, circumventing the Manchester Board.[38] The Ministry's response was to pacify the Board, by promises of orders for Stoke shell, 'provided the price was right',[39] but at the same time the Ministry restated the principal–agent relationship. It confirmed that the Board was responsible for the delivery of shell in its local area, and insisted that the Board's role as agent was to ensure that 'contractors meet their obligations in a business like manner'. In this, the Ministry asserted its authority by requiring that their Superintendent Engineer 'assist' the Board 'in bringing contractors up to scratch'.[40] The principal held the Board responsible for the organisation of local engineering, but how effective were local arrangements in raising the level of munitions output, and what were the major challenges and constraints?

Shells more shells: Lancashire and the drive for output

Firms producing shell were from a wide range of engineering backgrounds, they were making it for the first time, and consequently there were no previous benchmarks to gauge their performance. As a proxy of their effectiveness as munitions producers, Table 5 shows the trend of their deficit to contract ratio from late 1915 to mid-1916, for three different type of shell. A declining ratio would suggest that firms were making a successful transition to munitions production during a period of intense preparation for the Somme offensive. The ratio for all three types of shell fell, especially for 3.3-inch, the projectile supplied for the standard field gun used by the British Army, the 18-pounder.[41] The Board of the MDAOC could certainly congratulate itself on facilitating an enormous increase in output from the region's workshops over a short period, justifying the decision of the Ministry to organise via local committees.

The 'organisational strength of the Ministry lay not at the centre but in the localities',[42] the local committees aiding the munitions drive through their ownership of local knowledge and their experience of engineering practices, central characteristics of principal–agent relations.[43] With the priority on increasing the output of shell, the value of the MDAOC as local agents was that it possessed the necessary knowledge to identify those firms that had the production capability to make the transition from peacetime production to munitions. By July 1915 the MDAOC had identified on its list 43 firms (Appendix) with the potential to produce munitions, allocating contracts for 3.3-, 4.5- and 6-inch shells, as well as for components such as fuses, gaines, and plugs. These companies covered a wide spectrum of Lancashire engineering, ranging in size from large concerns such as British Westinghouse to small-scale machine tool makers such as Kendall & Gent, and formed the initial core of the local output drive. Raising output, however, was not a straightforward process, as a series of factors constrained production, and agency problems quickly emerged.

Table 5   *Manchester and District firms contracted to supply various types of shell*

Week ending	No. of firms	Contract total	Total delivered to date	Deficit	% Deficit to total
3.3-inch:					
30 October 1915	17	355,700	38,400	317,300	89.2
29 January 1916	17	794,400	249,710	544,600	68.5
30 June 1916	21	446,000	312,888	133,712	29.9
4.5-inch:					
6 November 1915	14	41,000	620	40,380	98.5
29 January 1916	15	140,850	24,610	116,240	82.5
1 July 1916	16	273,500	184,400	89,100	32.5
6-inch:					
6 November 1915	3	9, 450	0	9,450	100.0
29 January 1916	5	28,900	2,168	26,712	92.4
1 July 1916	4	31,200	16,816	14,383	46.1

Source: MA, MS F 623.4 M1 no. 5, 3 and 10 November 1915; no. 9, 1 February 1916; no. 20, 30 June and 1 July 1916.

Contractors' complaints focused on three interconnected issues: shortages of skilled labour, shortages of machine tools, and confusion over technical specifications. These were major concerns within the Ministry itself, Sir Fredrick Black, Director General of Munitions Supply, informing Lloyd George in

August 1915 of the need to 'assist' engineering firms by the provision of labour, expedition of the delivery of specialist machine tools, and the simplification of specifications.[44] At the local level, contractors informed the Manchester Board of failures to meet contracted targets on shell due to 'late delivery of machine tools and skilled men', which had delayed the production of 'tools and gauges' vital to conform to output and technical specifications.[45] As the Ministry acknowledged, there was a major problem in machine tool provision, available machinery being both inadequate for quantity production, and deficient in terms of the specialist machining required in making shells,[46] a situation that Lloyd George considered to be undermining the whole production drive.[47] Such problems did not lead to easy solutions, the Board raising alarm over the deployment of labour in 'making new machine tools' when there was a need for economy by using skilled workers to modify or adapt existing machines.[48] In addition, there were anomalies in the application of existing machines, with Ferranti Ltd (Hollingwell), for example, reported to have installed five new automatic lathes from the American Cleveland Co., while reports abounded of under-utilised automatics within the general vicinity of Manchester. In discussions, Bowden inferred the need for a 'definite policy' to economise on plant and 'avoid the placing of further orders until the existing automatics are fully occupied upon direct war work',[49] but this did not materialise, and the Board continued to rely on the good will of local firms. For example, Goodbehere and Mensforth met with representatives of the Fine Spinners and Doublers Association in July, to examine the adoption of their lathes to war work, but on inspection, they were unsuitable 'for the purpose of shell making'.[50]

As the pressure to increase output intensified, the Ministry's own strategic objectives conflicted with those of the Board and its contractors. A case in point was the priority given by the Ministry to National Projectile Factories, central to its output strategy, and managed by the dedicated munitions firms. In December 1915, private contractors in Lancashire complained to the Board that delays in delivering machine tools were related to the increasing orders to National Factories, with 'armament firms getting preference', and in addition that they were forced to compete for scarce skilled labour.[51] J. Bissett, the Secretary of the Board, informed Hubert Llewellyn Smith at the Ministry that advertisements had appeared in Lancashire to recruit skilled workers for National Factories, an accusation that Smith did not deny, but referred to the Defence of the Realm Act, which empowered the Ministry to prioritise government work. In this, Smith returned the problem to the Board, reminding them of the need for their own initiatives in widening the pool of local labour through utilising the stock of women 'suitable for employment on munitions work' registered with the Labour Exchanges.[52] Smith thus raised the contentious issue of dilution, a labour strategy designed to concentrate skilled labour on skilled tasks, leaving less skilled operations to semi/unskilled workers, including women.[53] The major contribution of females to dilution in the metal and engineering trades, however, occurred from 1916,[54] and consequently during 1915 and early 1916 private contractors and the Manchester Board remained deeply concerned over the scarce supply of skilled labour.[55]

Added to the problems of resource supply, local contractors faced the prospect of sudden changes in technical specifications that could result in existing tools and equipment becoming obsolete. In November 1915 the Ministry instructed Lancashire firms manufacturing 4.5- and 6-inch shells to switch from solid bars to forgings in their production processes, but the Board defended the interests of the contractors, reminding the Ministry of the delays that would ensue in meeting delivery targets, resulting from the need for several new machine tools to machine forgings. Bissett informed a Ministry official: 'I can assure you that all the Contractors feel very sore on the subject.' An experienced manufacturer berated the Ministry: 'Either a shell made from bar will or will not do. If it will do, why not let's go ahead now when our arrangements are complete. If it will not do, why let us have spent so much money and time in preparing for making shell in this manner.'[56] Reflecting on the issue of technical specifications in late 1916, Mensforth informed a Ministry conference that constant changes in design had resulted in the fact that manufacturers were 'either accelerating or decelerating … we have never concentrated our maximum output for any length of time.'[57] Despite its position as an agent to the Ministry, the Board did defend the interests of local contractors. On the bar/forging issue, for example, the Board demanded a meeting with Ministry officials, where Collingwood outlined the technical problems associated with converting to forgings, and demanded in future 'quick' decisions by the Ministry on design changes. In response, officials defended their position on the grounds of quality and military requirements, referring to the premature explosions associated with bar shell, and suggesting that 'it was desirable' to convert to forgings 'as soon as possible'.[58] The tone of their deliberation, however, signified the concession of a degree of discretion to the Board, the Ministry no longer insisting upon change but merely desiring it.

Although the Board was frequently prepared to defend the interests of local contractors, it also had an obligation to fulfil its agency responsibilities, leading it to challenge the behaviour of local engineering firms. For example, in November 1915, firms contracting for 4.5- and 6-inch shell complained over the reduction of prices by the Ministry from 23s. to 20s. from December to the completion date in March 1916. Contractors argued that the MDAOC should not concede the reduction, given that only a limited number of firms had delivered at prevailing prices, and that the Board should lobby the Ministry for an extension at the higher price. Mensforth saw little merit in their case, and in rejecting it pointed to the fact that the original contracts clearly stipulated the date of price reductions. 'It was not a nice job to try and get more than you know you ought to have,' Mensforth admonished, and maintained that even with the reduction 'they would get back the capital they had sunk.' In this game of persuasion, Mensforth gained the support of a contractor who acknowledged the efforts of the Board in negotiating the original price of 23s., and 'if they had delivered sooner' they would have incurred 'much less loss'.[59] The Board's monitoring role also led it into the area of opportunistic behaviour, as exemplified by the issue of 'fair shares'. In October 1915, following a request from Lloyd George, the Board investigated the distribution of munitions work in Lancashire, and in consultation with Bowden accepted that, 'all engineering firms shall be made to manufacture their fair share of munitions, failing which their machinery would be commandeered and installed where it could properly be used.' The Board focused attention particularly on textile machine makers, a sector where 'civilian work' constituted a larger proportion of production than in other engineering concerns, and cited Asa Lees as a company that had not contributed its 'fair share'.[60] Despite the Board's recognition of opportunistic behaviour, it now confronted the dilemma of constructing a benchmark for equitable distribution, a task that received little support from Bowden, who prevaricated on using Ministry sanctions to compel firms to increase the share of munitions work. Clearly there were limitations to the authority of the Board, and by February 1916 it conceded that it was unable to resolve the problem, identifying it as a matter that should be 'dealt with by the government'.[61]

In other areas the Board was more successful and exploited its local knowledge to advance munitions supply. For example, in March 1916 the Ministry requested a large order for adapters 'at very short notice', the Board rapidly providing a list of seven suitable contractors guaranteeing the 'earliest possible delivery': Asa Lees; Platt Bros (Oldham); Howard & Bullogh (Accrington); Lancashire Ordnance & Accessories (Heaton Manor); Butterworth & Dickinson (Burnley); Foden Ltd (Sandbach); and United Brassfounders (Manchester).[62] The Board was also proactive in responding to the Ministry's demands for heavy shell, preparing a report on the capabilities of Lancashire engineering to increase provision. This marked a shift in Ministry policy, which previously had focused production of heavy shell on the National Projectile Factories, confining small calibre shell to area boards. Among the recommendations of the report was the transfer of machine tools from those firms who under-utilised them to those that 'would use them more advantageously' on heavy shell.[63] Nevertheless the actions of the Ministry compromised the agency role of the Board, when it suddenly changed the contractual rules, threatening to undermine the trust of local contractors. At a meeting with contractors in May, the Board impressed the urgent need to switch from 3.3- to larger 4.5- and 6-inch shells and above, offering as an incentive extended contracts to December. However, the Ministry intervened, sanctioning contracts only until the end of September, which the Board considered a clear 'breach of their agreement' and 'felt honour bound' to keep its 'arrangement' with local contractors.[64] The episode illustrated the tenuous relations between principal, agent and contractor, and although the Board had successfully facilitated an enormous increase in supply prior to the Somme, following the battle the context changed as growing dissatisfaction among contractors heightened the tension between principal and agent.

War demands and the contractual problem: post-Somme

By mid-1917, relations between local contractors and the Ministry had reached breaking point, Goodbehere informing Sir James Stevenson, Shell Production Department, that the slow delivery of contracts from the district was partly due to labour difficulties, 'but a much more serious cause was a want of enthusiasm, and a feeling of dissatisfaction which had permeated the Contracting Firms'.[65] Why had relationships deteriorated to such an extent, resulting in what Stevenson condemned as 'prejudices against the Ministry',[66] and how did the Manchester Board respond as ministerial agents? Growing dissatisfaction resulted from ministerial pressure on the Board and contractors to meet delivery targets, which in turn raised issues concerning the quality of production, constraints on output, and a fair remuneration to firms faced with rising wage costs and falling prices.

In the aftermath of the Somme, there was intense pressure on local boards to raise output, especially of 18-pounder (3.3-inch) and 4.5-inch high explosive shell. A conference of local boards of management in November 1916, convened by E. S. Montague, who had succeeded Lloyd George in July, reflected on the decision before the Somme to reduce the output of these shell types, of which 'a large expenditure' was not anticipated. The battle, however, provided 'a valuable education in modern warfare', a lesson in the destructive power of artillery, and consequently in Montague's revised manufacturing programme for 1917 the 18-pounder and 4.5-inch were given priority 'to accommodate the new military uses found for them'. Thus the Ministry continued to push for quantity, insisting that local contractors, utilising 'the existing machine stock', should deliver these shells.[67] Responding to these demands, the Manchester Board informed Stevenson that they were 'willing and anxious to fall in line with the proposals', but at the same time outlined the potential constraints restricting output, which included rigid quality checks on finished munitions, and insufficient supplies of specialist machine tools, material supplies, and components.[68] During the first quarter of 1917, these factors seriously undermined the ability of contractors to meet targets, and by March there were 'serious' shortages of 18-pounder high explosive shell. In that month, only four firms – Brookes & Doxey, J. Stubbs, Heatherington Ltd, and Dobson & Barlow – registered surplus deliveries to total contracts, the remaining 28 contractors recording a total deficit of 23.3 per cent.[69] The deficit for 4.5-inch shell was 49.8 per cent, large makers such as British Westinghouse recording a deficit of 33.3 per cent.[70] As Goodbehere warned contractors, this situation was 'causing the Ministry serious alarm and must be at once improved'. Following Ministry instructions, the Board insisted upon the full utilisation of plant and labour, threatening contractors that if deliveries were not improved it would result in the Ministry taking direct action, constructing additional National Factories and redeploying machinery and labour.[71]

Demands to increase the output of specific types of shell raised serious issues for the Board in its agency role with local contractors. On the one hand, to appease Ministry demands the Board reluctantly used its 'authority' from the Ministry to sanction future 'continuation contracts' only to firms that would provide firm 'guarantees' of meeting delivery dates, power resting with the Board to redeploy machinery from unsatisfactory concerns to those 'capable of utilising them to their full capacity'.[72] On the other hand, the Board, possessing local knowledge, also felt obliged to support firms who faced increasing constraints. The drive towards expanding the output of particular types of shell accentuated the problems of adequate machine tool supply, contractors continually complaining of shortages of special-purpose machines for accurate shell work, which delayed full-capacity production.[73] At a meeting in April 1917 of boards of management with Christopher Addison, who had replaced Montague in December, Mensforth complained that Ministry promises to deliver balancing machinery had not been fulfilled, causing serious delays in the production of components and completed shell.[74] By June, although the deficit for 4.5-inch shell had fallen to 40.0 per cent, that for 18-pounder had risen to 47.6 per cent. Despite a renewed warning from Goodbehere of direct Ministry intervention,[75] the general consensus among contractors was that machinery acted as a considerable constraint, firms 'saddled with contracts for quantities of shell far in excess of what the plant was capable of producing, and machine tool utilisation varied markedly in favour of large rather than small producers'.[76] Deficient machine supply was evident also in the production of fuses, especially with the conversion from brass to cast iron in their fabrication. R. E. Hattersley, chairman of United Brassfounders, observed that experiments in cast iron had been successful, and machinery sanctioned by the Ministry for delivery in May, but this would not now arrive until the end of July, delaying full production until September.[77] Surveying the local machine stock in July, the Board concluded that contractors faced insurmountable constraints, 'MACHINERY STILL REQUIRED', and informed Stevenson of their support for contractors over the slow release by the Machine Tool Department of the Ministry.[78] Machine supply also opened up the question of quality, Mensforth acknowledging that the utilisation of inappropriate machine tools raised the issue of the trade-off between quantity and quality.[79] This trade-off became more marked after the Somme, because of the high number of duds fired by British artillery during the battle.[80]

The trade-off between quantity and quality led to direct support by the Board for their contractors. This was a crucial issue in the supply chain, given that the manufacture of shell was a complex process, involving, in the production of the 18-pounder, some 29 machining operations, 39 workshop gauges and 21 inspection gauges, and when finished the shell was inspected 'inside and outside' for faults and accuracy.[81] In December 1916 Mather & Platt complained to the Board that out of 23,480 shells they had delivered to the Belle Vue Inspection Bond in early November, only 9,303 had been examined a month later, and manufacturers generally complained over 'careless' inspection procedures.[82] Mensforth outlined the contractors' case at a meeting of the Management Representation Committee with Ministry officials in January 1917. Complaints included: serious delays to production by slow inspection at the area bonds; faulty inspection methods and lack of uniformity between bonds; delays by the Ministry in supplying adequate technical information and specifications for gauges; constant changes in design and standardisation of parts; and the general incompetence of 'travelling inspectors' in advising firms on quality control. Mensforth alleged that inspectors 'had less real knowledge of their subjects than the people they were attempting to advise', raising the paramountcy of local knowledge and what was felt to be excessive interference by Ministry officials. The meeting, chaired by Stevenson, concluded that inspection procedures in the Manchester area were 'not very satisfactory',[83] an issue debated at a meeting between the Board, contractors, and A. P. Sandberg, the Ministry Director of Inspection. At this meeting, Goodbehere recommended a reduction in the 'extreme severity of ... inspection' to facilitate a maximum delivery of shell, but as Sandberg observed this raised the trade-off between quantity and quality:

On the one hand, the Inspection Department were urged by the Ministry ... by the Filling Factories, and by the Boards of Management ... to pass through their hands the maximum possible quantity of shell ... and on the other hand the Army Officials and others who used the munitions on the front were continually urging the Inspection Department to increase the stringency of inspection, because of the number of premature and other failures at the front'.[84]

This issue opened tensions in the relationship between principal, agent, and contractor, and, as Mensforth insisted, 'this war was as much the Contractors' War as anybody's', and he reiterated the Board's position that inspection procedures, 'over which the contractors had no control', militated against quantity output, resulting in delayed delivery. At the same time he questioned the fairness of the system, in which contractors had to bear the costs of rectifying deficient shell and then had to accept lower remuneration under changes in the Ministry price scale.[85] Ensuring fair remuneration was even more difficult given the complexity of the supply chain, and the assembling of munitions from a variety of components. For example, J. R. Garner, of Lancashire Ordnance Accessories, observed that they supplied 140,000 shell tubes per week, supplying three different assemblers, adding to the problems of ensuring quality standards.[86] In the production of fuses, inter-firm disputes arose between assemblers and component suppliers over the culpability of contracting parties in relation to quality.[87]

Support for the contractors' case, however, was qualified, the Board recognising its responsibility to the Ministry. For example, in February, E. D. Simon of H. Simon & Co., referring to the meeting with Sandberg, acknowledged that the 'Board acted in a dual capacity … representing the Ministry and … Contractors'. Nevertheless, Simon interpreted the meeting as an opportunity to establish a regular forum for 'dialogue' between the Ministry, Board and 'a committee of local contractors', an ideal that was quickly dispelled by Mensforth. Reminding the contractors that the Board were 'Trustees of Government', Mensforth reinstated the principal–agent responsibility, which was to place contracts with individuals and not with 'collective committees of contractors'.[88] Although the Board accepted that it had a responsibility to communicate to the Ministry the complaints of contractors, and to arbitrate in disputes, the Board nevertheless rejected any idea of collusion with a collective group. Thus, in line with Ministry changes in inspection procedures, the Board informed contractors that inspection would 'be tightened', and methods of manufacture and shop inspection would be monitored more closely, an inducement for firms to improve their own quality control procedures.[89] The Board clearly recognised that despite problems in the quality control system, notably related to ministerial changes in designs and technical specifications, a fact recognised by the Ministry's own Shell Manufacturing Department, firms had a responsibility to self-inspect, and 'radically [to] change their methods'.[90] At the same time, the Board agreed concessions with the Ministry to compensate makers of 18-pounder and 4.5-inch shell, following rectification of defects after inspection, by paying them at the original contracted prices, removing a major issue of contention with local contractors.[91] Yet contractor discontent had intensified by the middle of 1917, as emphasised by a meeting of the Board with the Ministry to discuss 'an atmosphere' of dissatisfaction that prevailed over the 'action' of the Ministry and the continued problem of increasing deliveries. Representing the Ministry, Stevenson rhetorically remarked that it was 'rather difficult to deal with an atmosphere', but Mensforth cited a list of complaints justifying 'a general feeling of want of confidence among the different contractors'. These included constant alterations to design, lack of diligence in inspection and variations of standards between the local bonds,[92] imperfections in supplies of steel, and a failure to get prompt decisions from ministerial departments, notably over the release of machine tools. Added to these were the vexed question of profit margins, wages and prices, and the incentive to maximise output and fulfil contractual obligations.[93]

The increasing power of organised labour, especially in the munitions industries, characterised the last two years of the war. During 1917, wage demands escalated as inflation soared, leading to deteriorating industrial relations,[94] opening up a contentious issue in the local supply chain. In November 1916, Montague, in an attempt to appease local boards, had agreed that future contracts would be accompanied by price clauses compensating firms for increased costs if they could demonstrate that this had resulted from advances in wages ordered by the government's Committee of Production.[95] The Ministry, however, prevaricated in implementing this decision, and in February the Manchester Board took up their contractors' case. Price clauses, the Board insisted, constituted 'fair' practice in contractual relations when 'the whole question of controlling wages had been taken out of the hands of employers', in an effort to appease labour, and should be considered as 'a national charge' not borne by private business.[96] This received a positive response from the Ministry, Stevenson conceding that the insertion of compensatory price clauses 'was not only reasonable, but right' when 'a contract was being entered into by two parties, one of whom had the power to raise the cost of production and used that power'.[97] Despite these supportive overtones, and the efforts of the Board to assure contractors of ministerial commitments to price clauses, dissatisfaction remained. At a meeting between the Board and contractors in April, the Harland Engineering Co., on behalf of manufacturers, condemned the actions of the government in raising wages. This had made 'it more and more difficult for the Contractor to make ends meet', a problem compounded by the increasing introduction of female workers whom they were forced to pay 'at the rate of skilled men' and who 'materially' increased the cost of production because of their lower output and quality of work. Added to this, contractors complained of delays by the Ministry in communicating information on wage advances, and of undue interference by Ministry auditors who insisted upon detailed costing before granting the insertion of price clauses.[98]

In this context, complete contracts were never feasible because disputes arose over the actions of the principal in controlling wages and prices. Complicating this problem of contractual relations was the complexity of the local supply chain and the use of contracting for a variety of components. In February the Board, taking the side of contractors, condemned the decision by the Ministry to refuse to extend clauses to 'non-shell contracts', including a variety of components and importantly shell fuses.[99] As Mensforth informed Stevenson in March, 'this was illogical', as many firms were contracted to produce both shell and components and fuses, and 'if the Government was going to raise wages ad lib they ought to be made to feel the responsibility of their action by having to pay increased prices on their purchase'.[100] Despite the Board's strong representation, the Ministry rejected their overtures, offering no prospect of an immediate change in policy.[101] In a stark warning to H. D. McLaren, Deputy Director of Area Organisation, in April, Mensforth predicted that this would have 'a direct bearing on output', firms being already reluctant to accept new contracts for components and shells.[102] By June the situation had reached serious proportions, the Board observing that in the supply of vital brass fuses, 'the constantly increasing cost of production together with the constant reductions in prices have rendered the production of these stores so unattractive that all enthusiasm on the part of Contractors has disappeared'.[103] At a meeting McLaren urged the Board to ensure that they 'maximise output', especially of 18-pounder and 4.5-inch shell, as well as fuses, only to be confronted with the response that contractors would not sign new agreements until they had 'definite information' on the Ministry's intentions on prices.[104] As Mensforth informed Stevens, during the course of the war, prices for 18-pounder shell fell by 50 per cent, and the claims of the Ministry that they had saved 'large sums of money' on behalf of 'the nation', held little resonance with manufacturers. 'Mr. Lloyd George,' he claimed, may well desire to 'give labour its fair share,' but as the 'law' prohibited the reduction of piece rates when the Ministry reduced prices, this 'keenness on the part of the Ministry had caused a very bad atmosphere which had resulted in a loss of output,' as manufacturers switched back to more remunerative 'civilian work'.[105]

During the second half of 1917, the wages and price policy of the Ministry did much to create the 'atmosphere' of distrust that permeated contractual relations. In August Goodbehere informed contractors that 'the output of stores was still far below the quantities contracted for', especially for 18-pounder and 4.5-inch shells, as well as fuses, and they were 'letting down the Ministry' to the extent that firms should either ensure that they met targets or contract 'for less in the future'. Taking a strong line, Goodbehere referred to a meeting with McLaren, which had 'done a very great deal to destroy the Board's influence' with the Ministry, it being generally acknowledged that the 'Manchester contractors were practically the only people who were taking up the attitude that prices ... were too low'.[106] Despite this reprimand, the Board clearly faced a dilemma, well aware that the actions of the principal reduced the incentive of manufacturers to accept contracts and invest in machinery 'at anything like an economical price'.[107] For example, out of previous contracts for fuses, totalling 226,000 per week, by September contractors had only delivered 2.5 per cent. Attempts by the Board to increase delivery proved futile; out of 34 firms circulated in October to accept new contracts for fuse components only two accepted under the prices offered, resulting in the Ministry redirecting tenders outside Lancashire.[108] On shell output, a Ministry review of area boards compared Lancashire unfavourably, concluding that although the Manchester Board had 'secured reasonable conditions for contractors', output was only 60 per cent of total contracts, creating 'disorganisation' in the supply chain 'right up to the firing line'.[109] Such observations led the Board to take a firm line, classifying firms as 'delinquent' in their obligations to meet delivery targets.[110] A meeting of contractors in November observed the general reluctance of firms to increase output, some employers deliberately 'limiting' munitions output in the face of unremunerative prices.[111] Contractors aired their frustrations in December, reminding the Board that 'if the Ministry did not want [their] services, they should say so plainly and leave these contractors to manage their own businesses in their own way. They did not want excessive profits ... just sufficient to live on but they did not get the moral support from the Board that they felt they had the right to expect regarding prices.'[112] In early 1918 the Board accepted its 'moral' responsibility, reinforcing its obligations to the Ministry, and confining further contracts to concerns that it considered could provide firm delivery guarantees.[113]

Conclusion

The contractual relations between local engineering firms, the MDAOC, and the Ministry of Munitions were informed by reference to principal–agency theory. These relations were complex, open to moral hazard and opportunism, and marked by growing rather than reducing tensions, particularly following the Somme offensive. Indeed, the Manchester Board of Management was faced with a genuine set of dilemmas as it sought to reconcile the demands of the Ministry with the interests of local contractors. The Board, although sympathetic to contractor complaints, over inspection, constant design changes, contract pricing, skilled labour and machine tool supply, was nevertheless not slow to remind contractors that in its role as agent it was a 'trustee of government'. While it was the case that Lancashire's engineering concerns did make an important contribution to the increased production of shell, fuses, and components, it was also evident that contractual relations, especially during 1917, deteriorated. The Ministry's attempt to impose reduced contract prices in the context of frequent increases in wages, themselves controlled by government, coupled with an insistence on improving quality control, raised contractor complaints almost to breaking point, and threatened the integrity of the supply chain. In this context the Board strove to keep local contractors in line, using its local knowledge and negotiating skills in an attempt to close the growing gap between Ministry expectations and the increasing reluctance of contractors to supply. Despite the insatiable demands of the Western Front for munitions, and the increasing role of the state in business life, the remit of the authorities to control private business clearly had its limitations, and consequently in the absence of direct state control the activity of agents such as the MDAOC was critical in maintaining the drive for output at the local level.

Appendix

Forty-three firms contracted to supply MDAOC, November 1915

Location	Firm	Location	Firm
Ashton under Lyne:	National Gas Co.	Manchester:	British Westinghouse
	Hall & Kay		H. Simon
Belle Vue:	Kendall & Gent		Lancashire Dynamo & Motor
Blackburn:	Blackburn Bobbing Co.		Crossly Motors
Bolton:	Dobson & Barlow		J. Stubbs
	Hick, Hargreaves	Miles Platting:	Wests Gas Improvement Co.
Clayton:	Belsize Motors	Newton Heath:	Mather & Platt
Cornbrook:	Morrison, Ingbrook	Oldham:	J. J. Bradock
Duckenfield:	Danielle Adamson		Asa Lees
HO London:	Linotype Machinery		Platt Bros
	Schmidt Superheating		William Boden
Lanacashire	Eckstein, Heap & Co.	Patricroft:	Mitchell, Schackleton
Leigh:	Harrison, Macgregor	Rochdale:	Brierly Ltd.
Levenshulme:	Buffoline Noisless Gear Co.		Kelsall & Kemp
Manchester:	Heatherington Bros	Salford:	Harland Engineering
	Brookes & Doxey		Empire Engineering
	Galloways	Stalybridge:	Taylor & Lang
	United Brassfounders		Morton & Edwards
	Reliance Colliery	Stockport:	Thomas Robinson
	Hans Renold	West Gorton:	Higginbottom & Mannock
	A. Wood		
	Royce Ltd.		

Notes

1. *Through Terror to Triumph: The Speeches of David Lloyd George* (Hodder & Stoughton: London, 1915), p. 105.

2. Q.v. C. Wrigley, 'The Ministry of Munitions: An Innovatory Department' in K. Burk (ed.), *War and the State: The Transformation of British Government, 1914–18* (Allen & Unwin: London, 1982), pp. 32–56; D. French, 'The Military Background to the Shell Crisis of 1915', *Journal of Strategic Studies*, ii, no. 2 (1979), pp. 192–205; R. J. Q. Adams, *Arms and the Wizard: Lloyd George at the Ministry of Munitions, 1915–16* (Cassell: London, 1978); H. Strachan, *The First World War: Volume 1, To Arms* (Oxford University Press: Oxford, 2001), pp. 923–1005, 1065–84; D. French, 'The Rise and Fall of Business as Usual' in Burk (ed.), *War and the State*, pp. 7–31.

3. G. Sheffield, *Forgotten Victory: The First World War, Myths and Realities* (Review: London, 2002), p. 55.

4. The records of the MDAOC cover 84 volumes of minutes. Manchester Archives (MA), The Board of Management of the Manchester and District Armaments Output Committee, MS F 623.4 M1 nos 1–84.

5. H. Clay and K. R. Brady (eds), *Manchester at Work: A Survey* (Manchester Civic Committee, 1927), p. 110; R. H. Eastham, *Platts, Textile Machine Makers* (R. H. Eastham: Oldham, 1994), pp. 58–9; Lancashire Record Office, DDPSL/1, Platt Bros & Co. Ltd, Corporate and Financial Records.

6. Bolton Archive and Local Studies Service, ZDB, Agreement and Memorandum Books.

7. Clay and Brady, *Manchester at Work*, p. 111.

8. Clay and Brady, *Manchester at Work*, p. 110.

9. Clay and Brady, *Manchester at Work*, pp. 111–12.

10. J. Cantrell, *Naysmith, Wilson & Co.: Patricroft, Locomotive Builders* (Tempus: Stroud, 2005), p. 93.

11. G. T. Timmins, *Made in Lancashire: A History of Regional Industries* (Manchester University Press: Manchester, 1998), p. 229.

12. Clay and Brady, *Manchester at Work*, p. 112.

13. Timmins, *Made in Lancashire*, p. 229.

14. Speech at Manchester, 3 June 1915, in *Through Terror To Triumph*, p. 97.

15. W. M. Robertson (ed.), *Middlesbrough's Efforts in the Great War* (Jordinson & Co.: Middlesbrough, n.d.), p. 19.

16. Wrigley, 'The Ministry of Munitions', pp. 35–8.

17. National Archive (NA), MUN 5/180/1300/57, Statement of Requirement Made by Minister of Government Ordnance, Sir Stanley Von Donnop, 1 August 1914.

18. Q.v. D. Crow, *A Man of Push and Go: The Life of George Macaulay Booth* (Rupert Hart-Davis: London, 1965).

19. NA, MUN 5/7/17/1, Minutes of Meeting of the Armaments Output Committee, 20 April 1915.

20. J. Hussey, '"Without an Army, and Without any Preparation to Equip One": The Financial and Industrial Background to 1915', *The British Army Review*, no. 109

(1995): 76–84, p. 84.

21. NA, MUN 5/7/17/I Minutes of Meeting of Armaments Output Committee, 20 April 1915.

22. Wrigley, 'The Ministry of Munitions', p. 35.

23. Adams, *Arms and the Wizard*, pp. 62–70; Strachan, *The First World War*, pp. 1079–80.

24. Adams, *Arms and the Wizard*, p. 60

25. Q.v. D. Besanko *et al.*, *The Economics of Strategy* (John Wiley & Son: New York, 2007).

26. Strachan, *The First World War*, p. 1079.

27. MA, MS F 623.4 M1 no. 31, 14 December 1916.

28. Strachan, *The First World War*, pp. 1079–80; Adams, *Arms and the Wizard*, pp. 62–70.

29. Q.v. D. Sunderland, 'Principals and Agents: the Activities of the Crown Agents for the Colonies, 1880–1914', *Economic History Review*, lii, no. 2 (1999): 284–306, p. 286.

30. Besanko *et al.*, *Economics of Strategy*, p. 456.

31. MA, MS F 623.4 M1 no. 10, 9 February 1916.

32. MA, MS F 623.4 M1 no. 1, 27 July 1915.

33. MA, MS F 623.4 M1 no. 1, 9 August 1915.

34. MA, MS F 623.4 M1 no. 1, 24 August 1915.

35. MA, MS F 623.4 M1 no. 2, 8 September 1915.

36. Q.v. Besanko *et al.*, *Economics of Strategy*, p. 455.

37. MA, MS F 623.4 M1 no. 2, 8 September 1915.

38. MA, MS F 623.4 M1 no. 3, 24 September 1915; no. 4, 13 October 1915.

39. MA, MS F 623.4 M1 no. 4, 13 October 1915.

40. MA, MS F 623.4 M1 no. 3, 24 September 1915.

41. Q.v. P. Griffith, *Battle Tactics of the Western Front. The British Army's Art of Attack, 1916–18* (Yale University Press: New Haven, Conn., 1996), pp. 135–58.

42. Strachan, *The First World War*, p. 1,079; q.v. Adams, *Arms and the Wizard*, p. 64.

43. Q.v. Sunderland, 'Principals and Agents', p. 288.

44. NA, MUN 4/2369, Reply to Lloyd George by Sir Frederick Black Regarding Acceleration of Output, 11 August 1915.

45. MA, MS F 623.4 M1 no. 7, 22 December 1915.

46. NA, MUN 2/24, Ministry of Munitions, Secret Weekly Report, 30 October 1915, f. 10; 1 January 1916, f. 18.

47. NA, MUN 5/199/1700/14, Minutes of Conference with Machine Tool Manufacturers, 22 January 1916.

48. MA, MS F 623.4 M1 no. 2, 9 August 1915.

49. MA, MS F 623.4 M1 no. 3, 4 October 1915.

50. MA, MS F 623.4 M1 no. 3, 4 and 12 July 1915.

51. MA, MS F 623.4 M1 no. 7, 22 December 1915.

52. MA, MS F 623.4 M1 no. 3, 24 September 1915.

53. *Report of War Cabinet Committee on Women in Industry*, PP 1919, cmd. 135, pp. 181–3; K. Grieves, *The Politics of Manpower* (Manchester University Press: Manchester,

1988), pp. 14–22; MA, M8/2115, Manchester Chamber of Commerce, 8 December 1915, 11 January 1917.

54. Between August 1914 and December 1915, female employment in the metal trades increased by 74,000, but between 1916 and 1918 it accelerated by 350,000, representing 82.6 per cent of the overall increase during the war; PP 1919, cmd. 135, p. 181.

55. Q.v. MA, MS F 623.4 M1 no. 22, 2 August 1916.

56. MA, MS F 623.4 M1 no. 5, 3 November 1915.

57. NA, MUN 5/142/1121/32, Minutes of Conference on the 18-pounder Shell Situation, 1 November 1916.

58. MA, MS F 623.4 M1 no. 5, 10 November 1915.

59. MA, MS F 623.4 M1 no. 6, 24 November 1915.

60. MA, MS F 623.4 M1 no. 4, 27 October 1915.

61. MA, MS F 623.4 M1 no. 7, 9 February 1916.

62. MA, MS F 623.4 M1 no. 12, 8 March 1916.

63. MA, MS F 623.4 M1 no. 13, 12 March 1916.

64. MA, MS F 623.4 M1 no. 16, 3 and 10 May 1916.

65. MA, MS F 623.4 M1 no. 47, 6 July 1917.

66. MA, MS F 623.4 M1 no. 47, 6 July 1917.

67. NA, MUN 5/142/1121/32, Minutes of Conference on the 18-pounder Shell Situation, 1 November 1916.

68. MA, MS F 623.4 M1 no. 31, 14 December 1916.

69. MA, MS F 623.4 M1 no. 36, 16 March 1917.

70. MA, MS F 623.4 M1 no. 37, 29 March 1917.

71. MA, MS F 623.4 M1 no. 38, 4 April 1917.

72. MA, MS F 623.4 M1 no. 38, 4 April 1917.

73. Q.v. R. Lloyd-Jones and M. J. Lewis, *Alfred Herbert Ltd. and the British Machine Tool Industry, 1887–1983* (Ashgate: Aldershot, 2006), pp. 62–70, for deficiencies in the British supply of special-purpose machines, and reliance upon American imports.

74. MA, MS F 623.4 M1 no. 39, 17 April 1917.

75. MA, MS F 623.4 M1 no. 43, 7 June 1917.

76. MA, MS F 623.4 M1 no. 44, 8 June 1917.

77. MA, MS F 623.4 M1 no. 46, 27 June 1917.

78. MA, MS F 623.4 M1 no. 47, 6 and 12 July 1917.

79. MA, MS F 623.4 M1 no. 39, 17 April 1917.

80. Q.v. Strachan, *The First World War*, 1085–6; D. Stevenson, *1914–1918: The History of the First World War* (Allen Lane: London, 2004), p. 169.

81. NA, MUN 5/180/1300/62, Branch Memo. on Manufacture of a Complete Round of 18-pounder HE Ammunition, 11 June 1917.

82. MA, MS F 623.4 M1 no. 31, 14 and 21 December 1916.

83. MA, MS F 623.4 M1 no. 32, 3 January 1917.

84. MA, MS F 623.4 M1 no. 32, 12 January 1917.

85. MA, MS F 623.4 M1 no. 32, 12 January 1917.

86. MA, MS F 623.4 M1 no. 55, 16 October 1917.

87. MA, MS F 623.4 M1 no. 45, 28 June 1917.

88. MA, MS F 623.4 M1 no. 33, 2 February 1917.

89. MA, MS F 623.4 M1 no. 34, 15 February 1917.

90. MA, MS F 623.4 M1 no. 41, 17 May 1917; NA, MUN 5/180/1300/53, Shell Manufacturing Department, Replies to Reconstruction Committee Questionnaire, 28 July 1917.

91. MA, MS F 623.4 M1 no. 35, 1 March 1917.

92. For example, 78.6 per cent of shells delivered to the Belle Vue Bond in late June 1917 were accepted, compared to 94.5 per cent at Trafford Park and 98.6 per cent at Bolton; MA, MS F 623.4 M1 no. 48, 19 July 1917.

93. MA, MS F 623.4 M1 no. 47, 4 July 1917.

94. S. Pollard, *The Development of the British Economy, 1914–1980*, 3rd edition (Edward Arnold: London, 1991), pp. 43–4.

95. Q.v. MA, MS F 623.4 M1 no. 37, 15 March 1917.

96. MA, MS F 623.4 M1 no. 34, 15 February 1917.

97. MA, MS F 623.4 M1 no. 36, 16 March 1917; no. 37, 15 March 1917.

98. MA, MS F 623.4 M1 no. 39, 13 April 1917.

99. MA, MS F 623.4 M1 no. 36, 27–28 February 1917.

100. MA, MS F 623.4 M1 no. 37, 15 March 1917.

101. MA, MS F 623.4 M1 no. 38, 3 April 1917; no. 39, 13 April 1917.

102. MA, MS F 623.4 M1 no. 39, 17 April 1917.

103. MA, MS F 623.4 M1 no. 44, 14 June 1914.

104. MA, MS F 623.4 M1 no. 43, 5 June 1917.

105. MA, MS F 623.4 M1 no. 47, 6 July 1917.

106. MA, MS F 623.4 M1no 50, 10 August 1917.

107. MA, MS F 623.4 M1 no. 50, 23 August 1917.

108. MA, MS F 623.4 M1 no. 52, 14 September 1917; no. 54, 11 October 1917.

109. MA, MS F 623.4 M1 no. 52, 14 September 1917.

110. MA, MS F 623.4 M1 no. 54, 11 October 1917.

111. MA, MS F 623.4 M1 no. 57, 9 November 1917.

112. MA, MS F 623.4 M1 no. 59, 7 December 1917.

113. MA, MS F 623.4 M1 no. 61, 7 January 1918.

13

Wigan, 1540–1640:
Pre-industrial growth and
development in south Lancashire

A. J. H. LATHAM

Introduction

In the hundred years before the Civil War, the economy of Lancashire saw changes that prepared the way for the industrial revolution. South Lancashire was where the modern industrial world was created. In the centre of the region was Wigan, placed astride the great road north from London to Scotland, and equidistant between Manchester to the east and Liverpool to the west. This paper examines how Wigan, created a borough in 1246, grew and developed in these pre-industrial years.

The crucial issue is the internal economic dynamism created within the town at this time. This was not a static economy awaiting an external stimulus, but an economy already moving under its own initiatives towards economic development and industrialisation. A cluster of important primary sources from the period help us to map out the structure of the economy and the changes which were taking place in areas such as agriculture, the coal industry, and the pewter, copper, and bell-founding trades which were the speciality of the town. These sources include rare manuscript items, including Rector Bridgeman's Wigan Ledger. John Bridgeman became rector in 1616, and his ledger is crammed with details of the parish for these years, including tithe records. These give vital details on the agriculture of the parish. His ledger, however, is not to be confused with G. T. O. Bridgeman's *History of the Church and Manor of Wigan* of 1888, which also contains much information on the period. Another item is the Sherrington family account book, a vellum manuscript folder, which gives information on agriculture and coal mining. These sources are augmented by wills and inventories; Lancashire Quarter Sessions records; and many others. They show that the market driven urge to develop and manufacture lay with these determined Lancastrians at an early date.

Population

The population of south-west Lancashire increased from 1580 through to 1640. A comparative study of baptismal and burial entries shows that in every ten-year period in these years, there was a substantial surplus of baptisms over deaths, except for the years 1590–1600 when there was a small deficit.[1] The population was also growing in the Wigan area, and can be traced back to 1548. In that year there were 2,600 communicants in Wigan parish,[2] but the number had grown to 3,000 in 1590.[3] If communicants comprised two-thirds of the population this gives a total population of 3,903 in 1548 and 4,505 in 1590, a growth of some 15 per cent.[4] However, the pattern of growth fluctuated more than in the nearby parish of Standish (Table 1). Between 1580–81 and 1640–41 the net gain in Wigan parish was a mere 43, while in Standish parish the increase was 888. Wigan was one of the four largest Lancashire towns, perhaps even the largest, for its ship money assessment was the highest in Lancashire.[5] The assessment, however, was later reduced.[6] As a large town, more people would have moved into Wigan than Standish, and people would have died there who had not been born there.[7] Many indeed will have come from Standish, only three miles away. Thus Wigan (but not Standish) was hit by high death rates in consecutive years from 1589–60 to 1602–3, and probably from as early as 1584–85, although two years' figures are missing. These high death rates may be associated with the general unhealthy conditions of town life. But both parishes were hit badly by disease in the years 1621–22 to 1623–24, with the peak year being 1622–23, when Wigan saw a net loss of 180 and Standish a net loss of 51. Pneumonic plague is the most likely explanation for this, and there were isolated outbreaks elsewhere in the country in these years. This was just prior to the widespread outbreak of 1625–26 which Wigan and Standish missed, having just experienced it.[8] Despite the cumulative birth–death statistics of −24 for Wigan from 1591–92 to 1640–44, the town appears to have continued to grow from incomers, and the number of corn mills in the town increased from the original one to five in 1627, comprising two water mills, two horse mills and one hand mill.[9] This growth must have had other repercussions.

Table 1   *Population growth in Wigan and Standish, 1560–1640*

	Wigan				Standish			
	A	B	A–B	C	A	B	A–B	C
1560–61					55	25	30	30
1561–62					75	35	40	70
1562–63					42	42	0	70
1563–64					66	36	30	100
1564–65					56	44	12	112
1565–66					40	28	12	124
1566–67					58	43	15	139
1567–68					38	35	3	142
1568–69					41	30	11	153
1569–70					54	49	5	158
1570–71					44	36	8	166
1571–72					50	25	25	191
1572–73					34	29	5	196
1573–74					40	33	7	203
1574–75					48	28	20	223
1575–76					35	26	9	232
1576–77					42	39	3	235
1577–78					24	57	–33	202
1578–79					35	44	–9	193
1579–80					59	47	12	205
1580–81	124	71	53	53	43	55	–12	193
1581–82	84	29	55	108	43	32	11	204
1582–83	105	53	52	160	53	32	21	225
1583–84	104	85	19	179	59	34	25	250
1584–85	108	115	–7	172	41	40	1	251
1585–86	106	89	17	189	24	36	–12	239
1586–87	64	125	–61	128	42	45	–3	236
1587–88					55	43	12	248
1588–89					37	14	23	225
1589–90	66	76	–10	118				
1590–91	63	104	–41	77				
1591–92	67	127	–60	17	(60)	(43)	(17)	242

	Wigan				Standish			
	A	B	A–B	C	A	B	A–B	C
1592–93	87	95	–8	9	46	39	7	249
1593–94	64	102	–38	–29	41	16	25	274
1594–95	85	91	–6	–35	33	14	19	293
1595–96	85	128	–43	–78	36	13	23	316
1596–97	121	138	–17	–95	30	29	1	317
1597–98	59	107	–48	–143	40	33	7	324
1598–99	96	121	–25	–168	48	30	18	342
1599–1600	81	105	–24	–192	46	37	9	351
1600–01	87	101	–14	–206	53	38	15	366
1601–02	90	107	–17	–223	61	39	22	388
1602–03	89	141	–52	–275	65	46	19	407
1603–04	98	65	33	–242	60	31	29	436
1604–05	120	72	48	–194	64	42	22	458
1605–06	133	94	39	–155	55	32	23	481
1606–07	116	81	35	–120	72	57	15	496
1607–08	117	105	12	–108	57	35	22	518
1608–09	109	76	33	–75	70	47	23	541
1609–10	122	77	45	–30	59	48	11	552
1610–11	101	86	15	–15	75	35	40	592
1611–12	107	89	18	3	49	47	2	594
1612–13	106	135	–29	–26	40	47	–7	587
1613–14	131	101	30	4	47	20	27	614
1614–15	137	79	58	62	42	28	14	628
1615–16	143	105	38	100	46	32	14	642
1616–17	136	124	12	112	51	53	–2	640
1617–18	164	95	69	181	47	21	26	666
1618–19	141	109	32	213	36	29	7	673
1619–20	132	127	5	218	38	24	14	687
1620–21	155	133	22	240	47	28	19	706
1621–22	**158**	**166**	**–8**	**232**	**44**	**44**	**0**	**706**
1622–23	**78**	**258**	**–180**	**52**	**24**	**75**	**–51**	**655**
1623–24	**101**	**129**	**–28**	**24**		**28**	**–28**	**627**
1624–25	163	134	29	53	(38)	31	7	634

	Wigan				Standish			
	A	B	A–B	C	A	B	A–B	C
1625–26	141	103	38	91	54	32	22	656
1626–27	114	94	20	111	50	28	22	678
1627–28	109	97	12	123	43	28	15	693
1628–29	133	140	–7	116	65	34	31	724
1629–30	145	101	44	160	68	23	45	769
1630–31	134	97	37	197	59	31	28	797
1631–32	165	152	13	210	57	40	17	814
1632–33	133	122	11	221	68	41	27	841
1633–34	145	137	8	229	58	21	37	878
1634–35	173	136	37	266	59	34	25	903
1635–36	141	123	18	284	73	21	52	955
1636–37	126	122	4	288	59	30	29	984
1637–38	118	132	–14	274	58	32	26	1,010
1638–39	145	154	–9	265	61	26	35	1,045
1639–40	150	122	28	293	65	39	26	1,071
1640–41	153	110	43	336	61	39	22	1,093

A = births, B = deaths, C = cumulative gain

Notes:

Net gain in Wigan parish, 1580–81 to 1640–41 is 43. In Standish parish 1580–81 to 1640–41 it is 888. (1093–205). Note also the heavy death rate in both parishes (marked in bold) 1621–22 to 1623–24, with the peak in 1622–23, presumably due to plague.

Estimates of baptisms and deaths had to be made for some years, in Wigan parish 1587–90, and in Standish parish 1589–93, and 1623–26 (deaths only) because pages were missing or had not been kept. The figures for Wigan in the period 1625–41 were obtained from the actual registers at the parish church.

For Standish in 1592–93 there were 55 births from 14 May, and so 5 have been added to cover March–May to make 60. Deaths were 36 from 16 June, so 7 have been added to cover March–June, making 43. In 1601 deaths were 30 from 19 July, so 8 have been added to cover March–July, making 38. In 1625 there were 33 births from 6 May, so 5 have been added to cover March–May, making 38.

Sources:

J. Arrowsmith (ed.), 'Registers of the Parish Church of Wigan, 1580–1625', *Lancashire Parish Record Society Publication*, vol. 4. (1899).

J. Brierly (trs), 'Registers of the Parish Church of Standish, 1560–1653', *Lancashire Parish Record Society Publication*, vol. 46. (1912).

Agriculture

In 1941 Stamp wrote that, agriculturally, south-west Lancashire was dominated by the very fertile arable coastal plain. With the exception of wheat, crop yields were exceptionally high. Adjoining this arable plain was the grass belt which extended to the Pennines where dairying predominated. But these land use divisions, despite the soil and climatic conditions which gave rise to them, were of comparatively recent development. According to John Holt, as late as 1793 there was no apparent difference between the two areas, mixed farming being the practice.[10] Yet until the mid-fifteenth century arable farming was the chief agricultural activity of the entire area, although probably only land suitable for cultivation, and meadowland, came into agricultural use at that time. The extensive area of un-drained peat was not used in the medieval agricultural economy of the region; nor was the pasture land, as distinct from meadowland, or the moors and heaths. Only in the late fifteenth and the sixteenth centuries did grassland become important, not because of changes in land use within the old arable areas, but by bringing into use surrounding areas of less favourable land. Because there was so little conversion of grassland, and because most of Lancashire had been enclosed by common consent much earlier, no enclosure movement of significance took place at this time, unlike in some other parts of the country.[11] So by the mid-sixteenth century, a mixed farming economy had come into being, which was to last for over 300 years.

Wigan parish lies on the edge of the south-west arable region, just inside the grass belt. Up to the sixteenth century its agricultural evolution seems to have followed the general pattern outlined above.[12] By 1540 mixed farming was the agricultural order. But the tithe records for the parish exist for the years 1610–25;[13] and there are two more records probably for the years 1627 and 1628.[14] These imply quite clearly that of the factors which made up this mixed farming, arable farming predominated. In a normal year, such as 1616, tithe 'corne' receipts amounted to over double the value of all others put together. Tithe calves were not usually even entered, and on the one occasion they were, in 1627, the value was small, at £5 10s. 0d. While the value of lambs and wool was recorded regularly, they together only once amounted to more than £15 in a total never below £400. This was in 1627, when there was almost certainly a recording or transcription error, as lambs are valued at £45. The tendency in the years to 1627 was for lamb receipts to decline almost to nothing, and the following year the tithe was 'received in kind', usually an indication of small value. As the parson was entitled to a tenth of all agricultural produce, the greater importance of arable is obvious.[15]

However, livestock farming was not insignificant, as is indicated by the analysis of two series of parishioners' inventories, the first 1545–90, the other 1620–30.[16] There were 19 farmers in the first series, and 42 in the second, and the similarity of them makes analysis feasible. Clearly if they were widely different in content, such analysis would not make sense. Even though they may represent farmers in old age, and not at their most active, the overall similarity gives some indication of general farming practice. The impression that sheep farming was unimportant is reinforced, in that fewer than half the farmers in the first series kept sheep, and fewer than a third in the second, none keeping more than 37. However, cattle rearing was a significant feature, for each farmer had on average approximately 11 beasts in his herd, with a figure of 11.10 for the first series, and 10.78 for the second. The number of oxen per farmer declined, from 0.94 to 0.57, but not much can be inferred from this other than that it was common to have an ox on the farm. The number of horses averaged 2.61 in the first series, and 2.33 in the second, so it was usual to have couple of horses. Usually two or three pigs were kept by farmers and non-farmers alike. Geese, ducks and hens were similarly widely kept, but only in small numbers, a head of poultry of a dozen being exceptional.

Overall, then, the agricultural economy of the parish was based on corn and cattle, with cattle playing a secondary role. These cattle were almost certainly those Camden so much admired, having 'goodly heads and faire spread hornes and are in body well proportionate'.[17] These were the famous black Lancashire longhorns, the superb beef stock later chosen by Bakewell as the basis of his cattle breeding experiments.[18] Thus it is reasonable to assume that meat production was the main interest of the local herd owners. Certainly there are indications of an extensive trade in cattle both locally and outside the county. The Wigan three-day cattle fairs at St Luke's and Ascension attracted large numbers of animals, an average of 64 beasts being sold at each between 1561 and 1567. At ten of these twelve fairs, a certain Edmund Burscough attended and bought an average of 20 beasts on each visit, twice buying 40 animals or more.[19] Why Burscough bought these beasts is not known, but in 1620 Bishop Bridgeman recorded in his ledger that Charles Roby of Upholland bought many cattle during the year, 'yet he keeps them not past a week or two or some short tyme, and then sells them into other countryes'.[20] It may well be that Burscough was similarly employed.

The big market for meat was, of course, London, so that in all probability the animals from Wigan joined 'the great droves of Cattell [which] doe dayly passe upp to London from Lancashire, Shropshire [and] Cheshire'.[21] But inventory analysis reveals that beef production pure and simple cannot have been the only pursuit of herd managers. For in the first series there is a ratio of 2:1 milk and breeding stock (cows and heifers) to beef stock (oxen, steers and bullocks), while in the second series the ratio is 5:1. Too much significance must not be put on this change, as the ratio of 'indeterminate' cattle ('twinters' and calves) increases from 3.80 to 4.33 between the two series. Most of these were young animals, and might suggest an increase in breeding stock. It is possible that there was some increase in dairy production over the period, both through local demand for milk, and the growing London market for cheese, to which Wigan would have access via Liverpool. Nonetheless, the high ratios of breeding stock to beef stock imply that beef stock was not only finished for market, but was also bred locally. Indeed, it may well be that, as in Wales in this period, beef production was complementary to dairying, tithe steers and unwanted heifers being sold from the milking herds.[22] However, tithe cheese is never mentioned in the parish tithe accounts, and although milk tithes were customarily taken in cheese, it was not uncommon for no milk tithe to be taken.[23] Some cheese certainly was produced locally, as is clear from the inventories, and cheese was a major export from Liverpool, some of might have come from Wigan.[24] It is also possible that bloodstock production was an aim of the local farmers, for in the eighteenth century animals from Lancashire were in demand for herd improvement all over the country.[25] So cattle rearing would have been a major second activity for the local farmers, connected as it was to the growing London demand for meat and dairy products.[26] This was over and above any sales of bloodstock and the requirements of the local market.

The nature of arable production, the main agricultural activity of the parish, is indicated by Bridgeman's detailed tithe account of 1616.[27] Some of the tithe corn dues had been commuted by this time, but the most important townships of the parish still paid in kind, so that from their returns the approximate importance of each crop can be estimated. Oats were the leading crop, 1,536 thraves (58 per cent) being paid in tithe; barley came next, with 954 thraves (36 per cent), then wheat with a mere 83 thraves (3 per cent), and beans last with 64 thraves (2 per cent). A little rye was received from Billinge and Winstanley, and some flax and hemp were returned.[28] Peas are not mentioned. Oats predominated in all the townships, while barley was second in all; but in both Wigan and Aspull beans were the third most important crop. Unfortunately there are no similarly detailed accounts for other years, the later tithe returns simply covering all arable production by the word 'corn'. But there is no reason to suppose that the account for 1616 does not reveal the usual crop ratio. Certainly oats were always the primary grain in Lancashire, largely for climatic reasons, it being cold and wet.[29] Other contemporary evidence would suggest the same pattern.[30]

Such then were the crops, but it is perhaps less from the crops than from the methods used in cultivating them that the best indication of agricultural conditions in the parish can be obtained. While a backward area would linger on using old methods, a forward-looking district would utilize the most up-to-date practices. Crop rotation in the parish must remain a mystery, although there was some rotation, if the Sherrington Account Book is representative.[31] But it is not possible to gather in what order the crops were planted, or how much fallow there was. Probably rotation was mainly haphazard as was often the case even in the eighteenth century in Lancashire.[32] Yet this does not necessarily imply backwardness, as agricultural practices here were as advanced as anywhere in the country. The important development in agricultural technique in the sixteenth and seventeenth centuries was the extensive use of manures and fertilizers which resulted in a great increase in crop yields.[33] The ancient practice of marl spreading had become widely discontinued in the early sixteenth century.[34] But it was now being urged by many contemporary writers.[35] As a result it was becoming common again throughout the country by the end of the century, including Lancashire.[36] In Wigan, too, it was being used. Marl is referred to several times in the Bridgeman Wigan ledger.[37] Marl carts and marl wheels appear in the inventories of the period. But few can have favoured marl more than James Bankes of Winstanley, whose memorandum book is full of references to it.[38] He exhorted his heir 'in God's most holye name be a contenewall marler'[39] The value of marling is made clear by his estimation that a certain six acres worth £4 a year, would yield £12 if marled.[40] Marl, however, was not the only basis of improvement. Muck was widely used, for which farmers were 'willing to undertake the labours of Hercules'.[41] So it was in the Wigan area, and was valued in many of the inventories, for farmers and non-farmers alike. It was mentioned in Bridgeman.[42] Also it was mentioned in the Sherrington account book. Yet more indicative is the use of the new fertilizer, lime, which was being introduced elsewhere in the late sixteenth century.[43] It was, however, regarded as an 'extraordinarie charge and toyle'.[44] Nonetheless it was certainly used in the Wigan area, for the Sherrington family account book contains a complete account for lime to spread on the land in the summer of 1596, 459 & ⅔rds Winchester bushels of it being used.[45]

These practices, especially marling, were expensive, so it is fair to suppose that profits of farming were rising in Wigan, as elsewhere in England at this time.[46] This supposition is supported by the rarity of oxen when compared with horses listed in the inventories. As indicated above there were 2–3 horses on each farm, but on average less than one ox. Though more efficient, horses cost more, and were more expensive to maintain. Replacement of oxen by horses was a classic indication of modernisation in these years.[47] As profits rose, farmers re-invested in their fields using the new methods, or intensifying old, thereby increasing production and multiplying their returns. Indeed by the beginning of the seventeenth century the farmers' desire to maximise profits might have resulted in an increase in the area of arable, and Bankes advised his children to 'make as mych tillaig as possibyll … and to get corne for ther in is the most proffitt … for in bredying of cattel is grett loss'.[48] Camden too noticed that elsewhere in Lancashire hitherto unused land was now bearing corn.[49]

It appears therefore that agriculture was a highly profitable activity in the parish after the turn of the century, and although information is more scanty for the preceding sixty years, it is likely that it was also profitable then, though to a slightly lesser degree. For the inventories show a substantially similar agricultural structure in the two periods 1545–90 and 1620–30. Why then were the profits of farming rising? The increase in the number of corn mills in the town has already been referred to, these being suit mills held by the manor of Wigan which encompassed the town. This increase is a pointer to the solution of the question. The increase in mills resulted from the increase in the urban population and their rising demand for flour and meal. This linked directly to the need for more grain, meaning bigger sales for farmers, and the conversion of land to arable. So Wigan farmers were presented with a situation in which their local market was growing, which absorbed most of their grain and dairy produce, and so also was the London market, to which they could send what could not be sold profitably at home, particularly cattle and cheese.

Coal and cannel

The farmers in the parish appear to have been prospering, and investing more heavily in their land. But not all this investment was agricultural, for some, such as James Bankes,[50] Francis Sherrington,[51] and the Bradshaw family,[52] began to exploit the local coal seams.

The Wigan coalfield, an area comprising some 70 square miles, lies almost wholly within a radius of five miles from the town centre, and few areas in the country had more accessible seams.[53] The coal actually outcropped in many places,[54] and these conditions were ideal for the elementary techniques of extraction used in the sixteenth century.

The earliest reference to coal in the district is in deeds relating to Shevington, by which Margaret of Shuttlesworth exchanged land with Robert of Standish, while reserving to herself 'fyrestone and secole' should it be found.[55] Coal was possibly worked at Haigh at this time.[56] It was certainly dug at Hindley in 1475, but it was not until after 1500 that mining appears to have been of real importance, and there was a dispute at Hindley in 1528 over the right to dig coal.[57] Yet it was the cannel mines of Haigh that were to impress John Leland, when he noted in his *Itinary* of 1535: 'Mr Bradshau hath a Place caullid Hawe a Myle from Wigan. He hath found moch canel like se coole in his grounde very profitable to hym,' adding elsewhere that 'the great Myne of Canale is at Hawe 2 Miles from Wigan.'[58] These Haigh mines were worked through the 1550s.[59] By 1562 coal was being mined at Winstanley, as is clear from the will of Thomas Winstanley.[60] It had probably been mined nearby since early in the century on the property of John Orrell of Turton, and pits were flourishing there in 1573.[61] Mines were soon being dug in Whelley Lane, Wigan, to Parson Fleetwood's displeasure.[62] About 1580 there were six pits in Pemberton.[63] Also the Winstanley pits were still in existence in 1591, a Thomas Orrell 'of the Coale pitts' and a William Barton 'of the Coale pitts', both being mentioned in Edmund Winstanley's will of that year.[64] In 1595 Fleetwood took action against those who had 'digged delved and made mynes for cooles' unlawfully on his wastes.[65] The next year, 1596, saw the sale of the manor of Winstanley, with its coal measures, to James Bankes.[66] Bankes was greatly attracted by the presence of coal measures, noting in his memoranda book that 'there is a good stor of coles ther in praies god for the sam'.[67] Francis Sherrington, who also held land in the Winstanley/Orrell area, sank a coal pit in 1598, and bought a rope 'for ye coole pit in Orrell' that same year. Although Sherrington died that year, the family account book records in detail the digging of a new pit in 1600.[68] This may have been partly the root of the trouble between Sherrington's widow and William Orrell, the latter taking action against her in 1601 because the Sherrington prices were less than his own.[69]

After the turn of the century the new industry continued to expand. 'Wyllam barton of the cole pitt'[70] was still mining on the manor of Winstanley in 1600, much to the envy of Bankes, who suggested to his children that they 'bye the said tenement for money … and laie the sam to demayne'.[71] Bankes obviously had big plans for the Winstanley coal measures, for he began to reserve cottages on his estate for colliers about 1610.[72] It appears that Winstanley coal was still being mined in the second decade of the century, for in 1615 a James Winstanley of the Moor Hill was fined a shilling in the manor court 'for suffering his children to carry coals from the lord's pit on the Sabbath day', and in the same court a fine of sixpence was imposed in 1618 for unlawfully digging a coal pit in the highway.[73] When Bankes died in 1617 his wife and son took control of the collieries. His son gained sole control in 1619 and was still supervising the pits in 1625.[74]

In Wigan itself mines continued to be sunk, for in 1619 Peter Plat, a chandler, obtained permission from Bishop Bridgeman, the rector, to conduct water from his pit near Millgate over the lord's waste.[75] This pit, however, proved unsatisfactory because of flooding, although it was still working in 1621 after a temporary stoppage.[76] The Scholes cannel pits were well established in 1630,[77] but mining appears to have become almost frenzied in the next few years, even the town streets being dug up in search of coal, Bishop Bridgeman solemnly forbidding such doings in 1635.[78] This frantic activity was reflected in a long legal battle from 1634 to 1636 between Roger Bradshaw, owner of the Haigh pits, and Miles Gerrard of Aspull, who possessed the pits in that adjacent township, which were probably first excavated at the turn of the century.[79] The dispute (as in the Sherringto/Orrell case above) arose over a difference in the selling price of coal between the two owners. Considerable violence was involved, Gerrard having flooded Bradshaw's pits, killing a woman. The fact that each man spent over £1,000 on the case shows how important coal had come to be.[80]

That the number of pits had increased considerably since the middle of the sixteenth century of itself is no great indication of the extent of production. Only when the level of mining technique is understood does a rough picture of the size of output become appreciable, though it is not possible to calculate output tonnage.

It is likely that techniques varied from the crude to the most sophisticated in the country. The six pits in Pemberton in the 1580s were close together,[81] so they were probably primitive bell pits with small outputs.[82] Yet even from quite a primitive pit production may have reached 3,000 or 4,000 tons in a year. The Sherrington pit, sunk in 1600, does not appear to have involved much capital outlay – under £10 apparently. Yet it produced 859 loads in the first seven weeks; with a load being about 13 cwt, this amounted to 550 tons.[83] This would give an annual output of over 4,000 tons if maintained, at a time when usual output of a pit was 2,000–5,000 tons a year. It was, however, common for pits to be worked only intermittently.[84] Not all the pits in the Winstanley/Orrell area were so primitive, for as early as 1562 some were constructed on the pit and adit plan.[85] This was a more expensive and advanced system.[86] The output of these pits must have been substantial. But the most important pits in the area were the Haigh and Aspull cannel mines. The Haigh pits were clearly highly sophisticated in method by 1636. It was in that year, following a serious pit accident in 1632, that detailed and strict regulations were drawn up by Roger Bradshaw, the owner, to prevent similar disasters in the future.[87] Obviously the size of the operation had made the old haphazard methods unsustainable.[88] The regulations laid down that pillars of coal had to be left at regular intervals and of definite thickness, fines being enforced on those who failed to comply. Perhaps the most indicative of all the regulations laid down a maximum output per day for each face worker – 30 baskets on week-days, 20 on Saturdays, each basket containing about a hundredweight.[89] This necessary regulation took production pressure off the collier, thereby reducing the need to take risks cutting where it was unsafe. Moreover, to ensure that the colliers were experienced in the Haigh pits, they were bound by yearly bonds, some signing for life. The work at Haigh was continuous, the whole enterprise appearing surprisingly modern in concept. There is no way of estimating annual production, but if each miner cut as much as he was allowed, he must have produced about 442 tons a year, which implies a really sizeable yearly output.

That this is possible is suggested by information concerning the neighbouring rival cannel mines at Aspull. It has already been noticed that the rival owners spent £1,000 each in the legal dispute of 1634–36. Precisely what was at stake is revealed by the fact that the Gerrards had invested £400 in their newly dug pits in 1599 and probably £3,000 by 1626.[90]

Output in the Wigan coalfield was apparently considerable. Indeed, it was perhaps the largest in Lancashire at the time.[91] This poses the question of the market for coal. Of all commodities in general use coal was least valuable in proportion to its bulk. Transport costs therefore were inevitably high. In the sixteenth century, the cost of transport prohibited any considerable sale of coal at distances of more than ten to fifteen miles overland from the pit head, the price of coal doubling every two miles.[92] Wigan's high-quality cannel coal was 'the choicest coal in England'.[93] It was even marketed in places which could obtain ordinary coal more cheaply.[94] However, Wigan had no access to water transport, other than what little use might be made of the river Douglas, and the vast majority of the local coal must have been consumed within the neighbourhood. Local demand must therefore have been substantial, as the many pits and their high level of technical development does not imply a surfeit. Much of it must have been consumed by the local metal trades, a key part of Wigan's manufacturing economy (see below).

There were probably many more pits in the district than those discussed above, but absence of evidence makes further discussion of them impossible. Nor is it possible to discuss in much detail how capital, management and labour were co-ordinated in the Wigan mines. But from the pits of which there is information, it appears that the size of the pit went hand in hand with the level of its organisation. The Sherrington pit sunk in 1600 was a fairly simple operation. Although the family provided the capital and directed operations, the whole affair was very loosely organised. Labour was employed on a casual basis, the 'getters' paid sometimes by the day and sometimes by their output.[95] Previously it was thought that labour at the pit was organised on a more regular basis, but this was due to a misreading of the transcription of the expense sheets.[96] Pits of this kind must have been quite common, and William Barton's pit on the manor of Winstanley was probably much the same. Sherrington did not own the land on which he mined.[97] Nor did Barton.[98] But generally landowners in the district were loath to lease coal-bearing land, preferring to keep at least some control over the working of the pit, even if they had no time to exercise full entrepreneurship. Hence Bishop Bridgeman made a one-year covenant with a group of free miners to work his pits at Farnworth. These four 'colers' were to supply the necessary candles, bellows and tools, and find men to wind the coal up the shaft, the bishop providing them with a hovel, baskets and ropes, and paying them 8 pence for every quarter of coal dug. The men were 'to worke the works substantially, fairly, justly and honestly as may bee best for the safetie and upholding of the Mines and most for the p'fitt of the sd lod Bp'.[99] A 'quarter' apparently contained about 6 cwt (rather than the 5 cwt one might expect).[100]

Such agreements were probably not common.[101] In most cases the landowner exercised the full entrepreneurial function himself. Peter Plat, who ran a pit actually within the town in 1619, did so upon his own ground.[102] But as a chandler, he was a merchant, and it is not likely that he owned much land. There must have been other pits like Plat's in the town run by men of similar means, for encroachments by the townsfolk on the lord's waste to dig coal were a major source of contention between them and the rector.[103] However, the really important mines in the parish were on the property of the large landowners.[104] By the 1630s they had come to exercise full control over the pits personally. At Winstanley James Bankes, the lord of the manor, sought to buy out the tenants who had pits or coal upon their land.[105] William Orrell also seems to have tried to get control of leased coal-bearing property.[106] Both these men appear to have provided the capital and direction of their workings, and Bankes at least must have used full-time colliers, for he was even prepared to house them.[107]

But it is the Haigh pits of the Bradshaw family which give most insight into the development of pit organisation in the district. As late as 1554 these ancient pits were run by the tenants of the manor and the lord in conjunction, the tenants getting free cannel for use in their tenements, but jointly bearing the costs of boring and maintenance.[108] Yet, by 1636, the communal nature of the enterprise had completely disappeared. Roger Bradshaw was by then clearly responsible for both the capital and control of the pits.[109] No longer were the people engaged in getting coal 'husbandmen' as they had been in 1550.[110] Now they were full-time wage workers with separate tasks as 'editors, Hewars, Drawers, Wynders, Treaders [and] Takers'.[111] Surprisingly for one so capitalistic and entrepreneurial, Bradshaw was a Roman Catholic.[112] So was his neighbour and business rival Miles Gerrard.[113] He, too, was probably responsible for the capital and direction of the pits on his lands at Aspull.[114]

It seems, then, that as the industry expanded during the period, the mines were increasingly taken into the control of the owners of the mineral rights, the landowners. Customary rights and leases were thrust aside or bought out, and the loose organisation of the small pits was replaced, as they increased in size, by a more ordered system with a strong division of function between those who directed and finances and those who laboured. As the function of the entrepreneur became more distinct, so did that of the miner. For by the end of the period a growing class of full-time wage-earning miners is apparent, recruited from the growing population.[115]

Much of the capital which was put into the developing coal industry came from the growing profits of farming, as noted above. William Barton who mined in the manor of Winstanley was also a farmer, and no doubt all the large land-owning coal owners obtained much revenue from farming. But the smaller pits in the town, like Peter Plat's, must have been financed from the profits accruing to the thriving industries there.

Pewter, brass, bells and iron

Some of the extensive local coal production must have been used in the hearths of local houses. Iron chimneys indicated the use of coal in the house.[116] They were common items in contemporary inventories. But the major demand for coal must have come from the metal trades in the town, which boomed in this period, achieving a previously unrecognised importance in both Lancashire's and the national economy. While the pewter industry at Wigan has long been known, emphasis has been on the period after 1660.[117]

Coal was useless for smelting metal at that time, because of the impurities it transferred into the molten metal, but it was certainly used for working metal when it had been refined.[118] The inventories of local metal workers show that they used enormous amounts of coal and cannel. Rauff Markland, a metal worker who died in 1622, had ten shillings-worth, which represented several tons. Indeed, by the beginning of the seventeenth century, coal had become essential to local production processes, being a 'fyering … without which … divers artificers and other tradesmen cannot use their trades and occupations'.[119]

As noted, pewter working has usually been regarded as the most important local metal industry, and Wigan was definitely one of the leading pewter manufacturing centres in the country. Established as early as 1470, three years before the London Company of Pewterers received its charter, it was from the 1550s becoming very important in the town, several pewterers being mentioned in the extant records for this period. By the 1630s and 1640s large numbers of pewterers were working. A compilation of pewterers' names from various sources, which obviously does not contain the names of all the pewterers in the town, shows that there were at least 41 working in the craft between 1620 and 1630, and 51 between 1630 and 1640. This implies a very substantial output, and Wigan was possibly only second to London as a pewter centre. Some forty years later, in 1683, when there were only 79 pewterers in Wigan, they were handling between 40 and 50 tons of tin a year, London handling about 200 tons. This is shown in a draft petition made in this year, from which it is also known that the Wigan Company was considering seeking powers equal to the London Company.[120] The mere fact that the Wigan pewterers were an independent company reveals their importance.[121] In other towns pewterers were usually included in a company representing all the various metal trades.[122]

In Wigan, not only were the pewterers an independent company, but there was an entirely separate Company of Braziers (brassworkers) and Panners, who were in existence as early as 1573.[123] Brassworking in the town dates back to as early as 1539, when Adam Bankes, a brazier, was mayor.[124] Despite being so early and so important, the braziers seem to have been largely overlooked by the historians of Lancashire, and neither Phillips and Smith,[125] nor Crosby[126] even mention them. It seems likely that braziery and panwork were more important than pewter work in the town, with other references to braziery in 1557.[127] Extraordinarily, this was at a time when copper and brass working is thought not to have existed in England.[128] Strong measures by the government were required to stimulate it in the 1560s through the Company of Mines Royal and the sister company of Mineral and Battery works. It has usually been assumed that the techniques of battery and brass-working were imported after 1565, by attracting foreign artisans to England.[129] Yet quite apart from the early references above, in 1539 and 1557, William Hey who died in 1575 was clearly occupied in making metal pots, almost certainly of brass.[130] Again, in 1581, Alderman Hugh Forth died leaving nearly £70 worth of brass and all the instruments of a forge and for metal working – indeed 'all worke ... belonging to the potters occupation'.[131] It is significant, too, that Forth was an alderman, showing how important brass working already was in the town. It seems reasonable to assume that the techniques of pewtering were adapted to copper and brass.[132] In this way the Wigan craftsmen would have a home market previously almost entirely supplied from abroad.

By the 1620s and 1630s, the braziers and panmakers, like the pewterers, had become numerous, and it seems that all the metal workers in the town were producing brass and copper ware. From all twenty-three inventories of men who produced metal work in wills proved between 1620 and 1630, it is clear that brass was the predominant metal, even pewterers like Robert Bankes using substantial amounts of brass.[133] But the clearest evidence of the size of the Braziers and Panmakers Company comes from the 'Petition of the Company of Brasiers and Panners of the Towne and Burrowe of Wigan' to Manchester quarter sessions in 1636, in which the size of the company is stated to be 'one hundred p[er]sons and more w[i]th no other trade'.[134] This was probably more than the pewterers, as even in 1683 there were only 79 pewterers in Wigan (see above). This petition has not been previously been noted, and the finding of this single document revolutionises our understanding of the metal trades in Lancashire, and indeed England. In 1650 an early demarcation dispute is recorded, an action being brought by wardens of the Braziers Company against a pewterer who had cast some brass moulds necessary to his trade. From this it is clear that John Platt and six others including William Forth, pewterer, were all exercising the trade of braziers by casting pewterer's moulds and making 'morters and mill steps'.[135] Possibly Forth was the grandson or great grandson of Hugh Forth of 1581!

Although the Pewterers' Company and the Company of Braziers and Panners were so large, they were not the only metal workers in the town. For the comparatively heavy industry of bell-founding was also an important feature of the town's economic life. This trade almost certainly developed from the braziery industry.[136] Bells were cast in a kind of bronze made from copper and

The Woodley factory of Aspinall & Kay Ltd.

tin.[137] Robert Orrell, the first known founder, recast the great bell at Bodfari Church, Flintshire, in 1592, and probably worked between 1587 and 1614.[138] He was still alive in 1621, for Bishop Bridgeman refers to him as 'Old Orrell the bell founder'.[139] Orrell may have been preceded by a founder working as early as 1574.[140] He was certainly followed by the Scott brothers, who were already eminent in the town in 1627, when they were both bailiffs.[141] Their foundry seems to have continued working until the end of the seventeenth century.[142] There appears to have been a special peculiarity of the Wigan bellfounders, surely connected with the local coal and cannel. The bells were cast actually in Wigan, and then transported to the client church in a semi-finished state. Other bell-founders cast the bells close to the church for which they were intended.[143] This way the Wigan founders could use the best coal at the lowest price. Lest it be thought that bell-founding was an insignificant economic activity, it must be remembered that bells in themselves were very costly items, and that foundries employed many men. Bell-founders also produced other heavy cast metal goods, including the mortars in which apothecaries ground ingredients with a pestle.[144]

Even with bell-founding, the list of metal trades is not complete. About 1638 the latest techniques were being applied to iron manufacture in the district.[145] Ormskirk quarter sessions at Easter that year records the assault by William

Baitch, 'headworkeman and ingeneire att his masters slitting milne' at Haigh, on Margery, wife of his master William Brock 'ironmonger'.[146] Presumably this was down Brock Mill Lane, just north of the town off Wigan Lane, and by the river Douglas.

Vastly important as the metal trades were in the town, it has never been discovered exactly where the metals came from. Certainly they were not produced locally, with the possible exception of iron, of which there were local deposits.[147] So the lead, tin and copper must have been brought long distances, probably to Liverpool (or Preston) from Cornwall and the south-west peninsula, north Wales, Anglesey, the Lake District, or even abroad, especially Sweden.[148] Transport costs must therefore have been high, indicating that Wigan offered substantial local economies to the metal trades. Only the superb local coal and cannel can have yielded such a big advantage, and it is to this that the metal trades owed their existence in the town.

If there is virtually no evidence of the sources of the metals used by the metal workers in the town, there is nothing either to reveal the organisation of the trade in metals, or how the finished products were marketed. Bells, of course, were made on contract. Some brass ware and pewter ware was bought directly from the craftsmen locally, but there is nothing to indicate how the large area north of the Trent which they served was supplied.[149] But as the petition of the Company of Brasiers and Panners of 1636 made clear, it was illegal for those who had not been apprenticed with a free brazier or panner to 'hawke up and downe the country to buy and sell Brass: pann metle and made pannes in faires, marketts and in private houses'.[150] So perhaps certain time-served men in the brass and pewter trades specialised in marketing, but it is equally conceivable that each craftsman or his journeymen travelled to sell his stock of finished goods from time to time.

There is less doubt about the production side of the industry. For the most part, production was in the hands of independent craftsmen supplying their own capital and working on their own materials in their own workshops.[151] Each concern was only small, though men like pewterer Adam Bankes could employ at least two apprentices.[152] The brass and pewter trades can have provided little scope for wage labour, but some men may have been used for unskilled work. The bell-foundries were probably bigger enterprises than the average brazier's or pewterer's, yet they seem to have been essentially similar in organisation. Orrell and the Scott brothers were all working founders.[153] If they employed labourers for the heavy manual work involved, as they surely must, in no sense can it be supposed that there was any separation between entrepreneur and wage worker as was developing in the coal industry. Only in the iron industry was there a movement of this kind. Slitting mills were typical of the 'new and highly capitalistic' concerns that were transforming the industry elsewhere in the country.[154] Thus the division between capitalist entrepreneur and wage labourer was probably more evident at the Haigh slitting mill, which certainly employed workmen and engineers. In this it echoed the changes which were taking place at the Haigh collieries. This mill, however, was an exception to the general pattern of organisation in the district's metal industries, the most important sectors remaining in the control of individual craftsmen, who increased both in number and wealth in this period.

Textiles and other economic activity

If coal, pewter, brass, bells and iron dominated Wigan's manufacturing economy, there was also much other economic activity. The cloth industry was well established. In this period the Lancashire cloth trade was revolutionised, with output expanding and many new materials being produced. Spinning and weaving came to form a more important part in the economy of the smallholder, and a new class of cottagers almost entirely dependent on these crafts came in to being. Linking the cottagers to the market, both for raw materials and finished products, a network of middlemen grew up, often financing the small men with credit.[155] Yet much of this development is thought to have taken place in east Lancashire.[156] This was said to be due to the inhibiting controls of the old corporate towns in the west of the county, such as Wigan.[157] But it is clear that, if not as widespread as in the east, the cloth trade was both important and expanding in the Wigan area throughout this period, and experienced the same, characteristic changes of the east. The town had a fulling mill before 1535.[158] Between then and 1571 another was built, and both continued to function through to the 1640s.[159] However, it is the fact that the new domestic cloth workers existed there that reveals at least this corporate town was not lagging behind in the changes in the cloth industry. For it is not true that the first mention of the individual trade of weaver or 'webster' as an occupational description in the neighbourhood of Wigan is in 1625, as has been maintained.[160] On the contrary, the quarter sessions records for the county mention several between 1601 and 1605, in Aspull (three), Abram, Wigan, Pemberton and Ince.[161] There must have been many more, as these were the few unlucky enough to come before the courts! There were many more between 1626 and 1639.[162] One spinner is also mentioned.[163] Neither Peter Langton of Hindley,[164] nor William Cass,[165] were described as 'webster' in their wills and inventories, but obviously obtained most of their livelihoods from weaving. Thus the new workers typical of the changes in the textile industry were clearly found here almost as early as in east Lancashire, and nearly a century earlier than has been believed. This is not, however, to say that these weavers and spinners did not supplement their incomes from other sources. The inventories of the period show that most houses had their spinning wheels, and that agriculture still played an important part in the life of some of the cloth workers. As mentioned above, pigs were mentioned in many inventories. This must have been true of east Lancashire as well. The movement transforming the cloth industry was clearly running almost as strongly in Wigan as elsewhere in the county, the industry growing in importance and expanding. The constraints supposedly typical of neighbourhoods adjoining the corporate towns did not exist.

There were other textile industry crafts in the parish, and complementing the fulling mills already mentioned were several dyers, as their petitions in the 1630s show.[166] Similar petitions indicate that the leather industries were of some significance as well. Shoemakers are mentioned.[167] There were also tanners in the town, as shown by the wills of Hugh Ascow, tanner,[168] and William Higham, tanner.[169] Tanners are also mentioned in Bishop Bridgman's ledger.[170] The leather trades would use hides from the local cattle for their supplies. Yet more petitions mention skinners, glovers and whittawyers.[171] Another petition shows there were glaziers present, whether makers of glass or fitters of glass not being clear, although a glassmaker was prevented from working near the town in 1622.[172] Numerous persons described as potters worked in the town, and they certainly used clay in their work.[173] But they may not have been makers of pottery, but of brass, as discussed above, or even iron pots, 'pot' being widely used in the locality then for such items.[174] The clay that was being used may have been for moulds for cast metal.[175] On the other hand, there probably was some pottery made, as this was a flourishing industry in the eighteenth century.[176] The abundant coal would have been ideal for firing the local clay.

Service industries were also expanding in this period, for the Bridgman Wigan ledger mentions the construction of several new shops.[177] It seems likely that there was a movement from market stall to permanent premises in these years, although it would be misleading to overstate this. However, there were many local shopkeepers.[178] They seem to have been prospering, if Mathew Markland, a mercer who died in 1617, was typical. His stock in trade was valued at £343, a really immense sum for the time, much of it in luxury cloths, some costing 10–12 shillings a yard, a price more than equivalent to a skilled workman's weekly wage. There were more than 400 different items in his stock, mainly cloths, but there were some sweetmeats (for the ladies?) as well.[179] There must have been considerable purchasing power in the neighbourhood to support such a shop, as was also indicated by the fact that in 1634 there were 47 taverns in the town.[180]

Any survey of the town's general economic activity would be incomplete without some mention of the twin catalysts of economic development: education and finance. In both of these spheres great changes were taking place.

In 1540, as far as is known, there were no schools in the parish or surrounding districts. By 1614, however, there were two schools actually in the parish, one at Wigan and one at Hindley, and three more in the nearby districts of Ashton-in-Makerfield (founded 1588), Standish and Leigh.[181] The school at Hindley was already there about 1613.[182] The increasing number of schools must have increased the literacy of the district, and its economic growth. Better accounts could be kept, and new ideas and methods read about and adopted, for example from the numerous farming books of the day. By the 1620s books were commonly mentioned in the inventories of men,[183] and of women such as Eilen Hey[184] and Eilen Lord.[185]

This growth of literacy must have also helped the spread of the credit system so typical of the late sixteenth and early seventeenth centuries elsewhere in England.[186] Debts owing by bond, or 'specialitie' as they were called, were present in many parishioners' inventories. These included pewterers such as Robert Bankes[187] and Robert Smallshaw,[188] as well as tanners such as William Higham.[189] They included husbandmen like Laurance Heaton[190] and Richard Charnley,[191] and there were widows like Eilen Tunstall[192] and Alice Bankes.[193] These were all part-time rentiers, and some were apparently entirely dependent for income upon the earnings from the money they lent out, like Robert Orrell[194] and James Eden.[195] In this way frozen assets were released to help the development of the home based 'domestic' industries.[196] The demand for loans reflected a growing demand for capital, as production methods became more capital-intensive.[197] The demand for capital drew out the supply and in so doing created a new group of small capitalist rentiers symbolic of this period of transition. Wigan was in the forefront of the progressive move to capitalist industrialisation.

The rector, the burgesses and the struggle for the town

The main social change in the parish between 1540 and 1640 was the increasing wealth and power of the pewterers, braziers and bell-founders. As these men became wealthy they sought social advancement, and Thos Markland,[198] Rauff Markland,[199] James Pilkington[200] and Tho's Bankes[201] all described themselves as 'gentlemen' in their wills. More significantly they sought a say in the direction of local affairs as well. As they were dependent on trade and commerce, it was essential for them to have some control of these matters in the district.

In Wigan the burgesses supervised the commercial life of the town. By the original charter of 1246 by which Wigan was made a free borough for ever, they were granted a guild merchant with a hanse and all the liberties and free customs pertaining to such a guild. The rector, John Maunsel, lord of the manor, also gave the burgesses a charter in the same year, which made them free tenants of the manor, and allowed them the special liberty of a portmote. None but a member of the guild could do any business in the borough except by the consent of the burgesses, so it was to the burgess community that the new men aspired. To gain this, a burgess legally required a burgage of 5 roods of land, for which he paid the rector 12 pence a year.[202] But this limitation, by which the rector could select the burgesses, had apparently been cast aside: a petition of the town to the House of Commons in 1639 stated that 'all such p'sons as are or have beene Burgesses of that Corporation [of Wigan] have always beene received into that Corporacon by elecon made by the Burgesses for the tyme prsent of that Corporacon'.[203] A century earlier, in 1539, the burgesses were in the habit of electing their own mayor.[204] So it is not unlikely that they also elected newcomers to their ranks at that time. There was, therefore, no essential obstacle to prevent wealthy artisans becoming burgesses, and indeed the mayor of 1539, Adam Bankes, was a brazier.[205] Despite the fact that evidence is scanty, Hugh fforth, a metal worker,[206] and William Bankes, a pewterer,[207] are known to have been aldermen before 1600. There is more evidence for the first forty years of the seventeenth century, and the dominant position of the new men had come to assume in the burgess community is clearly evident. At least ten pewterers were aldermen in these years: Christopher Bankes, Thomas Bankes, William Bankes, Robert Barrow, William Ford, Hugh Ford, James Gerrard, Hugh Langshaw, Robert Markland and James Pilkington.[208] Five of them – Hugh fforth or Ford (1617–18), Robert Barrow (1620–21), William Ford (1622–23), James Pilkington (1619–20 and 1624–25) and Thomas Bancks or Bankes (1626–27) – became mayor, or six out of ten mayors in the years 1617–26, James Pilkington serving two terms. This is the most powerful evidence of the pewterers' influence in the town.[209] In 1626–27, as noted, the mayor Thomas Bankes, and William Forth and Robert Barrow, aldermen, were all pewterers.[210] The two bailiffs, the Scott brothers, were bell-founders.[211]

The burgesses were divided into two groups within the poll books. The 'out' burgesses were local gentry from the surrounding countryside. The 'in' burgesses were townsfolk, and these appear to have been the most active politically. In 1639 there were 134 'in' burgesses, and a comparison of their names with Shelley's list of pewterers plus those actually named in the list of braziers or pewterers implies that 31 of them were pewterers or braziers. In 1640 of 135 again 31 were pewterers or braziers.[212] This implies at least a quarter of the 'in' burgesses of the town were pewterers, braziers or bell-founders, and there may have been more.

But the power of the burgesses was not legally strong, for in law their authority was almost wholly dependent on the goodwill of the rector.[213] Nevertheless, about 1560 Bishop Stanley, then rector, found it necessary to assert his rights against the claim of the burgesses to hold markets, fairs and courts leet. However, although a commission was appointed to look into the matter, no conclusion was reached.[214] It is possible that Stanley dropped his action 'upon fear and for a fine of money received'.[215]

Probably both the rectors and the burgesses would have been content to leave the situation as it stood, with the burgesses in control of the markets, fairs and courts leet, though without legal right, were it not that the burgesses came to need the manorial wastes. As the town increased in population and prosperity, it began to increase in size. Consequently, the manorial wastes were required for building upon. Numerous encroachments for building are noted in the Wigan Rentall.[216] Not only this, but, as previously noted, coal was discovered under the wastes, which was needed by the pewterers, braziers and bell-founders. Coal dug within the town would not incur expensive transport costs, meaning cheaper fuel. However, the burgesses' only possible chance of taking over the wastes lay in claiming the manor for themselves, a claim to the wastes alone being implausible.

The struggle began as early as 1575, when Charles Banke and three other men seized part of the wastes, and deprived the rector 'of the profittes thereof in digginge coale pyttes and taking coales out of the same to great value'. Edward Fleetwood, then rector, therefore entered a bill of complaint in the Duchy Court which was probably inconclusive. In retaliation, ten years later Banke, then mayor, claimed the rights of the manor to be the burgesses', as having been given to them by the charters of King Henry III and Parson Maunsel. Maunsel's deed had recently been confirmed by Bishop Stanley, and with a view to strengthening their claim it was enrolled by the burgesses in the Court of Chancery.[217] Accordingly they began to take over the wastes. They 'improved dyvers parcells of the said comons and waste groundes late lyinge within the said mannor … erected and builded howses thereupon and … rented the same … and … likewise unlawfully digged delved and made mynes for cooles.'[218] Fleetwood was thus forced to take action against them, and in 1595 preferred a fresh bill in the Duchy Court complaining of their pretensions and usurpation, and asking for a remedy.[219] The suit resulted in a compromise quite favourable to the mayor and burgesses, for they acquired certain rights that formerly belonged to the parsons. The corporation was to keep such courts as they had been accustomed to keep, and the profits therefrom. The rector was to appoint a steward to sit with the mayor and burgesses at the leet, the profits of which were to be divided equally between the rector and the corporation. The markets and fairs and the profits thereof were also to belong to the corporation.[220] But the basic question of the wastes does not appear to have been settled, nor even the claim of the burgesses to the manor.

Twenty years passed before the struggle was resumed. In 1616 John Bridgeman became rector, and determined to reclaim some of the lost rights of the lordship. Having been Chaplain in Ordinary to the King, before whom he had preached by royal command on many occasions, he was able to use his influence at court to back his renewed claims.[221] Calling the mayor and burgesses to the pentice chamber on 17 October 1617, he re-opened the question by informing them of his right to the fairs, markets, courts leet, courts baron and other privileges.

The burgesses, however, replied that 'they had the right to them, and hoped to prove in law', although they did not challenge the rector's right to the manor or his landownership. They proceeded to deliver a private information to the king, asking him to signify to the Attorney General that the settlement of 1596 should stand good and that the present 'controversye between the parson and the Town may be decided by due course of Law. This His Majesty tore saying he knew Dr. Bridgeman would not wrong them'. Instead, King James accepted Bridgman's suggestion that he select a special tribunal of two bishops and two judges to decide the matter.[222] Not surprisingly, the tribunal returned a verdict very favourable to Bridgeman. The rector was recognised as lord of the manor, with a right to the wastes, court baron, and suit and service of the freeholders and inhabitants. The court of pentice plea and the court of pleas were to be the corporation's, as was the Michaelmas leet. The Easter leet was to be the rector's, the moot hall common to both parties. While the corporation kept the fair at St Luke's and the Friday market, the rector gained the Ascension fair and the Monday market.[223]

For a while after this setback the burgesses were content to bide their time. Yet as soon as the rector ceased to be resident in the town in the early 1630s, they again began to encroach on the wastes for, in 1635, Bridgeman had to 'forbid all & every of the inhabitants of the s[ai]d Town and mannor to dig for coles or make any soughes [i.e. drainage channels] under any of the streets or any p[ar]t of the Wast[e]'.[224] But it was not to be until thirty years later, after the Civil War and the Restoration, in 1662, that the burgesses were finally to achieve their ends. In this year, after a new dispute, it was ruled that although the rector was lord of the manor and must keep a court baron, yet in view of the municipal court of pleas, it was of little importance except for inquiring into the chief rents due to the rector, and preventing encroachments on the waste. The streets and wastes were to be regulated as to encroachments by the rector and mayor. The rector's Ascensiontide fair, weekly market and court leet, with all the tolls, courts, piccage, stallages, profits, commodities and emoluments belonging to them, were leased to the corporation on a renewable 21-year lease at a rent of five marks a year.[225] The fact that the mayor was given the right to regulate encroachments jointly with the rector gave the burgesses and corporation what they wanted. They had won.

Here then can be seen a political struggle taking place, triggered by the economic developments which were taking place. As the pewterers, braziers, bell-founders and other independent craftsmen increased in number and wealth, they sought their way on to the town's directing body in order to control the town's lands and matters affecting local commerce which was their livelihood. The need for room to expand, and cheap coal, caused by the rise in population and the expansion of the local economy, transformed the aims of the burgess community from the direction of trade to the possession of the manor. The success of this political movement resulted in a change in the town's legal constitution favourable to the new men.

Conclusion

From this study a distinct pattern of economic and political development emerges. The population expanded, exerting pressure on the resources of the district. The increased demand for food stimulated farmers into expanding production to maximise their profits. Some of these profits were diverted into opening the coal measures. The quality and quantity of the local seams attracted to the town the profitable pewter, brass and bell-founding industries, for whom cheap fuel was vital. These new industries created employment and sustained consumption. The cloth industry re-organised itself to meet demand, and the service industries prospered. Growing wealth sustained the establishment of schools, increasing literacy. Demand for capital meant that those with funds could lend to the developing industries and obtain income from their assets. The increasingly wealthy and numerous independent pewterers, braziers and bell-founders found themselves increasingly frustrated in their need for coal and room to expand by the powers of the rector, the lord of the manor; they sought, therefore, to wrest from him control of the town. In this they were eventually successful.

Thus, in the hundred years before the Civil War, the economy of this area of Lancashire was being transformed rapidly. If the parish of Wigan is representative, then south Lancashire early underwent fundamental changes which were to culminate in the Industrial Revolution.

Notes

1. W. G. Howson, 'Plague, Poverty and Population in Parts of North West England, 1580–1720', *Transactions of the Historic Society of Lancashire and Cheshire*, cxii (1960), p. 42.

2. F. R. Raines (ed.), *A History of the Chantries within the County Palatine of Lancaster*, Chetham Society, old series, 59 (1862), p. 67fn.

3. G. T. O. Bridgeman, *History of the Church and Manor of Wigan*, vol. I, Chetham Society, new series 15 (1888), p. 175.

4. Raines, *History of the Chantries*, p. xxvii.

5. E. Baines, *The History of the County Palatine and Duchy of Lancaster*, vol. II (Routledge: London, 1870), p. 179. G. T. O. Bridgeman, *History of the Church and Manor of Wigan*, vol. II, Chetham Society, new series 16 (1889), p. 391.

6. State Papers Domestic, ccclxiii (1637), nos 53 and 54.

7. Lt. Col. Fishwick, *Distribution of Surnames in Lancashire in the Sixteenth and Seventeenth Century*, *Transactions of the Historic Society of Lancashire & Cheshire*, new series, xvii (1865), p. 135.

8. Susan Scott, and Christopher J. Duncan, *Biology of Plagues: Evidence from Historical Populations* (Cambridge University Press: Cambridge, 2005), p. 240.

9. Bridgeman, *Church and Manor of Wigan*, vol. II, pp. 240, 239, 243, 309.

10. L. D. Stamp, *Land of Britain*, vol. 45 (Longmans, Green & Co.: London, 1941) pp. 69–70, 72, 74.

11. F. Walker, *Historical Geography of South West Lancashire before the Industrial Revolution*, Chetham Society, new series, 103 (1939), pp. 38–40, 54, 55.

12. Walker, *Historical Geography*, pp. 39, 40, 55–7.

13. Wigan Public Library, Reference Case 6, Top, Bridgeman Wigan Ledger, fol. 1.

14. Bridgeman, *Church and Manor of Wigan*, vol. II, p. 307.

15. Sir Simon Degge, *The Parsons Counsellor with the Laws of Tythes or Tything*, 5th edn (Richard Sare and Jos Hindmarsh: London, 1695), book 2.

16. Lancashire Record Office: Wills and Inventories.

17. William Camden, trs. P. Holland, *Britain* (Andrew Hebb: London, 1637), p. 745.

18. John Holt, *General View of the Agriculture of the County of Lancaster* (G. Nicol: London, 1795), p. 143. See also R. Trow-Smith, *History of British Livestock Husbandry to 1700* (Routledge & Kegan Paul: London, 1957), p. 220.

19. Book of Tolls for Wigan Market, Lord Kenyon's Deeds, Historical Manuscript Commission Report 14. Appendix IV 4.

20. Bridgeman Wigan Ledger, fol. 50.

21. J. U. Nef, *The Rise of the British Coal Industry*, 2 vols (Routledge: London, 1932), p. 101 *cit.* Privy Council Register xlii 65–6, letter to justices of the peace of Warwick County, 1 June 1632.

22. Trow-Smith, *British Livestock Husbandry*, p. 214.

23. Degge, *The Parsons Counsellor*, p. 253.

24. T. S. Willan, *The English Coasting Trade, 1600–1750* (Manchester University Press: Manchester, 1938), pp. 48–9.

25. Holt, *Agriculture*, pp. 143fn, 144.

26. F. J. Fisher, 'The Development of the London Food Market, 1540–1640', *Economic History Review* V (2) (1935), pp. 46–64.

27. Bridgeman, *Church and Manor of Wigan*, vol. II, pp. 188–92.

28. Bridgeman, *Church and Manor of Wigan*, vol. II, pp. 189–90.

29. Walker, *Historical Geography*, p. 41. Holt, *Agriculture*, p. 56.

30. Wigan Public Library, Reference, Strong Room: Sherrington Family Account Book.

31. Sherrington Family Account Book.

32. Holt, *Agriculture*, pp. 51–2.

33. G. E. Fussell, 'Crop nutrition in Tudor and Stuart England', *Agricultural History Review* iii (1958) p. 105. See also E. Kerridge, *The Agricultural Revolution* (Allen & Unwin: London, 1967).

34. Fussell, 'Crop nutrition', p. 99.

35. John Norden, *The Surveiors Dialogue*, 3rd edition (I. Busby: London, 1618), pp. 222–3. Fussell, 'Crop nutrition', p. 99, cited in John Fitzherbert, *Boke of surveying and improvementes* (R. Pynson: London, 1523), p. 82.

36. Camden, *Britain*, p. 745.

37. Bridgeman Wigan Ledger, fols 154, 182.
38. Wigan Library, Reference W615. B2: J. H. M. Bankes (trs.), The Memoranda Book of James Bankes of Wigan, 1586–1617, pp. 8, 12, 13, 14.
39. Joyce H. M. Bankes, 'James Bankes and the Manor of Winstanley, 1595–1617', Transactions of the Historic Society of Lancashire and Cheshire xciv (1942), p. 72.
40. Bankes, Memoranda Book, p. 30. Also see pp. 8, 12, 15, 19.
41. Fussell, 'Crop nutrition', p. 105.
42. Bridgeman Wigan Ledger, fol. 155.
43. Fussell, 'Crop nutrition', p. 100.
44. Norden, Dialogue, p. 224.
45. Sherrington Family Account Book, Tithe Book, Back Page.
46. Joan Thirsk, 'Agrarian history, 1540–1950', in Victoria County History: Leicestershire, vol. II (1954), p. 199. W. G. Hoskins, 'The Rebuilding of Rural England, 1570–1640', Past & Present, iv (1953), p. 50.
47. See B. H. Slicher van Bath, trs. O. Ordish, The Agrarian History of Western Europe, AD 500–1850 (Arnold: London, 1963), pp. 289–90.
48. Bankes, Memoranda Book, p. 23.
49. Camden, Britain, p. 745.
50. Bankes, 'James Bankes and the Manor'.
51. Sherrington Family Account Book.
52. A. J. Hawkes, 'Sir Roger Bradshaigh of Haigh', Supplement to Transactions of the Lancashire & Cheshire Antiquarian Society (1945). Also in Chetham Miscellanies 8, Chetham Society, new series 109. Nef British Coal Industry, vol. II, p. 7.
53. Wigan Public Library. Reference WTN623, L2, C6: H. M. Clegg, 'Historical Notes on the Wigan Coalfield', Presidential address to the Manchester Geological Society, October 1957.
54. Joyce H. M. Bankes, 'Records of Mining in Winstanley and Orrell near Wigan', Transactions of the Lancashire & Cheshire Antiquarian Society, liv (1939), p. 33.
55. T. C. Porteus, Calendar of the Standish Deeds, 1230–1575 (Wigan Free Public Library, 1933), pp. 27–8.
56. Porteus, Calander, p. vi.
57. Victoria County History: Lancashire, vol. iv (1906-), p. 108.
58. John Leland, Itinary, 3rd edition (J. Fletcher and J. Pote: Oxford, 1770) vii. fol. 56, pp. 47, 49.
59. Hawkes, 'Sir Roger Bradshaigh', pp. 2–3.
60. J. P. Earwaker (ed.), Lancashire and Cheshire Wills, Chetham Society, new series 3 (Manchester, 1884), p. 25.
61. Bankes, 'Records of Mining', pp. 32, 33.
62. Bridgeman, Church and Manor of Wigan, vol. I, pp. 146–7.
63. Lancashire Record Office: DDSc 32/1, Scarisbrick of Scarisbrick Muniments.
64. Lancashire and Cheshire Wills, pp. 116–17
65. Bridgeman, Church and Manor of Wigan, vol. I, p. 151.
66. Victoria County History: Lancashire, vol. iv, pp. 87–8.
67. Bankes Memoranda Book, p. 2.
68. Sherrington Family Account Book.

69. Bankes, 'James Bankes and the Manor', p. 35. *Victoria County History: Lancashire*, vol. iv, p. 90 fn. 18.

70. Bankes Memoranda Book, p. 10.

71. Bankes Memoranda Book, p. 10.

72. Bankes Memoranda Book, pp. 18–19.

73. Bankes, 'Records of Mining', p. 38.

74. Bankes, 'Records of Mining', pp. 38–9.

75. Bridgeman Wigan Ledger, fol. 33. Bridgeman, *Church and Manor of Wigan*, vol. ii, p. 264.

76. Bridgeman Wigan Ledger, fol. 59.

77. Bridgeman Wigan Ledger, fol. 144.

78. Bridgeman Wigan Ledger, fol. 176.

79. Bridgeman Wigan Ledger, fol. 113. Nef, *British Coal Indusrty*, vol. i, p. 62.

80. John Rylands Library Manchester, extracted from papers at Haigh: Haigh-Aspull Mining Dispute, 1634–36, D. A. R. Lindsay, by David, 28th Earl of Crawford, October 1941. Wigan Public Library, Reference Mun. Rm. 3: 5. Add MSS 215.

81. Scarisbrick of Scarisbrick Muniments.

82. R. L. Galloway, *Annals of Coal Mining and the Coal Trade* (Macmillan: London, 1898), pp. 32–4.

83. Clegg, 'Wigan Coalfield'.

84. Nef, *British Coal Industry*, vol. i, pp. 359, 377fn.

85. Bankes, 'Record of Mining', pp. 33–4.

86. J. U. Nef, 'The Progress of Technology and the Growth of Large Scale Industry in Great Britain, 1540–1640', *Economic History Review* v (1934), pp. 9–10.

87. Hawkes, 'Sir Roger Bradshaigh', p. 4. Wigan Public Library, Reference, Safe: A. J. Hawkes, Haigh Colliery Orders, 1635–98, transcript of manuscript of original regulations.

88. Clegg, 'Wigan Coalfield'.

89. Nef, *British Coal Industry*, vol. ii, p. 374.

90. Nef, *British Coal Industry*, vol. ii, p. 378.

91. *Victoria County History: Lancashire*, vol. ii, p. 357.

92. Nef, *British Coal Industry*, vol. i, pp. 78, 102, 103.

93. Nef, *British Coal Industry*, vol. i, p. 115 *cit.* Guy Miege, *The New State of England* (J. Robinson: London, 1691), part 1, p. 128.

94. Nef, *British Coal Industry*, vol. i, p. 115.

95. Sherrington Family Account Book.

96. Bankes, 'Record of Mining', p. 37. H. T. Crofton, 'Lancs. and Chesh. Mining Records', *Transactions of the Lancashire & Cheshire Antiquarian Society* vii (1889), pp. 50–3.

97. Bankes, 'Record of Mining', p. 39.

98. Bankes Memoranda Book, p. 10.

99. Bridgeman, *Church and Manor of Wigan*, vol. ii, pp. 397–8.

100. Nef, *British Coal Industry*, vol. ii, p. 376.

101. Nef, *British Coal Industry*, vol. i, p. 416.

102. Bridgeman Wigan Ledger, fol. 33.

103. Bridgeman, *Church and Manor of Wigan*, vol. i, pp. 146–7, 151. See also Bridgeman

Wigan Ledger, fol. 176.

104. Nef, *British Coal Industry*, vol. ii, p. 7.

105. Bankes Memoranda Book, pp. 10, 14.

106. *Victoria County History: Lancashire*, vol. iv, pp. 90 fn. 18.

107. Bankes Memoranda Book, pp. 18–19.

108. Hawkes, 'Sir Roger Bradshaigh', p. 3.

109. Hawkes, Haigh Colliery Orders. Also Haigh-Aspull Mining Dispute.

110. Nef, *British Coal Industry*, vol. ii, p. 136 *cit*. Duchy of Lancs Pleadings 25/B/1.

111. Hawkes, Haigh Colliery Orders.

112. *Victoria County History: Lancashire*, vol. iv, p. 117.

113. Bridgeman Wigan Ledger, fol. 113. *Victoria County History: Lancashire*, vol. iv, p. 103.

114. Haigh-Aspull Mining Dispute. Bridgeman Wigan Ledger, fol. 113. Nef, *British Coal Industry*, vol. i, p. 378.

115. Hawkes, Haigh Colliery Orders. Lancashire Record Office: Lancashire Quarter Session Rolls 1. E.g. Qsb/1/46 46. Qsb/1/62 32. Qsb/1/242 13, Qsb/1/142 3, Qsb/1/166 47.

116. Nef, *British Coal Industry*, vol. i, p. 199.

117. C. B. Phillips and J. H. Smith, *Lancashire and Cheshire from AD 1540* (Longman: London, 1994), p. 102, *cit*. J. Hatcher and T. C. Barker, *A History of British Pewter* (Longmans: London, 1974), p. 285.

118. Nef, *British Coal Industry*, vol. i, p. 11.

119. Nef, *British Coal Industry*, vol. i, pp. 11, 108, 203.

120. R. J. A. Shelley, 'Wigan and Liverpool Pewterers', *Transactions of the Historic Society of Lancashire and Cheshire* xcvii (1945), pp. 5, 9–13, 21–6.

121. G. H. Tupling, 'Early Metal Trades and the Beginings of Engineering in Lancashire', *Transactions of the Lancashire and Cheshire Antiquarian Society* lxi (1949), p. 18.

122. Shelley, 'Pewterers', p. 2.

123. Tupling, 'Early Metal Trades', p. 19.

124. Bridgeman, *Church and Manor of Wigan*, vol. ii, p. 108. Also Bankes, 'Records of Mining', p. 58.

125. Phillips and Smith, *Lancashire and Cheshire*.

126. Alan Crosby, *A History of Lancashire* (Phillimore & Co.: Chichester, 1998).

127. Crosby, *History of Lancashire*.

128. R. H. Tawney and Eileen Power, *Tudor Economic Documents*, vol. i (1924), p. 242.

129. H. Hamilton, *English Brass and Copper Industries to 1800* (Longmans: London, 1926), pp. 3, 3fn.

130. Lancashire Record Office: William Hey, Inventory, 30 July 1575.

131. Lancashire Record Office, Will and Inventory: Hugh Forth (fforth), 29 May 1581.

132. Tupling, 'Early Metal Trades', p. 19.

133. Lancashire Record Office, Will and Inventory: Robert Bankes, 1626.

134. Lancashire Record Office: Manchester Quarter Sessions, 1636. Qsb/1/175 82.

135. Shelley, 'Pewterers', p. 3.

136. Tupling, 'Early Metal Trades', p. 20.

137. J. W. Clarke, 'Bells and Bell Founding', *Transactions of the Lancashire and Cheshire Antiquarian Society*, liv (1939) p. 22.

138. F. H. Cheetham, 'Church Bells of Lancashire', *Transactions of the Lancashire and Cheshire Antiquarian Society*, xlv (1930). pp. 103–4.

139. Bridgeman Wigan Ledger, fol. 61.

140. F. H. Crossley, 'Bells of Cheshire', *Transactions of the Lancashire and Cheshire Antiquarian Society* lviii (1946). p. 232.

141. D. Sinclair, *History of Wigan*, vol. I (Wall: Wigan, 1882), p. 204.

142. Cheetham, 'Church Bells', pp. 107–8.

143. Sinclair, *History of Wigan*, vol. I, p. 204.

144. J. R. Nichols, *Bells thro' the Ages* (Chapman and Hall: London, 1928), p. 82. Timothy Giles, Bronze mortars of Somerset, *Sunday Times*, 7 September, 1969, p. 62. A. B. Flemming, Mortars by English Bell Founders, *The Connoisseur* June 1934. J. Llewellin, *Bells and Bellfounding* (J. W. Arrowsmith: Bristol, 1879).

145. Nef, 'Progress of Technology', p. 13.

146. Lancashire Record Office: Ormskirk Quarter Sessions 1638. Qsb/1/202 57. See also Lancashire Record Office: Wigan Epiphany Sessions 1636/7. Qsb/1/178 85.

147. Nef, *British Coal Industry*, vol. ii, p 136.

148. Ryuto Shimada, *The Intra-Asian Trade in Japanese Copper by the Dutch East India Company during the Eighteenth Century* (Brill: Leiden, 2006).

149. Shelley, 'Pewterers', pp. 11, 15.

150. Lancashire Record Office: Manchester Quarter Sessions.

151. Tupling, 'Early Metal Trades', p. 17.

152. Shelley, 'Pewterers', p. 9.

153. Cheetham, 'Church Bells', pp. 103–5.

154. Nef, 'Progress of Technology', p. 11.

155. A. P. Wadsworth and Julia de Lacy Mann, *The Cotton Trade and Industrial Lancashire, 1600–1780* (Manchester University Press: Manchester, 1931), pp. 5, 10–12.

156. J. J. Bagley, 'Mathew Markland, a Wigan Mercer', *Transactions of the Lancashire and Cheshire Antiquarian Society*, lxviii (1953), p. 61.

157. Wadsworth and Mann, *The Cotton Trade*, pp. 55–6.

158. Bridgeman, *Church and Manor of Wigan*, vol. ii, p. 321.

159. Bridgeman, *Church and Manor of Wigan*, vol. i, p. 143.

160. Bagley, 'Mathew Markland', p. 60.

161. *Lancashire Quarter Session Records, 1590–1606*, Chetham Society, new series 77 (1917), pp. 130, 181, 191, 245, 248, 273, 283.

162. Lancashire Record Office: Lancashire Quarter Sessions Rolls 2. 1628 Qsb/1/42 40. 1628 Qsb/1/46 36. 1629 Qsb/1/66 34. 1630 Qsb/1/ 73 25. 1631 Qsb/1/94 15. 1631 Qsb/1/94 33. 1633 Qsb/1/126 6. 1633 Qsb/1/126 46. 1634 Qsb/1/142 8. 1636 Qsb/1/174 39. 1637/8 Qsb/1/195 14. 1637/8 Qsb/1/195 42. 1639 Qsb/1/222 28.

163. Lancashire Record Office: Lancashire Quarter Session Rolls 3. 1629/30 Qsb/1/66 34.

164. Lancashire Record Office, Will and Inventory, 1625: Peter Langton.

165. Lancashire Record Office, Will and Inventory, 1629: William Cass.

166. Calendar of the State Papers Domestic 1. 1635 ccciv December 1. 45. 1635–36 cccvii

68, 69

167. Wadsworth and Mann, *The Cotton Trade*, p. 61. *cit.* Privy Council Register May 10, and December 18, 1633.

168. Lancashire Record Office, Will and Inventory, 1624: Hugh Ascow.

169. Lancashire Record Office, Will and Inventory, 1624: William Higham.

170. Bridgeman Wigan Ledger, fol. 130.

171. Calendar of the State Papers Domestic 2. 1633 ccliv Dec 18. 3. 1635 ccciv Dec 17. 44. 1635 ccciii Dec 1. 9.

172. Acts of the Privy Council of England, 23 September 1621, 10 January 1621–22.

173. Bridgeman, *Church and Manor of Wigan*, vol. ii, p. 222. Bridgeman Wigan Ledger, fol. 130.

174. Lancashire Record Office, Will and Inventory, 1621: Thomas Markland.

175. Clarke, 'Bells and Bell Founding', p. 23.

176. H. T. Folkard, R. Betley and C. M. Percy, *Industries of Wigan* (T. Wall & Sons: Wigan, 1889), p. 50.

177. Bridgeman Wigan Ledger, fols 41, 66.

178. Bridgeman, *Church and Manor of Wigan*, vol. ii, pp. 308–9, 315, 249.

179. Bagley, 'Mathew Marklnad', pp. 47, 56.

180. Wigan Public Library. Reference W160 H3: A. J. Hawkes, Earliest List of Wigan Taverns, 1634–5.

181. J. J. Bagley, *A History of Lancashire*, 2nd edition revised (D. Finlayson: London, 1961), p. 31.

182. Bridgeman Wigan Ledger, fol. 113.

183. E.g. Lancashire Record Office, Will and Inventory, 1622: Rauff Markland. Lancashire Record Office, Will and Inventory, 1622: Peter Orrell. Lancashire Record Office, Will and Inventory, 1623: Thomas Gerrard. Lancashire Record Office, Will and Inventory, 1626: John Prescott.

184. Lancashire Record Office, Will and Inventory, 1620: Eileen Hey.

185. Lancashire Record Office, Will and Inventory, 1622: Eilen Lord.

186. R. H. Tawney, *Business and Politics under James I: Lionel Cranfield as Merchant and Statesman* (Cambridge University Press: Cambridge, 1958), pp. 114–15. R. H. Tawney, Introduction in T. Wilson, *Discourse on Usury* (G. Bell & Sons: London, 1925).

187. Lancashire Record Office, Will and Inventory, 1627: Thomas Bankes.

188. Lancashire Record Office, Will and Inventory, 1623: Robert Smallshaw.

189. Lancashire Record Office, Will and Inventory, 1624: William Higham.

190. Lancashire Record Office, Will and Inventory, 1622: Laurance Heaton.

191. Lancashire Record Office, Will and Inventory, 1623: Richard Charnley.

192. Lancashire Record Office, Will and Inventory, 1625: Eileen Tunstall.

193. Lancashire Record Office, Will and Inventory, 1630: Alice Bankes.

194. Lancashire Record Office, Will and Inventory, 1622: Robert Orrell.

195. Lancashire Record Office, Will and Inventory, 1625: James Eden.

196. Wadsworth and Mann, *The Cotton Trade*, p. 6.

197. See Nef, 'Progress of Technology'.

198. Lancashire Record Office, Will and Inventory, 1621: Thos. Markland.

199. Lancashire Record Office, Will and Inventory, 1622: Rauff Markland.

200. Lancashire Record Office, Will and Inventory, 1627: James Pilkington.

201. Lancashire Record Office, Will and Inventory, 1628: Tho's Bankes.

202. *Victoria County History: Lancashire*, vol. VI, pp. 70–1.

203. Sinclair, *History of Wigan*, vol. I, p. 222.

204. Bridgeman, *Church and Manor of Wigan*, vol. I, p. 108.

205. Bridgeman, *Church and Manor of Wigan*, vol. I, p. 108. Bankes, 'James Bankes and the Manor', p. 58.

206. Lancashire Record Office, Will and Inventory, 1581: Hugh fforth, see Hugh Forth.

207. Shelley, 'Pewterers', p. 22.

208. Shelley, 'Pewterers', pp. 21–6.

209. Shelley, 'Pewterers', pp. 21–6. Bridgeman, *Church and Manor of Wigan*, vol. II, pp. 223, 265, 274, 251, 197.

210. Sinclair, *History of Wigan*, vol. I, p. 197. Shelley, 'Pewterers', pp. 21–6.

211. Sinclair, *History of Wigan*, vol. I, pp. 204–5.

212. Sinclair, *History of Wigan*, vol. I, pp. 214–21; vol. II, pp. 3–9. Shelley, 'Pewterers', pp. 21–6.

213. *Victoria County History: Lancashire*, vol. IV, p. 71.

214. Bridgeman, *Church and Manor of Wigan*, vol. I, pp. 134, 137–8.

215. Bridgeman, *Church and Manor of Wigan*, vol. II, p. 213.

216. Bridgeman, *Church and Manor of Wigan*, vol. II, pp. 314–16.

217. Bridgeman, *Church and Manor of Wigan*, vol. I, p. 146–7.

218. Bridgeman, *Church and Manor of Wigan*, vol. I, p. 151.

219. Bridgeman, *Church and Manor of Wigan*, vol. I, p. 148.

220. Bridgeman, *Church and Manor of Wigan*, vol. I, pp. 157–8.

221. Bridgeman, *Church and Manor of Wigan*, vol II, pp. 183–7.

222. Bridgeman, *Church and Manor of Wigan*, vol. II, pp. 213–17.

223. Bridgeman, *Church and Manor of Wigan*, vol. II, pp. 221–2.

224. Bridgeman Wiagan Ledger, fol. 176.

225. *Victoria County History: Lancashire*, vol. IV, p. 73.

Manuscript sources

Book of Tolls for Wigan Market. Lord Kenyon's Deeds. Historical Manuscript Commission Report 14, Appendix IV 4.

Bridgeman Wigan Ledger. At Wigan Public Library. Reference Case 6. Top.

Lancashire Quarter Session Records. At Lancashire Record Office. QSR.

Parish Registers at Wigan Parish Church.

Scarisbrick of Scarisbrick Muniments. At Lancashire Record Office. DDSc.

Sherrington Family Account Book. At Wigan Public Library. Reference: Strong Room.

Wills and Inventories from the Bishop's Registry, Chester. At Lancashire Record Office.

WCW.

Printed Sources only at Wigan Public Library

J. H. M. Bankes (transcriber), The Memoranda Book of James Bankes of Wigan, 1586–1617. Reference W615. B2.

H. E. Clegg, Historical Notes on the Wigan Coalfield. The Presidential Address to the Manchester Geological and Mining Society, October 1957. Reference WTN623. I2. C6.

Haigh-Aspull Mining Dispute, 1634–36. D. A. R. Lindsay. Reference Mun. Rm. 3: 5. Add MSS 215.

Haigh Colliery Orders, 1635–98. Reference. Safe.

A. J. Hawkes, Earliest List of Wigan Taverns, 1634–35. Reference W160 H3.

A. J. H. Latham, Economic Growth in the Parish of Wigan, 1540–1640. Typescript at Wigan Public Library.

14

Textile colonies and settlement growth in Lancashire, c.1780–c.1850

GEOFF TIMMINS

Introduction

J. D. Marshall's pioneering work on the formation of industrial colonies in Lancashire has provided an invaluable means of investigating the process of settlement growth in the county, and elsewhere, during the Industrial Revolution period. As his work has demonstrated, industrial colonies took varied forms and featured strongly both in the emergence of *clean-slate* or *primary* settlement, where no significant inhabitation had previously occurred, and in the growth of *secondary* settlement, where development occurred on the fringes of pre-existing towns and villages. He put forward the idea that industrial colonies comprised distinct communities with their own range of social amenities that might well be provided by the main employer or employers. He also observed that town growth could take place in stages, with colonies based on different industries emerging, and that the rise of industrial colonies could occur well beyond the classic Industrial Revolution period, in some cases playing a major role in urban growth. Though he commented on the impact of industrial colonisation on the evolution of the built environment, he recognised that a great deal more could be said on the matter.[1]

John Marshall's analysis focused on industrial settlements based on centralised forms of production, both within and beyond textiles, and has been extended by the examination of industrial colonisation linked with domestic industry, especially handloom weaving.[2] Unlike colonies associated with factories and mines, these colonies do not appear to have been created by entrepreneurs, though entrepreneurs may have played some part in their formation. Nor did they contribute much, if anything, to settlement growth beyond the 1820s, when the handloom weaving trade was at its peak. Even so, their role in the growth of settlement as industrialisation gathered pace needs to be acknowledged and assessed if the manner in which the built environment emerged in textile Lancashire is to be fully appreciated.

This essay furthers Marshall's analysis of industrial colonisation by considering the role that both factory and handloom weavers' colonies played in developing the built environment in textile Lancashire during the Industrial Revolution period. Separate sections are devoted to colonies that were created on hitherto unexploited sites in rural areas and to colonies that added to existing settlement in towns and villages. The nature of the colonies is examined, along with the natural and acquired advantages of site from which they benefited and the local settlement patterns to which they gave rise. Various types of primary evidence are utilised, especially that drawn from the first edition Ordnance Survey maps dating from the mid-1840s to the early 1850s, to present case studies relating to several towns and rural districts. Though the emphasis is on the expansion of the built environment that resulted from the formation of textile colonies, consideration is also given to the changes these colonies brought to the appearance of the built environment. Taking into account both these dimensions, the argument is made that the emergence of textile colonies brought a profound degree of change to Lancashire's built environment, both in rural and urban areas, giving strong support to the argument that, at regional level, the Industrial Revolution was associated with marked economic and social discontinuities.[3]

Primary colonisation

Figure 1, an extract from the six-inch to the mile OS map surveyed during the mid-1840s, shows the two types of nucleated settlement that, during the Industrial Revolution era, came to characterise the rural districts of textile Lancashire.[4] One, the factory village, is represented by the settlement at Lower Darwen, situated some two miles south of Blackburn and a similar distance north from the village of Over Darwen. The origins of the village can be traced to 1784, when Thomas Eccles (1743–1818) and John Taylor (1740–95) built a water-powered cotton carding mill alongside the river Darwen. Three years later, they added a cotton spinning mill. The mills were relatively small, that used for spinning being four-storeys high but with only an eight-bay frontage.[5] In 1823, when Thomas Eccles' son Joseph was in charge, each of the mills gave employment to around 50 operatives.[6] By the 1840s, however,

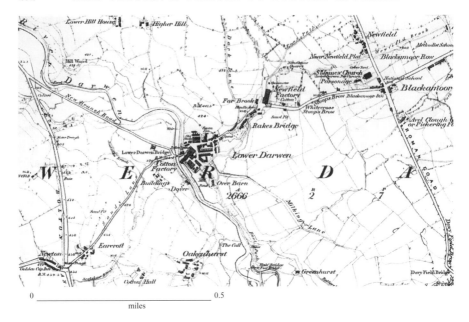

0   0.5

miles

Figure 1. The Lower Darwen and Blackamoor area in the mid-1840s.

Figure 2. Rows of two-up two-
down cottages at Lower Darwen,
situated to the west of the Swan
Inn.

under the proprietorship of Thomas Eccles' grandsons, Thomas and Richard, major developments had taken place on the site, including the rebuilding of the carding mill and the addition of a power-loom weaving shed.[7] At the time of the 1851 census, the firm was employing 613 hands in spinning and weaving cotton.[8] As the map extract reveals, several rows of cottages, comprising almost 100 dwellings in total, were erected adjacent to the mills, and community facilities, including a public house and a police station, were provided. There was also a factory school. The nearby Newfield factory, situated on a tributary of the Darwen, generated less settlement than the Eccles' family mills, but another public house was nonetheless provided.

The second type of settlement, the handloom weavers' colony, can be exemplified by the rows of houses bordering each side of the road at Newton, about half a mile to the south-west of Lower Darwen. Again, most of the houses survive. The settlement is not shown on Yates' map of 1786, but there is an 1811 datestone on one of the houses. In common with those at Lower Darwen, the houses exhibit the vernacular characteristics of buildings erected during the Industrial Revolution period, and some display partially blocked rows of windows that indicate the existence of former loomshops. According to the 1851 census returns, few handloom weavers were still at work in the colony. Much of the other settlement shown in Figure 1 was linked with handloom weaving, including that at Oakenhurst, which is recorded on Yates' map, but has not survived. In 1813 two of the cottages there were for sale, each containing a loomshop for two pairs of looms,[9] while in 1851, nearly all the households still relied on some income from handloom weavers. Most were middle-aged or elderly, however; their children were working in factories, probably at Lower Darwen or Newfield.[10]

It is quite evident from Figure 1 that the size and nature of rural textile colonies varied considerably. As far as those related to centralised production are concerned, settlement might consist of nothing more than a factory with a short row of houses nearby. However, housing was not always built as close to factories as at Lower Darwen, the building space available in valley floors often being limited and required for reservoirs and factory buildings. Yet the inhabitants of small factory settlements could often take advantage of social amenities, including schools, places of worship and public houses, which were available in the vicinity. In fact, this could be the case with the more sizeable factory colonies, too. The inhabitants of Lower Darwen, for example, could avail themselves of religious facilities, including a Methodist school, by walking the half mile or so to Blackamoor, although they had to cope with the steep incline at Stoops Brow. Equally, the rural factory owner might draw on labour that lived some distance away. Both in terms of meeting the need for community facilities and labour, therefore, factory colonies might depend appreciably on neighbouring rural settlements, even if the larger ones, such as that developed by the Ashworth Brothers at Egerton, to the north of Bolton, could mostly meet these needs on site.[11] And if, perhaps through paternalistic ideals, factory owners sought to discourage their employees from drinking, the frequency with which rural inns occurred, both within or near to settlements, would scarcely have aided their cause.

The need for adequate supplies of running water to generate power meant that river valleys assumed greatly enhanced importance as settlement sites. As at Lower Darwen, river water was stored in reservoirs excavated from the valley side and located upstream from the mill. In this way, falls of water could be created at the downstream end, next to the mill, that permitted backshot and overshot waterwheels to be installed rather than the less efficient undershot wheels.[12] Those selling land were certainly alert to the advantages that could arise in this respect, as at Entwistle, near Bolton, in 1796, when the vendor maintained that 35 foot and 13 foot falls of water were available.[13] In some cases, remote sites in upland locations were exploited, though numerous sites within the vicinity of towns were also occupied, bringing advantage in terms of accessing raw material supplies and labour, as well as easing product distribution. Moreover, some rural mill owners turned at least in part to steam power, and since much of Lancashire's textile area lay on the county's coalfield, the availability of local coal added to the natural advantages of site from which they could benefit.

River valley sites were also of crucial importance with regard to the location of factory colonies concerned with cotton finishing – bleaching, dyeing and printing. These processes required large quantities of soft water and the premises in which they took place were often serviced by several reservoirs, which had gravel beds for filtration purposes. Ashmore has noted the concentration of bleaching and printing works along the Irwell and its tributaries, including no fewer than twenty in the Bolton area, which were situated in the valleys of Bradshaw Brook, Eagley Brook, Dean Brook and the river Croal.[14] Among

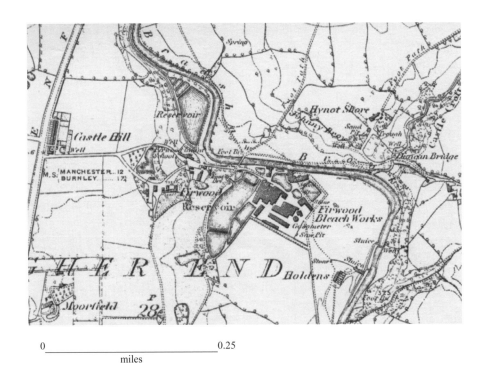

0 ———————————————— 0.25
miles

Figure 3. Firwood Bleachworks in the mid-1840s.

them was Firwood bleachworks, sited alongside Bradshaw Brook about a mile and a half from to the north-east of Bolton centre (Figure 3).[15] As can be seen, two large reservoirs and a number of smaller ones were provided, along with a range of factory buildings, indicating that a considerable amount of fixed capital expenditure was required to develop the site. Additionally, a row of three-storey, back-to-back housing associated with the works was erected at Castle Hill and an infants' school at Firwood.[16] The location of the settlement alongside the Bolton to Burnley turnpike road brought a useful site advantage, both in terms of goods transportation and in enabling the inhabitants to access community facilities, including the public houses that were situated about half a mile away in either direction.

As far as handloom weavers' colonies were concerned, small settlements with just a short row of up to a dozen or so cottages predominated, though, as at Oakenhurst and at Newfield (adjoining Roman Road to the north of Blackamoor) clusters of settlement emerged with detached houses and short terraces laid out irregularly. And more substantial settlements also developed, as at Mile End, to the west of Blackburn (Figure 4).[17] This colony comprised five rows of cottages – over fifty in total – and of the 279 people who lived there in 1851, 130 wove at the handloom.[18] As was commonly the case, the inhabitants relied at least in part on a well for their domestic water supply. Moreover, that their cottages had little or no land attached indicates that they did not supplement their income from agricultural pursuits, a tendency that would have been reinforced during the early decades of the nineteenth century because of the relatively high earnings that handloom weaving families could still achieve. In weaving animal fibres (wool and silk) weavers' cottage loomshops were located above ground-floor level, thereby lessening light obstruction from surrounding buildings and natural features. However, in weaving vegetable fibres (cotton and linen), or at least the finer grades, ground-floor and cellar loomshops with earth floors were preferred, thereby maximising the advantage that could be derived from the naturally high levels of humidity that prevailed (Figure 5).[19] Quite commonly, a handloom weaver's cottage might have loomshop capacity at more than one level, while the size of loomshops could vary, thereby catering for differing family circumstances. That rows of windows were often provided in domestic loomshops to facilitate natural lighting gave rise to new types of cottage that appeared in their tens of thousands throughout the county's textile zone, bringing a highly distinctive change to the appearance of the built environment.[20]

Adding to the natural locational advantages on which the creators of Lancashire's industrial colonies could draw was the availability of local supplies of building stone. Particularly well known are the Haslingden flags, a fine-grained, grey sandstone that was much valued for building purposes because of its durability and the ease with which it could be split to produce thin roofing

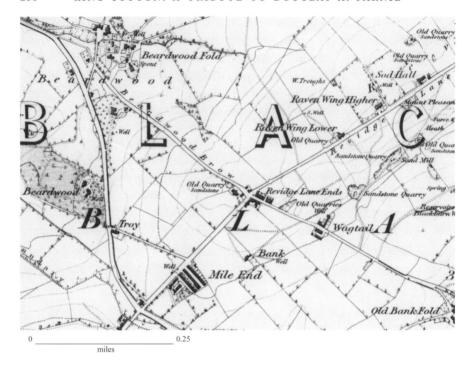

0 _____ 0.25

miles

Figure 4. The rural area to the west of Blackburn during the mid-1840s.

Figure 5. Former handloom weavers' cottages at
Mile End, Blackburn. The loomshop windows rose
above ground level and may have had light wells in
front. Key stone arches above the doors offer some
architectural relief, but they display pronounced
vernacular features.

slates and paving slabs.[21] But variety was available, including the white and the
mixed white and brown building rocks that stone mason and quarryman James
Parkinson offered for sale at Wensley Fold, Blackburn, in 1833. He claimed that

these stones were the best in the county for fine work.[22] In fact, as the early Victorian six inch to the mile OS maps reveal, quarrying of sandstone and gritstone was widely distributed in upland Lancashire, with some sites having been worked extensively. The use of local stone gave rise to mills and domestic premises that exhibited pronounced vernacular qualities, even though some architectural detail was increasingly incorporated. And such detail might be seen to extend to the 'watershot' walling techniques that were extensively used in Pennine districts during the Industrial Revolution period.[23]

The formation of rural industrial colonies also benefited from acquired advantages of site. As is well known, the labour force required in many of Lancashire's early rural factory colonies was partly supplied by pauper apprentices, often, though not always, imported from distant parts, who supplemented the labour provided by local families, young adults and children alike.[24] That they were required reflects the strong competition that, over the long term, emerged for labour in Lancashire as industrialisation gathered pace. Of course, country factory owners were helped by the growth of rural populations, in general up to the 1820s, and in many cases beyond.[25] Yet they had to compete with other types of rural industry, most notably textile weaving, which stuck stubbornly to hand technology and therefore remained labour-intensive. Moreover, profound short-term labour shortages could beset rural factory masters as they could industrialists more generally. These shortages were associated with major peaks in the trade cycle, including that of the mid-1830s, when rural factory owners became involved in a scheme established by the Poor Law Commission to transfer unemployed labour into Lancashire from the southern counties.[26]

Whether native or immigrant, the growing labour supply available to Lancashire's rural entrepreneurs proved to be a crucial acquired advantage of site. So, too, were improved transport facilities. The emerging canal network, which linked the county's major manufacturing towns, facilitated the bulk transportation of the raw materials required in textile mills.[27] However, raw material supplies for rural mills still had to be transported by road from canal-side wharves located in, or near to, urban areas, while spun thread and woven cloth might be returned to urban warehouses or perhaps carried directly between rural production sites specialising in spinning, weaving or finishing. Accordingly, the rural manufacturing colonies relied heavily on road transportation and gained considerably from the major additions and amendments that were made to the county's road network. Not only were better road surfaces provided by developing improved paving as well as broken-stone techniques – sometimes a combination of both – but also by securing marked gradient reductions and the provision of wider carriageways with gentle bends.[28] Thus the Newton handloom weavers' colony was situated close to the main road between Blackburn and Bolton, which was turnpiked by an Act of Parliament passed in 1797. More generally, as is evident from the map extracts shown in

Figures 1 and 4, handloom weavers' colonies were built adjoining roads, thereby easing the transportation of yarn and cloth and of general movement between households. As with the factory colonies at Abbey Village, near Chorley and the Ainsworth cotton mills, which were located between Bolton and Bury, particularly advantageous siting could be obtained where turnpike roads crossed rivers or streams.[29]

The infrastructural changes associated with rural settlement and communications development drew on a further acquired advantage, namely the availability of local finance. The quickening pace of Lancashire's economic growth generated unprecedented levels of investment income that could be used to finance the creation of industrial buildings and equipment, as well as infrastructure improvements. As has often been noted, family savings and those of trusted friends and acquaintances were much utilised, with partnerships commonly being formed. As far as rural factory colonies were concerned, the relatively small amounts of power that could normally be generated on each site from the available water supply tended to limit the size of factories and hence the level of fixed capital expenditure. Costs could rise appreciably, however, if steam-powered equipment was installed or, as in the case of bleaching concerns, extensive reservoir and workshop provision was necessary.[30] In such circumstances, partnerships were often required. Thus, of 36 bleaching firms listed in the Manchester section of Baines' 1824 trade directory, no fewer than 24 were partnerships.[31] Moreover, rural factory owners often needed to build housing for their employees, some of which has been seen to have set high standards, although, reflecting the amount of rent that families were able and willing to pay, the quality could vary appreciably, both within and between settlements.[32] The same point can be made with regard to premises erected in handloom weavers' colonies. Thus the larger dwellings had the advantage of loomshops that were separated from the living accommodation and, as field observation of the numerous extant examples demonstrates, they were often built to high constructional standards.[33]

How far cotton industry entrepreneurs provided funds for the construction of handloom weavers' colonies is unclear. In many instances, however, the sums required were generated by terminating building societies, the subscribers to which, who were local people, sought relatively safe and profitable investments from renting out the houses they came to own.[34] Local landowners, too, played their part, not only by making land available on long-term leases for the creation of all types of industrial colonies, but by doing so at affordable ground rent levels. With regard to handloom weavers' colonies, for example, a row of four cottages with loomshops erected close to the Millstone public house at Mellor, near Blackburn, were subject to a ground rent of £3 18s. 4d. (a rate of 1d. per square yard) over the 999-year period of the lease.[35] Furthermore, landowners might also offer mortgage facilities to prospective buyers of their property. Thus the sale of a freehold estate near Wensley Fold, Blackburn, which comprised a house with loomshop for seven looms, a cowhouse and several acres of meadow and pasture land, was accompanied with the offer that half the purchase money could 'remain for a term of years on security of the premises', presumably subject to an interest payment.[36]

As well as differing in the form they took, Lancashire's rural industrial colonies gave rise to varying patterns of local settlement. In some cases, notable concentrations emerged. This could be so where, as in the Lower Darwen and Blackamoor area, factory colonies were juxtaposed with handloom weavers' colonies. But it could also be the case with factory settlements alone, as in the Cheesden Brook Valley, to the west of Rochdale (Figure 6).[37] Here the steepness of the valley permitted sizeable falls of water to be created in close succession, giving rise to a virtually continuous series of reservoirs and factories, with associated houses nearby. At Croston Close Upper Mill, for example, the

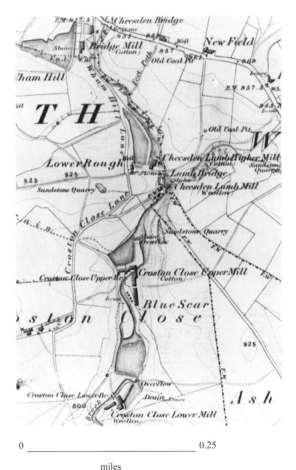

0 _____ 0.25

miles

Figure 6. Water-powered textile mills in Cheesden Brook Valley during the mid-1840s..

factory buildings ranged at the foot of the reservoir, with the southernmost block comprising a row of eight or nine cottages, or double these numbers if they were back-to-backs.[38] Usually, however, rural factory settlements were more widely dispersed. In the Spodden Valley to the north of Rochdale, for example, ten were to be found within a distance of about four miles between Shawforth and Spotland, while the nearest ones to the Lower Darwen settlement were about a mile downstream at Ewood and around the same distance upstream at Hollins Paper Works.[39] But whatever the settlement pattern to which they gave rise, factory colonies became a ubiquitous feature of river valleys, both major and minor, in Lancashire's upland textile zone.

In rural districts where handloom weaving dominated economic activity, scattered patterns of settlement tended to emerge. This was the case in the area to the north and west of Blackburn, for example (Figure 4). No factories were built here – water power was lacking – and the boundary of the coalfield lay some distance to the south. As at Mile End, some of the small pockets of settlement were associated entirely, or nearly so, with handloom weaving alone. Thus at Wagtail, fifteen out of the seventeen households recorded in the 1851 census contained handloom weavers, with no household being headed by a farmer.[40] Other settlement, however, was associated with pastoral farming as well as with handloom weaving. This was the case with the estates at Lower and Higher Raven Wing, each of which comprised a farmhouse with a loomshop, along with a barn, shippon and other outbuildings. Additionally, there were two other dwellings with loomshops at the former and one other dwelling with a loomshop at the latter.[41] Similarly, settlement on the Beardwood estate, which extended to about forty-five acres of land, consisted of four dwellings with loomshops and various farm buildings.[42] Settlements of this type plainly maintained a long-standing link between agriculture and industry, but also represented a new form of settlement that arose in response to the massive expansion of the handloom weaving trade.

Secondary colonisation

The 1840s OS maps of Lancashire reveal that the creation of factory settlements on the fringes of towns and villages was commonplace. In some instances, as at Brookhouse, to the north-east of Blackburn and Low Moor to the west of Clitheroe, substantial amounts of housing might be provided by the factory owner, along with a range of community facilities. In the case of the former, the location of which is shown in Figure 7, development started in 1828 with the construction of a small, three-storey spinning mill driven by a waterwheel.[43] Four years later, a much larger mill was erected on the site. The mill was owned by Tory paternalist John Hornby, who erected several double rows of houses alongside the mill and adjoining Whalley New Road.[44] As Figure 8 reveals, all

Figure 7. The location of the Brookhouse factory colony..

were through houses with their own rear yards – albeit small ones – and privies that were serviced by means of narrow back passages, indicating that they offered high-quality accommodation for working-class families at that period.[45] Housing of such a uniformly high standard no doubt helped to promote community identity and cohesion among Hornby's employees and may well have been seen by Hornby as a useful means of helping to exercise control over them. Some of the premises fronting Whalley New Road occupied a larger ground-floor area than the majority of the houses and may well have been shops. A school with playground and a spacious, walled gymnasium (seemingly a general recreational area) were also provided for the Hornby families, the former being opened in 1841 and the latter during the following year.[46]

At Low Moor, where the first mill was erected in 1782 by John Parker, 234 dwellings housing 1,272 people could be found by 1851, along with a school, shopping facilities and a church.[47] In other cases, however, map evidence indicates that comparatively little housing, if any, was built close to factories, at least by the time the map survey was undertaken. The factories built on the northern outskirts of Preston alongside Moor Brook provide a case in point, their closeness to the built-up area lessening the need for factory owners to incur the expense of providing any housing or community facilities (Figure 9).[48] Even so, considerable residential development was taking place immediately south of the mills, where, as several private estates were sold for development

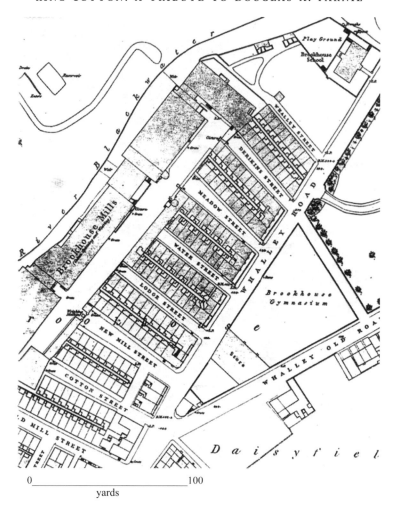

Figure 8. Housing at the Brookhouse factory colony, Blackburn, in the mid-1840s.

purposes, new streets were laid out in grid-iron fashion to accommodate working-class terraces.[49]

The Brookhouse, Low Moor and north Preston factory colonies were all located in river valleys, the water being harnessed in reservoirs for power generation or raising of steam.[50] But roads and canals could also have a strong bearing on the siting of secondary colonies. With regard to roads, the growth of Over Darwen, some four miles to the south of Blackburn, offers a striking example (Figure 10). The late 1840s six-inch OS map shows the Bolton to Blackburn turnpike road (labelled Market Street and Duckworth Street) providing a

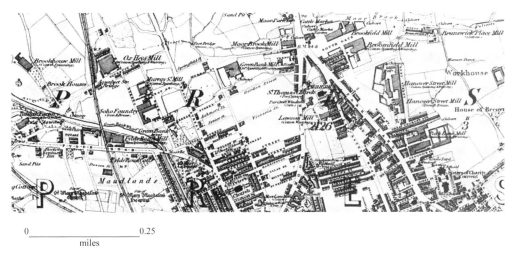

0 _____ 0.25
miles

Figure 9. Cotton factory development on Preston's northern fringe, c. 1845.

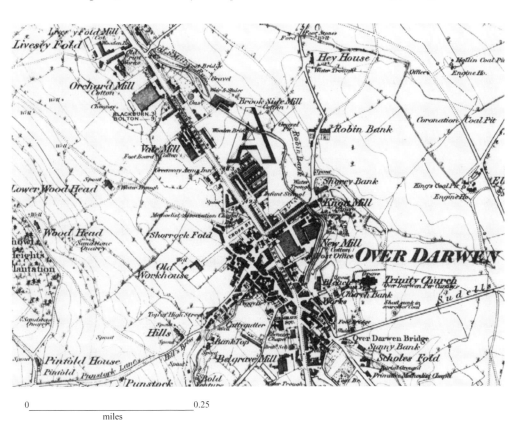

0 _____ 0.25
miles

Figure 10. Over Darwen in the mid-1840s.

straight, wide carriageway running through the village centre.[51] The road was constructed during the closing years of the eighteenth century and it by-passed the established settlement, which was enclosed by Cross Street and Market Street and was characterised by winding streets of varying width. By following the floor of the valley, the turnpike route avoided short inclines leading to and from the old centre. And it brought advantage by providing a greatly improved line of communication along which factories with workers' houses nearby could be erected. Indeed, a new industrial zone was emerging in the Darwen valley, with factory settlements arising by the side of both road and river.

Over Darwen was never joined to the canal network, but in those towns that were, a further corridor became available along which factory colonies could be created. Developments in Burnley illustrate the point. As can be seen from the late 1840s six-inch OS map (Figure 11), the Leeds and Liverpool Canal enclosed the main built-up area on three sides, passing along a lengthy viaduct to the east. Several mills, mainly concerned with cotton processing, had been constructed alongside the canal, with accompanying rows of houses.[52] For the most part, sites on the town side of the canal were selected, easing

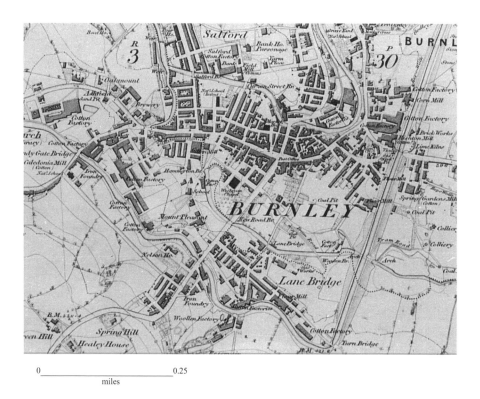

0 ⎯⎯⎯⎯⎯⎯⎯⎯⎯⎯⎯⎯ 0.25
miles

Figure 11. Burnley during the 1840s.

access to facilities in the town for both employers and employed. From an employer's perspective, the need to incur the cost of providing housing facilities was lessened or avoided, while canal-side locations eased transport costs and provided a source of water for steam raising and condensing. From an employee's point of view, the workplace was normally a short walk from home, as were a full range of town centre facilities.

As the nineteenth century progressed and the textile and ancillary manufacturing industries grew apace, canal and river valley sites in Lancashire's textile towns increasingly became the favoured location for steam-powered factories, along with associated terraces of working-class houses and social facilities. Accordingly, zones of heavily concentrated manufacturing activity emerged. In Manchester, as map evidence reveals, such zones had already been formed by mid-century along the Ashton-under-Lyne and Rochdale canals, and along the river Medlock.[53] During the latter half of the nineteenth century, the same type of development also occurred in the other major textile towns. Burnley provides a case in point, as is evident by comparing the area to either side of Sandy Lane Bridge on the late 1840s and early 1890s OS maps (Figures 11 and 12).[54] As can be seen, not only had infilling of the available space occurred on the northern bank of the canal by the 1890s, but a continuous line of mills flanked by housing laid out in grid-iron streets had also emerged on the southern bank.

As was commonly the case, especially in north-east Lancashire, multi-storey spinning blocks were interspersed with single-storey, roof-lit weaving sheds, and the skyline was dominated by round- or octagonal-section factory chimneys, the minimum height of which was regulated through by-law provision.[55] Plainly, the emergence of such industrial zones played a major role in achieving the striking transformation that, during the Victorian era, was made to the built environment in urban Lancashire.

In addition to factory colonies extending established towns and villages, so, too, did handloom weavers' colonies. Nigel Morgan's work on Preston has revealed that handloom weavers' cottages probably comprised about a quarter of the town's total housing stock during the early nineteenth century and that they were concentrated on the north-western and south-eastern fringes of the town.[56] Morgan made particular use of the 1840s five foot to the mile Ordnance Survey maps to identify cottages that were likely to have contained cellar loomshops, which, as Figure 5 reveals, projected above ground level to improve natural lighting. Such cottages are indicated by the flights of steps that were provided, sometimes with an accompanying light well, to the front and/or back doors in order to reach the living accommodation.

Similar analysis relating to towns and villages elsewhere in Lancashire remains to be undertaken, though attention has also been drawn to examples of rows of handloom weavers' cottages having been erected on the edge of other towns and villages between the 1780s and 1820s, including Blackburn, Leyland

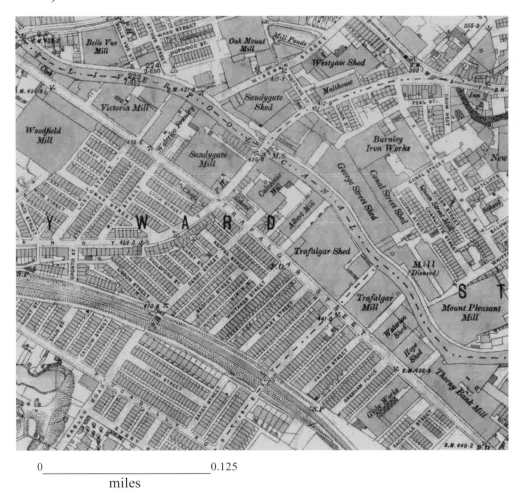

0   0.125

miles

Figure 12. Burnley during the early 1890s.

and Horwich, all of which added appreciably to existing settlement.[57] In the case of Blackburn, such colonisation is evident in several parts of the periphery of the built-up area and can be identified on the 1840s five-foot OS map by projecting door steps recorded at the front and/or rear of small houses, many of which were back-to-backs. As Morgan points out, this approach has limitations in determining the actual numbers of handloom weavers' cottages, because there is some doubt as to how accurately the map makers recorded doorstep details and because some weavers' cottages would have been equipped with loomshop at, or above, ground-floor level.[58] Nonetheless, when supplemented by physical and sale notice evidence, sufficient information is available to demonstrate

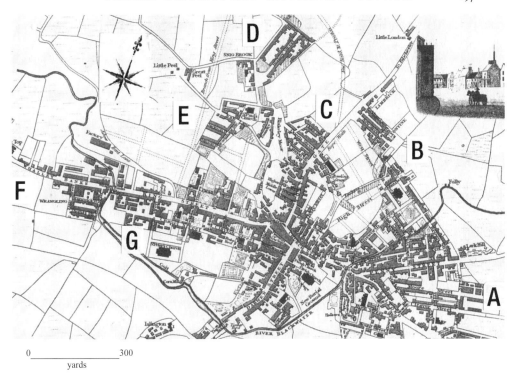

Figure 13. Handloom weavers' colonies in Blackburn during the early 1820s.

where the main areas of handloom weavers' colonisation occurred in the town and to enable an assessment to be made of the impact it had on the town's physical expansion.

For both these purposes, Gillies' map of Blackburn, which was surveyed in 1824, is particularly useful, because it depicts the town at a time when the expansion brought about by handloom weavers' colonisation was complete, or nearly complete, and before the rise of factory industry made any marked impact on the town's growth (Figure 13). The main areas of handloom weavers' colonisation that can be identified are marked A to G on the map and the type of analysis that can be undertaken for each of them can be illustrated in the case of the Moor Street and Cleaver Street area, which formed the north-eastern limit of the town's built-up area. The area is designated A in Figure 13. As the 1840s five foot to the mile OS map reveals, the handloom weavers' cottages were mainly back-to-back, though their quality varied considerably, as, for example, with regard to yard provision (Figure 14).[59] Photographic evidence shows that the houses in Cleaver Street serviced via Back Moor Street had two storeys above the cellars, providing, therefore, only two rooms

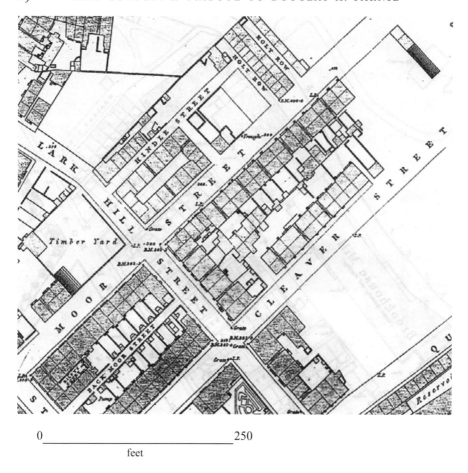

0 ———————————————————— 250

feet

Figure 14 Handloom weavers' cottages in Moor Street and Cleaver Street, Blackburn, in the mid-1840s.

for domestic purposes, besides the workshop.[60] In the block beyond Lark Hill Street, however, four of the Cleaver Street back-to-backs were double-fronted, as were six others opposite them in Moor Street; the ground-floor area they occupied was up to twice that of the other back-to-backs and the steps to the doors were centrally placed. These dwellings offered as much internal living space (or nearly as much) as two-up two-down through houses.[61] In common with those in rural areas, urban colonies of handloom weavers were frequently associated with building society activity, as was the case at both Moor Street and Lark Hill Street.[62]

The number of handloom weavers' cottages that can be identified in the Moor Street and Cleaver Street area using large-scale map evidence is 222. Given the limitations of the evidence, however, this can only be regarded as an approximate figure. So, too, can the numbers for the town's other handloom weaving areas that are given in Table 1. As can be seen, with the exception of the Snig Brook area (D), appreciable numbers can be identified in each area, amounting in total to some 750.[63] However, from the 1851 census returns, nearly fifty households that contained handloom weavers can be identified in streets of the Snig Brook colony. The 1821 census for Blackburn township gives a total of 4,119 houses, but the enumeration included settlement in the surrounding rural districts, including most, if not all, of that shown in Figure 4. Without the aid of census enumerators' schedules, it is difficult to know what discount should be made from the 1821 house total to allow for the houses in these settlements. However, using 1851 census schedule evidence for this purpose gives a total of some 620 dwellings, probably the majority of which existed in 1821. If, therefore, some 3,500 houses were to be found in Blackburn's built-up area in 1821, then approaching a quarter of them would have been handloom weavers' cottages, a proportion similar to that at Preston. Despite the uncertainty of these figures, what can be said with confidence is that, as industrialisation gathered pace, handloom weavers' colonies had a marked impact on Blackburn's outward expansion. By the 1820s, they had extended the built-up area by a considerable degree, perhaps doubling it. Their impact was particularly marked to the east and west of the town, where they thickened and extended settlement along the main roads and, as at Snig Brook, established new pockets of settlement beyond the existing limits of the built-up area.

Table 1   *Handloom weavers' cottages in Blackburn streets*

Area	Streets	Number of hand weavers' cottages
A	Cleaver, Moor (including Mount Pleasant), Penny, Syke, Lark Hill and Brown	222
B	Limbrick, Kirkham Lane, Tontine, James, Henry and St John's Place	90
C	Duke, Queen and Cannon	62
D	Snig Brook (Peel & Old Bank)	22
E	Montague, Mary Ann, Adelaide, William Henry, Victoria, Hanson, Jackson, St Paul's and Nab Lane	110
F	Whalley Banks, Throstle, Richard. Radcliffe, Stout and Bank Top	114
G	King, Bent, Back King, Chapel, Byrom, Clayton	128
Total		748

Conclusion

While much more research could usefully be undertaken into the nature and extent of industrial colonisation associated with the rise of the textile industry, the evidence presented in this paper gives a clear indication of the fundamental role it played in developing the built environment in Lancashire during the Industrial Revolution period. And this was so both in rural and urban areas and with regard to settlement arising from the growth of centralised and dispersed forms of production. As this role was played out, existing settlements were appreciably extended and numerous new ones were created. Moreover, these settlements brought into existence new types of buildings in which industrial activity took place and in which working people lived. Factories and small terraced houses, with or without loomshops, that displayed pronounced vernacular qualities emerged as ubiquitous and distinctive features of the built environment.

In rural districts, industrial colonisation increased the density of settlement appreciably, albeit to varying degrees from one locality to another, as established communities were extended and new ones were formed. The more populous among them generated their own community facilities, though some of the everyday needs of their inhabitants might have been met by itinerant traders. Moreover, in order to extend the range of facilities available to them, or to obtain choice, they were reliant on facilities in neighbouring settlements or even further afield. Meeting religious needs provides a case in point. In all probability, too, the inter-dependency of rural industrial communities was strengthened as earnings from domestic weaving declined and the inhabitants of handloom weavers' colonies – at least the younger ones – sought work in nearby factory colonies. This development would arise where, as at Lower Darwen during the 1840s, the owners of more favourably located rural factories expanded their production facilities.

In urban areas, industrial colonisation brought major peripheral extensions to the built environment, adding the same type of distinctive buildings that were erected in the rural districts, though normally in greater concentrations. Much of the urban growth that occurred between the 1790s and 1820s depended on the formation of handloom weaving communities, with handloom weavers' cottages coming to comprise sizeable proportions of the urban housing stock. Often they extended settlement along major roads and were within short walking distance of warehouse facilities located in central business districts, which were themselves expanding. As is evident in the case of Blackburn, they could also constitute planned zones of settlement in which streets were laid out in grid-iron fashion. The indications are that urban handloom weavers' colonies were far more likely to have featured back-to-back dwellings than their rural counterparts, perhaps reflecting notably higher land values in urban areas. Even so, the accommodation standards and loomshop capacities available varied appreciably within urban and rural handloom weavers' colonies alike, a recognition of the differing income levels and housing preferences of their inhabitants.

Notes

1. J. D. Marshall, 'Colonisation as a Factor in the Planting of Towns in North-West England' in H. J. Dyos (ed.), *The Study of Urban History* (Edwin Arnold: London, 1968), pp. 215–30; J. D. Marshall, 'Industrial Colonies and the Local Historian', *The Local Historian*, 23 (1993), pp. 146–54.

2. J. G. Timmins, *Handloom Weavers' Cottages in Central Lancashire* (Centre for North West Regional Studies: Lancaster, 1977), pp. 48–57; N. Morgan, *Vanished Dwellings: Early Industrial Housing in a Lancashire Cotton Town* (Mullion Books: Preston, 1990); G. Timmins, 'Domestic Weaving Premises in Lancashire: a contextual analysis' in P. S. Barnwell, M. Palmer and M. Airs, *The Vernacular Workshop: From Craft to Industry, 1400–1900* (Council for British Archaeology: York, 2004), pp. 90–6; G. Timmins, 'Domestic Industry in Britain during the 18th and 19th centuries: Field Evidence and the Research Agenda', *Industrial Archaeology Review* (2005), pp. 70–3.

3. See especially P. Hudson and M. Berg, 'Rehabilitating the Industrial Revolution', *Economic History Review*, 45 (1992), pp. 24–50.

4. The extract is taken from sheet 70, published in 1849.

5. C. Aspin, *The Water-Spinners* (Helmshore Local History Society: Helmshore, 2003), pp. 275–6; W. A. Abram, *A History of Blackburn Town and Parish* (Toulmin: Blackburn, 1877), pp. 475–6.

6. Lancashire Record Office, Factory Visitors' Report, 1823, QSP 2479/1.

7. M. Rothwell, *Industrial Heritage: A Guide to the Industrial Archaeology of Blackburn. Part One: The Textile Industry* (Hyndburn Local History Society: Hyndburn, 1985), p. 15.

8. Lower Darwen census enumerators' schedules, 1851, district 4d.

9. *Blackburn Mail*, 24 November 1813.

10. Lower Darwen census enumerators' schedules, 1851, district 4a.

11. See R. Boyson, *The Ashworth Cotton Enterprise* (Clarendon: Oxford, 1970), pp. 115–40. and G. Timmins, 'Housing Quality in Rural Textile Colonies c. 1800–c. 1850: the Ashworth Settlements Revisited, *Industrial Archaeology Review*, XXII (2000), pp. 21–37.

12. For a discussion of different types of waterwheel and water-power systems, see D. Crossley, *Post-Medieval Archaeology in Britain* (Leicester University Press: Leicester, 1990), pp. 137–52.

13. *Blackburn Mail*, 17 August 1796.

14. O. Ashmore, *Industrial Archaeology of Lancashire* (Augustus M. Kelly: New York, 1969), pp. 58–9.

15. The extract is from the six inch to the mile OS map, 1850, sheet 87.

16. The houses survive as six-roomed dwellings. Dwellings of this size for working-

class houses were unusual at the time, so the row was likely to have been built as back-to-backs.

17. The extract is from the six inch to the mile OS map, 1848, sheet 62.
18. Timmins, *Cottages*, p. 51.
19. Timmins, *Cottages*, pp. 20–3.
20. The one computation that has been made suggests that between 40,000 and 70,000 were constructed. See G. Timmins, *Made in Lancashire* (Manchester University Press: Manchester, 1998), pp. 33–4.
21. H. Bolton, *The Geology of Rossendale* (Tyne & Shepherd: Bacup, 1890), pp. 50–1.
22. *The Blackburn Alfred*, 7 August 1833.
23. F. Atkinson, 'Water-shot Stonework: A Building Technique', *Transactions of the Lancashire and Cheshire Antiquarian Society*, 69 (1959), pp. 141–3.
24. M. B. Rose, 'Social Policy and Business: Parish Apprenticeship and the Early Factory System', *Business History*, 31 (1989), pp. 5–12.
25. Population figures for towns and villages in Lancashire for each of the census year between 1801 and 1901 are set out in W. Farrer and J. Brownbill (eds), *Victoria County History: Lancashire*, vol. II (Constable: London, 1908), pp. 332–49.
26. Boyson, *Cotton Enterprise*, pp. 184–99.
27. For a description and map of Lancashire's canal system, see Ashmore, *Lancashire*, pp. 165–80.
28. For discussion of these improvements see G. Timmins 'Road Gradient Easing during The Industrial Revolution: A Case Study of the Lancashire Textile District', *Industrial Archaeology Review* (2003), pp. 97–117 and G. Timmins, 'Paving the Way: Developments in Road Building Techniques in Lancashire, *c*.1770–*c*.1870', *Journal of Transport History* (March, 2005), pp. 19–40.
29. See the six inch to the mile OS maps sheet 70 (1849) and sheet 87 (1850).
30. See, for example, the plan and description of Heaton Mersey bleachworks in Ashmore, *Industrial Archaeology*, pp. 62–4.
31. E. Baines, *History, Directory, and Gazetteer of the County Palatine of Lancaster*, vol. II (1968 reprint of 1825 edition), p. 296. The list includes bleachers in areas around Manchester, including Bolton.
32. S. D. Chapman. 'Workers' Housing in the Cotton factory Colonies, 1770–1850, *Textile History*, 7 (1976) pp. 117–29: R. Dennis, *English Industrial Cities of the Nineteenth Century* (Cambridge University Press: Cambridge, 1984), pp. 50–2 and 176–80. and G. Timmins, 'Housing Quality in Rural Textile Colonies *c*.1800–*c*. 1850: the Ashworth Settlements Revisited', *Industrial Archaeology Review*, XXII (2000), pp. 21–37.
33. Timmins, 'Domestic Weaving', pp. 96–100 and Timmins, 'Domestic Industry', pp. 73–5.
34. J. G. Timmins, 'Early Building Societies in Lancashire' in S. Jackson (ed.), *Industrial Colonies and Communities* (1988), pp. 19–24.
35. The cottages were offered for sale in 1817 (*Blackburn Mail*, 1 January 1817).
36. *Blackburn Mail*, 1 October 1800.
37. Six inch to the mile OS map, sheet 80 (1851).
38. D. Nugent, *et. al*, *Cheesden Valley Mills* (Preston Polytechnic: Preston, 1981), p. 21.

39. For the Spodden valley settlements, see the six inch to the mile OS map, sheet 80 (1851).

40. Blackburn census enumerators' schedules, 1851, district 11.

41. *Blackburn Mail*, 5 February 1812 and 1 December 1819.

42. *Blackburn Mail*, 10 June 1807.

43. Figure 7 is extracted from the 1848 six inch OS map, sheet 62.

44. G. C. Miller, *Blackburn: The Evolution of a Cotton Town* (Blackburn Town Council: Blackburn, 1951), pp. 329–30.

45. Figure 8 is extracted from the 1848 five foot to the mile OS map of Blackburn, sheet 2.

46. P. Joyce, *Work, Society and Politics: The Culture of the Factory in Later Victorian England* (Methuen: London, 1980), pp. 149–50, 173. Joyce sees such provision as examples of industrial paternalism that developed in Britain from the 1840s.

47. O. Ashmore, 'Low Moor, Clitheroe: A Nineteenth Century Factory Community', *Transactions of the Lancashire and Cheshire Antiquarian Society*, 73–4 (1966), pp. 124–52.

48. Figure 8 is extracted from the 1848 six inch OS map, sheet 61.

49. Marshall, 'Colonisation', p. 229.

50. For discussion on the reservoirs built for Preston's mills, see T. C. Dickinson, *Industrial Archaeology of the Preston Cotton Industry* (Lancashire Education Committee: Preston, 1981), pp. 29–30.

51. The extract is from sheet 70.

52. The extract is from sheet 64.

53. See Alan Godfrey reproductions of the late 1840s five foot to the mile OS maps for Manchester illustrate these developments, especially sheets 29, 33, 34 and 35.

54. The 1890s map was published on a scale of twenty-five inches to the mile.

55. For a succinct discussion of the development of textile mill design, see Ashmore, *Industrial Archaeology*, pp. 47–52. Detailed local studies of Lancashire's textile mills include M. Williams with D. Farnie, *Cotton Mills in Greater Manchester* (Carnegie: Preston, 1992).

56. Morgan, *Vanished Dwellings*, pp. 47–64.

57. D. Hunt, *The History of Leyland and District* (Carnegie: Preston, 1990), pp. 74–82 (Leyland); J. G. Timmins, 'Handloom Weavers' Cottages in Central Lancashire: Some Problems of Recognition', *Post-Medieval Archaeology* (1979), pp. 251–72 (Blackburn); Timmins, *Cottages*, pp. 552–6 (Horwich).

58. Morgan, *Vanished Dwellings*, pp. 40–7.

59. Ordnance Survey, five foot to the mile map of Blackburn, sheet 5 (1848).

60. See G. Timmins, *Blackburn, A Pictorial History* (Phillimore: Chichester, 1993), illustration 10. The original of the illustration is held in Blackburn Reference Library.

61. Double-fronted back-to backs were commonly built in east Lancashire and adjoining parts of Yorkshire during the Victorian period. For further comment see G. Timmins, 'Healthy and decent dwellings: the evolution of the two-up, two-down house in nineteenth-century Lancashire' in A. Crosby (ed.), *Lancashire Local Studies* (Carnegie: Preston, 1993), pp. 106–7.

62. *Blackburn Mail*, 17 January 1810.

63. The figure for Snig Brook area is too low. The 1840s OS map does not show houses with steps at either Snig Brook or the adjoining Blakey Street. Yet, in 1810, twelve houses in Blakey Street, each with a loomshop, were offered for sale. See the *Blackburn Mail*, 2 May 1810.

15

Buildings in the landscape:
the offices of the Lancashire cotton
trade unions

ALAN FOWLER AND TERRY WYKE

We beg to introduce our readers to a necromancer, to whom Aladdin's genie was a nonentity, to whom the bright fairies of the east and the fearful wizards of the north were mere shufflers, and before whom all the mighty genii of all ages 'hide their diminished heads'. This mighty potentate has fixed the cardinal points of his dominion in the length, and breadth and depth, and height of Manchester with a grasp and certainty that only Cotton could assume. Cotton is Lord of the Ascendant in the Manchester house of destiny; or rather Cotton is that creative, vivifying, radiating power from which emanates the suns and stars and comets, the life and light and being of the Manchester 'system'.

Wheeler's Manchester Chronicle, 5 October 1833

And who visiting Manchester in 1833 would have disagreed? Streams of visitors came in these years to the south-east corner of Lancashire to look in amazement at the new industrial order. And what most impressed them, burning itself into their memories, to be captured in the letters, articles and books they wrote, were the buildings: the massive smoke-stained brick mills, the plain symmetrical warehouses, Harrison's neoclassical Exchange and the rest. Curiously, so long after Baines and Butterworth began to carve out the history of this the most pivotal of all modern industries, we still await a detailed social and architectural history of many of the building types that made up the fabulous landscape of Textile Lancashire. It is embarrassing to detail the omissions: the different types of Manchester textile warehouse that together formed one of the most distinctive urban landscapes in the world has attracted only a handful of serious studies.[1] Nor do we possess an adequate history of the Manchester exchanges – 'the parliament of the cotton lords' as the penny-a-line journalists writing yet another description of 'Change liked to call it – though, fortunately, we do have an exemplary guide to its membership.[2] Perhaps if Degas had painted the Manchester instead of the New Orleans Exchange there would be more historiographical threads to twist together here.[3] And moving outside Manchester, what of William Brakspear's Cotton Exchange in Blackburn, or the Baroque confection that was the Liverpool Exchange, the creation of Matear and Simon.[4] But the mills, the warehouses and the exchanges were not the only silhouettes that blocked the skyline of Textile Lancashire. A less obvious group of buildings were those associated with its trade unions, and it is these that are our concern.

Cotton trade union buildings have not been considered sufficiently distinctive to warrant the attention of either architectural historians or to find a place on the growing list of textile buildings studied by industrial archaeologists. Labour historians have also shown little interest in the buildings of the trade union movement, either when narrating the histories of individual unions or in analysing the wider role of trade unionism in society.[5] It was only in the mid-1990s that the Archives and Resources Committee of the Society for the Study of Labour History drew attention to the historical and architectural importance of the buildings of the Labour movement in general, setting in motion the compilation of a list of significant buildings.[6] This essay provides a preliminary study of union buildings that ought to be included and discussed on such a list. It focuses on the administrative headquarters built by the spinning and weaving trade unions in the late Victorian and Edwardian years. Six buildings, taken from a much a larger number, are highlighted and a brief history of each provided: Oldham Spinners' Hall (1876), Burnley Weavers' Institute (1896), Nelson Weavers' Institute (1905), Todmorden Weavers' Institute (1914), Bury Textile Operatives' Hall (1894) and Bolton Spinners' Hall (1887).

Cotton trade unionism

Trade unionism in the Lancashire cotton industry can be traced back to the trade clubs of the late eighteenth century, but it was not until the second half of the nineteenth century that the struggle to establish permanent trade unions bore fruit. These unions became an important force in the industry and Lancashire life. Their influence was also evident on British labour. At their peak in the early 1920s, they represented nearly 400,000 operatives, three-quarters of the industry's labour force. There were three principal unions or amalgamations, covering the main branches of the industry: the preparatory processes, spinning and weaving. Their real strength varied but was especially evident in the spinning sector where the Spinners' Amalgamation, founded in 1870, organised and defended a skilled male workforce whose working practices allowed them to exercise considerable power. Carefully managed high union subscriptions allowed the Spinners to build up substantial financial reserves, funds that became a pre-eminent factor in negotiations with employers. Established in 1884, the Amalgamated Weavers' Association represented both male and female workers, the latter making up the majority. They had a larger membership than the Spinners – in 1914 the Weavers' Amalgamation numbered almost 200,000 members, the Spinners' Amalgamation fewer than 25,000. Founded in 1886, the Cardroom Amalgamation was the final major cotton union. It organised male and female workers in the preparatory phases of the mill, though the dominant group in the union was the strippers and grinders, a male elite who were to become among the highest paid workers in the industry. In 1914 the Cardroom's membership was just over 50,000.

Sectionalism was one of the defining features of cotton trade unionism. The three main unions were federal associations, each Amalgamation consisting of district associations usually based on a town. The district organisation was as important as the central body, and it was the former that pioneered purpose-built union offices. There were differences in the administrative organisation of the unions: the collection of weekly subscriptions, for instance, was carried out by the Spinners in the workplace, while the Weavers and Cardroom employed paid collectors who visited members in their own homes. An important but overlooked feature in operating these trade unions in the late Victorian and Edwardian years was the absolute increase in administration. Rising membership, an increase in meetings needed to operate the landmark Brooklands settlement, and the work associated with legislation such as the National Insurance Act of 1911 all contributed to heavier workloads for union officials. There was also the routine work associated with monitoring the wage lists, a complex system of calculations that mystified outsiders, and required would-be officials to pass rigorous examinations to demonstrate their under-standing of the lists and mathematical competence.

Administrative pressure was one of the factors that contributed to the decision to forsake rented premises and to open dedicated union buildings. As is indicated in Tables 1 and 2 (Appendix), which refers to the leading spinning and weaving towns in 1913, this process was already under way by the 1870s. One of the first places where it began was the most important centre of the spinning industry, Oldham.

Figure 1:
Oldham Spinners' Hall
(Oldham Local Studies
and Archives)

Oldham Spinners' Hall

In what can be regarded as one of the stock scenes in Edwardian recollections of the Victorian trade unionism, Thomas Ashton, the central figure in Oldham cotton trade unionism, recalled attending his first union meeting in the late 1860s. It was in a public house. The landlady directed him to the 'spinners' office' – the taproom – commenting that the spinners 'usually sat there playing dominoes with the navvies'.[7] By the 1870s the main Oldham cotton union had a new address, their first dedicated offices being two rented 'pill-box' garret rooms in Union Street. Ashton was appointed secretary of the Province in 1868, and it was under his stewardship that a professional trade union was established. By 1876 the union was in a position to spend £3,000 on its own purpose-built offices which included a council room and a large public room, together with cellars and lavatories.[8] As well as meeting the needs of the Province, the building also provided accommodation for the Oldham No. 1 branch and the local twiners' union. The Rock Street building was to become an address known throughout Oldham as the union expanded and became involved in historic struggles with the employers' association.

The Edwardian period saw an increase in work for the union, an increase reflected in the appointment of further full-time officials and clerical staff. In 1904 the Rock Street premises were extended with the addition of new offices for the secretary, treasurer and assistant secretary. David Shackleton MP ceremonially unlocked the doors of the new extension with a key presented to him by the architect, Thomas Taylor. Praising the achievements of the Oldham Spinners in improving wages and working conditions, Shackleton recalled the early meetings of trade unionists in pubs when the President of the Association would 'carry the books under his hat'.[9] The Rock Street offices continued to be the administrative headquarters of the Oldham Province until the 1960s when the rapidly contracting union moved out. The building was demolished in 1970.

Figure 2: Burnley Weavers' Institute
(Burnley Weavers' Report, 1897; Lancashire Record Office)

Burnley Weavers' Institute

By the late nineteenth century Burnley was a classic cotton town, boasting more looms than any other Lancashire weaving town. It also had the largest number of weaving trade unionists, many of whom were women, of any of the district associations. By 1896 its 11,000 members were contributing a weekly income of £165, and the accumulated reserve fund exceeded £14,000. Burnley was one of the first weaving towns to have its own purpose-built union headquarters. The building, erected in 1896 at a cost of £7,000, was located in Charlotte Street, near the Leeds and Liverpool Canal. Designed by a local mill architect, Samuel Keighley, it was a substantial three-storey building, covering an area of 500 square yards: the ground floor contained offices, committee rooms and reading rooms; a lecture room was the principal feature of the first floor, while the top floor was given over to a large public room with a capacity for 1,000 people. It was an impressive building, warranting the *Cotton Factory Times*'s assessment of it as 'the best class of buildings of any district in the textile trades'.[10]

It was in this building that the officials conducted the day-to-day business of the union and over the years met to discuss the problems and crises that came to define the industry. The institute also operated as an educational centre for the union. The union finally left the institute for smaller premises in 1958.[11] For a time the building was occupied by the Ministry of Labour before being demolished in 1977.[12]

Nelson Weavers' Institute

The decision taken by the Nelson Weavers' Association in 1903 to move from rented premises into its own building was the public expression of the union's increasing power in this parvenu weaving town.[13] The union's growth mirrored that of the town's. A place that had not troubled the surveyors of the Ordnance Survey in the 1840s, Nelson's first major weaving factory did not open until the 1850s; by 1901 it was recognised as one of Lancashire's main weaving towns; the borough's population was in excess of 30,000, the majority of whom were employed in its weaving sheds. The Nelson union was strong and politically active – in 1902 its membership was approaching 7,000 and it had been important in the election of David Shackleton as the first Labour MP in the north of England. Thirty years before the union counted its members in scores rather than thousands and had its headquarters in a public house.[14]

The Weavers' Institute was a large three-storey building, sited in Pendle Street, adjacent to the town centre. The ground floor was given over to a suite of offices and committee rooms, and a lecture room for 150 people. The first floor was dedicated to the leisure of members, including a reading room, debating room, conversation room and a billiards room. An assembly hall on the top floor,

Figure 3: Weavers' Institute, Nelson. (Authors)

one of the largest such public rooms in the town, reinforced the institute's role as a social centre. Even so, the institute was not an architecturally ostentatious building. For its architect, Thomas Bell, the building epitomised the town and its cloth: 'plain, good, substantial'. The union was mindful of building costs but while the final bill of £4,000 exceeded the original estimate, it felt itself able to afford the building. Reserves of £20,000 and a rising membership placed it in a financial position which made it an exemplar of trade union organisation. The institute was opened in July 1905.[15]

In the following years the Nelson Weavers' Institute operated in ways that made it more than the union's administrative headquarters. It functioned as a political centre for labour, most obviously as a meeting place at times of local and national elections. For many more people its importance was as a social and leisure centre, the venue for dancing and socialising. Its fortunes, of course, changed with those of the cotton industry. The eventual decline in union membership – it peaked in 1921 – meant that the institute proved too large and expensive for the union to maintain. The long drawn-out struggle to keep the building operating came to a head in the mid-1960s when the decision was finally taken to sell it. The purchaser was the local authority which re-opened it as a public hall.[16]

Todmorden Weavers' Institute

Founded in 1880, the early years of the Todmorden Weavers' Association saw the union renting rooms in terrace houses. Todmorden was both a spinning and weaving town, and as such membership of the weavers' union was smaller compared to the main weaving towns. By 1902, against a background of increasing membership and an improving financial position, the union decided to purchase its own premises. York Place, a substantial stone dwelling house in the centre of the town, was converted into offices by the union. It proved to be a temporary home. The continued growth of the union resulted in the decision to erect its own dedicated building.

Opened in May 1914, the Todmorden Weavers' Institute was designed to impress. Its name carved in raised capitals above the central doorway left no one in any doubt about the building's ownership and purpose. Offices, committee rooms, reading room and a large assembly hall featured in the interior, reflecting the fact that the institute was to be a place of business, education and leisure. There was also a billiards room, the latter having proved popular in York Place.[17]

Located on the Burnley Road, adjacent to Centre Vale Park, the institute,

Figure 4: Todmorden Weavers' Institute. (Authors)

designed by J. Edward Stott, who had only recently established his practice in the town,[18] was sufficiently impressive to be added to the list of Todmorden's public buildings. Some £3,000 had been spent but it was clearly within the means of a union whose annual subscriptions amounted to £3,200. As with any voluntary association, owning its own building was a declaration of permanence and probity; the Todmorden Weavers had come of age. It was not long before orders were being placed for cups and saucers emblazoned with the union's name.[19] The building served as the union's headquarters for over fifty years, before the contraction of the industry made it redundant. The premises were sold and eventually converted into residential flats.

Bury Textile Operatives' Hall

Opened in 1894, the Bury Textile Operatives' Hall differed from the institutes already noted in that it was the result of a collaborative effort involving the town's three main cotton unions: the Weavers, Spinners and Cardroom. In Bury, where there was a considerable numbers of both spinning and weaving firms, there appears to have been a recognition that cooperation was likely to result in the building of more substantial premises. By the late 1880s the Bury cotton unions were finding rented premises less satisfactory places in which to conduct business. Cramped accommodation was one problem, while the tenants sharing the building used by the Cardroom reportedly complained of the noise made by the clogs of operatives visiting the union office.[20]

The erection of purpose-built offices was the response to these difficulties. That the unions were intent on providing something more than prosaic offices was evident from their willingness to spend a substantial sum of money – £5,000 was the final amount – on the building.[21] David Hardman, a local architect, was commissioned to design the building. The ground floor contained offices for the three unions plus additional rooms intended to be rented to other trade unions, while a large public room capable of accommodating 1,000 people and a council room seating 150 persons comprised the first floor. The building, faced in Yorkshire stone, had an elaborate projecting central entrance culminating in a short tower. Sculptural panels – the weavers represented by a loom, the spinners by a mule and the cardroom by a frame tenter – embellished the façade.[22] It was a building that dignified its location, Manchester Street, an extension of the town's prestigious Silver Street. This choice of location was to be further enhanced when the borough's grandest public building, the Art Gallery and Library, was erected on the adjoining site. Bury Textile Operatives Hall 1893 – the name was incised on a moulded stone above the parapet – articulated solidity and respectability; a declaration in stone that the cotton trade unions were no longer marginal institutions in the town. From a distance it might have been mistaken for a bank.

Figure 5: Carved stone panels on Manchester Street façade,
Bury Textile Operatives' Hall. (Stephen Yates)

Such a building required to be opened in style. A massive procession was organised, thousands of trade unionists from Bury and other cotton towns walking through the streets parading banners. Emilia Dilke, the tireless campaigner for the improvement of women's working conditions, was the principal speaker.[23]

The hall was soon in use as union offices and, as intended, other unions rented rooms in the building. The large hall was also hired out, establishing itself as a venue for dances and other social events. Fire damaged part of the building in 1952. The contraction of the cotton industry eventually raised questions over maintaining such a large building, and finally in 1964 it was decided to sell it.[24] The hall passed into the hands of the borough council who still own and occupy it.

Bolton Spinners' Hall

Victorian cotton trade unionism followed a complex trajectory in the fine-spinning town of Bolton where until 1880 there were separate associations for mule spinners and self-actor minders. The increased strength, both organisational and financial, that followed the creation of a single union greatly enhanced the ability of the spinners to become a focus for trade union activity in the town. In 1886 under the dynamic leadership of John Fielding, the Bolton Operative Spinners' Provincial Association underlined its increasing importance by purchasing the premises of the Junior Reform Club for the not inconsiderable sum of £3,000. Located on St George's Road, this building had been designed by John Jonas Bradshaw, the founder of what was to become Bolton's leading architectural practice.[25] This large building was adapted to meet the union's needs, some of the rooms being rented out to other unions, including the cardroom, weavers and engineers.

Figure 6: Bolton Spinners' Hall.
(John Rylands University of Manchester Library)

Such an arrangement made financial sense for the Operative Spinners as well as furthering Fielding's wider vision of Bolton trade unionism. This arrangement appears to have worked successfully and in 1910–12 the building was extended to double its size at a cost of over £10,000.[26] The architects, the Bolton and Manchester firm of Potts & Hennings, produced a far more ornate Renaissance- and Baroque-inspired building, which included a tower and cupola. The new accommodation included a basement hall capable of holding 300–400 people (for smaller public events) and a much grander hall on the first floor. In all, the building included 22 offices, chiefly for the use of local trade unions. It was a *de facto* trades club.

Bolton Spinners' Hall, the most architecturally impressive of all the cotton union buildings, was re-opened in 1912 by A. H. Gill, secretary to the Bolton Province and the town's MP, who received the ceremonial key from the architect, William Potts. For much of the twentieth century the new hall played a prominent role in the labour politics of the town, establishing itself as the natural meeting place for labour groups. The decline of the cotton unions inevitably raised questions over its future, and in 1964 the Amalgamated Union of Engineers became the owners of the building, although the Spinners continued to occupy offices until their final demise.[27] The Spinners' Hall, now a listed building, continues to be one of the most recognisable buildings in this historic part of Bolton, and at the time of writing its tenants include a nonconformist church and Chinese restaurant.

Perspectives

By the 1980s all of the main cotton unions were no longer independent associations, the rump of their memberships having become part of either the General Municipal Workers Union or the Transport and General Workers Union. The National Union of Associations of Loom Overlookers was one of the last cotton trade unions to survive as an independent body. In short, the Lancashire cotton unions had become part of history. Many of the union buildings were sold off in the final years of the industry's long decline; some were demolished; others found new uses. A crop of histories of the cotton unions were published in the following years, all of which paid little attention to the physical remains of one of the major social movements in the modern history of Lancashire.[28] This brief survey suggests that this was a mistake.

It is evident that the key period for erecting cotton trade union buildings coincided with the expansion of the industry and union membership in the late Victorian and Edwardian years. Negotiating with employers, taking up issues of health and safety, keeping track of money paid in by and out to members required the unions to develop a professional bureaucracy, which itself necessitated the provision of suitable accommodation in which elected officials could create, file and store the necessary written documents. The time when the union's affairs could be kept informally, 'under the secretary's hat', was fast disappearing. This professionalisation of administration was no more evident than in the appointment of full-time salaried union officials and their selection by examination. By the Edwardian period the introduction of superannuation schemes by unions such as the Spinners, and the new administrative duties that arose out of the National Insurance Act further added to the unions' workloads.[29]

For trade unions with increasing administrative functions and full-time officials, it made sense at first to rent accommodation and then, as we have seen, to own their own office buildings. These dedicated buildings met obvious administrative needs but they also proclaimed the new social standing of the cotton unions. The new offices were solid rather than architecturally flamboyant buildings but, nonetheless, they commanded notice and respect, visible evidence of the changing public position of the trade unions and the growing confidence of its leadership. They suggested to some that the age of rough trade unionism, when unions were regarded as a disturbing and disruptive force in a capitalist society, was coming to an end.

Cotton union leaders frequently contrasted their present position with that of the early and mid-Victorian years. In earlier times the public house had necessarily occupied a prominent place in trade unionism. Publicans had played an essential part in the emergence of the movement. Friendly societies, of course, had been based in public houses, landlords often being one of the trusted holders of the keys to the cash box. Trade unionists frequented and were encouraged to frequent sympathetic pubs, and in the absence of other meeting places, the pub was the natural venue for union meetings. The new world of the modern union office did not entirely replace the tradition of conducting business over a glass of beer. For reasons of convenience, comfort and cost, public houses continued to be used as meeting places, especially by the smaller union branches,[30] but the conducting of important union business was transformed, a change that union officials, and not just those with temperance sympathies, had been calling for since the middle decades of the century.[31]

The emergence of the district associations and the provinces made the hired room in the public house unsuitable for conducting the business of a modern union. Rising membership rolls and the ensuing financial strength enabled unions to rent and, finally, to own their premises. These institutes and halls did not fall into the category of great buildings but in the context of their communities they did rank as public buildings. Their design was not to be settled by commissioning a known architect or organising a competition; rather the process was one of requesting designs and estimates from local architects. Competent as the chosen architects were, all of those identified – Samuel

Keighley, Thomas Taylor, William Potts – ran local or regional practices, producing largely bread-and-butter work that rarely attracted the attention of the specialist architectural press. Contracts were fulfilled using union labour. Budgets left little room for show – what Lancashire folk would have called swank – though, as we have noted, some money was spent, as in Bury, on symbolic sculptural decoration. Burmantofts tiles and representations of textile machines were in evidence on the Rock Street façade in Oldham, while inside the entrance of Bolton Spinners' Hall there was a coloured frieze depicting Samuel Crompton (who else?) seated by the machine which had been at the centre of the cotton spinning revolution.[32]

The opening of union institutes were red-letter days, public occasions defined by the ceremonials one usually associates with the opening of municipal libraries, swimming baths or parks. Such occasions helped further to embed the values of trade unionism into the town's culture, confirming their position and status, and the acceptance of them by the local community. These ceremonies were orchestrated to demonstrate the power of the unions, their success in advancing the membership, both economically and socially. The speeches were confirmations of the road that trade unionism had travelled, resulting in the acceptance by employers of collective bargaining. The difference between contemporary trade unionism and earlier trade unionism was emphasised, often by asking the oldest member or lay official to speak, or, as at Ashton-under-Lyne and Todmorden, to open the building.[33] Looking beyond the rhetorical self-congratulations of these occasions, a definite sense of achievement is evident. Trade unionism and the social class it represented were a force to be reckoned with, a power that was to be read in the numbers of paid-up members, the size of its bank balance and, now, in bricks and mortar.

It is also important to recognise the opening of these trade union buildings in the Lancashire cotton towns as part of those wider changes discussed by historians: the 'forward march of labour'. These developments coincided with the growth of labour politics and the election of cotton trade union leaders to public offices. The buildings were indicative of labour's impact on the public sphere in their local communities as trade union offices took their place alongside those more familiar municipal and charitable buildings that comprised the public buildings of the Lancashire cotton towns. In this, as the buildings celebrated in the rich array of histories and souvenir brochures published by local cooperative societies in these years testify, they were part of much wider process of the remaking of the public townscape, especially in the small and medium-size cotton towns. Together, these buildings were highly visible reminders of the organised presence of a labour movement able to challenge both of the two main political parties, liberals and conservatives, reflecting the changing social relationship between the classes in communities numerically dominated by the working classes.

These changing perceptions of the union were both encouraged and reinforced by the social rise of union leaders who were beginning to occupy public positions in their communities, serving as councillors, justices of the peace and members of parliament.[34] In the cases of John Fielding and William Wilkinson this culminated in the erection of impressive public memorials.[35] For men of talent, and they were exclusively men in spinning which excluded women from the trade, rising to become a full-time trade union official presented an opportunity for career advancement and securing 'a job in the office' was the beginning of this path. They helped to confirm the view held by some observers that cotton unions such as the Spinners represented a new type of trade union. Central to this new image was the idea of the union official as professional administrator, an individual competent in the rigours of bookkeeping and the arcane calculations of the wage lists. However, it also raised the spectre of the paid official in the union offices becoming detached from the problems of the ordinary members, a position that might be compounded, or so the Webbs feared, by the bureaucrat turning to drink.[36] In the case of the cotton unions, where trade and local identities remained strong and efforts to concentrate power at the centre were resisted, this does not appear to have been a serious problem.

The Lancashire cotton unions were in the vanguard of providing permanent trade union offices, a new type of building in the Victorian town. Such buildings were declarations in stone of the unions' new position and status in society, declarations underwritten by the investment of not insignificant sums of money. That money, of course, had to be paid for by union members, yet while careful expenditure was implicit in the agenda of all building committees, when estimates were exceeded, members were generally forbearing and ready to admire the 'architecture, strength and accommodation' of their new building.[37] It was significant that these buildings were not used solely by union officials but that they were also places in which the members could socialise and relax.

Looking back across this landscape from the vantage point of 1914 it is also evident that these new institutes continued to reflect the inherent sectionalism of cotton trade unionism. Cotton was never to have an effective industry-wide trade union, and the cooperation evident in Bury was not the model followed in most towns. Further research is required to tease out and order the reasons behind the establishment and operation of the Bury hall, but it is reasonably clear that many district associations shunned such collaboration, preferring to fund their own premises. Cooperation may have held out the possibility of more substantial premises that were also cheaper to run, but even in those communities that were not specialist spinning and weaving towns, there was a reluctance to embrace cooperative projects. Such attitudes also worked against those who wished to see trade unions advancing broader policies of social change, using institutes as educational centres and as meeting places for other trade unionists and workers, not directly connected to the mill.

These buildings also reveal much about the structural organisation of the union. The Amalgamated Association of Operative Cotton Spinners was a federal union based on districts and provinces and though the union's constitution had been devised to strengthen the centre, with an executive consisting of full-time officials determining, in particular, issues associated with industrial disputes, much of the union's policy was decentralised. The two major provinces of Bolton and Oldham dominated the union and their secretaries were considered as influential as the General Secretary. They were housed, as we have seen, in suitably impressive buildings. In contrast the Association's offices in Manchester remained modest. To find the Amalgamation's secretary – a post held by one of the most influential of all late-Victorian trade unionists, James Mawdsley – one sought out his offices in a rented house in Blossom Street, Ancoats, one of the city's poorest working-class districts. Even quite small union meetings in Manchester required the hiring of larger premises. Likewise the headquarters of the Weavers' Amalgamation was an ordinary two-up, two-down terrace house in Accrington. In contrast the employers' organisation maintained high-status accommodation in the commercial centre of Manchester.

We have said little about how the buildings were used or how the different purposes of the institutes – administrative, educational and leisure – altered over time. It is important to recognise that apart from serving as offices these institutes and halls were also recreational centres. Thomas Banks recalled with some pride the opening of its union rooms to all the town's operatives during the dismal years of the Cotton Famine, where they had 'the privilege of reading books, newspapers and playing at draughts' without payment.[38] Billiards proved to be an especially popular attraction in these institutes. The hiring out of the larger rooms for social events came to provide an important source of revenue.[39] The Colne Institute boasted a dance floor that had once graced the Tower Ballroom in Blackpool.[40] We should also remind ourselves that these institutes and halls were male-dominated spaces. The original designs of the weavers' institutes, for example, showed little concern about female members, even though in the weaving sector women comprised the majority of workers and union members.[41] It was not until after the First World War that women began to be active as committee members and serve as union officials, but anecdotal evidence suggests that the institutes remained largely masculine domains.

At a first or even a second glance the social and architectural history of trade union buildings in the Lancashire cotton towns may not appear to rank highly in the research priorities of textile historians. But as we have argued in this essay these building are sufficiently important to warrant a place in any full discussion of the making and re-making of that unique landscape that became the visual epitome of the industrial society with which Manchester and its satellite cotton towns will forever be associated. Neither were they the only buildings in which the cotton unions were directly involved. Trade unions began to provide convalescent homes as part of their expanding role as friendly societies during the late nineteenth century. In the case of the cotton industry buildings such as the Joseph Cross Convalescent Home, Poulton-le-Fylde, deserve further attention.[42]

The buildings of the Lancashire cotton industry still offer enormous research opportunities for many different types of historian. Our purpose in this essay has been to point out that amid these opportunities, attention needs to be given to those buildings that were erected by the cotton unions. The weavers' institutes and spinners' halls of the cotton towns may not be as immediately obvious and eye-catching as some other building types, but neither should they be dismissed as an insignificant feature of the landscape of Textile Lancashire. The buildings identified here are among the earliest purpose-built trade union buildings in this country, an expression of the values, ambitions and public standing of trade unionism in the cotton communities. For that reason alone they should not to be overlooked in any serious study of social history of the cotton towns. They should also be recognised and contextualised as part of a much larger neglected group of urban buildings, including cooperatives stores and halls, political clubs and Oddfellows halls, whose presence re-defined the late Victorian and Edwardian public townscape.

Appendix

Table 1   *Number of spindles in principal spinning towns, date of union formation, union membership in 1913, opening date of permanent union office*

District	Number of spindles 1913	Formation of Provincial or District Association	Union members 1913	Permanent offices established
Oldham	16,573,004	1864	7,400	1876 (1904)
Bolton	6,777,243	1880	2,996	1887 (1912)
Rochdale	3,619,202	1868	1,056	1907
Stockport	2,349,128	1873	417	1879 *
Preston	2,144,544	1814	766	1873
Ashton	2,010,080	1875	1,147	1905
Blackburn	1,325,934	1866	680	1884
Bury	971,208	1869	325	1894
Hyde	752,120	1853	707	1906

* first mentioned in Amalgamation Report

Table 2   *Number of looms in principal weaving towns, date of union formation, union membership in 1913, opening date of permanent union office*

District	Number of looms 1913	Formation of Provincial or District Association	Union members 1913	Permanent offices established
Burnley	110,215	1870	28,740	1896
Blackburn	93,529	1854	20,000	c. 1890
Preston	67,490	1858	11,102	1890
Nelson	57,524	1870	16,082	1905
Accrington	39,193	1858	6,240	1894
Darwen	38,361	1857	9,102	1923
Colne	25,543	1879	8,338	1903
Bolton	23,701	1865	7,946	1887
Bury	22,632	1884	6,850	1894
Rochdale	20,712	c. 1878	4,572	c. 1890
Todmorden	17,959	1880	4,426	1914
Oldham	16,602	1859	7,200	c. 1901
Padiham	15,612	1856	5,100	1905
Great Harwood	14,541	1858	5,668	c. 1891

Sources: *Amalgamated Association of Operative Cotton Spinners Annual Reports* (1879–1959); *Cotton Spinners and Manufacturers' Directory* (Oldham: Worralls, 1914); *Amalgamated Weavers' Association Annual Report* (1914); *Amalgamated Weavers' Association Directories* (1907, 1928, 1939), E. Hopwood, *A history of the Lancashire cotton industry and the Amalgamated Weavers' Association* (1969).

Notes

1. The important published work would begin with H. R. Hitchcock, 'Victorian monuments of commerce', *Architectural Review*, 105 (1949) pp. 61–74 and end with S. Taylor *et al.*, *Manchester. The warehouse legacy: an introduction and guide* (English Heritage, 2002).

2. D. A. Farnie, 'An index of commercial activity: the membership of the Manchester Royal Exchange, 1809–1948', *Business History*, 21 No. 1 (1979), pp. 97–106.

3. G. Feigenbaum, *Degas in New Orleans. A French impressionist in America* (New Orleans Museum of Modern Art, 1999).

4. *Manchester Guardian*, 11 March 1863; *Architectural Review*, 21 (1907) pp. 270–84.

5. Union buildings are given short shrift in most of the standard histories of individual unions as well as in the general histories of trade unionism.

6. Of the published work arising from this project see in particular Bob Hayes, 'Heritage, commemoration and interpretation: Labour and radical movements and the built environment', *North West Labour History Journal*, 29 (2004), pp. 48–51.

7. *Cotton Factory Times*, 25 March 1904.

8. *Oldham Operative Cotton Spinners Annual Report, 1876–7* (Oldham, 1877), pp. 23–4.

9. *Cotton Factory Times*, 25 March 1904.

10. *Cotton Factory Times*, 2 October 1896.

11. *Burnley Express and Advertiser*, 12 April 1958.

12. *Burnley Express and Advertiser*, 1 May 1970, 4 January 1978.

13. *Cotton Factory Times*, 17 July 1903.

14. A. Fowler and L. Fowler, *The History of the Nelson Weavers Association* (Burnley, Nelson and Rossendale Textile Workers' Union: Nelson, 1984), pp. 1–24.

15. *Nelson Leader*, 7 July 1905; *Cotton Factory Times*, 30 June 1905, 7 July 1905.

16. The Institute was renamed Silverman Hall in memory of Sydney Silverman, the town's campaigning Labour MP.

17. *Cotton Factory Times*, 20 February 1914, 29 May 1914; *Todmorden Advertiser*, 29 May 1914.

18. Architect's plans of Weavers' Institute, Todmorden Weavers' Archive, Calderdale Archives, TU/36. Stott does not appear to have been related to the well-known family of Lancashire cotton mill architects. Information from Roger Holden.

19. Our thanks to the late Pat McDougall, weaver and trade unionist, for showing us examples of the union crockery on a stopping train somewhere between Bobbinopolis and Cottonopolis.

20. *Bury Times*, 5 May 1894.

21. *Cotton Factory Times*, 5 and 26 August 1892.

22. *Cotton Factory Times*, 4 and 11 May 1894.

23. *Bury Times*, 5 May, 9 May 1894; *Manchester Guardian*, 7 May 1894.

24. *Bury Times*, 5 December 1964.

25. M. Williams with D. A. Farnie, *The Cotton Mills of Greater Manchester* (Carnegie/Greater Manchester Archaeological Unit with the Royal Commission on Historical Monuments, 1992), p. 31; A. Redman, 'Bolton Civic Centre and the Classical Revival Style of Bradshaw Gass & Hope', in C. Hartwell and T. Wyke (eds), *Making Manchester. Aspects of the history of architecture in the city and region since 1800. Essays in honour of John H. G. Archer* (Lancashire and Cheshire Antiquarian Society, 2007), pp. 158–9.

26. Spinners' Hall Extension, BSC1/10/6–9, Operative Cotton Spinners and Twiners' Provincial Association of Bolton, University of Manchester John Rylands University Library; C. Hartwell, M. Hyde and N. Pevsner, *Lancashire: Manchester and the South-East* [The Buildings of England] (Yale University Press: New Haven, 2004), p. 150.

27. Conversation in 2007 with Joe Richardson, aged 95, last Secretary of the Amalgamated Association of Operative Spinners, who started work in the hall as a full-time union official in 1947.

28. The authors' edited volume *The barefoot aristocrats. A history of the Amalgamated*

Association of Operative Cotton Spinners (G. Kelsall: Littleborough, 1987) and Alan and Lesley Fowler, *The history of the Nelson Weavers Association* (Nelson, 1984) are cases in point; *noster culpa*, as we say in Hebden Bridge.

29. E. H. Phelps Brown, *The growth of British industrial relations* (Macmillan: London, 1959), p. 308.

30. Twenty-nine of the district associations in the Spinners' Amalgamation are listed as meeting in pubic houses in 1909, almost half of all districts. Other venues included schoolrooms, mechanics' institutes, Oddfellows halls and, intriguingly, in Ripponden the Chartist Room. The Spinners' Amalgamation's annual report in 1920 identifies 20 branches meeting in public houses.

31. For example the report on strike of self-acting minders in *Manchester Guardian*, 15 November 1855.

32. A. Foley, *A Bolton childhood* (Manchester: Workers' Educational Association, 1974), p. 87.

33. *Cotton Factory Times*, 3 October 1905.

34. A. Fowler, 'Lancashire to Westminster: A study of cotton trade union officials and British Labour, 1910–1939', *Labour History Review*, 64 No. 1 (1999), pp. 1–22.

35. T. Wyke with H. Cox, *Public sculpture of Greater Manchester* (Liverpool University Press: Liverpool, 2004), pp. 212–14.

36. S. and B. Webb, *History of British Trade Unionism, 1616–1920* (Authors: London, 1920), pp. 467–8.

37. *Report of Burnley and District Weavers, Winders and Beamers' Association* (1907).

38. T. Banks, *A short sketch of the cotton trade of Preston in the last 67 years* (Toulim: Preston, 1888), p. 10.

39. See Registers of Room Bookings for Spinners' Hall, 1937–64, BSC1/10/19–21, Bolton, Operative Cotton Spinners and Twiners' Provincial Association of Bolton, University of Manchester John Rylands University Library.

40. *Colne and Nelson Times*, 9 February 1932.

41. See, for example, the evidence collected from female weavers in Nelson by Barbara Hutchins, Webbs Papers, London School of Economics, Trade Union Collection Section H/49/59–60.

42. Established by the Weavers' Amalgamation, *Cotton Factory Times*, 15 May 1931; *Blackburn Times*, 16 May 1931. There appears to be no published study of convalescent homes established and operated by trade unions.

16

Occupational health and the region: the medical and socio-legal dimensions of respiratory diseases and cancer in the Lancashire textile industry

GEOFFREY TWEEDALE

O N 27 February 2007, a group of people gathered in Albert Square in Manchester beneath the imposing architecture of Manchester Town Hall. At midday, 200 balloons were released to commemorate the 2,000 people who die in the UK every year from the virulent asbestos cancer mesothelioma. Similar gatherings took place across the country, in cities such as York, Newcastle and Glasgow, and wherever mesothelioma has become a major health concern. However, not every city and town in Britain has been affected similarly. Asbestos-related diseases have a strongly regional dimension that is well reflected in Lancashire's own experience, where mesothelioma has become an 'epidemic'.

This regional component in occupational disease – which can be seen in the history and distribution of other industrial illnesses, besides asbestos – is, at one level, no more than a reflection of Britain's commercial history, where specific products were strongly linked with a particular locality. This linkage has received its due in the writing of economic history. Historians such as J. D. Marshall, Sidney Pollard and Clive Lee have identified the region – in terms of its geography, language, shared values, and industrial location – as a prime factor in industrialisation. Douglas Farnie and his colleagues, besides Geoffrey

Timmins, have underlined the key influence of the 'region' in explaining the rise of industry in Lancashire.[1] None of these studies, however, has extended this interest in regionalism to occupational health.

In fact, occupational diseases have featured little in accounts of industrialisation in Lancashire (or indeed in any other region), since the emphasis has traditionally been on the 'engines' of industrial advance. Almost all the recent standard histories of the Lancashire textile industry – by Mary Rose, John Singleton and not least Douglas Farnie – have done a brilliant job at uncovering and describing the production, technology, marketing and entrepreneurship involved with textiles in the region.[2] But the history of occupational diseases has been almost totally ignored. When Terry Wyke and Nigel Rudyard compiled a bibliography of the cotton industry in 1997, less than four pages of references (from 295 pages) related to health and safety, and hardly any of the references related to modern historical work.[3] To be sure, Arthur McIvor's survey of the relevant historiography presented a more detailed listing, but many of the citations were to broadly relevant works that did not focus specifically on Lancashire.[4] Until very recently,[5] the only work on an occupational health issue was Wyke's pioneering study of cancer among spinners, published in 1987.[6]

Perhaps the neglect simply reflects the conservatism of much economic and business history writing, with its heavy emphasis on management, production, multinationals and the Whiggish advance of capitalism. Or perhaps it simply reflects the view – one that has its roots in the nineteenth century – that cotton was a relatively safe industry, with little associated morbidity and mortality.[7] However, for two reasons it seems to be a surprising subject for historians to neglect. First, occupational disease was a crucial aspect of working conditions in the Lancashire textile industry, which – aside from causing untold suffering – was responsible for many thousands of deaths. Certainly, early critics of industrialisation did not neglect the impact of the factory system on workers' well-being or the way in which it legitimised what Engels described as 'social murder'.[8] Britain's first health and safety laws and the evolution of the factory inspectorate were strongly shaped by experiences in the Lancashire textile mills.[9] Second, in the nineteenth and twentieth centuries, the rise of the textile industry in Lancashire was concomitant with the development of several distinctly regional occupational diseases. Respiratory illnesses and occupational cancers, in particular, had a strongly regional bent. This article discusses the historical development of these diseases, focusing on their recognition, and the response of government, doctors and trade unions. It compares the development of these diseases, the evolution of medical knowledge, and the problems in securing compensation. The regional setting provides the backdrop throughout, but the Lancashire contribution to the development of international knowledge of industrial disease is also emphasised.

Occupational respiratory diseases

Medical expertise in the study of occupational health was bred in the locality by the observations of town and city physicians. This was true of leading nineteenth-century physicians, such as Charles Turner Thackrah (1795–1833) in Leeds, who noted the deleterious effects of dust on the health of workers in the flax industry. It was also true of Thomas Arlidge (1822–99), who treated workers in the Potteries and wrote the classic Victorian text, *Hygiene, Diseases, and Mortality of Occupations* (1892). Manchester physicians, too, made their own contribution to the study of occupational disease by identifying distinctive illnesses associated with the Lancashire textile industry.

As McIvor has noted, respiratory diseases caused by inhalation of fine particles of dust within the factory or mine were probably the most prevalent of all industrial hazards – a hazard to which cotton workers were not immune.[10] The first observations were made by Manchester physician, James Kay, who publicised the link between respiratory illnesses and cotton textile manufac-turing in 1831. An experienced physician from the Ardwick and Ancoats areas of Manchester, Kay saw many cotton workers with a lung disorder that appeared to him 'to differ from ordinary chronic bronchitis', in which 'the patient suffers a distressing pulmonary irritation from the dust and filaments which he inhales … these symptoms become gradually more severe … [and] He experiences a diffused and obscure sensation of uneasiness beneath the sternum …'[11] Kay stressed that the symptoms appeared to relate uniquely to cardroom workers and were more frequent 'in mills where coarse and therefore dirty cotton is spun, than where a finer and cleaner material is used'.[12] Although Kay's findings did not evoke universal sympathy – one writer complaining that Kay was more concerned with training men for the Grecian games, than 'their necessary subjection to the toils of trade'[13] – other sources highlighted the dust problem. The heroine in Elizabeth Gaskell's *North and South* (1855) is told how cotton dust in carding 'winds round the lungs and tightens them up,' so that workers fell 'into a waste, coughing and spitting blood, because they're just poisoned by the fluff.'[14]

These comments were the harbingers of a new respiratory condition that was to be increasingly noted in the medical literature after the mid-nineteenth century. It was a disease – characterised by acute dyspnoea and cough – that was associated with the dust in cotton manufacture, especially the blowing and carding processes (where stripping and grinding the cards was particularly injurious). The symptoms, which could become disabling, affected workers most at the start of the week (causing what became known as the 'Monday feeling').[15] By the 1850s, workers had a name for the disease: strippers' and grinders' asthma. Doctors named it byssinosis: a term first used by Marcel Proust's father in 1877. The name derived from the Greek *bossos*, meaning fine linen, and signified that byssinosis could also be found in the flax and linen trade. But byssinosis was essentially a Lancashire disease and was soon known as such.[16]

Consequently, the pioneering medical work on byssinosis was conducted in the Manchester cotton region. The world's first epidemiological study of byssinosis was conducted in the late 1920s on Lancashire card room workers by Dr Bradford Hill – later one of the most renowned epidemiologists in the country. Hill's study, under the aegis of the Medical Research Council (MRC), confirmed the existence of byssinosis and the excess of respiratory sickness suffered by card room workers and others.[17] Most of the affected workers felt worse on Monday mornings. A fuller government report in 1932 provided a three-stage model of the impact of the dust: temporary irritation (that was reversible); temporary disablement or incapacity; and total disablement or incapacity.[18] The report recommended various measures to control dust, and also regular medical examinations. The MRC's efforts continued into the early 1930s, with a series of studies conducted at Manchester University that was designed to investigate the allergens in cotton dust.[19]

By the 1930s, byssinosis had 'arrived' medically, with a diagnostic model that endured as the 'Manchester criteria'. Lancashire's pre-eminence in the field of byssinosis research was due to its regional setting: it was where cotton manufacture was heavily concentrated and where the influence of the cotton trade unions was very marked. The trade unions had underpinned the medical studies (by providing sickness records and access to workers) and had also campaigned for less dusty conditions. They also pushed for compensation.[20] Sadly, the latter was only partly and belatedly realised. It was unfortunate that the government accepted byssinosis as a medical condition only after the industry had passed its zenith in the 1920s and was about to enter the Depression. A government compensation scheme of sorts was introduced in 1941, but it excluded many workers (only those permanently disabled could apply, after working twenty years in the card rooms), offered paltry compensation, and led to a widely held view by government and doctors (though not by workers) that by the Second World War byssinosis had disappeared.

However, the disease was 'rediscovered' in the early 1950s by Dr Richard Schilling (1911–97), an occupational physician who had joined the Nuffield Department of Occupational Health at Manchester University in 1947.[21] Schilling demonstrated that byssinosis was still rife in the industry and that it was not only widespread among card and blow room workers, but also among mule and ring spinners.[22] Schilling's work moved byssinosis back onto the occupational health agenda and prompted a steady stream of medical studies through the 1960s and 1970s. Over 4,600 cases were diagnosed between 1953 and 1977, and for many years byssinosis was second only to coal miners' pneumoconiosis as a cause of industrial lung disease. Yet not until 1974 was government compensation widened to include all affected workers (from waste cotton through to beaming and winding) and the permanent disablement qualification abolished. Starting in the late 1970s, litigation filled this compensation void, as solicitors like John Pickering (based in Oldham and Manchester) launched thousands of successful actions against employers and insurers. In doing so, important legal precedents were set in Lancashire (such as legally restoring bankrupt firms to the Register of Companies, so that their insurers could be sued).[23]

Schilling himself refined the Manchester criteria and became a world authority on the disease. His work had an international impact. In 1960 Schilling was invited to America, where official ignorance and neglect (and the weakness of trade unions) had nurtured a belief that byssinosis did not exist in the US cotton industry.[24] Schilling helped demonstrate otherwise, which led to recognition in America that byssinosis was a health hazard in all sectors of the cotton industry. In Lancashire, byssinosis disappeared after the 1980s, along with the cotton industry and the trade unions. But there was a coda. Byssinosis became a problem elsewhere, in Eastern European countries and especially in the developing world.[25] It remains so today in South Africa, India, and the Far East, where the diagnostic and preventive methods developed in Lancashire remain relevant.[26]

Byssinosis was not the only respiratory disease with a strong Lancashire bent. In the late nineteenth century, another spinning and weaving industry evolved on the back of traditional Lancashire cotton. This industry was based not on cotton but on asbestos, a naturally occurring fibrous mineral, which – when the fibres were released from the rock, opened out, carded and spun – behaved in much the same way as its fluffy cousin. The pioneering asbestos company in the UK was Turner & Newall (T&N), based in Rochdale, a textile town to the north of Manchester. This company and the asbestos industry – producing a huge variety of engineering products – followed a separate trajectory from the older cotton industry. While the latter went into a protracted decline after the 1920s, asbestos thrived and until the 1960s enjoyed a period of virtually uninterrupted economic growth. T&N so dominated the industry that it became known as the Asbestos Giant – a huge multinational that dwarfed its competitors. In the UK the asbestos industry was controlled by three firms – T&N, Cape Asbestos, and British Belting & Asbestos – whose respective positions can be shown by their approximate issued capital in the early 1970s, when asbestos use was reaching a peak: T&N £65m, BBA £9m and Cape £5m. For most of the twentieth century, therefore, the history of the asbestos industry was synonymous with this North West firm, though until recently that industry had been little studied.[27]

However, although the trajectories of cotton and asbestos manufacture differed, the respiratory diseases had uncanny similarities. Workers in asbestos textiles inhaled fibres in exactly the same way as their counterparts in the cotton industry, especially in the carding and spinning sectors of the factories. But the fibres of asbestos proved much more damaging than the relatively innocuous fibres of cotton. Asbestos is virtually indestructible, and the minute mineral fibres, once inhaled, scarred the lungs of asbestos operatives and resulted in the 1920s in unprecedented morbidity and mortality.

In 1924 the world's first inquest on an asbestos worker – a young mother named Nellie Kershaw at Turner Brothers' plant in Rochdale – reported that she had died from asbestosis (lung fibrosis) caused by inhaling asbestos dust.[28] Such was the prevalence of asbestosis in the industry by the late 1920s, that the government instructed its Factory Inspectors to conduct a survey of the workforce. The survey was organised by Dr Edward Merewether, a Medical Inspector of Factories, whose report drew heavily on an examination of T&N workers.[29] In 1931, this led to the introduction of government Asbestosis Regulations, which aimed at the protection, compensation and medical examination of asbestos workers. These were the first asbestosis regulations in the world.

The asbestosis compensation scheme failed to compensate workers adequately – indeed most workers were excluded, because the Regulations only applied to the dustiest areas of a few factories (such as the Rochdale plant).[30] As with byssinosis, claims were restricted by a raft of legal limitations and bureaucracy. Unlike byssinosis, asbestos-related diseases proved not only difficult to eradicate in the long term, but difficult to contain. In the late 1950s and early 1960s, while other occupational respiratory diseases began to decline, the incidence of asbestosis began to increase. In Britain T&N, as the leading company in the industry, remained at the centre of this problem. By the 1950s, it was the largest asbestos textile factory in the world and was regarded as the flagship of the T&N organisation. Nevertheless, despite the introduction of dust control measures in the aftermath of the 1931 regulations, asbestosis was never eradicated at the plant. In the 1950s the disease was still apparent in Rochdale, and becoming more common in other T&N subsidiaries, where the company had made little effort to limit dust exposures.

Further control measures were introduced by the government in the late 1960s, including a dust threshold that was devised using data supplied by T&N from its plant in Rochdale. Key individuals involved in collecting these data included the company physician Dr John Knox and industry hygienist Dr Stephen Holmes. The threshold aimed to limit workers' dust exposure to 2 fibres per cubic centimetre (in lay terms, two fibres per thimbleful of air) – a level that would still mean that workers inhaled billions of fibres a day. This was supposed to cut the risk of asbestosis to *only* one per cent during a working life. These thresholds proved highly controversial, not least because the industry influenced the setting of the dust standard through its lobbying organisations, such as the Asbestosis Research Council (based in Rochdale).[31]

As with most such standards brokered between the industry and government, the dust thresholds were acceptable to both parties because it was believed that the standard was already in operation (or could soon be achieved) at Rochdale and other plants around the country.[32] Despite these deficiencies, the 2-fibre threshold, based on the experience of the Rochdale factory, became the gold standard around the world. It was eventually taken on board in America, where it was incorporated into government guidelines in the 1970s. The standard also influenced regulatory dust limits in other countries, such as France, Germany and Canada.

In the 1980s, as the adverse health effects of asbestos began to worsen, the UK government tightened dust thresholds further. In 1979 a major government enquiry – the Simpson Committee – reported on the dust problems in the industry. As before, the medical and dust level data derived from the Rochdale factory remained key to the formulation of government strategy. And, as before, the influence wielded by the industry's lobby group was a key factor in helping the industry survive as workers' deaths mounted and publicity became increasingly negative. Even as the industry unravelled, it retained its regional focus.

Occupational cancer

By the end of the twentieth century, thirty per cent of the total mortality in some industrialised countries was due to cancer, with the incidence rising each year.[33] Several hypotheses have been advanced to explain the observed increases, including lifestyle and diet. Inevitably, given that economic development has been expanding rapidly, industrial agents have been suspected of increasing cancer rates. This question has still to be resolved, but Lancashire has provided crucial evidence and experience for any discussion of occupational and environmental carcinogens.

Even in such a 'safe' industry as cotton, these insidious risks were never entirely absent: they merely needed time to show themselves. The earliest textile machines were lubricated with readily available animal oils, but by the mid-nineteenth century the 'wheels' of the Lancashire textile industry – especially the spinning mills – were oiled by mineral lubricants (especially the shale oils available in Scotland). By the 1870s, the occurrence of skin cancer among shale oil workers had been recognised; by then, cases of cancer of the groin had also been reported in cotton workers. It became apparent that such skin cancers had a predilection for the scrotum of male mule spinners, whose clothing at below waist level was soaked in oil from the horizontal bars of the spinning machines. In 1910, S. R. Wilson, a surgeon at Manchester Royal Infirmary (MRI) wrote a scholarship report in which he pointed out that of 35 patients admitted to the MRI with cancer of the scrotum, 25 were spinners ('mostly mule spinners') and five were labourers, three of whom had been mule spinners. However, for reasons that have never been explained, this work was not published until it appeared in 1922 in a paper jointly authored by Wilson and his colleague A. H. Southam. This suggested that the mineral oil caused the cancer: it also supplied evidence of 141 cases of scrotal cancer between 1902 and 1922, about half of whom were cotton mule spinners.[34]

It was evident that a new occupational disease, mule spinners' cancer (epithelomatous ulceration), had appeared – though scrotal cancers themselves were not new, having been first observed in 1775 among chimney sweeps. As with byssinosis, this knowledge triggered meetings between the Factory Inspectorate, the employers and the leading cotton spinning trade union (the Amalgamated Association of Operative Cotton Spinners & Twiners). As the Amalgamated warned: 'The scourge of our occupation can have the most fearful consequences if contracted and allowed to develop to a stage where successful surgical operation is impossible.'[35] By the mid-1920s, therefore, a government departmental committee investigating the disease had set out several lines of action. The help of a Manchester Committee on Cancer was enlisted (involving Manchester Corporation, the University of Manchester, local hospitals, the oil companies, charities, and the Amalgamated). The emphasis was on the search for a safer oil, the introduction of safety improvements (such as splashguards), and campaigns for worker awareness. The keynote was voluntarism, and progress was limited during the 1930s.

It was soon apparent that sick workers would struggle to get compensation, since claims were vigorously rejected by the employers. In 1924, however, a mule spinner with epithelioma (backed by the Amalgamated) won a test case in the courts and opened the way for compensation. In 1930 the government recognised mule spinners' cancer as a compensatable disease. But there were snags. For workers who had left the industry, claims had to be launched within one year. Yet the Factory Inspectorate knew that typically the disease took years – even many decades – to manifest itself and that most workers were in retirement when they first sought medical advice.[36] This effectively excluded the majority of workers from any compensation payments (inadequate though these were). For many workers, accident insurance from the trade union was the only 'benefit'. The Amalgamated's reports in the inter-war period are regularly punctuated with horror stories, such as the experience of:

Thomas Taylor, spinner member, 66 years of age, of Shaw District, [who] was employed at the Dawn Mill. He was compelled to cease work on September 5th, 1936, suffering from scrotal epithelioma, and is now unable to walk any appreciable distance, because of the effect of the disease and subsequent operations, a medical certificate to this effect being submitted.[37]

In 1945, another government advisory committee on mule spinners' cancer ordered yet more research on the safest oils to use in the industry, even though these had now been available for some years. Not until 1953, when Special Regulations were drawn up, did the government move to deal more effectively with epithelioma. These specified the mandatory use of non-carcinogenic ('white') oils, instituted compulsory medical exams every six months, and included epithelioma within the Industrial Diseases Benefits Scheme (while removing the invidious 12 months rule). As Wyke has observed, some spinners never lived to read the new regulations. By the late 1950s, well over 1,600 Lancashire cotton workers had contracted this cancer, with over 500 deaths (see Table 1). However, these figures were only compiled after 1920 and, given the inadequacies of the compensation system and the fact that death certification failed to log many cases, undercounting was inevitable (the sudden increase in cases in 1953 should be noted). The minimum figure by the 1960s was certainly over 2,000 cases.

Throughout, it remained very much a regional disease, with about 80 per cent of the cases and deaths involving Lancashire cotton workers (see Table 1). As with byssinosis, treating and monitoring the disease drew upon the skills at local institutions, such as the Christie Hospital (founded as a cancer hospital in 1892), the MRI, and the department of occupational health at Manchester University. The disease had its own local medical experts, such as Dr Edward M. Brockbank at the MRI and Dr Sydney Henry, a Rochdale physician who became a Medical Inspector of Factories in Manchester during the 1920s. Henry conducted detailed investigations of the occurrence of mule spinners' cancer, in which he 'footslogged through remote towns and villages ferreting out the occupational history of the musician, the egg dealer, and the parish clerk, who had died of scrotal cancer'.[38]

Table: 1 *Cases of epitheliomatous ulceration relating to exposure to mineral oil among mule spinners/piecers reported to Chief Inspector of Factories, 1923–57*

	Cases	*Deaths*
1923	15 (94)	1 (50)
1924	79 (88)	17 (94)
1925	78 (84)	35 (76)
1926	88 (81)	20 (57)
1927	101 (92)	31 (78)
1928	101 (96)	36 (92)
1929	54 (73)	24 (69)
1930	82 (85)	21 (81)
1931	60 (77)	19 (61)

	Cases	*Deaths*
1932	57 (95)	22 (88)
1933	39 (85)	23 (88)
1934	61 (90)	24 (88)
1935	62 (93)	20 (95)
1936	41 (89)	12 (80)
1937	63 (91)	25 (96)
1938	58 (94)	12 (92)
1939	47 (90)	20 (87)
1940	41 (89)	10 (91)
1941	34 (89)	5 (83)
1942	24 (86)	6 (100)
1943	44 (92)	13 (93)
1944	38 (84)	13 (76)
1945	29 (81)	8 (100)
1946	36 (86)	21 (84)
1947	24 (83)	9 (90)
1948	29 (85)	10 (83)
1949	22 (79)	7 (70)
1950	21 (75)	8 (100)
1951	13 (68)	1 (100)
1952	25 (81)	1 (100)
1953	55 (92)	37 (88)
1954	23 (77)	6 (67)
1955	40 (83)	9 (69)
1956	36 (80)	8 (73)
1957	23 (92)	3 (60)
Total	1643 (80)	537 (82)

Bracketed numbers are Lancashire spinners/piecers as percentage of UK total.
Source: John Rylands Library. Archive of Amalgamated Association of Operative Cotton Spinners & Twiners. ACS/6/7/2.

As the workforce at risk declined (from about 50,000 in the 1920s to under 15,000 by the end of the 1950s) and mule technology fell into abeyance, mule spinners' cancer too declined. By the end of the twentieth century, the disease was in the past and scarcely remembered. However, as with byssinosis, the knowledge acquired in researching the effects of oil in triggering cancer was an important component in world knowledge about this disease, even if the government failed to use the information fully.

The actions of the Factory Inspectorate regarding mule spinners' cancer were hardly pro-active. As the Inspectorate itself admitted, its softly-softly approach was designed 'not so much to stimulate action as to put the seal of approval on a situation' that had mainly occurred by the actions of interested parties or simply by events.[39] This policy was to reap a disastrous dividend with a carcinogen which refused to 'go away'.

The first warnings that asbestos could cause cancer came in the 1930s, when medical case reports described lung cancer among asbestos workers in America and Europe. The fact that lung cancer was still a relatively rare disease meant that the occupational link with asbestos was easier to recognise. In 1935 a London pathologist suggested to the government an association between the two diseases; and, by 1943, the German government became the first in the world to recognise asbestos-induced lung cancer as a compensatable occupational disease. In Britain, the Factory Inspectorate, first alerted to the trend in the late 1930s, featured the rising incidence of asbestosis/lung cancer deaths in its publications in the late 1940s. By 1947, the Factory Inspectorate had accumulated figures which showed that the percentage of asbestosis cases with lung cancer was about 13 per cent – a highly significant percentage when the lung cancer rate for those with silicosis was the same as the general population (only 1 per cent).

No specific action was taken by the government (and it was to be nearly forty years before lung cancer was recognised as a compensatable disease – and only then in association with asbestosis). The threat of lung cancer to its workers, however, did provoke a reaction from the asbestos companies, including T&N. Through its American subsidiary, Keasbey-Mattison, the Rochdale company joined other US asbestos producers in sponsoring a research programme at a private research facility, the Saranac Laboratory in upstate New York. In 1943 this programme showed that mice exposed to asbestos showed an excessive incidence of pulmonary cancer (findings that the sponsors refused to publish).[40]

By the early 1950s, however, the growing number of lung cancers in the asbestos factories forced the industry's hand. Somewhat reluctantly, it was T&N that led the way. In the early 1950s, the company asked a young epidemiologist, Richard Doll, to conduct a study of lung cancer among its asbestos textile workers in Rochdale. Using data supplied by Dr John Knox, Doll was able to confirm that asbestos was indeed associated with a heavy risk of lung cancer; and the order of risk – in those exposed twenty years or more – was estimated to be ten times that in the general population. However, when Knox and Doll planned to publish their results in a medical journal, the company directors vetoed the idea, because they feared bad publicity. Doll went ahead and published the findings under his own name in 1955, but not before T&N had tried to persuade the journal editor to reject the article.[41]

Doll's paper on Rochdale workers, however, became a landmark in asbestos epidemiology: it fostered the reputation of its author (who later became even more famous for his work on smoking and lung cancer) and highlighted a worrying additional health risk in the asbestos mills. In Britain the proportion of lung cancer cases among those with asbestosis published in the Factory Inspectorate's annual reports rose inexorably throughout the 1950s and 1960s. But what transformed the 'magic mineral' into a 'killer dust' in the popular mind was its ability to cause mesothelioma. This is a highly malignant tumour of the pleura (the lining of the chest) or the peritoneum (the lining of the abdomen). Once a rare condition, it is now (alongside asbestos-induced lung cancer), the leading cause of asbestos-related deaths. Its only known occupational cause is asbestos.

Autopsies on T&N workers from the 1920s had shown that the tiny, needle-like fibres of asbestos could work their way through the lung tissues to damage the pleura. It was also known that asbestos workers suffered from rare pleural cancers (described in the early literature as 'endotheliomas'). Perhaps the first mesothelioma for which written records survive relate to Rochdale asbestos worker William Pennington, who died in 1936 from asbestosis and endothelioma of the pleura.[42] Evidence accumulated during the early 1950s, when the term 'mesothelioma' was increasingly used and when peritoneal mesotheliomas in asbestos workers were also noted. However, mesothelioma excited little interest, because it was still a rare disease. That situation changed dramatically in the late 1950s, when a team of South African pathologists uncovered a mesothelioma 'epidemic' around the asbestos mines in Cape Province. The research, published in a British industrial medicine journal in 1960, was a bombshell, because it firmly connected asbestos with mesothelioma and also showed that non-occupational (i.e. neighbourhood/environmental) exposure might cause the disease. Mesothelioma was now revealed in all its horror – as a cancer that could stay latent for anything between 30 and 60 years, that could be caused by brief and non-occupational exposure, and that could kill painfully within months and with no hope of a cure.

Mesothelioma deaths began rising steadily after the 1960s. This was partly due to the fact that doctors were looking for them, but the increase also reflected the widespread exposures suffered by workers in the 1940s and 1950s. In the 1970s and 1980s, the asbestos industry was hit first by an avalanche of bad publicity, and then by the largest wave of litigation in history. Researching asbestos-related diseases was an international affair, but Rochdale remained a focus of attention. Sir Richard Doll had continued to track workers' health at the factory and in the 1970s was joined by another Oxford epidemiologist, Julian Peto. They devised complex formulations which, it was hoped, would provide an 'acceptable' level for working with asbestos and so allow the industry to continue. Data from their work was used to set government thresholds and these, in turn, influenced thresholds abroad, especially in America.[43] Ultimately, these safety standards failed to save an industry and in the early 1990s asbestos manufacture in Rochdale ceased. A decade later, crippled by its asbestos liabilities, T&N was absorbed by an American multinational (which promptly filed for bankruptcy because of the asbestos claims).

By then epidemiologists had realised that most victims of mesothelioma were (and will be) building workers, carpenters, electricians and metal workers, whose employment was outside the factories and whose only contact with asbestos was transient. Focusing on factory dust exposures in places like Rochdale had proved a mistake.[44] Not only that, but in the 1990s it was suddenly realised that mesothelioma deaths, far from levelling off and falling, would continue to rise for decades. Asbestos industrialists had wanted the world to remember the benefits of using asbestos: instead, the monument to the industry in the UK is a grisly roll call of some 3,500 deaths a year from asbestos-related diseases (about 2,000 of these from mesothelioma). The deaths affect all sectors of society – from labourers to company executives, from schoolteachers to film stars – though the distribution of asbestos deaths still follows a strongly regional imprint. Mesothelioma occurs in 'hot-spots', not only where asbestos was manufactured in the factories, but also where the mineral was used in downstream industries, such as shipbuilding, railway engineering and building work.[45] Thus Clydeside has an elevated incidence of mesothelioma.[46] So too do areas in the North West, such as Merseyside, Crewe and Nantwich, while in Greater Manchester mesothelioma deaths are also rising.

Conclusion

Douglas Farnie has described Lancashire cotton as the 'most widely and deeply studied of all manufactures'.[47] That description does not yet apply to the study of occupational diseases in the industry, although research in this area is gathering momentum. This article has attempted to show that these work-related illnesses do not deserve this neglect, especially from those sensitive to the regional aspects of Lancashire's industrial history.

Byssinosis, mule spinners' cancer, and asbestos-related diseases would merit attention in their own right. But they were also very region-specific diseases – sometimes almost purely 'Lancashire diseases', which generated their own local expertise and responses. Nor were they the only such diseases. Other occupational illnesses that have not been included in this article include cotton twisters' cramp (a repetitive strain injury, due to workers continually twisting cotton ends). It was listed by the government as a compensatable illness in 1921 and provided six months' compensation if the worker was totally disabled. It was probably the first time in the world RSI had been officially recognised. Regional approaches would therefore appear to offer useful insights into medical history, though this line of research has yet to be fully appreciated.[48]

Besides this regional component, the history of these diseases provides other interesting features. Perhaps the most striking is the glacial development, not necessarily of knowledge, but of health and safety measures and compensation. All these diseases provide evidence of the way in which, as one critic has asserted, the figures for occupational disease 'are washed and shrunk in the statistical laundries of industry and government ... [so that] ... it is hard to believe that the system is not designed to conceal the truth'.[49] Certainly the system was not designed to dispense fair and adequate compensation for what were sometimes mortal illnesses. In these circumstances, the role of the trade unions was creditable. As the Amalgamated remarked about mule spinners' cancer, 'we have sought to discover the cause and its removal, and we have fought a long battle to achieve working conditions aimed at the prevention of this lethal disease'.[50] The unions were not always successful, but this was mainly because these problems took place within a declining industry.

Perhaps the most striking feature of occupational diseases 'made in Lancashire' is that the knowledge accumulated in fighting them had more than merely local significance. In the same way that the region's products and technology found their way overseas, so too did its occupational diseases and then eventually its medical expertise. Byssinosis, asbestosis, epithelioma, and mesothelioma generated knowledge that could be transferred abroad. In America, it was Schilling's studies of byssinosis that in the 1970s had the effect of 'catalyzing ... the American discovery of byssinosis'.[51] Data on scrotal cancer that stretched over half a century fed into international debates over the incidence of occupational carcinogenesis.[52] In the 1970s data generated in Rochdale was – for better or worse – the basis for dust thresholds world-wide. As with its cotton and asbestos textile products, so too with occupational health: the repercussions of Lancashire industry were manifold and profound.

Notes

1. D. Farnie *et al.* (eds), *Region and Strategy in Britain and Japan: Business in Lancashire and Kansai, 1890–1990* (Routledge: London, 1999); G. Timmins, *Made in Lancashire: A History of Regional Industrialisation* (Manchester University Press: Manchester, 1998).

2. D. A. Farnie, *The English Cotton Industry and the World Market, 1815–1896* (Oxford University Press: Oxford, 1979); M. Rose (ed.), *The Lancashire Cotton Industry* (Lancashire County Books: Preston, 1996); J. Singleton, *Lancashire on the Scrapheap: The Cotton Industry, 1945–1970* (Oxford University Press: Oxford, 1991).

3. T. Wyke and N. Rudyard, *Cotton: A Select Bibliography* (Manchester Central Library: Manchester, 1997), pp. 118–22.

4. A. McIvor, 'Health and Safety in the Cotton Industry: A Literature Review,' *Manchester Region History Review* 9 (1995), pp. 50–7.

5. Alan Fowler, *Lancashire Cotton Operatives and Work, 1900–1950: A Social History of Lancashire Cotton Operatives in the Twentieth Century* (Ashgate Publishing: Aldershot, 2003); Janet Greenlees, '"Stop Kissing and Steaming!": Tuberculosis and the Occupational Health Movement in Massachusetts and Lancashire, 1870–1918', *Urban History* 32 (2005), pp. 223–46; Ian Convery and J. Welshman, 'Mills, Migration, and Medicine: Ethnicity and the Textile Industry', in M. Nelson (ed.), *Occupational Health and Public Health: Lessons from the Past – Challenges for the Future* (National Institute for Working Life: Stockholm, 2006), pp. 145–64. Accessed at: www.arbetslivsinstitutet.se/ebib/ah/2006/ah2006_10.pdf

6. T. Wyke, 'Mule Spinners' Cancer,' in A. Fowler and T. Wyke (eds), *The Barefoot Aristocrats: A History of the Amalgamated Association of Operative Cotton Spinners* (Kelsall: Littleborough, 1987), pp. 184–96.

7. A. McIvor, *A History of Work in Britain, 1880–1950* (Palgrave: Basingstoke, 2001), pp. 120, 124–5.

8. Friedrich Engels, *The Condition of the Working Class in England* (1845: Penguin edition, 1987), pp. 127–8.

9. E. Crooks, *The Factory Inspectors: A Legacy of the Industrial Revolution* (Tempus Publishing: Stroud, 2005), pp. 8–23.

10. McIvor, *History of Work*, pp. 124–5.

11. James Phillips Kay, 'Observations and Experiments Concerning Molecular Irritation of the Lungs as One Source of Tubercular Consumption; and on Spinners' Phthisis', *North of England Medical & Surgical Journal* 1 (1830–1), Art. IX, pp. 348–63, 360.

12. Kay, 'Observations', p. 359.

13. Edward Baines, *History of the Cotton Manufacture in Great Britain* (Cass, 1966 reprint of 2nd edition, 1835), p. 460.

14. E. Gaskell, *North and South* (1855; Penguin edition, 1995), p. 102. See also John Roberton, 'A Model Warehouse', *Transactions of Manchester Statistical Society* (1859–60), pp. 42–57, for comments attributing ill-health in cotton shipping warehouses to the dusty environment. Reference courtesy of Douglas Farnie.

15. *Third Report of the Medical Officer of the Privy Council. 1860* (HMSO, 1861), Appendix, pp. 37–194.

16. P. Neild, *Byssinosis – 'The Lancashire Disease'* (Chartered Insurance Institute: London, 1982).

17. A. Bradford Hill, *Sickness among Operatives in Lancashire Cotton Spinning Mills (With Special Reference to Workers in the Cardroom)* (HMSO, 1930).

18. Home Office, *Report of the Departmental Committee on Dust in Card Rooms in the Cotton Industry* (HMSO, 1932).

19. C. Prausnitz, *Investigations on Respiratory Dust Disease in Operatives in the Cotton Industry. MRC Special Report Series 212* (HMSO, 1936).

20. S. Bowden and G. Tweedale, 'Mondays without Dread: The Trade Union Response to Byssinosis in the Lancashire Cotton Industry in the 20th Century', *Social History of Medicine* 16 (2003), pp. 79–95.

21. R. F. S. Schilling, *A Challenging Life: Sixty Years in Occupational Medicine* (Canning Press: London, 1998).

22. R. F. S. Schilling, 'Byssinosis in Cotton and Other Textile Workers', *Lancet* ii (1956), pp. 261–5, 319–24.

23. S. Bowden and G. Tweedale, 'Poisoned by the Fluff: Compensation and Litigation for Byssinosis in the Lancashire Cotton Industry', *Journal of Law & Society* 29 (December 2002), pp. 560–79.

24. C. Levenstein, G. F. DeLaurier and M. L. Dunn, *The Cotton Dust Papers: Science, Politics, and Power in the 'Discovery' of Byssinosis in the US* (Amityville: New York, 2002).

25. R. Schilling, 'The Worldwide Problems of Byssinosis', *Chest* 79 (1981), pp. 3–5.

26. Xaio-Rong Wang and David C. Christiani, 'Occupational Lung Disease in China', *International Journal of Occupational & Environmental Health* 9 (2003), pp. 320–5.

27. G. Tweedale, *Magic Mineral to Killer Dust: Turner & Newall and the Asbestos Hazard* (Oxford University Press, 2000, reprinted, 2001).

28. I. J. Selikoff and M. Greenberg, 'A Landmark Case in Asbestosis,' *Journal of American Medical Association* 265 (20 February 1991), pp. 898–901.

29. E. R. A. Merewether and C. W. Price, *Report on Effects of Asbestos Dust on the Lungs and Dust Suppression in the Asbestos Industry* (HMSO, 1930).

30. G. Tweedale and P. Hansen, 'Protecting the Workers: The Medical Board and the Asbestos Industry, 1930s–1960s,' *Medical History* 42 (1998), pp. 439–57.

31. G. Tweedale, 'Science or Public Relations?: The Inside Story of the Asbestosis Research Council', *American Journal of Industrial Medicine* 38 (December 2000), pp. 723–34.

32. M. Greenberg, 'British Asbestos Standard Setting: 1898–2000', *American Journal of Industrial Medicine* 46 (2004), pp. 534–41.

33. C. Maltoni and I. J. Selikoff, Preface, in Maltoni and Selikoff (eds), 'Living in a Chemical World: Occupational and Environmental Significance of Industrial Carcinogens', *Annals of New York Academy of Science* 534 (1988), pp. xv, 1–1044.

34. J. C. Bridge and S. A. Henry, 'Industrial Cancers', in *British Empire Cancer Campaign Report of the International Conference on Cancer, London, 17–20 July 1928* (Simpkin, Marshall Ltd: London, 1928), pp. 258–62.

35. John Rylands Library, University of Manchester: Archive of Amalgamated Association of Operative Cotton Spinners & Twiners. *Report of Council. Quarter ending … 31 July 1960.*

36. *Annual Report of Chief Inspector of Factories and Workshops for 1936* (HMSO, 1937), p. 49, admitted that it took between 13 and 70 years for the cancer to appear after a worker joined the industry.

37. John Rylands Library, University of Manchester: Archive of Amalgamated Association of Operative Cotton Spinners & Twiners. *Executive Council Meeting, 18 December 1937.*

38. R. S. Schilling, 'Obituary of S. A. Henry', *British Journal of Industrial Medicine* 27 (1960), p. 161. See also S. A. Henry and E. D. Irvine, 'Cancer of the Scrotum in the Blackburn Registration District, 1837–1929', *Journal of Hygiene* 36 (1936), pp. 310–40; S. A. Henry, 'Cutaneous Cancer in Relation to Occupation', *Annals of*

Royal College of Surgeons of England 7 (December 1950), pp. 425–54;

39. Health & Safety Executive, *Cotton and Allied Fibres: Health and Safety, 1971–1977* (HMSO, 1979), p. 12.

40. D. E. Lilienfeld, 'The Silence: The Asbestos Industry and Early Occupational Cancer Research – A Case Study,' *American Journal of Public Health* 81 (June 1991), pp. 791–800.

41. M. Greenberg, 'A Study of Lung Cancer Mortality in Asbestos Workers: Doll, 1955', *American Journal of Industrial Medicine* 36 (1999), pp. 31–47.

42. Report of a Post-Mortem Carried out by J. S. Pooley, Rochdale Mortuary, 16 October 1936. Copy in author's possession.

43. R. Doll and J. Peto, *Asbestos: Effects on Health of Exposure to Asbestos* (HMSO, 1985).

44. G. Tweedale, 'What You See Depends on Where You Sit: The Rochdale Asbestos Cancer Studies and the Politics of Epidemiology', *International Journal of Occupational and Environmental Health* 13 (January/March 2007), pp. 70–9.

45. Health & Safety Executive, *Mesothelioma Mortality in Great Britain: An Analysis by Geographical Area, 1918–2000* (n.d.). Accessed at: www.hse.gov.uk/statistics/causdis/area8100.pdf

46. R. Johnston and A. McIvor, *Lethal Work: A History of the Asbestos Tragedy in Scotland* (Tuckwell: Glasgow, 2000).

47. D. A. Farnie and D. J. Jeremy (eds), *The Fibre that Changed the World: The Cotton Industry in International Perspective, 1600–1990s* (Oxford University Press, 2004), p. 15.

48. The only work that appears to use 'region' as an analytical tool in medical history is Megan J. Davies, 'Mapping "Region" in Canadian Medical History: The Case of British Columbia', *Canadian Bulletin of Medical History* 17 (2000), pp. 73–92.

49. Patrick Kinnersly, *Hazards of Work: How to Fight Them* (London: Pluto Press, 1973), p. 10.

50. John Rylands Library, University of Manchester: Archive of Amalgamated Association of Operative Cotton Spinners & Twiners. *Report of Council. Quarter ending … 31 July 1960.*

51. E. H. Beardsley, *A History of Neglect: Health Care for Blacks and Mill Workers in the Twentieth-Century South* (University of Tennessee Press: Knoxville, 1987), p. 236.

52. W. R. Lee, 'Occupational Aspects of Scrotal Cancer and Epithelioma', in U. Saffiotti and J. K. Wagoner (eds), 'Occupational Carcinogenesis', *Annals of New York Academy of Sciences* 271 (1976), pp. 138–42.

The Chetham Society

FOR MANY YEARS Douglas Farnie was a member of the Council of the Chetham Society, and the society is proud and honoured to be associated with the present volume, a worthy tribute to Douglas and his great contribution to our understanding of the history of Lancashire and Cheshire. This volume, although published by Crucible Books, has been designated no. 47 in the Chetham Society's third series.

Founded in 1843, the Chetham Society (its formal title is The Chetham Society for the Publications of Remains Historical and Literary connected with the Palatine Counties of Lancaster and Chester, a typically early Victorian mouthful) publishes monographs and editions of texts on aspects of the history of the two ancient counties. Its scope is very wide – the subjects of recent volumes have included Anglicanism in south-east Lancashire, 1847–1914; the maritime history of Parkgate in Wirral, the seventeenth- and eighteenth-century passenger port for Ireland; the Act Book of the Ecclesiastical Court of Whalley, 1510–1537; and Macclesfield in the later fourteenth century.

Since its foundation the society has published a total of 270 volumes, an immensely valuable contribution to historical studies in north-west England, and many of its contributing authors have been historians of great eminence and distinction. Plans for future volumes include the civil war in Lancashire, the book trade in Stockport, and biographical studies and editions of diaries from key figures in the region's development. The society welcomes new members. The current annual subscription is £13 (which entitles members to a copy of each volume published during that year), and we aim to publish an average of a volume per year.

For membership queries please contact the secretary, Mr Christopher J. Hunwick, 10 Beacon Road, Hampeth, Morpeth, NE65 9LH, or chrishunwick@hotmail.com